D1188287

THE BIBLICAL RESOURCE SERIES

THE FAITH OF JESUS CHRIST

The Narrative Substructure of Galatians 3:1–4:11

RICHARD B. HAYS

WILLIAM B. EERDMANS PUBLISHING COMPANY
GRAND RAPIDS, MICHIGAN / CAMBRIDGE, U.K.

DOVE BOOKSELLERS
DEARBORN, MICHIGAN

Main text originally published as
The Faith of Jesus Christ: An Investigation of the Narrative Substructure of Galatians 3:1–4:11,
Number 56 in the Society of Biblical Literature Dissertation Series
© 1983 by The Society of Biblical Literature

Appendixes 1 and 2 originally published in *Pauline Theology*
Volume 4: *Looking Back, Pressing On,*
part of the Society of Biblical Literature Symposium Series
© 1997 by The Society of Biblical Literature

Foreword by Luke Timothy Johnson and new introductory essay by Richard B. Hays
© 2002 by Wm. B. Eerdmans Publishing Co.
All rights reserved

Published 2002 by Wm. B. Eerdmans Publishing Co.
2140 Oak Industrial Drive N.E., Grand Rapids, Michigan 49505 /
P.O. Box 163, Cambridge CB3 9PU U.K.
www.eerdmans.com
and by
Dove Booksellers
13904 Michigan Avenue
Dearborn, Michigan 48126

Printed in the United States of America

07 06 05 04 03 02   7 6 5 4 3 2 1

Library of Congress Cataloging-in-Publication Data

Hays, Richard B.
The faith of Jesus Christ.
(Dissertation series/Society of Biblical Literature; no. 56)
Thesis (Ph.D.) — Emory University, 1981.
Bibliography: p.
ISBN-10: 0-8028-4957-1 / ISBN-13: 978-0-8028-4957-1
1. Bible. N.T. Galatians III, I–IV, 11 — Criticism, interpretation, etc.
2. Bible. N.T. Epistles of Paul — Criticism, interpretation, etc.
I. Title.   II. Series: Dissertation series (Society of Biblical Literature); no. 56.
BS2685.2 H39 1983
227'.406   82-10660

Excerpt from "East Coker" in FOUR QUARTETS, copyright 1940 by T. S. Eliot and renewed 1968 by Esme Valerie Eliot, reprinted by permission of Harcourt, Inc. and Faber & Faber Ltd.

Contents

CONTENTS

Contents

Foreword

Most Ph.D. dissertations in New Testament studies are read only by the committee for whom they were written, are bound and shelved in the research library, and are happily forgotten by everyone except the author. A few dissertations find publication in a monograph or dissertation series, or even a university press, and can claim readers beyond the boundaries of the writer's department. This is known as academic success. But when a dissertation has stayed in print for twenty years and is then reissued by a major publisher — without alteration — for a still wider readership, we can speak of real influence and importance. As a scholarly colleague and friend of Richard Hays who has profited from the book and who has exploited some of its key ideas perhaps even more enthusiastically than its author, I am delighted to celebrate the occasion of its re-publication by noting some features of this study that make it an original and significant contribution to New Testament scholarship.

Even when considered as a dissertation, the study has qualities that demand attention. First, it has both scope and ambition. Although Hays focuses on a single passage in Paul's Letter to the Galatians (3:1–4:11), he seeks from the perspective of that analysis to engage one of the most difficult of all questions concerning Paul the Apostle, whether he had any coherence to his thought at all, and if he did, where it is to be found. Hays rejects the available options: that Paul has a single theological principle (like righteousness by faith) or a specific symbolic framework (like eschatology) that governs his thought. He offers instead the daring thesis that what appears explicitly in Paul's arguments is really directed by what seldom appears explicitly and directly but is always present implicitly, namely the story of Jesus the Messiah. Hays invites us to read Galatians (and perhaps Paul's other letters) as discourse that clarifies and corrects an implicit narrative about Jesus that is shared by Paul and his readers. And the heart of that story of Jesus is the faith of the Messiah. Paul does believe that humans are put into right relationship with God through faith. It is not through their own faith, however, but through the faith of Jesus.

The book's argument, then, cuts to the very heart of Pauline theology. Hays's conversation partners, consequently, are not the random set of scholars who have commented on this passage of Galatians, but those major figures who have addressed the central themes in Paul's theology that he has taken on. We find him responding to Bousset, Schweitzer, Bultmann, Käsemann, Cullmann, Dodd, Beker, Sanders, Via, and Dahl, among New Testament scholars: figures who have made major contributions but whom Hays engages with the quiet confidence of one who considers his thesis to be better than theirs. More surprising, Hays also joins in conversation with literary and philosophical figures like Amos Wilder, Steven Crites, William Beardslee, Northrop Frye, and Paul Ricoeur.

His effort to place his narrative analysis within the framework of contemporary literary criticism and hermeneutics prepares for the substantial use he makes of A. J. Greimas's actantial analysis in the heart of his study, and indicates how Hays's dissertation was distinctive from the beginning also in the way in which it eschews the customary historical-critical questions — he never asks about the situation Paul faced in Galatia — in favor of a strictly literary approach. He is aware of the (then) innovative application of ancient rhetorical theory to Paul's letters, especially the pioneering effort of H. D. Betz on Galatians, but although he recognizes the limited value of such analysis, his own interest is less with the technique of Paul's discourse than with the deep narrative logic out of which that discourse emerges and of which it is a fresh expression.

Hays's argument moves in three stages. He begins with the puzzle presented by two short passages in Galatians (4:3-6 and 3:13-14) that all scholars perceive both as having a certain formal pattern and as standing in some sort of relationship with each other, but that no other scholar has been able satisfactorily to solve. By applying Greimas's actantial analysis, Hays identifies the two passages as narrative fragments that represent "two tellings ('performance manifestations') of the same story" (p. 107 below), one formulation from a Gentile point of view and the other from a Jewish point of view (pp. 107-8). The story is how God sent his Son to redeem humans. In this story, Hays says, "Jesus Christ [is] in the role of Subject, with πίστις as the power or quality which enables him to carry out his mandate" (p. 115). In Greimas's terms, πίστις appears in the analysis as the "helper." Critical to this entire analysis, however, is the fact that "faith" is clearly a quality or power exercised by the human person Jesus, not something directed to Jesus by others.

Having shown the narrative function of faith through the analysis of these two story fragments, Hays moves to the second stage of his argument, in which he contends, against the majority position within scholarship, that the subjective reading of πίστις Χριστοῦ best corresponds to the narrative logic and best expresses Paul's theological point. This section of the dissertation patiently leads the reader through the grammatical nuances of the disputed Greek phrase. When Paul uses the expression, does he intend the genitive Χριστοῦ to be subjective or objective with respect to the nominative πίστις? Does he, in other words, think of faith as something that Jesus Christ has or exercises, or does he think of it as something that humans direct toward Jesus Christ? Hays marshalls an impressive set of arguments in support of the subjective reading. What is particularly impressive here is that he makes this case independently of his narrative analysis, that is, he shows the superiority of the subjective position strictly on grammatical grounds. His two lines of analysis reinforce each other: what the actantial analysis demands, the grammatical analysis supplies.

The significance of Hays's accomplishment here should be noted. The long-standing debate over "faith of/in Christ" — a one-sided debate, to be sure — had tilted in favor of the objective reading for three major reasons: the supporters of the subjective reading tended to be quirky, they failed to face all the problems head-on, and, above all, they could not really account for Paul's usage in Galatians. Hays's dissertation decisively turned the debate (though it has not entirely ended) toward the subjective reading precisely because he established it in the hardest passage. The arguments being made simultaneously by other scholars on the basis of Romans therefore became more persuasive because of the heavy lifting Hays had done in Galatians.

The third major stage of Hays's argument is to follow the entire argument of Galatians 3:1–4:11 in light of the analysis he had already carried out on 3:13-14 and 4:3-6. How do these narrative fragments fit within Paul's clearly nonnarrative discourse? Once more the boldness of Hays's attack is impressive, for if there is any section in all of Paul's letters that would seem to demand a strictly logical apprehension, it is this part of Galatians. Hays considers in turn three efforts at cracking Paul's dense argumentation. G. M. Taylor thinks that a juridic logic is at work; N. A. Dahl argues that Paul is using midrashic logic, and H. D. Betz reads the section in terms of rhetorical logic. Hays recognizes that each suggestion contributes something but falls short of grasping the real point of the passage, which is to clarify the import of the story of how God has made humans righteous through the faith of the Messiah Jesus. What holds Galatians 3:1–4:11 together, Hays says, is an implicit participationist soteriology, or, to use simpler terms, a story in which Paul and his readers have been caught up: "Paul's reasoning is most fully comprehensible when this section of Galatians is understood as Paul's attempt to articulate in discursive language the meaning *(dianoia)* of a story whose protagonist is Jesus Christ" (p. 209 below). Christ is not only the ground of their salvation; through baptism, Paul's readers have come to participate in the story of Jesus. They are the ones Paul refers to as οἱ ἐκ πίστεως, "those who are out of faith," and the work of the Holy Spirit is to shape them according to the pattern of the one whose faith has saved them (p. 203).

Hays himself presents a number of corollaries to his thesis beyond his claim to having solved the puzzle of Gal 3:1–4:11.

1. He proposes that his position helps solve the long-standing debate between Pauline scholars over the question whether "justification by faith" or "participation in Christ" is more central to the Apostle's thinking. Hays says that it is a false opposition. If one grasps that the faith that makes righteous is Jesus' own faith and that his story is one in which, by baptism, Christians have been incorporated, the two sides of the debate can best be seen as moments in the same narrative process.

2. He suggests as well that such a reading of Paul raises questions about Paul's place in earliest Christianity: "theologically speaking, Paul may have been less sharply distinctive within his contemporary environment than is often supposed" (p. 217 below). In particular, real lines of continuity can be shown between the Paul of Galatians, Romans, and Philippians, the Letter to the Hebrews, and even Irenaeus.

3. In particular, Hays's study suggests a closer link between Paul and the Gospels than has often been seen. Simply to state that Paul's thought has a narrative substructure is to make stronger the connection between his letters and the Gospel genre. But Hays also sees in the narrative fragments of Galatians an implicit link between the proclamation of the cross, the incarnation, and even pre-existence.

4. Hays perceives that his thesis has real implications for Pauline ethics in the way that the Christ story serves to shape the readers' sense of the self and the world. Once more he sees that a constant conflict within Protestant theology between faith-righteousness and works-righteousness is relieved in this reading of Paul, in which the faithful obedience of Jesus *shapes* the story of the believer, so that the faithful obedience of Christians does not replace but continues the story of Jesus.

5. Finally, Hays thinks that Paul can be much more fruitfully read when

his discourse is seen as more reflexive and responsive than is sometimes thought. Galatians is not "foundational language" in which Paul lays down for his readers what they do not already know. Instead, his language serves a more indirect, even poetic, function. Unless we understand that Paul and his readers share a story and that Paul seeks both to allude to and to apply that story in ways that correct their misapprehensions and clarify the story's implications, we do not read him right.

Like the thesis concerning Galatians 3:1–4:11 itself, this set of corollaries is bold and ambitious. Fortunately, much of subsequent scholarship has shown it to be correct in the directions it proposes. Some of these corollaries have been worked out in Hays's own subsequent research. Through a series of articles, he has shown the significance of the faith of Jesus for Paul in Romans. In his major work on New Testament ethics, *The Moral Vision of the New Testament* (San Francisco: HarperSanFrancisco, 1996), he further developed the implications of the Christ-story, not only for Pauline but also for all New Testament ethics. And in his influential work *Echoes of Scripture in the Letters of Paul* (New Haven: Yale University Press, 1989), he showed another side to Paul's "allusive" discourse, this time with respect to Scripture: Paul's sense of story includes all that God did with Israel as well as what God did in and through the Messiah Jesus. It would be tedious to show how much attention these two monographs in particular generated, and how much effect Hays's work has had (positively) on other scholars. By no means do his views command universal consent. But for those who find this way of approaching the New Testament not only profoundly right but also deeply enriching, Richard Hays's work is of great significance. You have in your hands the first expression of his vision, already in its way remarkably mature, and still, in every way, worth careful study.

LUKE TIMOTHY JOHNSON

Preface

This study grew from seeds planted during Professor Leander Keck's seminar in the Fall of 1978 on Paul's use of traditions. From Professor Keck I acquired the vision for seeking to distinguish "what Paul preached" from the particular matters at issue in his letters. The seedling project was further nourished by a subsequent seminar under Professor Hendrikus Boers which afforded me the opportunity to employ linguistic methodologies for investigating the function of πίστις in Romans and Galatians. Professor Boers has made many incisive criticisms that have contributed substantially to the sharpening of my investigation. To both Professors Boers and Keck I am grateful for their example of passionate engagement with the text and determination to confront the ultimate theological questions raised by it.

Professor William Beardslee, who served as director of the dissertation, guided my work not only with erudition but also with a generous catholic spirit which has served to broaden my vision and refine my thinking in countless ways. Thanks are due also to the other members of my committee, Professor Fred Craddock, Professor Carl Holladay, and Professor Paul Borgman, for their encouragement and suggestions. Professor Holladay's assistance was particularly invaluable in "tightening the bolts" at the final stage of the project.

I would also like to express my appreciation for several others who contributed materially to the completion of this study. Rev. Ben Witherington of Coleridge, North Carolina, read a draft of the first five chapters and made numerous helpful comments and criticisms. Professor Luke Johnson of Yale Divinity School offered encouragement at several crucial points along the way. Mrs. Orrin Branson proofread the manuscript in its entirety, and Ms. Sharon Cole undertook with diligence and good humor the formidable task of typing the dissertation under the pressure of various deadlines.

My thanks are due also to the trustees of A Foundation for Theological Education, whose John Wesley Fellowship grant has helped to support me and my family over the past three years, and to the United Methodist Church, which provided support through a Cokesbury Graduate Award during 1979-80.

Finally, my gratitude goes out above all to my family: to my mother and father who, in their separate ways, have had faith in me and supported me; to my wife Judy, whose love and endurance over these trying years of student life have been a living out of Paul's exhortation to "serve one another in love"; and to my children Christopher and Sarah, who have taught me much about the importance of stories.

Atlanta, Georgia   Richard B. Hays
11 July 1981

An additional word of thanks is now due to several people who assisted in preparing this study for publication: to the Council of Fellows of the Whitney Humanities Center of Yale University, whose award of a grant from the A. Whitney Griswold Faculty Research Fund has made possible the typing of this manuscript; to Peter Jonas, who compiled the indices; and to Joann River Burnich for her careful and professional preparation of the text.

All abbreviations in this study follow the system set forth in the *Journal of Biblical Literature* 95 (1976) 335-46.

New Haven, Connecticut
25 May 1983

Acknowledgments

I would like to say a few words of appreciation for several people who have made this book possible. First of all, the editorial staff at Eerdmans graciously initiated this project and moved it forward with professionalism and dispatch; I am grateful particularly to Sam Eerdmans and Michael Thomson for their roles in bringing this book into its new edition. The collegial cooperation of Rex Matthews and his staff at the Society of Biblical Literature was also instrumental in facilitating this edition. I also want to thank Jimmy Dunn for agreeing to the reprinting of his essay, in counterpoint to mine, as an appendix to the book; I have found him a delightfully collegial and formidable debating partner, and I have learned much from him. Two recent students, Sigve Tonstad and Kevin Adair, did a reading course with me on πίστις Ἰησοῦ Χριστοῦ; their excitement about the issues renewed my conviction of the theological urgency of the topic. My wife Judy, as always, encouraged me to quit ruminating and get on with it. The new introduction was written during a research leave at The Center of Theological Inquiry in Princeton, NJ. I am grateful to Wallace Alston, Robert Jenson, and Kathi Morley for their support and for the wonderful facilities of the Center. Cory Hall provided timely research assistance.

Finally, I want to offer a word of thanksgiving for Will Beardslee, the director of my dissertation, who died on January 25, 2001, and so did not live to see this reprint edition. Twenty years ago, Will patiently read my rough drafts and tried to polish the rough edges of my brash and overly ambitious project. (I had originally planned not only to write about Galatians 3:1–4:11 but also to include chapters on Romans 5, 1 Corinthians 15, and Philippians 2. Will wisely talked me out of this plan; had I entered the labyrinth of secondary literature on those texts, the present book might be a first edition rather than a reprint.) He was in every way a gentleman and a model of scholarly integrity. I am indebted to him for making this a far better book than it could have been without his guidance. Those of us who were privileged to know him will miss him.

Introduction to the Second Edition

This book was originally written on a Smith-Corona portable electric typewriter. That fact highlights the span of time elapsed since I submitted *The Faith of Jesus Christ* as my doctoral dissertation at Emory University in 1981. During my dissertation-writing years, no one owned a personal computer. To employ Greek and Hebrew characters, I had to leave blank spaces in the typed text and later write them in by hand. Typing errors had to be scraped off the page with a special eraser or blotted out with a fast-drying white liquid solution. Any significant revision necessitated retyping all pages from the point of revision forward. When my dissertation was accepted into the SBL Dissertation Series, it had to be retyped from scratch in order to meet the formatting guidelines of the series. (Happily, the cost of paying a professional typist to do this work was covered by a grant from the Whitney Humanities Center of Yale University, where I was then beginning my teaching career.) My students today, accustomed to correcting their computer-processed papers at will and reprinting with a couple of mouse clicks, can hardly conceive that their professor once labored under such primitive conditions.

I call to mind these mundane facts about the technology of text production in order to mark the distance we have traversed in the past twenty years — and to suggest, by analogy, that the field of Pauline studies has also covered a large stretch of new ground in the same period. When this dissertation was finished in 1981, J. D. G. Dunn had not yet written his essay on "The New Perspective on Paul";[1] Wayne Meeks had not yet published *The First Urban Christians;*[2]

---

1. J. D. G. Dunn, "The New Perspective on Paul," *BJRL* 65 (1983) 95-122.
2. W. A. Meeks, *The First Urban Christians: The Social World of the Apostle Paul* (New Haven: Yale University Press, 1983).

the SBL Pauline Theology Group was still years in the future; and J. Louis Martyn's paradigm-shifting essays on Galatians as an apocalyptic text had not yet invaded the discipline.[3] Nor had I yet encountered the (diverse) ideas of scholars such as N. T. Wright, Beverly Gaventa, Daniel Boyarin, John Barclay, Francis Watson, and A. Katherine Grieb, who were destined to become my friends and conversation partners.[4] Nor had I yet addressed in more than a rudimentary way the task of integrating New Testament exegesis into the wider study of Christian Scripture and theology — a challenge clarified for me in recent years through my participation in the Scripture Project at the Center of Theological Inquiry in Princeton. All of this is to say that if I were setting out to write this book today it would be a different book, because I have learned much in twenty years and because the conversation within the discipline has moved forward.

When, therefore, Eerdmans approached me about producing a new edition of *The Faith of Jesus Christ,* I could not help recalling T. S. Eliot's lines from "East Coker":

> So here I am, in the middle way, having had twenty years —
> Twenty years largely wasted, the years of *l'entre deux guerres* —
> Trying to learn to use words, and every attempt
> Is a wholly new start, and a different kind of failure
> Because one has only learnt to get the better of words
> For the thing one no longer has to say, or the way in which
> One is no longer disposed to say it. And so each venture
> Is a new beginning, a raid on the inarticulate
> With shabby equipment always deteriorating
> In the general mess of imprecision of feeling,
> Undisciplined squads of emotion. And what there is to conquer
> By strength and submission, has already been discovered
> Once or twice, or several times, by men whom one cannot hope
> To emulate — but there is no competition —
> There is only the fight to recover what has been lost
> And found and lost again and again: and now, under conditions
> That seem unpropitious.

3. Especially "Apocalyptic Antinomies in Paul's Letter to the Galatians," *NTS* 31 (1985) 410-24; see also the other essays collected in idem, *Theological Issues in the Letters of Paul* (Nashville: Abingdon, 1997).

4. I did have the opportunity to discuss my work with Luke Timothy Johnson during the writing of the dissertation, and his essay on "Romans 3:21-26 and the Faith of Jesus" (*CBQ* 44 [1982] 77-90) appeared in time to be included in my final revision of the work for publication.

I was pleased at the prospect of having my work on the narrative substructure of Paul's theology reprinted in a more attractive format than the old typescript edition, and I dared to hope that some good might come of making the work available to a wider audience. On the other hand, acutely aware of the shortcomings of this early work, I found the prospect of undertaking a revision daunting. It would not do simply to revise a few paragraphs and add some additional bibliographical notes: a revision would be "a wholly new start." I would have to rethink and rewrite the whole book to bring it up to speed with the important conversations that have developed in the interim. The conditions for such rewriting, however, were not propitious, for new projects and commitments demanded my time and attention. It seemed best, therefore, to reprint the dissertation just as I originally wrote it, accompanied by a new introduction and by the essays that Jimmy Dunn and I wrote for the Pauline Theology Group in 1991, debating the πίστις Χριστοῦ question.[5] Thus, this reprint edition offers, as it were, a time capsule, a record of how I approached Paul's thought twenty years ago. At the same time, this edition also provides the occasion for some fresh reflections about the arguments I made and about how the discussion might fruitfully go forward.

I. How to Interpret *The Faith of Jesus Christ*

Just as parents may not be the best judges of their children's accomplishments, authors are not necessarily the best interpreters of their own books: we stand too close and have too much at stake. On the other hand, we may also have revealing insights. I therefore will begin this introduction by presuming to offer the reader three suggestions about how to interpret this book.

A. The Central Thesis: The Narrative Substructure of Paul's Theology

First of all, this is a book about the narrative elements that undergird Paul's thought. Despite its title, the book is *not* just a discussion of how to translate the contested expression πίστις ᾽Ιησοῦ Χριστοῦ. Although my treatment of

---

5. These essays were subsequently revised for inclusion in E. E. Johnson and D. M. Hay (eds.), *Pauline Theology Volume IV: Looking Back, Pressing On* (Society of Biblical Literature Symposium Series; Atlanta: Scholars, 1997). The essays as reprinted in this volume are taken from that edition.

this issue in Chapter IV has attracted insistent response and attention within the scholarly guild,[6] this problem of translation plays a subsidiary role in the larger argument. The central thesis of the book is stated forthrightly in the opening pages and reiterated in the concluding chapter: *a story about Jesus Christ is presupposed by Paul's argument in Galatians, and his theological reflection attempts to articulate the meaning of that story.* Thus, the book's subtitle is a better guide to its content than the main title.

The point may be underscored by noting that the *Problemstellung* in the opening chapter makes only a single passing allusion to the "faith of Christ" question (p. 10), and that the survey of previous research in Chapter II focuses on how major treatments of Pauline theology have dealt with the narrative dimension of Paul's thought — *not* on the question of how they have translated πίστις Ἰησοῦ Χριστοῦ. (For a survey of scholarly positions on the latter question, the reader must await a brief six-page account in Chapter IV [pp. 142-47].) Similarly, the concluding chapter makes only slight reference to the "faith of Christ" problem.

My point here is not that the πίστις Χριστοῦ debate is inconsequential: far from it. Rather, I want to insist that discussion of this problem should be placed in the framework of a more comprehensive debate about the story-shaped character of Paul's theology. Some critiques of my work have focused narrowly on the translation of a single phrase and thereby have lost their way, overlooking the larger contours of the argument.[7]

The theological education I had received at Yale during the 1970s prepared the way for my book's emphasis on narrative. I had appreciatively read great chunks of Karl Barth, and I had been fascinated by David Kelsey's description of Barth's reading of Scripture as "one vast, loosely structured nonfictional novel."[8] (Chapter II of my dissertation originally included a brief section on Barth's treatment of narrative in Paul, but I was dissatisfied with it and deleted it, realizing that a much lengthier discussion would be necessary

---

6. For a survey of the literature up to the mid 1990s, see R. B. Hays, "ΠΙΣΤΙΣ and Pauline Christology: What Is at Stake?" in Johnson and Hay (eds.), *Pauline Theology Volume IV: Looking Back, Pressing On*, 35-60; see especially pp. 35-37 nn. 2-4. For other recent surveys, see P. Pollard, "The 'Faith of Christ' in Current Discussion," *Concordia Journal* 23 (1997) 213-28; J. Dunnill, "Saved by Whose Faith? The Function of πίστις Χριστοῦ in Pauline Theology," *Colloquium* 30/1 (1998) 3-25.

7. The recent article of R. Barry Matlock ("Detheologizing the ΠΙΣΤΙΣ ΧΡΙΣΤΟΥ Debate: Cautionary Remarks from a Lexical Semantic Perspective," *NovT* 42 [2000] 1-23) is a particularly clear example of this tendency.

8. D. H. Kelsey, *The Uses of Scripture in Recent Theology* (Philadelphia: Fortress, 1975), 39-50. The quoted phrase appears on p. 48.

to do justice to Barth.) At the same time, I had encountered the work of Hans Frei — whom I was later privileged to know as a colleague, before his untimely death. Frei had stimulated a theological revolution by contending in *The Eclipse of Biblical Narrative* that biblical criticism, especially in Germany, had gone astray by failing to grasp the narrative sense of Scripture.[9] Furthermore, Frei had offered a constructive account in *The Identity of Jesus Christ* of what it might mean to give hermeneutical primacy to the narrative renderings of the character of Jesus in the Gospels.[10] I was not uncritical of Frei: his sketch of the story of Jesus failed to do justice to the narrative particularities of the four different canonical gospels, and his emphasis on narrative left important questions about the relation between story and history unresolved — or at least so it then seemed to me. Nonetheless, Frei's appeal for a theological recovery of narrative was a timely and important word. It is no accident that my dissertation contains half a dozen references to Frei and that in attempting to explain the narrative logic of Paul's christology, I twice quote Frei's description of "the pattern of exchange" in which Jesus "enacts the salvation of men in obedience to God."[11] Frei never attempted to apply his insights about narrative to Pauline texts, but his work provided the indispensable background for the questions I was asking.

My interest in exploring the relation between narrative and theology in Paul also had a polemical edge. The great adversary whose shadow looms over *The Faith of Jesus Christ* is Rudolf Bultmann. Bultmann's once dominant influence in NT studies has waned strikingly over the past twenty years — the reasons for this shift in intellectual fashion need not detain us here — but in the 1970s his work was still a force to be reckoned with by every student of theology. His *Theology of the New Testament* was the benchmark against which any new hermeneutical proposals had to be measured, and the spirited debate sparked by Ernst Käsemann's attacks on the hermeneutical program of his mentor defined the issues that preoccupied me as a graduate student.[12]

9. H. Frei, *The Eclipse of Biblical Narrative: A Study in Eighteenth and Nineteenth Century Hermeneutics* (New Haven: Yale University Press, 1974).

10. H. Frei, *The Identity of Jesus Christ: The Hermeneutical Bases of Dogmatic Theology* (Philadelphia: Fortress, 1975).

11. Frei, *Identity*, 75. The "pattern of exchange" is cited on pp. 179, 220 in my book. See also Morna Hooker's important essay on "Interchange in Christ," in *From Adam to Christ: Essays on Paul* (Cambridge: Cambridge University Press, 1990), 13-25.

12. E. P. Sanders's watershed book, *Paul and Palestinian Judaism,* had appeared in 1977. Sanders had transformed my picture of Palestinian Judaism, but in 1981 I was only beginning to grapple with the consequences of this transformation for the construal of Paul's theology. Another way of putting this point would be to say that I found Sanders's account of

Anyone who wants to understand the battles I was fighting in this dissertation should read with care my brief exposition and critique of Bultmann on pp. 5-6 and 47-52). Even where Bultmann is not mentioned explicitly, he is often the unnamed elephant in the room, as in my laborious explanation of why I prefer to speak of "story" and "narrative" rather than "myth" in Paul's thought-world (pp. 15-18).

In brief, it seemed to me that Bultmann had made two interrelated and fatefully mistaken hermeneutical decisions in his reading of Paul: he sought to "de-narrativize" Paul's thought world, and he understood the gospel principally as a message about human decision, human self-understanding. The theological burden of my argument is to show that Bultmann was wrong on both counts. One of Bultmann's chief reasons for seeking to strip away narrative mythological elements in Paul was his belief — rooted ultimately in Kantian philosophical assumptions — that a narrated kerygma would necessarily become merely one more event in the phenomenal world, susceptible to human manipulation and detached from authentic encounter with God's word. My dissertation, however, presents a diametrically opposed view: the story *is* the word of God, and we know God in no other way than as the God who has acted through the faithfulness of Jesus Christ to "rescue us from the present evil age" (Gal 1:4).

Of course, my dissertation barely scratches the surface of the hermeneutical issues involved, but it seeks to offer a demonstration of how to read Galatians 3:1–4:11 in accordance with a narrative model for interpretation. I believed then and still believe strongly that this approach yields a more coherent reading of the Pauline letters.

In order to fight this battle I enlisted the aid of whatever methods came to hand. In Chapter I, I cobbled together an eclectic assemblage of insights from various critics, with the work of Northrop Frye, Paul Ricoeur, and — strange as it now seems — Robert Funk playing the most important parts.[13] No one of these critics provided a comprehensive methodological framework, but each contributed something significant to my proposal about how reflective theological discourse can be grounded in a narrative substructure.

In Chapter III, I turned to structuralist methodologies for analyzing the

---

Palestinian Judaism more immediately illuminating than his sketch of Paul's "pattern of religion." Given the relative attention that Sanders gives to each in his book, this result is not entirely surprising. Still, as my concluding chapter demonstrates, it seemed to me that by focusing on participation in Christ as the central theme of Pauline soteriology, Sanders had put his finger on the heart of the matter.

13. Funk's subsequent Jesus Seminar follies should not be allowed to obscure the usefulness of his earlier work.

syntax of narratives, drawing particularly on the work of A. J. Greimas, which in turn had been influenced by Vladimir Propp's studies of the morphology of Russian folktales. This chapter particularly reflects the intellectual gravitational pull of Hendrikus Boers, one of my teachers at Emory, who was then engaged in dialogue with structuralism — a theoretical movement much discussed in the 1970s but now as thoroughly superseded as disco music, or as my Smith-Corona typewriter. Candidly, I thought even then that structuralism offered a singularly mechanistic and barren approach to reading texts, but Professor Boers strongly encouraged his graduate students to work with these methods. Thus, Chapter III constituted a thought experiment for me. I took it as a challenge first of all to give a concise and understandable explanation of Greimas's schema (or, more precisely, the part of the schema that I found useful) and then to make it work as a heuristic tool for outlining narrative structures in Galatians. To my own surprise, this "shabby equipment" yielded more interesting results than I expected. I found the model particularly helpful for explaining how Paul's differing kerygmatic summaries can be read synthetically as part of a single story. In my view, however, the argument of the dissertation does not ride upon these methods or upon the results produced by them. Readers who find their eyes glazing over as they seek to decipher the actantial diagrams in Chapter III are hereby absolved of responsibility for making sense of this material and given permission to skip on to Chapter IV. Since departing from Emory I have not used structuralist methods in my subsequent exegetical work, nor do I expect that I shall do so in the future.

The thing that matters is the message of the text, the story that it tells and interprets. Methodology is a secondary and instrumental concern. As Frei opined, "the theoretical devices we use to make our reading more alert, appropriate, and intelligent ought to be designed to leave the story itself as unencumbered as possible."[14] It would, therefore, grieve me if the earnest methodological reflections of Chapters I and III of my book stood in the way of substantive engagement with the issues I have sought to raise about interpretation of the text. Readers who want to see how my proposals about "narrative substructure" work out in a sustained, integrative reading of Galatians may now consult my recent commentary in the New Interpreter's Bible.[15]

14. Frei, *Identity,* xv.
15. R. B. Hays, *The Letter to the Galatians* (NIB 11; Nashville: Abingdon, 2000). For other readings that proceed along similar — though hardly identical — lines, see especially J. L. Martyn, *Galatians* (AB 33A; New York: Doubleday, 1997), and B. W. Longenecker, *The Triumph of Abraham's God: The Transformation of Identity in Galatians* (Edinburgh: T&T Clark, 1998).

In any case, I am gratified to see that the shape of the conversation about Pauline theology has changed significantly, at least in the English-speaking world, so that claims about narrative features in Paul's thought are now much more widely accepted than they were twenty years ago.[16] A single example will serve to illustrate the point: Wayne Meeks, the distinguished social historian of early Christianity, now writes about Paul in a way that acknowledges his theological use of narrative:

> We have not thought of Paul as a storyteller, for the Jesus stories of the Gospels are absent from his letters. Yet his use of narrative is very important . . . , because Paul's central concern was to use the narrative to form a moral community. . . . Paul's most profound bequest to subsequent Christian discourse was his transformation of the reported crucifixion and resurrection of Jesus Christ into a multipurpose metaphor with vast generative and transformative power. . . . In that gospel story Paul sees revolutionary import for the relationships of power that control human transactions. . . . Thus Paul's use of the metaphor of the cross resists its translation into simple slogans. Instead he introduces into the moral language of the new movement a way of seeking after resonances in the basic story for all kinds of relationships of disciples with the world and with one another, so that the event-become-metaphor could become the generative center of almost endless new narratives, yet remain a check and control over those narratives.[17]

16. See, for example, N. R. Petersen, *Rediscovering Paul: Philemon and the Sociology of Paul's Narrative World* (Philadelphia: Fortress, 1985); S. Fowl, *The Story of Christ in the Ethics of Paul: An Analysis of the Function of the Hymnic Material in the Pauline Corpus* (JSNTSup 36; Sheffield: JSOT Press, 1990); N. T. Wright, *The Climax of the Covenant: Christ and the Law in Pauline Theology* (Edinburgh: T&T Clark, 1991); B. Witherington III, *Paul's Narrative Thought World: The Tapestry of Tragedy and Triumph* (Louisville: Westminster/John Knox, 1994); F. Thielman, "The Story of Israel and the Theology of Romans 5–8," in D. M. Hay and E. E. Johnson (eds.), *Pauline Theology Volume III: Romans* (Minneapolis: Fortress, 1995), 169-95; S. C. Keesmaat, *Paul and His Story: (Re)-Interpreting the Exodus Tradition* (Sheffield: Sheffield Academic Press, 1999); M. J. Gorman, *Cruciformity: Paul's Narrative Spirituality of the Cross* (Grand Rapids: Eerdmans, 2001); A. K. Grieb, *Romans: The Story of God's Righteousness* (Louisville: Westminster/John Knox, 2002). Of course, this change is part of a larger shift towards an appreciation of the importance of narrative for Christian theology. For a helpful discussion and selection of key essays, see S. Hauerwas and L. G. Jones (eds.), *Why Narrative? Readings in Narrative Theology* (Grand Rapids: Eerdmans, 1989).

17. W. A. Meeks, *The Origins of Christian Morality: The First Two Centuries* (New Haven: Yale University Press, 1993), 196-97. A footnote to this passage cites *The Faith of Jesus Christ* in support of Meeks's claims about the "underlying narrative in Paul's letters" (p. 240 n. 16).

Meeks's discerning description of Paul's moral reasoning represents a clear gain over older, nonnarrative accounts.[18] It is to be hoped that the reprinting of *The Faith of Jesus Christ* will reinforce and clarify the growing recognition of the narrative roots of Paul's theology.

B. Participation in Christ as the Key to Pauline Soteriology

A second suggestion for readers of this book is to observe its insistent claim that we are caught up into the story of Jesus Christ. *In a mysterious way, Jesus has enacted our destiny, and those who are in Christ are shaped by the pattern of his self-giving death. He is the prototype of redeemed humanity.* Thus, for Paul, "the faithfulness of Jesus Christ" has an incorporative character. That is why Paul says, "I have been crucified with Christ; and it is no longer I who live, but it is Christ who lives in me. And the life I now live in the flesh I live by the faithfulness of the Son of God, who loved me and gave himself for me" (Gal 2:19b-20). Jesus is not merely a good moral example; rather, his story transforms and absorbs the world. The old world has been crucified and new creation has broken in through Jesus' death and resurrection (Gal 6:14-15).

Another way of putting the point would be to say that Irenaeus, in his doctrine of "recapitulation" (ἀνακεφαλαίωσις) grasped the logic of Paul's christology and soteriology far more clearly than have most subsequent Western theories of atonement. The greatest weakness of the traditional post-Reformation understanding of "faith" and "justification" in Paul is, as Gerhard Ebeling rightly observed, that it offers no coherent account of the relation between the doctrine of justification and *christology*.[19] The greatest strength of the exegesis set forward in *Faith of Jesus Christ* — and in the work of others who have come to understand the expression πίστις Ἰησοῦ Χριστοῦ as a shorthand reference to Christ's action — is that it explains how Paul's understanding of the πίστις of Jesus is integrally related to his understanding of δικαιοσύνη. As Leander Keck has commented, "in every case, construing πίστις Ἰησοῦ as the fidelity of Jesus . . . clarifies the key point — the role of Jesus in salvation."[20] In order to explain this a little more fully, let us consider three as-

18. See also my discussion of Pauline ethics in *The Moral Vision of the New Testament: Community, Cross, New Creation* (San Francisco: HarperSanFrancisco, 1996), 16-59.

19. See the passage from G. Ebeling (*Word and Faith* [London: SCM, 1963], 203) cited as an epigraph to Chapter IV of *Faith of Jesus Christ*.

20. L. E. Keck, "'Jesus' in Romans," *JBL* 108 (1989) 454.

pects of the logic of "participation in Christ" that are touched upon but perhaps not forcefully enough thematized in my dissertation.

(1) *"The faithfulness of Jesus Christ" refers first of all to his gracious, self-sacrificial death on a cross.* The cross is the dramatic climax of the Jesus-story, and Paul uses the expression πίστις Ἰησοῦ Χριστοῦ by *metonymy* to suggest and evoke that focal moment of the narrative. The death of Jesus can be characterized as πίστις for at least two reasons. First, Jesus "humbled himself and became obedient to the point of death — even death on a cross" (Phil 2:8). In contrast to the ἀπιστία of Israel (Rom 3:3), in contrast to the unbroken ἀδικία of all the rest of rebellious humanity (Rom 1:18-32; 3:9-20), Jesus Christ is the one human being who embodies radical obedience by remaining faithful to God, to the painful end.[21] For that reason, his fidelity overcomes Adam's rebellion, and he constitutes in himself a new, faithful humanity: "For just as by the one man's disobedience the many were made sinners, so by the one man's obedience the many will be made righteous" (Rom 5:19). Second, and equally important, this death of Jesus is mysteriously also a gracious act of God. As Paul formulates it in Rom 5:8, *"God* proves his love for us in that while we still were sinners *Christ* died for us." For that reason, the death of Jesus is also an act of divine πίστις, embodying and revealing the faithfulness of God (Rom 3:3, 21-22). In the death and resurrection of Jesus, we see God's fidelity to the promises made to Abraham.[22] Rather than abandoning or de-

---

21. B. W. Longenecker has argued persuasively that διὰ [τῆς] πίστεως in Rom 3:25 is not a Pauline editorial insertion but an integral part of the traditional formula that Paul is citing, which should be interpreted to mean "whom God put forward as an atoning sacrifice, through (Jesus') faithfulness by means of his blood" ("ΠΙΣΤΙΣ in Romans 3.25: Neglected Evidence for the Faithfulness of Christ?" *NTS* 39 [1993] 478-80).

22. This dimension of "the faith of Christ" is given particular emphasis in the work of George Howard (see *Paul: Crisis in Galatia: A Study in Early Christian Theology* [SNTSMS 35; Cambridge: Cambridge University Press, 1979], 57-58). Howard's discussion of "justification by faith," which contains a number of insightful observations about the construction of Paul's argument in Galatians 3, is unfortunately so terse and apodictic that it has made a limited impact on Pauline scholarship. I find now, rereading Howard twenty years later, that some of his points would have been helpful to me if I had then grasped more fully what he meant. In particular, his attention to the way that "the faith of Jesus Christ" is related to the justification of *Gentiles* provides an important additional dimension to the problem. (See further comment on this below.) Howard's rather grudging review of my book (*JBL* 105 [1986] 156-59) perhaps reflects his disappointment that his work was not given more prominence in my analysis. Certainly, had I been writing a dissertation that focused primarily on the πίστις Χριστοῦ question, Howard's work would have merited a larger role. In attempting to understand the *narrative* substructure of Paul's thought, however, I did not concentrate on Howard, since he was pursuing different issues.

stroying his unfaithful people, God constitutes Abraham's σπέρμα by his own gracious action in Christ (Gal 3:16, 29). Thus, the expression "the faith of Jesus Christ" signals that the death of Jesus is *simultaneously* an act of human fidelity to God and an act of divine fidelity to humanity.[23]

This observation carries an important negative corollary. Paul does not use "the faith of Jesus Christ" to extol Jesus' own religious disposition or subjective God-consciousness. It is *not* an expression that describes what many today would fondly call Jesus' "spirituality." Nor does Paul use it to call attention to Jesus' exemplary lifelong piety. (Indeed, this sort of habitual piety is precisely the aspect of Paul's own religious past that he now regards as σκύβαλα ["dung"; Phil 3:8].) Rather, the sense of πίστις ᾽Ιησοῦ Χριστοῦ is anchored consistently in the story's climactic event, the crucifixion of Jesus. Readers who fail to understand the metonymic character of "the faith of Jesus" as a reference to the story of Jesus' death will pervasively misread my argument.

(2) *Jesus Christ embodies the new creation and embraces us in his life.* All who are baptized into union with him share his destiny and his character. His fidelity to God is the pattern for the new life that he has inaugurated. That is why Paul can equate the coming of Christ with the coming of πίστις (Gal 3:23, 25): in a definitive way, he has now instantiated πίστις as a historical reality. Sam K. Williams has argued that, for Paul, Jesus actualized and exemplified faith in such a way that he is the creator of a new domain or "power field" characterized by faith.[24] This would be entirely consistent with the christol-

---

23. Thomas Torrance, informed by Barth's theology, quite correctly understood this complex bivalent sense of πίστις Χριστοῦ ("One Aspect of the Biblical Conception of Faith," *ExpTim* 68 [1957] 111-14). Unfortunately, he tried to attribute this complexity to a distinctive *linguistic* property of the noun πίστις as a "bipolar expression" whose sense depended on an underlying "Hebrew meaning." He thereby exposed himself to the withering critique of James Barr (*The Semantics of Biblical Language* [London: Oxford University Press, 1961], 161-205). I would suggest that Torrance's interpretation of Paul is nonetheless substantially correct, not because of distinctive linguistic features of πίστις but because of the distinctive identity of Jesus in the story to which Paul alludes by speaking of πίστις ᾽Ιησοῦ Χριστοῦ. As A. Katherine Grieb writes, "Jesus Christ is both Israel's representative (the Israelite who keeps covenant with God) and God's representative (the righteousness of God enacted through his own faithfulness, his faithful obedience unto death on the cross). . . . Paul's argument for the righteousness of God in Romans stands or falls precisely here: unless the faithfulness of Jesus Christ is also the righteousness of God as shown in his resurrection from the dead, then, as Paul says elsewhere, 'our preaching has been in vain and your faith has been in vain' (1 Cor 15:14)" (*Romans: The Story of God's Righteousness* [forthcoming]).

24. S. K. Williams, "Again *Pistis Christou*," *CBQ* 49 (1987) 431-47. Williams has developed this interpretation also in his commentary, *Galatians* (ANTC; Nashville: Abingdon,

ogy of the Letter to the Hebrews, which calls its readers to look to Jesus as τὸν τῆς πίστεως ἀρχηγὸν καὶ τελειωτὴν ("the author and finisher of faith"; Heb 12:2 — the text does not say ". . . of *our* faith," as in many English translations).[25] Thus, as a result of Jesus' faithfulness, the life that we now live in Christ we live "by the faith of the Son of God" (Gal 2:20). We are taken up into his life, including his faithfulness, and that faithfulness therefore imparts to us the shape of our own existence.[26] As Morna Hooker — in her 1988 presidential address at the Studiorum Novi Testamenti Societas in Cambridge — argued, Paul's use of the πίστις Χριστοῦ formula must be understood in light of his "interchange" soteriology: "Paul presents redemption in Christ as a radical restructuring of human nature: it is in effect a new creation (2 Cor 5:17). Christ became what we are in order that we might become what he is." Consequently, πίστις Ἰησοῦ Χριστοῦ should be understood as "a concentric expression, which begins, always, from the faith of Christ himself, but which includes, necessarily, the answering faith of believers, who claim that faith as their own."[27] In short, the soteriological logic of Galatians is participatory. It is not only in Romans 5 that Jesus is depicted as the founder and paradigm of a new humanity; indeed, this christological pattern is everywhere presupposed by Paul.

E. P. Sanders has rightly emphasized that participatory soteriology stands at the center of Paul's thought — though Sanders does not link this observation to the proposals made here about narrative and the faith of Christ, and he confesses himself unable to explain what Paul means by this "real participation in Christ."[28] My own guess is that Sanders's insights would be supported and clarified by careful study of participation motifs in patristic theology, particularly the thought of the Eastern Fathers.

1997). For an appreciative discussion of Williams, with some caveats, see my essay "ΠΙΣΤΙΣ and Pauline Christology: What Is at Stake?" at the end of this volume.

25. The relationship between the narrative portrayals of Jesus in Hebrews and in Paul's letters is a topic that would reward further inquiry. I made this suggestion briefly in the concluding chapter of *Faith of Jesus Christ* (p. 217). For a slightly different way of formulating the comparison, see also Ben Witherington III, "The Influence of Galatians on Hebrews," *NTS* 37 (1991) 146-52.

26. Surely something like this transformative incorporation in Christ is in Paul's mind when he writes that in the gospel the righteousness of God is revealed ἐκ πίστεως εἰς πίστιν (Rom 1:17a). Note the parallels to Rom 3:22 (διὰ πίστεως Ἰησοῦ Χριστοῦ, εἰς πάντας τοὺς πιστεύοντας) and Gal 3:22 (ἐκ πίστεως Ἰησοῦ . . . τοῖς πιστεύουσιν). On this point, see also Ebeling, *Word and Faith*, 303.

27. M. D. Hooker, "ΠΙΣΤΙΣ ΧΡΙΣΤΟΥ," *NTS* 35 (1989) 321-42; the quotations are from pp. 338 and 341.

28. Sanders, *Paul and Palestinian Judaism*, 522-23.

(3) *The cross, as Christ's saving action, is God's action of πίστις, God's demonstration of fidelity to the promise made to Abraham.* We have already noted this point above, but it deserves specific attention in its own right. While Jesus is "sent forth" by God (Gal 1:4; 4:4-5), there is a mysterious sense in which he is more than simply an intermediary or an agent of God's will. For Paul, Christ's death becomes God's own act, so that here, as, for example, in Rom 8:9-11, there is an overlay and fusion of the agency of Christ and the agency of God. Ultimately, being united with Christ is salvific because to share his life is to share in the life of God. Once again, this claim is explicable only in relation to the story in which Jesus is not just an exemplary human being but in fact God's own Son sent forth for our deliverance from slavery to the στοιχεῖα τοῦ κόσμου. The entire argument of Galatians presumes the following claims as axiomatic: God made a covenant with Abraham, promising to bless all nations through him; even though Jews and Gentiles alike were in a state of longstanding slavery, that promise remains unbroken; God fulfilled the promise through the death of Jesus, who is both Abraham's true seed and the revelation of God's fidelity to the promise. Thus, the πίστις Ἰησοῦ Χριστοῦ is the demonstration of God's righteousness, God's πίστις. (This last point is made more explicit in Romans 3 than in Galatians, but a similar underlying story is necessary for either argument to make sense.)

Nowhere in *The Faith of Jesus Christ* did I enter into theological reflection about the person of Christ or the doctrine of the Trinity, but analyzing the narrative substructure of Paul's thought inescapably leads us to the threshold of such questions. If the story that Paul told the Galatians is true, how are we to understand the apparent coinherence of God and Christ as characters in the story? Here as in other matters, we see the tensive character of Paul's discourse, its capacity to generate continually fresh reflection about the story in which it is grounded.

C. The Poetic Character of Paul's Language

The last observation leads to the final suggestion I want to impress upon the reader of this book. *Paul, the missionary preacher, is at least as much a poet as he is a theologian.* Not only in obviously poetic effusions such as Rom 8:31-39 and 1 Corinthians 13, but throughout his writings, Paul's language sparkles with the veiled energy of metaphor and allusion. I have made repeated pleas for recognition of this quality of Pauline discourse. (For a sustained argument about the poetic character of Paul's use of OT allusions and echoes, see my programmatic study *Echoes of Scripture in the Letters of Paul.*)[29] My investigation of narrative substructure in Galatians is intended not only to expose the narrative roots of Paul's argument but also thereby to free up our reading of the text, to make our reading more supple, more witty, and therefore more responsive to the character of the rich language that confronts us in the letter.

A passage such as Gal 6:14-15 calls upon us to read with lively metaphorical imagination: "But for me, let me not boast, except in the cross of our Lord Jesus Christ, through whom the world is crucified to me and I to the world. For neither circumcision is anything, nor uncircumcision, but — new creation!" Can anyone seriously suppose that the best way to interpret the writings of an author capable of this astonishing riff is to paraphrase his ideas into univocal concepts? On the contrary, Paul is constantly calling his readers to a conversion of the imagination.[30] That conversion entails not only the adoption of a new belief system but also learning to speak, pray, and sing the new confessional language summoned into existence by the gospel story. The phrase "the faith of Jesus Christ" belongs to that new language of new creation: it beckons us to ride the waves of signification unleashed by the impact of the cross. To speak this language is to be always alert to the possibilities of metaphor, typology, allusion, and polyvalence.

This is the intuition that informs my decision to approach Paul using various methods and categories derived from literary criticism. I am convinced that many of our disagreements about πίστις Ἰησοῦ Χριστοῦ and about whether Paul alludes to a story of Jesus Christ have their origins in differing prior construals of the character of Paul's discourse. Consequently, I call the reader's attention especially to the brief section on "The Character of Paul's Language" in the concluding chapter of the dissertation and to the final two paragraphs of my reply to Jimmy Dunn in the essay on "ΠΙΣΤΙΣ and Pauline Christology" that is appended at the end of the book. In these passages I state the case for reading Paul as a poetic writer who draws upon the allusive and evocative power of language. My book will make more sense if the reader adopts, at least as a thought experiment, the assumption that Paul writes as a preacher engaged in lively intertextual interplay with an audience that knows well the story of Jesus' crucifixion (as Paul reminds them in Gal 3:1) and the broad framework of the story of Israel. Because the audience knows these stories, Paul need not retell them from scratch; he can evoke

29. R. B. Hays, *Echoes of Scripture in the Letters of Paul* (New Haven: Yale University Press, 1989).

30. See R. B. Hays, "The Conversion of the Imagination: Scripture and Eschatology in 1 Corinthians," *NTS* 45 (1999) 391-412.

them allusively. (Indeed, such evocative references are rhetorically most effective.) Our interpretative task, then, is to trace the allusions to the story and to reconstruct the narrative framework that the Galatian congregations shared with Paul.

II. Moving the Discussion Forward

Thus far I have been looking backwards, advising the reader on how to understand what I wrote twenty years ago. The more interesting question, however, might be to ask how the discussion should proceed from here. If I were going to undertake a "wholly new start" on the issues addressed in *The Faith of Jesus Christ*, what topics would have to be addressed? I offer here a brief enumeration of the questions and dialogue partners that I would want to engage.

A. The Story of Israel in Galatians

Because *The Faith of Jesus Christ* concentrated on the analysis of a few kerygmatic formulations such as Gal 2:16; 3:13-14; 3:22; and 4:3-6, the focus of my work was on the christological elements of the "topical sequence" of Paul's foundational story, the dramatic events of Jesus' death and its immediate consequences. Once we discern the outlines of this story, however, another question quickly comes into view: how does the story of Jesus fit into the wider story of Israel, the story of election and promise told in the Old Testament? This question is of urgent importance for the interpretation of Galatians, a letter in which Paul was engaged in fervent debate with Jewish-Christian missionaries who placed the Jesus story within the story of Israel in a way that Paul regarded as disastrous.

My book contains a few observations about such questions, but the problem is not brought into focus as a primary topic for discussion. To continue the discussion today, my analysis of the narrative substructure of Galatians would need to be brought into conversation with the work of J. D. G. Dunn and N. T. Wright, who have argued in various ways that Paul's gospel message stands in continuity with the story of Israel[31] — as well as the

31. J. D. G. Dunn, "The Theology of Galatians: The Issue of Covenantal Nomism," in J. M. Bassler, (ed.), *Pauline Theology Volume I: Thessalonians, Philippians, Galatians, Philemon* (Minneapolis: Fortress, 1991), 125-46; idem, *The Theology of Paul's Letter to the Galatians* (Cambridge: Cambridge University Press, 1993); N. T. Wright, *The Climax of the*

work of J. Louis Martyn, who has made a forceful case for the gospel's radical discontinuity with that story.[32]

The problem is particularly complicated in the case of Galatians. At the simplest level Paul seems to be arguing for the gospel's continuity with the story of Abraham and discontinuity with the story of the giving of the Law at Sinai. Yet, as generations of voluminous commentary attest, the matter is not entirely that simple, for Paul insists that the Law is *not* contrary to the promises of God (3:21), that the Law, allegorically interpreted, proclaims the gospel of inheritance and freedom (4:21-31), and that the Law has been fulfilled in the words of Lev 19:18 about loving the neighbor (5:14). He can even speak, in a notorious paradox, about "the Law of Christ" (6:2).[33] Consequently, to carry forward my analysis of the narrative substructure of Paul's theology in Galatians, I would want to widen the frame of reference beyond the selected kerygmatic formulae and grapple more extensively with the problem of how to understand the story of Christ's faithfulness in relation to the story of Israel.

Some important hints about how to approach this problem are given in the analysis of narrative structure in Chapter III. Israel's situation under the Law must, it seems to me, be placed in the *initial sequence* of the narrative, in which there is a situation of lack or deprivation. The Law has proven powerless to bring the promises into fulfillment. Indeed, according to Paul, it was never intended to do so. Within this initial sequence the Law itself seems to have fallen into the hands of an enemy power so that it becomes an oppressing force in the narrative role of Opponent. Christ's act of deliverance, however, not only sets Israel free from bondage to the Law but also recasts the role of Law in the story's *final sequence,* where it becomes no longer the enemy but now a herald prefiguring the gospel, perhaps even a servant of Christ.[34]

Covenant: Christ and the Law in Pauline Theology (Edinburgh: T&T Clark, 1991; "Gospel and Theology in Galatians," in J. A. Jervis and P. Richardson (eds.), *Gospel in Paul: Studies on Corinthians, Galatians and Romans for Richard N. Longenecker* (JSNTSup 108; Sheffield: Sheffield Academic Press, 1994), 222-39. See also R. Scroggs, "Salvation History: The Theological Structure of Paul's Thought (1 Thessalonians, Philippians, and Galatians), in Bassler, *Pauline Theology Volume I*, 212-26.

32. Martyn, *Galatians.* B. W. Longenecker *(The Triumph of Abraham's God)* attempts to work out a mediating position between these poles of the argument.

33. On this passage, see R. B. Hays, "Christology and Ethics in Galatians: The Law of Christ," *CBQ* 49 (1987) 268-90.

34. For an outworking of this suggestion in relation to the argument of Romans, see R. B. Hays, "Three Dramatic Roles: The Law in Romans 3-4," in J. D. G. Dunn (ed.), *Paul and the Mosaic Law* (WUNT 89; Tübingen: J. C. B. Mohr [Paul Siebeck], 1996), 151-64.

If this sketch is along the right lines, it seems to me that Dunn underplays the plight of Israel in the initial sequence and therefore underestimates the dramatic force of the *peripeteia* in the topical sequence; the narrative movement from Law to Christ in Dunn's reading is too smooth. The story as Paul tells it in Galatians involves a world-shattering event — the crucifixion — that requires radical judgment upon and reassessment of all that has gone before it. The accounts of Wright and Longenecker more adequately recognize the hermeneutical discontinuity introduced by the story of the cross, and Wright's suggestions about the exile as a picture of Israel's situation of deprivation before the coming of Christ provide numerous helpful insights into the argument of Galatians 3. Martyn, on the other hand, while insightfully describing the dramatic discontinuity of Paul's gospel with the story of Moses and the Law, underplays the indicators in Galatians, noted above, that the story of Jesus' death and resurrection is somehow the consummation of Israel's story. All of this would of course require fuller analysis and demonstration. (Again, I refer the reader to my commentary on Galatians for an attempt to sort out these issues.)

One important part of that demonstration would be a sustained investigation of Paul's actual use of OT quotations and allusions in the argument of Galatians. To what extent do these citations correspond to or clarify the gospel story? My book *Echoes of Scripture in the Letters of Paul* undertook to address this question, at least in a preliminary way, focusing particularly on Gal 3:1-14 and 4:21-31.[35] Douglas Campbell has argued persuasively that Hab 2:4, understood as christological prophecy, is a key to understanding Paul's πίστις formulations throughout Galatians and Romans.[36] It seems to me that Campbell is on the right track. We can make further progress in our understanding of Paul's theology by attending more carefully to the way in

35. *Echoes*, 105-21. My student Andy Wakefield has recently completed a dissertation on "The Hermeneutical Significance of Paul's Use of Citations in Galatians 3:6-14" (Ph.D. dissertation, Duke University, 2000).

36. D. A. Campbell, "The Meaning of πίστις and νόμος in Paul: A Linguistic and Structural Perspective," *JBL* 111 (1992) 91-103; idem, "Romans 1:17 — A *Crux Interpretum* for the πίστις Χριστοῦ Debate," *JBL* 113 (1994) 265-85. On the messianic reading of Hab 2:4, see also my essay, "'The Righteous One' as Eschatological Deliverer: Hermeneutics at the Turn of the Ages," in J. Marcus and M. L Soards (eds.), *The New Testament and Apocalyptic: Essays in Honor of J. Louis Martyn* (JSNTSup 24; Sheffield: JSOT, 1988), 191-215. R. E. Watts ("'For I Am Not Ashamed of the Gospel': Romans 1:16-17 and Habakkuk 2:4," in S. K. Soderlund and N. T. Wright, *Romans and the People of God: Essays in Honor of Gordon D. Fee on the Occasion of His 65th Birthday* [Grand Rapids: Eerdmans, 1999], 3-25) questions the messianic interpretation of Hab 2:4 but shows in greater detail how this text is nonetheless foundational for the argument of Romans.

which he reads Scripture as figuring forth the story of Israel's Messiah and the eschatological people that he gathers to himself. This formulation constitutes a reshaping of my earlier argument in *Echoes of Scripture in the Letters of Paul*, where I contended that Paul's hermeneutical strategy for reading Scripture is relentlessly ecclesiocentric. That is a good example of something that I once put in a way that I am "no longer disposed to say it": I would now prefer to say that Paul finds in Scripture the story of Israel as a prefiguration of the story of Jesus the Messiah *and* of the church that he brings into being, "the Israel of God" (Gal 6:16).

B. An Apocalyptic Story?

If the narrative substructure of Galatians must somehow include the story of Israel, what of the still wider frame of reference provided by other biblical texts that situate Israel's story within a cosmic narrative stretching from creation to the eschatological judgment? Elsewhere (e.g., Romans 8; 1 Corinthians 15; 1 Thess 4:13-18) Paul explicitly narrates elements of this cosmic story and its eschatological conclusion. Does Galatians also presuppose this cosmic epic framework, and are there any signs that Paul draws upon it in his arguments in this letter?

In *The Faith of Jesus Christ*, I hardly addressed this issue at all, and in the few places where it did arise, I opined that Galatians "lacks the apocalyptic themes that appear so prominently elsewhere in Paul. . . . Paul traces the story backwards no farther than Abraham and forwards no farther than the immediately controverted future of the Galatian churches."[37] This is among the very few statements in the book that I would now repudiate. I was influenced in this judgment by J. Christiaan Beker's description of Galatians as the contingent exception to Paul's general proclamation of a gospel centered on the cosmic triumph of God,[38] but in light of subsequent insights and a fuller consideration of the evidence I now think the case is very strong for reading Galatians, no less than Paul's other letters, within an apocalyptic narrative framework.[39]

37. *Faith of Jesus Christ*, 226.
38. J. C. Beker, *Paul the Apostle: The Triumph of God in Life and Thought* (Philadelphia: Fortress, 1980), 58.
39. Doubts about the usefulness and clarity of the term "apocalyptic" have been raised by, *inter alia*, L. E. Keck, "Paul and Apocalyptic Theology," *Int* 38 (1984) 229-41; R. B. Matlock, *Unveiling the Apocalyptic Paul: Paul's Interpreters and the Rhetoric of Criticism* (JSNTSup 127; Sheffield: Sheffield Academic Press, 1996). I cannot enter this debate here except to reg-

The work of J. Louis Martyn has been the chief catalyst that has led me, along with many others in the NT guild, to rethink the role of apocalyptic elements in Galatians. The watershed essay on this question was Martyn's "Apocalyptic Antinomies in Paul's Letter to the Galatians," published in 1985.[40] The issue was subsequently sharpened tellingly in an exchange of papers in the SBL Pauline Theology Group between Martyn, Dunn, and Beverly Gaventa.[41] It now seems to me that Martyn has made a compelling case: Paul's theology in Galatians rests upon an apocalyptic narrative about the end of the old age and the beginning of a new one. Within that story, the death of Christ is the crucial turning point, the event in which he rescues humanity from slavery. Martyn, in his commentary on Galatians, has emphatically endorsed the interpretation of πίστις Ἰησοῦ Χριστοῦ as "the faith of Jesus Christ," understanding it as a reference to the cross as Christ's act of giving himself up to rescue us from the present evil age.[42]

Once we see the death of Jesus as the decisive act in God's eschatological invasion of a world previously held in thrall to hostile powers, several elements of the letter become clearer when read within the framework of Paul's cosmic story of liberation. Consider the following examples: Paul's reference to being in the pangs of childbirth until Christ is formed (4:19) employs a familiar metaphor for the sufferings of the endtime.[43] His reference to the "Jerusalem above" (4:26) draws on the apocalyptic image of a heavenly Jerusalem that will descend to earth when God finally sets all things right (cf. Rev 21:2). His declaration that "we eagerly await the hope of righteousness" (5:5) expresses the same eschatological longing found in Rom 8:18-25, a hope that looks for a redemption we do not yet see. Martyn's vivid interpretation of

---

ister my own opinion that the term "apocalyptic," as employed by Martyn, is in fact a valid and illuminating category. Paul does, after all, declare that he received his gospel δι' ἀποκαλύψεως Ἰησοῦ Χριστοῦ (Gal 1:12).

40. J. Louis Martyn, "Apocalyptic Antinomies in Paul's Letter to the Galatians," *NTS* 31 (1985) 410-24; reprinted in Martyn, *Theological Issues*, 111-23.

41. All three essays appear in Bassler (ed.), *Pauline Theology, Volume 1:* Dunn, "The Theology of Galatians: The Issue of Covenantal Nomism," pp. 125-46; Gaventa, "The Singularity of the Gospel: A Reading of Galatians," pp. 147-59; Martyn, "Events in Galatia: Modified Covenantal Nomism versus God's Invasion of the Cosmos in the Singular Gospel: A Response to J. D. G. Dunn and B. R. Gaventa," pp. 160-79.

42. ". . . [P]istis Christou is an expression by which Paul speaks of Christ's atoning faithfulness, as, on the cross, he died faithfully for human beings while looking faithfully to God" (Martyn, *Galatians*, 271).

43. Gaventa, "The Maternity of Paul," in R. T. Fortna and B. R. Gaventa (eds.), *The Conversation Continues: Studies in Paul and John in Honor of J. Louis Martyn* (Nashville: Abingdon, 1990), 189-201.

Paul's account of the struggle between Spirit and Flesh (5:17) convincingly characterizes this opposition as a manifestation of eschatological warfare between suprahuman powers. In Gal 5:21, Paul warns that those who do the works of the flesh "will not inherit the kingdom of God," certainly a reference to future judgment. Similarly, when he employs the maxim "Each will bear his own load" (6:5) and draws on the imagery of reaping and harvest (6:7-9), Paul is using traditional eschatological judgment language.[44] Finally, the wish for peace and mercy upon "the Israel of God" (6:16) is to be understood as a blessing on God's eschatological people.

None of the examples given here is taken from Gal 3:1–4:11, the section of the letter on which my dissertation concentrated; my judgment about the absence of apocalyptic eschatology in Galatians resulted, in part, from a failure to take the entire message of the letter into account. In any case, in these passages, Paul gives a number of allusive hints to a final act of the cosmic drama in which there will be a judgment of the wicked and a vindication of God's people, the establishment of a new righteous order ("Jerusalem") in which the saints will receive their promised inheritance. In light of other Pauline texts, we should certainly also infer that the "hope of righteousness" (5:5) includes the resurrection of the dead. A fresh reading of the narrative substructure of Galatians would have to factor all these passages into the analysis.

C. The Political Implications of Paul's Gospel Story

In *The Faith of Jesus Christ* I did not deal in any detail with the specific rhetorical and pastoral function of Paul's appeals to the gospel story. What was the impact of Paul's use of this story on the Gentile churches in Galatia that were under pressure to adopt the practice of circumcision? What political impact did Paul's gospel story have in the communities to which it was originally addressed?[45]

There are two distinguishable issues here. First, how does Paul's evocation of the story of Jesus Christ bear upon intra-ecclesial political problems about relations between Jews and Gentiles and the applicability of Jewish identity markers to Gentile converts? In brief, the answer is that the story un-

44. D. Kuck, "'Each Will Bear His Own Burden': Paul's Creative Use of an Apocalyptic Motif," *NTS* 40 (1994) 289-97.

45. This is one of Howard's primary criticisms: "the book places little or no emphasis on the issue of unity between Israel and the nations which dominates the letter to the Galatians as a whole" (*JBL* 105 [1986] 158).

dercuts any theological basis for ethnic divisions within the community of faith. Because all are adopted children and heirs of the promise only in Christ, by virtue of his faithful death, the Law should no longer function as a dividing wall to separate God's people from one another. The promise to Abraham, after all, was that *all nations* would be blessed in him. The Law had a temporary role as a παιδαγωγός, but that role is now ended. Now that Christ, the one seed of Abraham, has come and the Spirit has been given, the distinctions between Jew and Gentile have been rendered *adiaphora*.[46] Therefore those who try to build up again a wall of separation by insisting on circumcision or by withdrawing from table fellowship with Gentiles are working against the logic of the story, seeking wrongly to return to a time that is now past. I have discussed these matters at length in my commentary, as have other recent commentators such as Dunn, Matera, and Williams.[47]

The second issue, however, is the more intriguing one for ongoing conversation. How did Paul's retelling of the Jesus story engage the surrounding political culture of the pagan world? In particular, how did his narrative about Jesus confront the Roman imperial cult and the claims of Caesar to create a symbolic world in which justice (δικαιοσύνη) and peace prevailed? This question was nowhere on the radar screen for me when I wrote my dissertation. In 1987, however, Dieter Georgi published a little collection of essays, "Gott auf den Kopf stellen," subsequently translated into English as *Theocracy in Paul's Practice and Theology*,[48] in which he suggested that Paul's proclamation of an εὐαγγέλιον should be read as counter-imperial rhetoric, challenging the Empire's pretensions to create a sovereign and just political order. These claims have subsequently been taken up and explored by several other scholars.[49] Georgi's proposals are of particular interest in relation to my work because he rejects the objective genitive reading of πίστις Ἰησοῦ Χριστοῦ, cit-

46. As Daniel Boyarin has observed in his acutely insightful study of Paul, the abolition of such distinctions would hardly be welcomed by all parties to the discussion. In Boyarin's view, Paul creates a "particularist universalism" that annihilates Jewish identity, replacing it with a new identity "in Christ" (*A Radical Jew: Paul and the Politics of Identity* [Berkeley: University of California Press, 1994]).

47. J. D. G. Dunn, *The Theology of Paul's Letter to the Galatians* (Black's New Testament Commentaries; London: A. & C. Black, 1993); F. J. Matera, *Galatians* (Sacra Pagina; Collegeville, MN: Liturgical Press, 1992); Williams, *Galatians;* see also B. W. Longenecker, *Triumph,* and P. F. Esler, *Galatians* (London: Routledge, 1998).

48. D. Georgi, *Theocracy in Paul's Practice and Theology* (Minneapolis: Fortress, 1991).

49. See the collections of essays in R. A. Horsley (ed.), *Paul and Empire: Religion and Power in Roman Imperial Society* (Harrisburg, PA: Trinity Press International, 1997); and in idem, *Paul and Politics: Ekklesia, Israel, Imperium, Interpretation: Essays in Honor of Krister Stendahl* (Harrisburg, PA: Trinity Press International, 2000).

ing my dissertation in support of this rejection, and proposes to interpret the phrase as "the trust (or even better 'loyalty') of Jesus, indeed the trust and loyalty Jesus stands for; and this establishes and preserves social solidarity."[50] Georgi goes on to argue that *fides* (= πίστις) was an important term in imperial propaganda: "Beginning in the time of Augustus, *fides*, the Latin synonym [*sic*] of *pistis*, was reassessed and assumed weightier dimensions. The Caesar represented the *fides* of Rome in the sense of loyalty, faithfulness to treaty obligations, uprightness, truthfulness, honesty, confidence, and conviction — all, as it were, a Roman monopoly. The ancient cult of the goddess Fides was revived under Augustus. It is significant too, in the period of the principate, that the word appears frequently on coins."[51] From this and other observations, Georgi concludes that "Paul's gospel must be understood as competing with the gospel of the Caesars. . . . The *sōtería* represented by Caesar and his empire is challenged by the *sōtería* brought about by Jesus."[52]

It must be said that Georgi's essays, epigrammatic in their brevity, fall far short of proving his case. The parallels that he adduces are few and imprecise, and he gives no convincing explanation of how this alleged counter-imperial discourse is pertinent to the situation that Paul is addressing in Galatia. (His suggestions may actually make better sense in relation to Romans.) Still, Georgi has gestured provocatively in the direction of issues that demand more careful investigation. Paul does make claims about Jesus as sovereign Lord that would necessarily appear subversive in the eyes of the Roman imperium. One task of a new study of the narrative substructure of Paul's theology in Galatians, therefore, might be to compare the structure and language of the Jesus-story to the structure and language of narratives about Caesar and his rule. What would such a close comparison show? I pose this as an open question for ongoing research.

D. Paul's Gospel Story within the Matrix of Early Christianity

The concluding chapter of *The Faith of Jesus Christ* contains two brief sections that reflect on "Paul's Place within Early Christianity" and "Paul's Gospel and the Gospel Genre." The burden of both these sections is to ask whether the basic narrative pattern of Paul's christology was held in common with other early Christian traditions and writings. I proposed that in fact Paul was less theolog-

50. Georgi, *Theocracy,* 36 n. 9.
51. Georgi, *Theocracy,* 84.
52. Georgi, *Theocracy,* 87.

ically distinctive than is generally supposed — that is, that his Christology and soteriology are closely in sync with Hebrews, with the Deutero-Pauline letters, and with the writings usually thought to represent "early catholicism" — and that, despite the near-total absence of synoptic Jesus tradition in Paul's letters, his story-grounded preaching marks a point on a historical trajectory towards the composition of written gospel narratives. These proposals, deliberately designed to provoke a rethinking of New Testament theology and of the development of early Christianity, mark out for me an unfinished agenda.

It is impossible here to take up this discussion in any substantive way. For now it must suffice to draw attention to two other scholarly contributions that point in the same direction as my suggestions, though from very different vantage points. First, Craig Hill's book *Hellenists and Hebrews: Reassessing Division within Early Christianity* — an excellent study still too little known and heeded in the NT guild — makes a painstaking argument that NT scholarship since F. C. Baur has formed exaggerated constructs of radical divisions within the early Christian movement between a "liberal" Pauline-Hellenistic faction and a "conservative" Jewish-Petrine faction.[53] Without denying tensions and differences, Hill argues that the historical evidence suggests a greater degree of complexity: the texts "bear witness to a complicated situation in which the Jerusalem church was neither in direct opposition to nor in complete agreement with the apostle to the Gentiles."[54] There was not only diversity but also commonality of faith and practice among first-century Christian groups. Hill's detailed critique of the handling of the evidence by NT scholarship deserves to be read closely. One of the strangest legacies of German biblical criticism is its widespread assumption that when Paul quotes Jewish-Christian confessional traditions (e.g., Rom 3:24-26), he does so primarily to rebut or correct them. The findings of my study point in precisely the opposite direction: Paul quotes these narrative kerygmatic traditions in order to affirm them and argue from them to the conclusions he wishes to draw. Thus, both Hill and I see Paul's thought as growing organically and constructively within the matrix of early Christianity.[55] (The myth of Paul the isolated religious genius who shared little or nothing with his Jewish-

---

53. Craig C. Hill, *Hellenists and Hebrews: Reappraising Division within the Earliest Church* (Minneapolis: Fortress, 1992). Hill's book is a revised version of his doctoral thesis at Oxford, written under the direction of E. P. Sanders.

54. Hill, *Hellenists and Hebrews,* 192.

55. Cf. the helpful approach of J. D. G. Dunn (*The Theology of Paul's Letter to the Galatians* [Cambridge: Cambridge University Press, 1993]), who outlines "the fundamental agreements" between Paul and his Jewish-Christian interlocutors before tracing the distinctive claims for which Paul argues.

Christian contemporaries has the suspiciously convenient result of reinforcing the iconoclasm of scholars who are themselves alienated from the traditions and practices of their own contemporary faith communities.)

My other suggestion, that Paul's gospel story presages the development
of the gospel genre, is a bit more fanciful. Still, I note with interest a recent essay by Joel Marcus, "Mark — Interpreter of Paul," which makes a fairly impressive case that "plausible reasons can be advanced for a later Paulinist wanting
to write the story of the earthly Jesus" and that Mark, with his decided emphasis on a theology of the cross, could be understood as performing exactly such
a task.[56] Marcus — addressing this topic while working on a commentary on
Mark — appears unaware of my earlier suggestion; if so, the convergence of
our ideas is all the more interesting. If my earlier proposal has any substance, it
should be possible to demonstrate a common framework, not only at the level
of theological concepts but also at the level of narrative substructure, that links
Mark's Gospel to Paul's letters, despite their different literary genres.

E. Πίστις Χριστοῦ: Lexical Semantics and Ancient Parallels

As I noted in my essay for the Pauline Theology Group ten years ago, one of
the weaknesses of my dissertation was its lack of attention to the cultural/se-
mantic background of the term πίστις.[57] Apart from my detailed critique of
Greer M. Taylor's attempt to explain Paul's use of πίστις in light of the Roman
legal device of *fidei commissum* (pp. 184-89), I did not provide a sustained
discussion of uses of πίστις in ancient sources outside the New Testament. My
reason for this was simple: I took the task as already accomplished by the essays of George Howard and others.[58] I had nothing new to add to the discussion, and the weight of the evidence seemed to show that the objective genitive following πίστις was rare — especially in Hellenistic Jewish sources —
but possible. Thus, while the lexical evidence seemed to support my reading,
the debate on this front appeared inconclusive, and I thought it necessary to
argue the case primarily by showing how this language actually functioned
within the context of Paul's argument in Galatians.

---

56. J. Marcus, "Mark — Interpreter of Paul," *NTS* 46 (2000) 473-87. The quotation is
from p. 473.

57. Hays, "ΠΙΣΤΙΣ and Pauline Christology," 38 (p. 275 in the present edition).

58. See especially Howard, "Notes and Observations on the 'Faith of Christ,'" *HTR* 60
(1967) 459-84; idem, "The 'Faith of Christ,'" *ExpTim* 85 (1974) 212-15; D. W. B. Robinson,
"'Faith of Jesus Christ' — A New Testament Debate," *Reformed Theological Review* 29 (1970)
71-81.

We now find ourselves in a changed situation because of the availability of computerized search tools such as the *Thesaurus Linguae Graecae*, which make it possible to comb rapidly through vast quantities of ancient Greek texts looking for specific constructions such as πίστις + genitive noun. A recent article by R. Barry Matlock has culled out several instances of the objective genitive with πίστις in the writings of Strabo and Plutarch.[59] While Matlock's survey does not attempt to report all uses of πίστις with the genitive in these authors or to compare the relative frequency of subjective and objective constructions, his note provides a corrective qualification to Howard's findings and helpfully underscores the need for further studies of this kind.

Along similar lines, David Hay's 1989 article on "*Pistis* as 'Ground for Faith' in Hellenized Judaism and in Paul" correctly observes the widespread use of πίστις, particularly in ancient rhetoric, to mean "proof" or "basis for belief."[60] On the other hand, as Hay also notices, this sense is generally absent from the LXX, which is the immediate background for Paul's use of πιστεύειν (Gen 15:6) and πίστις (Hab 2:4). Thus, while Hay provides interesting information about the wider cultural context of this language, his proposed interpretation fails to make sense of the way that Paul uses πίστις in his arguments, with the possible exception of Rom 3:22, 25.

We have also noted above Georgi's proposal to set Paul's use of πίστις in juxtaposition to imperial claims about *fides* as a distinctive attribute of Caesar. This is the most stimulating new suggestion that has emerged so far in the attempt to explore the cultural/semantic background to Paul's use of the term.

Alongside these examples, I would reiterate that the most interesting parallel to Paul's discussion of Abraham's faith occurs in Philo, *De Abr.* 273. In the course of extolling Abraham's faith as a praiseworthy virtue, Philo writes of God's response to this faith: ὃς τῆς πρὸς αὐτὸν πίστεως ἀγάμενος τὸν ἄνδρα πίστιν ἀντιδίδωσιν αὐτῷ, τὴν δι' ὅρκου βεβαίωσιν ὧν ὑπέσχετο δωρεῶν ("[God], marvelling at Abraham's faith in Him, repaid him with faithfulness by confirming with an oath the gifts which He had promised").[61]

---

59. Matlock, "Detheologizing," 19 n. 59. Several of Matlock's examples are debatable: for example, his single instance of this construction in Polybius's *History* 2.4.8.1 seems to me not to support his case, but many of his examples validly support his point that the objective genitive does sometimes appear with πίστις. That point, however, was never in doubt (cf. my comments on Mark 11:22 in *Faith of Jesus Christ*, 149).

60. D. M. Hay, "*Pistis* as 'Ground for Faith' in Hellenized Judaism and in Paul," *JBL* 109 (1989) 461-76. See my comments in Hays, "ΠΙΣΤΙΣ and Pauline Christology," 45 n. 24 (p. 283 n. 24 in the present edition).

61. The translation is that of F. H. Colson, *Philo*, LCL 6 (Cambridge, MA: Harvard University Press and London: Heinemann, 1935).

The passage is significant because Philo refers several times to "faith in God," using the construction ἡ πρὸς θεὸν πίστις (see also 268, 271), *not* πίστις θεοῦ, and — more importantly — because he uses πίστις in two different senses in the same sentence: it refers first to Abraham's faith/trust towards God and then, immediately thereafter, to God's faithfulness in keeping his promise to Abraham. This example nicely illustrates the multivalence of πίστις and the need to interpret it contextually. If Philo can pivot about in this way in a single sentence, we should hardly be surprised that Paul can similarly speak in the same breath both of our faith in God (καὶ ἡμεῖς εἰς Χριστὸν Ἰησοῦν ἐπιστεύσαμεν) and of the faithfulness of Jesus Christ (διὰ πίστεως Ἰησοῦ Χριστοῦ . . . ἐκ πίστεως Χριστοῦ; Gal 2:16).

The exploration of parallels should certainly continue, but we should always beware of "parallelomania."[62] Parallels are useful only if they actually illuminate the usage of terms in Paul's writings. There is therefore finally no substitute for contextually sensitive readings of the way Paul actually uses πίστις in his letters.

For that reason, the attempt of Matlock to "detheologize" the πίστις Χριστοῦ debate is a sure prescription for misinterpretation. Paul is, after all, using this language in the context of *theological* arguments, and there is no way to understand the sense of the terminology without attempting to understand the shape and coherence of the argument. That is what the study of Pauline theology seeks to do. Matlock, however, writes as though there were an objective science of lexical semantics that permits him to perform theologically "neutral" interpretations of linguistic units,[63] in contrast to all the other foolish participants in the debate who have allowed theological considerations to warp their judgment. This is an astonishingly naive claim. Matlock's "exegetical" procedure is basically nothing more sophisticated than to look up the word πίστις in various lexicons, with particular emphasis given to Louw and Nida's *Greek-English Lexicon of the New Testament Based on Semantic Domains,* and to see how these lexicons classify the range of Paul's uses of the word.[64] Can anyone seri-

---

62. See the classic essay of Samuel Sandmel, "Parallelomania," *JBL* 81 (1962) 1-13.

63. The very first paragraph of Matlock's article disclaims the possibility of ruling on "a properly exegetical decision from some 'neutral' standpoint above the fray" (Matlock, "Detheologizing," 1). He then proceeds for the next 23 pages to ignore this disclaimer. By page 2, he writes, "Ideally, lexical semantics might offer a more or less stable and agreed set of terms and principles for the analysis of word-meaning, worked out in general application and thus 'neutral,' at least, to the specific interpretative issues arising over πίστις Χριστοῦ." In light of the opening disclaimer, we expect this sentence to be followed by another to balance the "ideally" with a "however, in reality" — but the shoe never drops.

64. Matlock, "Detheologizing," 6-20.

ously believe that the lexicographers are not making *theological* judgments about the meaning of the sentences in which the word πίστις appears?

The argument of my book is that the conventional judgments of lexicographers and commentators since the Reformation have been mistaken, precisely because they have focused narrowly on the apparent semantic equivalence established in Gal 2:16 and failed to see the larger context provided by Paul's narrative christology. Matlock nowhere engages the argument in the terms that I have tried to pose it. When he does finally, in the last three pages of the article, attempt to offer some constructive exegetical comments, he does nothing other than to fall back on the well-worn argument that Gal 2:16 is the "entry-point" for solving the problem because it places πίστις Χριστοῦ in opposition to "works of law." Matlock appears to think, like Dunn (whom he does not cite), that because ἔργα νόμου refers to a human activity, πίστις Χριστοῦ must also refer to a different sort of human activity. He does not engage at all the arguments made by Martyn and by me that the whole point of the sentence is to juxtapose futile human activity to gracious divine initiative. But that would, of course, be a "theological" argument, and so Matlock rules it out of court.

I do not mean to suggest that lexical semantics is of no value for exegesis. Matlock makes several useful observations and poses some clarifying questions. This is not the place for me to engage in detailed debate with his article. The main point I want to make, however, is that lexical semantics, insofar as it seeks to make judgments about the meanings of words in Paul's letters, must attend to larger sense units that are inescapably theological. The attempt to do non-theological exegesis of the New Testament is self-defeating. In fact, Matlock's own interpretation of Galatians 2 — to the extent that he offers us one — is itself theological, despite his efforts to transcend theology.

F. The History of Interpretation

Finally, considerably more light might be shed on the themes of this book by a study of the history of interpretation. In *The Faith of Jesus Christ*, my account of the history of research focuses almost exclusively on twentieth-century studies. The footnotes are thick with detailed references to books and essays of modern New Testament critics, but almost no attention is given to the church's long history of reading Paul, except for occasional sidelong disapproving glances at Luther. Now, however, one of the important growing edges of my own work — and of the field more generally — is the recognition that we have a great deal to learn by broadening the conversation to include the questions and insights of our predecessors who lived before the so-called "Enlightenment."

I know of two significant studies that have taken up this challenge in relation to the interpretation of πίστις Χριστοῦ in patristic theology: Ian G. Wallis, *The Faith of Jesus Christ in Early Christian Traditions,* and Roy A. Harrisville III, "ΠΙΣΤΙΣ ΧΡΙΣΤΟΥ: Witness of the Fathers."[65] Anyone who hopes that a study of this material will put the debate to rest, however, will be disappointed to learn that these two authors arrive at very different findings. Harrisville concludes that the patristic evidence favors "faith in Christ," while Wallis finds that "the faith *of* Jesus" played a significant ongoing role in Christian theology during the first three centuries but disappeared from Christian thought as a casualty of the christological controversies of the fourth century, particularly the struggle against Arianism. The difference between the two studies is partly methodological: Harrisville, using the *Thesaurus Linguae Graecae,* focuses on passages in which the expression πίστις Χριστοῦ (or a close equivalent) appears explicitly, while Wallis casts the net more widely, looking not just at this verbal formulation but at a range of material that might describe the pattern of Christ's faithfulness as salvific and/or paradigmatic. (Harrisville's search method, if I understand his description correctly, would not locate citations of Gal 2:20, for example.)

The evidence that Harrisville adduces is surprisingly slight. He offers a substantial list of citations that he classifies as "ambiguous," where a Pauline πίστις Χριστοῦ passage is quoted either without comment or without sufficient surrounding context to determine how the expression is being used. He then lists only four subjective genitives, always πίστις αὐτοῦ used in reference to "human faith" rather than Christ's faith (this way of putting the distinction is unsettling, since it seems to suggest a view that Jesus was not human).[66] He then enumerates half a dozen passages in the Greek Fathers that he regards as

65. Ian G. Wallis, *The Faith of Jesus Christ in Early Christian Traditions* (SNTSMS 84; Cambridge: Cambridge University Press, 1995); and Roy A. Harrisville III, "ΠΙΣΤΙΣ ΧΡΙΣΤΟΥ: Witness of the Fathers," *NovT* 36 (1994) 233-41.

66. Actually, this unspoken presupposition lies at the root of much of the opposition to the subjective genitive interpretation: if Jesus was God, he could not possibly have needed to have faith. See the very telling citation from Thomas Aquinas with which Wallis opens his study: "The field of faith is divine reality that is hidden from sight. . . . Hence, where divine reality is not hidden from sight there is no point in faith. But from the moment of conception [!] Christ had the full vision of the very being of God, as we will hold later on. Therefore he could not have had faith" (*Summa Theologiae,* 3a.7.3, cited in Wallis, *Faith of Jesus Christ,* 1). Note that Aquinas's position depends on understanding *fides* as "belief."

supporting an objective genitive interpretation. In several of these cases I would contend that Harrisville is probably wrong, or that the evidence is more ambiguous than he allows. In the examples cited from *Acta Petri*, Chrysostom's *In Epistulam ad Galatas* on Gal 2:15, and Origen's *In Joannem*, the passages probably refer to "the faith" as a body of doctrine that Christians believe or, by metonymy, "the faith" as the community constituted by such beliefs — just as in Gal 1:23.

Harrisville's other two examples from Origen, on the other hand, appear to provide clear support for the objective genitive reading — especially the commentary on Romans 3:26.[67] If one reads the whole section on Rom 3:21-26, however, the matter becomes more complex. For example, Origen paraphrases 3:22 by saying that Jesus Christ is the *teacher* (διδάσκαλος) of the righteousness of God, which suggests a paradigmatic interpretation of Jesus' faith rather than Jesus as object of faith.[68] Then, a few lines later, still commenting on 3:22, he speaks of "those who trust Jesus Christ (πιστεύοντας . . . Ἰησοῦ Χριστῷ)[69] *or* contain the faith which Jesus Christ creates for them in the father (ἢ πίστιν χωροῦντας ἣν Ἰησοῦς Χριστὸς αὐτοῖς ἐνεποίησεν εἰς τὸν Πατέρα)."[70] This rhetorical device of self-correction, reminiscent of Gal 4:9, suggests that Origen feels the need to explicate what looks like an "objective genitive" reading of Rom 3:22 by speaking of faith as a phenomenon of trust created by Jesus Christ which has God the Father as its proper "object." This comes very close to the idea expressed by Ignatius of Antioch: ἡ πίστις ἡ δι' αὐτοῦ, "the faith which is through him" (Letter of Ignatius to the Philadelphians 8:2; see also my description of participation in Christ's faith in I.B., above, and the essays of Hooker and Williams).

These remarks only scratch the surface of the matter, but they demonstrate, I think, that it will not suffice merely to classify a list of short phrases churned out by a computer search. What is required is more patient in-depth exegesis of the wider context of each of the pertinent references in the Fathers. I would hope that others more expert than I in these texts would take up this investigation.

Before leaving Harrisville's essay, however, I must comment on the quo-

67. Harrisville's example from Chrysostom's *De Incomprehensibili Dei Natura* should probably be conceded to this category as well.

68. *Le Commentaire d'Origène sur Rom III.5–V.7*, ed. by J. Scherer (Cairo: L'Institut Français d'Archéologie Orientale, 1957), p. 150.

69. Note the use of the dative case here.

70. *Commentaire sur Rom III.5–V.7*, p. 154. (It should be noticed, by the way, that Harrisville's method of searching the *TLG* did not catch this passage in the net; one suspects that there must be many other such passages.)

tations from Augustine with which he concludes his discussion. Augustine (who, it should be noted, was not competent in Greek) is the one author turned up by Harrisville who explicitly rejects the idea of a subjective genitive interpretation of "faith of Jesus Christ." Here, for instance, is the passage that Harrisville cites from *De Spiritu et Littera*, chapter 9:

> [The righteousness of God is] not that whereby he Himself is righteous, but that with which he endows man when he justifies the ungodly. . . . 'But righteousness of God by faith of Jesus Christ,' that is by the faith wherewith one believes in Christ; for just as there is not meant the faith with which Christ Himself believes, so also there is not meant the righteousness whereby God is Himself righteous.

I would suggest that Augustine's exegesis is mistaken on both points, and that the two are closely connected. Though the citation appears to support Harrisville's case, it actually demonstrates the extent to which Augustine's objective genitive reading is linked with an otherwise questionable interpretation of Paul's message. Augustine exemplifies the shift that Wallis describes, a shift away from the early patristic reading of Christ as embodying the pattern of faith into which we are conformed, towards the later insistence that Christ can only be the object, never the subject of faith.

Wallis's study, which is in every respect more sympathetic to the interpretation of πίστις Ἰησοῦ Χριστοῦ for which I have contended, focuses primarily on the New Testament material, with separate chapters on the Synoptic Gospels, the Pauline Epistles, the deutero-Pauline and Pastoral Epistles, and Hebrews and Revelation. The final chapter of the study, however, is most pertinent to my concerns here, for it discusses "Jesus' faith in extrabiblical sources," carrying the survey up to the fourth century C.E.[71] I make no attempt here to summarize Wallis's wide-ranging and richly theological discussion, except to report that he finds significant references to Jesus' faith in Origen, Clement of Alexandria, Polycarp, the Shepherd of Hermas, Ignatius of Antioch, the Odes of Solomon, and Tertullian, among others. Some of his examples seem a bit strained, but others are unimpeachable, and the cumulative effect is highly persuasive. A citation from the final paragraph of Wallis's summary of what he calls "the theological function of Jesus' faith" elegantly sums up the tradition he finds in these early Christian sources — and at the same time demonstrates how closely convergent this evidence is with the interpretation of πίστις Χριστοῦ in Paul that I have advocated.

---

71. Wallis, *Faith of Jesus Christ*, 175-212.

Most if not all of the passages discussed demonstrate an intimate association between Jesus' faith and his death, the latter being interpreted in terms of God's salvific purposes and provision. As a result, because Jesus' faith is epitomised in the circumstances surrounding a death which mediates God's salvation, he becomes the source of faith for others. Because of what he achieved on behalf of all, others may now share his faith and its benefits.[72]

If that is what Christian writers of the second and third centuries thought about Jesus' faith, is it improbable that they derived some of their understanding from Paul, and that we should see their testimony as a guideline that might help us read Paul more clearly?

Of course, the history of interpretation cannot be confined to the patristic period. To trace the debate forward through the centuries would exceed both my competence and the patience of the reader. We may, however, conclude with a single example from the nineteenth century. In a fascinating brief essay, J. Gerald Janzen has shown that Samuel Taylor Coleridge held an understanding of πίστις Χριστοῦ closely aligned with the patristic views I have just summarized.[73] Janzen adduces a number of quotations in which Coleridge reflects on Gal 2:20 as a key to understanding the phrase. Coleridge's concise summary of the meaning of this verse is as follows: "Thus we see that even our faith is not ours in its origin: but is the faith of the Son of God graciously communicated to us."[74] After surveying a number of Coleridge's reflections on these themes, Janzen sums up Coleridge's views: "Christian life receives its shape and character by entry into a divine intent and activity first of all embodied in Christ. Insofar as Christian life may be summed up as a 'life of faith,' the individual Christian's faith is a participation in the fidelity of Christ."[75] (I cannot resist remarking that Coleridge, who was not only a scholar but also a poet, was perhaps well equipped to understand the metonymic function of Paul's language.) Janzen then goes on to observe the close correspondence between Coleridge's reading of Paul and that of Morna Hooker: both understand πίστις Χριστοῦ in terms of participation in the faith of Christ.

All of this serves to warn us that what we now describe as the "tradi-

72. Wallis, *Faith of Jesus Christ,* 194.

73. J. G. Janzen, "Coleridge and *Pistis Christou,*" *ExpTim* 107 (1993) 265-68.

74. Cited in Janzen, "Coleridge," 266 from G. Whalley (ed.), *The Collected Works of Samuel Taylor Coleridge: Marginalia II* (London: Routledge & Kegan Paul, 1984 and Princeton: Princeton University Press, 1984), 591-92.

75. Janzen, "Coleridge," 268.

tional" objective genitive understanding of πίστις Ἰησοῦ Χριστοῦ may be in some respects a modern, or at least post-Reformation, innovation that offers a truncated account of what the broader Christian tradition has heard in Paul's language about "the faith of Christ."[76] By studying the history of interpretation, we seek to overcome "exegetical amnesia"[77] and "to recover what has been lost/and found and lost again and again." Thus, if I were starting afresh to write my dissertation, I would feel compelled to devote far more attention to this recovery effort.

Conclusion

I have looked back in order to highlight what I take to be significant about the argument of my book, and I have looked around in order to indicate the new lines of conversation that I hope a fresh appearance of the book might invite. To pursue all of these lines would require me to write a new book — a book that the pressure of other commitments now prevents me from writing. I offer these reflections, therefore, in the hope that they may be helpful to other students of Paul who want to take up the pursuit of these issues.

Even though this book remains, I fear, unreadable for most people outside the guild of New Testament scholarship, the issues pursued here are of serious significance for the church. I have grown increasingly convinced that the struggles of the church in our time are a result of its losing touch with its own gospel story. We have gotten "off message" and therefore lost our way in a culture that tells us many other stories about who we are and where our hope lies. In both the evangelical and the liberal wings of Protestantism, there is too much emphasis on individual faith-experience and not enough grounding of our theological discourse in the story of Jesus Christ. My hope, therefore, is that this book will continue to play some role in calling the church back to focused primary reflection about the story of the Son of God who loved us and gave himself for us in order to rescue us from the present evil age.

Richard B. Hays
The Center of Theological Inquiry
Princeton, New Jersey
August 27, 2001

76. As rightly noted by Hooker, "ΠΙΣΤΙΣ ΧΡΙΣΤΟΥ," 321-22.
77. I am indebted to Dale Allison for this expression.

Chapter I

The Search for the Constant Elements
of Paul's Gospel

A. Statement of the Problem and Elaboration of the Thesis

1. The Quest for the "Core" of Paul's Thought

Upon reading the Pauline letters we find ourselves cast *in medias res*, into a network of unexplained assumptions and allusions.[1] With no advance briefing, we can pick up a Platonic dialogue or Descartes' *Discourse on Method* and read it from start to finish with a sense of being able to "follow" the reasoning that undergirds the text, but not so with a Pauline letter, which is a much more challenging object for exegesis because of its "occasional" character.[2] Paul is speaking to particular situations and events within the communities to which he writes; he brings his gospel into an encounter with these situations and draws out applications for the concrete problems of the community's life. As J. C. Beker has formulated it, Paul's letters bring the "core" of the gospel into dynamic interaction with particular circumstances: "The 'core' then is not a frozen unity, but has interpretive fluidity, which consists in a steady interaction between the constant elements of the gospel and the variable elements of the situations, so that in each new situation the gospel comes to speech again."[3]

---

1. Cf. G. Bornkamm, *Paul* (New York: Harper & Row, 1971) 109.

2. It is, of course, debated whether Romans may constitute an exception to this general statement. See, for statements on both sides of the argument, *The Romans Debate* (ed. K. P. Donfried; Minneapolis: Augsburg, 1977). In any case, whether Romans is directed to a specific situation or not, it is perhaps the most difficult of all the letters to "follow."

3. J. C. Beker, "Contingency and Coherence in the Letters of Paul," *USQR* 33 (1978) 148. This distinction between "the constant elements of the gospel" and "the variable ele-

Historical-critical exegesis attempts, of course, to reconstruct the particular situations *into which* Paul was speaking. (Who were the opponents of Paul at Galatia and what were they really saying?)[4] Important as this task of historical reconstruction is, however, critical exegesis must reckon equally with the question of what Paul brought *to* these encounters: what constitutes the framework *out of which* Paul reacted to the pastoral problems that appear in his letters? What are, in Beker's phrase, "the constant elements of the gospel" which Paul brings into contact with various situations?

When the question is posed in this way, NT critics have almost invariably tended to seek the answer in Paul's "ideas," the doctrinal content of his thought. Older orthodox Protestant exegesis treated Paul as a systematic theologian whose teaching could be understood as a compendium of theological propositions, or *Lehrbegriffe*. In the late nineteenth century there emerged a growing awareness that Paul was not, after all, a systematic theologian, and that his letters, if read as theological tractates, must be judged as peculiarly rambling and unsatisfactory ones, riddled with non sequiturs and contradictions.[5] Nonetheless, as Beker remarks, the attempt to grasp the "core" of Paul's gospel was still conceived by critics as "a quest for doctrinal centers,"[6] a quest for conceptual formulations. Even W. Wrede, with his acute awareness of the nonsystematic character of Paul's thought, was still persuaded that "the religion of the apostle is theological through and through: his theology is his religion."[7]

---

ments of the situation" may correspond roughly to the "ideational" and "interactional" "macro-functions" of discourse, as defined by M. A. K. Halliday (*Explorations in the Functions of Language* [New York: Elsevier, 1977] 91-93).

4. For recent proposals and literature on the question of Paul's opponents in Galatia, see J. Eckert, *Die urchristliche Verkündigung im Streit zwischen Paulus und seinen Gegnern nach dem Galaterbrief* (Biblische Untersuchungen 6; Regensburg: Friedrich Pustet, 1971); W. Schmithals, *Paul and the Gnostics* (Nashville: Abingdon, 1972) 13-64; Joseph B. Tyson, "Paul's Opponents in Galatia," *NovT* 4 (1968) 241-54; F. F. Bruce, "Galatian Problems 3: The 'Other' Gospel," *BJRL* 53 (1971) 253-72; R. Jewett, "The Agitators and the Galatian Congregation," *NTS* 17 (1971) 198-212; G. Howard, *Paul: Crisis in Galatia* (SNTSMS 35; Cambridge: Cambridge University, 1979) 1-19.

5. W. Wrede (*Paul* [Boston: American Unitarian Association, 1908; reprinted, Lexington, KY: American Theological Library Association, 1962] 77) remarks that "It is no great feat to unearth contradictions, even among his leading thoughts." For recent efforts to confront contradiction in Paul's thought, see R. Pregeant, "Grace and Recompense: Reflections on a Pauline Paradox," *JAAR* 47 (1979) 73-96; P. Richardson, "Pauline Inconsistency," *NTS* 26 (1979-80) 347-62.

6. Beker, "Contingency and Coherence," 148. My formulation of the interpretive problem in this discussion (though not my solution to it) is significantly indebted to Beker.

7. Wrede, *Paul*, 76.

The great difficulty with this approach, of course, is that it has inevitably forced critics to play Paul off against himself: if the "core" of Paul's thought is a central theological idea, then all the ideas expressed in the letters, if not derived from this central idea, must be tangential (and therefore unimportant) or even in conflict with it. E. P. Sanders' study *Paul and Palestinian Judaism*, for example, represents a vigorous attempt to restate Albert Schweitzer's position that "justification" is a "subsidiary crater" within Paul's thought and that eschatological participation in Christ is the real center.[8] This interpretation, however, results in the rather odd judgment that Romans 1–5, for example, is peripheral to Paul's theology and that major portions of the letters are argued using theological categories unrelated to the doctrinal center of Paul's thought.

An alternative interpretive strategy is to expand the concept of justification so that it subsumes all the other conceptual schemata in Paul's letters. Among contemporary NT scholars this strategy (which can trace its origins to Martin Luther) has been most resourcefully advocated by Ernst Käsemann.[9] Some of his proposals must be evaluated in the course of this study, but one can hardly avoid the impression that, on the whole, Käsemann's highly elastic interpretation of "righteousness" stretches the concept nearly to its breaking point.

Attempts to discover the "core" of Paul's gospel in something other than a set of theological ideas have taken two fundamental directions: (1) the attempt to interpret Paul's theology as an expression of his personal subjective religious experience, and (2) the attempt to interpret Paul's gospel within existentialist categories. Let us consider each of these briefly in turn.

Early in this century, Adolf Deissmann reacted against the prevalent interpretation of Paul as a dogmatic theologian and argued that his letters should be read as expressions emerging from his personal experience of mystical union with Christ.[10] To understand Paul, according to Deissmann's romantic interpretation, it is less important to worry over his accidental theo-

---

8. E. P. Sanders, *Paul and Palestinian Judaism* (Philadelphia: Fortress, 1977) esp. 434-42.

9. The extension of the doctrine of justification for Käsemann is most concisely illustrated in his essay "Justification and Salvation History in the Epistle to the Romans" (*Perspectives on Paul* [Philadelphia: Fortress, 1971] 60-78). Now see also H. Hübner ("Pauli Theologiae Proprium," *NTS* 26 [1979-80] 445-73), who attempts to refute the Schweitzer-Sanders position and to reassert against it the centrality of the doctrine of justification in Paul's thought.

10. A. Deissmann, *Paul: A Study in Social and Religious History* (2nd ed.; New York: Doran, 1926); see, for example, pp. 165-68.

logical formulations than to grasp the experiential intensity of this unitive mysticism. Wilhelm Bousset, writing from the perspective of the *religionsgeschichtliche Schule,* also stressed Paul's religious experience, emphasizing especially that Paul's encounter with the *Kyrios Christos* had its locus within the cultic experience of the early Hellenistic Christian communities.[11] These approaches, by insisting on placing Paul within the religious environment of his time, served as a valuable corrective against the 19th-century tendency to interpret Paul as if he had been a professor of theology, and Bousset's proposals for interpreting the Pauline letters against the backdrop of cultic myth provide some suggestive clues for the alternative thesis argued in this study. (See the discussion of Bousset in Chapter II, below.) Nonetheless, these heavily "experience"-centered interpretations do not provide an adequate basis for answering the question about the "core" of Paul's thought. No one contests the fact that Paul underwent intense personal religious experience, but the question is this: what were the structures of thought within which this experience took place and by means of which he tried to communicate it to others? This question cannot be answered by an appeal to a nonverbal mystical experience, because the experience receives its shape in, with, and through the language with which it is apprehended and interpreted.

The same criticism applies also to the effort of Joachim Jeremias to find the "key" to Paul's theology in his conversion experience on the road to Damascus.

> Es gibt nur einen Schlüssel zur paulinischen Theologie. Er heisst Damaskus. . . . In diesem Erlebnis die ganze Theologie des Apostels verwurzelt ist.[12]

Apart from the dubious historical propriety of according the "key" place in Pauline theology to an event which is known to us only through the book of Acts, we must still ask whether a single "experience" can provide a sufficient explanation for Paul's diverse and rather fully articulated theological formulations. The "experience" may provide a causal explanation of how Paul the persecutor of the church became Paul the apostle, but it hardly accounts for the shape and content of Paul's thinking.[13]

---

11. W. Bousset, *Kyrios Christos* (Nashville: Abingdon, 1970) 153-210.

12. J. Jeremias, *Der Schlüssel zur Theologie des Apostels Paulus* (Stuttgart: Calwer, 1971) 20.

13. As A. Schweitzer (*The Mysticism of Paul the Apostle* [London: A. & C. Black, 1931; reprinted, New York: Seabury, 1968] 35) comments concerning the efforts of Deissmann and others to derive the content of Paul's thought from the Damascus Road experience, "This

The case of the "existentialist" interpretation of Paul, as exemplified by Rudolf Bultmann, is somewhat more complicated. By proposing that the "core" of Paul's gospel is to be found in a new existential "self-understanding," Bultmann finds a center which defies classification within the categories posited in this discussion so far. This "self-understanding," as exposited by Bultmann, is experiential without being mystical and conceptual without being doctrinal. It is experiential because it "determines one's living in its manifold historical reality,"[14] and it is conceptual because "faith contains a knowing."[15] Faith has a "'dogmatic' character insofar as it is the acceptance of a word."[16] At the same time, Bultmann is insistent that this self-understanding of faith is never reducible to doctrinal propositions: faith also has "'undogmatic' character insofar as the word of proclamation is no mere report about historical incidents. It is no teaching about external matters which could simply be regarded as true without any transformation of the hearer's own existence. For the word is *kerygma,* personal address, demand, and promise."[17] The subtlety of this Bultmannian interpretive synthesis of concept and experience may explain in part its widespread influence and staying power. We should note, however, that at least formally, if not materially, Bultmann treats Paul's thought as a structure of theological concepts that may be elucidated through systematic exposition: anthropological concepts,[18] "grace," "faith," and so forth. At the same time, moreover, major portions of Paul's language are declared "mythological" and therefore immaterial to the *Sache,* the theological substance of Paul's thought.[19]

This aspect of Bultmann's interpretive program has been, of course, the subject of much controversy. Is Paul's thought so readily translatable as Bultmann thinks into non-"mythological" categories?[20] Would it not be pos-

---

method amounts to explaining the obscure by the more obscure." See also the cogent remarks of C. H. Dodd, *According to the Scriptures: The Sub-Structure of New Testament Theology* (London: Nisbet, 1952) 133-35.

14. R. Bultmann, *Theology of the New Testament* (2 vols.; New York: Charles Scribner's Sons, 1951-55) 1.324.

15. Ibid., 318.

16. Ibid.

17. Ibid., 318-19.

18. Cf. the critique of Bultmann's use of Paul's anthropological terms as fixed theological concepts in R. Jewett, *Paul's Anthropological Terms: A Study of Their Use in Conflict Settings* (AGTU 10; Leiden: Brill, 1971).

19. R. Bultmann, "Neues Testament und Mythologie," *Kerygma und Mythos I* (ed. H. W. Bartsch; Hamburg/Bergstedt: Herbert Reich-Evangelischer Verlag, 1960) 23.

20. This question has been raised forcefully by H. W. Boers, "Interpreting Paul: Demy-

sible to give an account of the "constant elements of the gospel" which would be more faithful to the forms in which Paul actually thought?

This is Beker's basic concern when he charges other critics with having bypassed "the investigation of the nature and method of Paul's theological language."[21] If Paul is not working on the basis of a system of theological propositions, what does give form to his thinking? Surely his statements are not purely random. In this study, I propose the thesis that any attempt to account for the nature and method of Paul's theological language must reckon with the centrality of *narrative* elements in his thought. As we shall see through an examination of Gal 3:1–4:11, in certain key theological passages in his letters, the framework of Paul's thought is constituted neither by a system of doctrines nor by his personal religious experience but by a "sacred story,"[22] a narrative structure. In these texts, Paul "theologizes" by reflecting upon this story as an ordering pattern for thought and experience; he deals with the "variable elements" of the concrete situation (for instance, the challenge of his opponents in Galatia) by interpreting them within the framework of his "sacred story," which is a story about Jesus Christ. Thus, this study will explore the hypothesis that if there are "constant elements of the gospel" for Paul, they are to be sought in the structure of this story.

Paul does not, of course, simply retell the story in his letters, although he alludes to it constantly. He assumes that his readers know the gospel story, and his pervasive concern is to draw out the implications of this story for shaping the belief and practice of his infant churches. Thus, because the text of any particular Pauline letter is a complex "production" shaped by many factors, it is impossible to isolate the story as though it were a mathematical coefficient capable of being factored out of an equation.[23] It is possible, however, to identify Paul's allusions to his story of Jesus Christ, to discern some features of its narrative "shape," and to examine the way in which this story operates as a constraint governing the logic of Paul's argumentation.

thologizing in Reverse," *The Philosophy of Order: Essays on History, Consciousness, and Politics* [*for Eric Voegelin on His Eightieth Birthday*] (ed. P. J. Opitz and G. Sebba; Stuttgart: Klett-Cotta, 1981) 153-72.

21. Beker, "Contingency and Coherence," 148.

22. The expression is taken from S. Crites ("The Narrative Quality of Experience," *JAAR* 39 [1971] 295).

23. Here again, Halliday's model (*Explorations*, 92) may be useful. His "macro-functions" are theoretical "general categories of meaning potential" which are present in almost any actual text: "With only minor exceptions, whatever the speaker is doing with language, he will draw on all three components of the grammar [i.e., ideational, interpersonal, and textual]."

This claim must be stated very carefully: the gospel story does not *determine* Paul's discourse in the sense that the latter follows directly and inevitably from the former — indeed, Paul's letters may be read as running arguments with opponents who draw different inferences from the same story[24] — but the story provides the foundational substructure upon which Paul's argumentation is constructed.[25] It also provides, therefore, certain boundaries or constraints for the logic of Paul's discourse. Thus, the narrative structure of the gospel, while not all-determinative, is *integral* to Paul's reasoning. The task of this study will be to demonstrate the truth of this hypothesis with reference to the text of Gal 3:1–4:11.

At this point, the distinction between my undertaking and Beker's may be usefully clarified. In his major study, *Paul the Apostle*, Beker works out in considerable detail his understanding of the interplay between contingency and coherence in Paul's letters. There he declares that "the coherent center of Paul's gospel is constituted by the apocalyptic interpretation of the Christ-event."[26] The basic theme of the book is Beker's claim that for Paul the Christ-event is permanently welded into the framework of Jewish apocalyptic thought, so that this framework itself is constitutive of the "core" of Paul's message. Although Beker has ably formulated the problem of contingency and coherence, my differences with him concern the substance and structure of the gospel "core," which Beker tends to describe in general phrases about the cosmic triumph of God. As Luke Johnson remarks in a review of Beker's work, "the frame is sharp, but the picture within it somewhat fuzzy."[27] I do not propose, however, to engage in a critique of Beker, with whose position I am, in fact, in general agreement; instead, I intend to undertake a more precise examination of the gospel "core" as it is manifested in Galatians, a letter that, as Beker acknowledges, "threatens to undo what I have posited as the coherent core of Pauline thought, the apocalyptic coordinates of the Christ-event that focus on the imminent, cosmic triumph of God."[28] Before we can attend, as Beker wants to do, to the *process* whereby the gospel core is brought into conjunction with various particular situa-

---

24. Another way of putting this same observation is to say that christology is never the subject of argument in Paul's letters. The christological formulations, rather than being the point at issue, form the warrants from which Paul draws soteriological inferences.

25. Some of the possibilities of "substructure" as an architectural metaphor are developed by Dodd (*Scriptures*, 12-13).

26. J. C. Beker, *Paul the Apostle: The Triumph of God in Life and Thought* (Philadelphia: Fortress, 1980) 135.

27. L. T. Johnson, [critical note] *RelSRev* 7 (1981) 164.

28. Beker, *Paul the Apostle*, 58.

tions in Paul's churches, it is necessary to identify more carefully the *structure* of the "core" itself.

In Galatians, the gospel message is manifested in a kind of shorthand through allusive phrases such as "Jesus Christ crucified" (3:1). My thesis is that these allusive phrases are intended to recall and evoke a more comprehensive narrative pattern and that we may learn something new through a fresh attempt to delineate this pattern, tracing its structure through Paul's various allusions to it. Thus, my project in some respects closely parallels Leander Keck's attempt to sketch "The Gospel Paul Preached" in distinction from "What Paul Fought For."

> The letters do not summarize what Paul preached to elicit faith, but interpret aspects of that preaching and its foundations. In developing his arguments, he alludes to his prior preaching/teaching; these references furnish the foundation of any reconstruction of Paul's preaching.[29]

At the same time, however, I go beyond Keck's position by suggesting that the heart of "what Paul preached" was a story of Jesus Christ, and that Paul's "gospel" therefore has a narrative structure. In this way I hope to do justice to Beker's concern for attention to the nature and method of Paul's theological thinking. The "interpretive fluidity" that Beker observes in the "core" of Paul's message is a direct consequence of that core's narrative character; stories are by nature polyvalent, i.e., susceptible to various levels of interpretation and application. If Paul's theological thinking is grounded in a narrative structure, this raises some provocative questions for our understanding of his "method," and it also requires us, as I hope to demonstrate, to reconsider the meaning of certain key passages in Galatians and Romans. The central contention of this study is that we can best "follow" Paul's thought when we know the outline of the story; otherwise, when we read a Pauline letter, we are overhearing one side of an argument over the interpretation of a story that we have never heard.

Two clarifications are necessary to avert possible misunderstanding. First of all, this investigation intends neither to deny nor to minimize the importance of *non*-narrative elements in Paul's letters. The letters are, after all, *letters,* and their form is certainly influenced by epistolary and rhetorical conventions. Furthermore, among the diverse contents of the letters there are, of course, blocks of material, such as the "halakic" material in 1 Corinthians 7, which are not in any discernible way related to a narrative substructure. No claim is made here that everything in Paul's letters must be explained on the

---

29. L. E. Keck, *Paul and His Letters* (Philadelphia: Fortress, 1979) 31.

basis of a narrative structure; instead, I am seeking to highlight a dimension of Paul's thought which has heretofore received insufficient emphasis by suggesting that a gospel story is foundational for the explicitly theological portions of Paul's discourse, the sections in which he seeks to articulate the fundamental features of his proclamation. This suggestion will be tested in detail through an analysis of Gal 3:1–4:11.

The second necessary clarification concerns a more difficult problem: is it really possible to suppose that Paul's thinking is rooted in a single story? Pauline scholars have long recognized that Paul employs mythic or traditional motifs that may come from a variety of backgrounds or sources. How then can we speak of a coherent unitary story undergirding Paul's discourse? One of the tasks of this study will be to show with reference to Galatians that Paul's eclectic absorption of diverse traditions is made possible precisely because he interprets them within the framework of a narrative pattern. The unity of this pattern — and the unity that it imparts to Paul's argumentation — can be demonstrated in Gal 3:1–4:11. Whether the same pattern informs Paul's thought always and everywhere is a question too complicated to pursue in this study. However, *if* a particular narrative pattern can be shown to be integral to Paul's reasoning in Galatians, then it is arguable that this pattern may be more central to his overall theological method and position than has generally been recognized.

2. Intimations of Narrative Elements in Paul

The suggestion that Paul's thought is rooted in a narrative order is not unprecedented. Several interpreters, including such widely influential figures as A. Schweitzer, O. Cullmann, and C. H. Dodd, have offered readings of Paul that stress various aspects of what I am calling the narrative substructure of Paul's theology, but none of them carries through an interpretation of Paul's theology as being rooted in story; consequently, their treatment of narrative aspects in Paul remains, although essential, implicit. Their contributions must be sketched and evaluated in Chapter II, below.

There have also been, however, a number of scholars who explicitly speak of Paul's thought as grounded in some sort of narrative paradigm. Many of their insights are expressed in "throwaway" comments, brief provocative remarks about Paul that occur in the course of essays about some other topic. None of these critics has attempted to develop these casual insights into a more comprehensive interpretation of Pauline theology, yet their observations, taken together, suggest that some such larger inquiry is requisite.

9

(a) Amos Wilder

We must begin with Amos Wilder, whose seminal works began to bridge the once enormous gap between literary criticism and biblical scholarship and thus made him the progenitor of a growing group of contemporary literarily-oriented biblical critics.[30] In *Early Christian Rhetoric*, his discussion of "The Story" as a literary form in the NT includes the following passing reference to Paul.

> That which makes the peculiar mystery of the life of the Christian is that the world plot plays itself over in him, yet in such a way that it is always unprecedented; that, as Paul says, "It is not I that live but Christ liveth in me," yet as he goes on to say, "The life that I life [*sic*], I live by the faith of him that gave himself for me."[31]

Two points are of interest here. First of all, Wilder regards Paul's claim that "Christ liveth in me" as equivalent to a claim that the "world plot" is "playing itself over" in Paul's own life, that a paradigmatic pattern which was played out in Christ is now being recapitulated in Paul. Although this is a richly suggestive approach to interpreting the text, it is not self-evidently correct, and it will have to be tested through exegetical investigation of Galatians. Secondly, Wilder's rendering of Gal 2:20b is noteworthy: not, as in nearly all modern translations, "I live by faith in him . . ." but "I live by the faith *of* him. . . ." Wilder does not draw attention to this unusual translation, because his primary intention is to comment upon the synthesis of pattern and uniqueness in the daily experience of the Christian. Nonetheless, his choice of this translation, which essentially follows the *KJV,* may be linked to his insight that "Christ" defines for Paul a paradigmatic plot-structure.

Wilder goes on to remark that even though the NT epistles themselves are not in story form, they do contain embedded within them a narrative element in the form of confessions and hymns, which have a narrative structure.[32] This is not coincidental, for Christian confession has an irreducible

---

30. For an assessment of Wilder's influence, see W. A. Beardslee, "Amos Niven Wilder: Poet and Scholar," *Semeia* 12 (1978) 1-14.

31. A. Wilder, *Early Christian Rhetoric: The Language of the Gospel* (2nd ed., Cambridge: Harvard University, 1971) 58.

32. J. T. Sanders (*The New Testament Christological Hymns* [SNTSMS 15; Cambridge: Cambridge University, 1971] 24-25) is able to sketch a "pattern" which is common to all the NT christological hymns, a pattern which he describes as a "mythical drama." Whereas Sanders is primarily concerned to inquire after the "historical religious background" of this

narrative aspect: "When the Christian in any time or place confesses his faith, his faith turns into a narrative."[33] If Wilder is right about this, it must carry significant implications for our understanding of the core-structure of Paul's gospel.

(b) Stephen Crites

In the course of a witty and provocative essay on, of all things, angels, Stephen Crites argues the point that the agents that move the action in stories are always "persons," not "mere behaviors or minds or motives or symptoms but characters that are mysterious and whole, undivided, underway. . . . Even if it is a god or an angel who appears as a character in a story, he can appear only in the form of a person."[34] To illustrate this point he turns, rather surprisingly, to *Paul's* use of the literary device of personification.

> Even what we would have to regard, outside a narrative context, as an abstraction or a general power, like Death or Eros, must appear in a story under a personal aspect. One thinks of St. Paul in the narrative-dramatic mode typical of him, snapping his fingers under Death's nose, taunting: O Death, where is thy sting! Paul, of course, also had a theology of resurrection. But its source, which his every theological utterance on the subject attempted to interpret, was clearly the drama played out before his imagination in the most concrete way: Death as the demonic-personified tyrant over the sons of Adam being overthrown by Christ the Lord, risen in power from the tomb.[35]

Now, everyone would admit that Paul, in 1 Cor 15:55, personifies and apostrophizes Death. Crites, however, is making the bolder claim that this personification is not a passing figure of speech but a reflection of the way that Paul usually thought: "the narrative-dramatic mode typical of him." Crites is proposing that Paul's reference to Death must be understood in a "narrative con-

---

pattern, my primary purpose is to investigate the way in which it informs Paul's argumentation.

33. Wilder, *Early Christian Rhetoric*, 59.

34. Crites, "Angels We Have Heard," *Religion as Story* (ed. J. B. Wiggins; New York: Harper & Row, 1975) 26. Note the stark contrast between Crites' view and the structuralist dogma that characters in stories are not persons, but illusory "narrative effects." For a clear statement of this position, see J. Calloud, *Structural Analysis of Narrative* (Semeia Supplements 4; Philadelphia: Fortress, 1976; Missoula: Scholars, 1976) 19.

35. Crites, "Angels," 27.

text." Furthermore, Crites makes the additional claim, closely parallel to the thesis of this study, that Paul's *theological* utterances have their *"source"* in a "drama" and that they should be uniformly understood as attempts to interpret that drama. Following these bare assertions, Crites' essay leaves Paul behind and moves on to its more central concerns; this inquiry, however, will take Crites' remarks as signposts toward a more detailed investigation.

(c) James A. Sanders

In an essay intended to offer a fresh approach to the problem of law and gospel, James A. Sanders proposes that the Torah itself should be understood as "a balanced intermingling of story and law,"[36] and he illustrates his proposal in the following diagram.[37]

$$\text{Torah} \begin{cases} \textit{muthos} - \text{gospel} - \text{story} - \text{identity} - \textit{haggadah} \\ \textit{ethos} - \text{law} - \text{ethics} - \text{life style} - \textit{halachah} \end{cases}$$

In light of this schema, Sanders suggests that "Paul's conversion may be seen . . . as a move on his part from emphasis on the *ethos* aspect of Torah to the *muthos* aspect."[38] According to Sanders' interpretation, Paul reads the Torah as the "story of God's works of salvation and righteousness for ancient Israel" and finds in the story of Jesus Christ an instance in which God "committed another righteousness, in Christ just like the ones of old but an even greater one!"[39] Thus, argues Sanders, the story of Jesus Christ becomes for Paul the climax and culmination of the "Torah story."[40] Sanders then concludes the essay by pointing to the Christ-hymn in Philippians as an example of the way in which Paul relates the "Torah-Christ story" to "the kind of life of obedience the Christian should try to live."[41] In other words, Sanders finds a specifically Christian analogue to the Torah in Phil 2:1-13, in which, just as in the Jewish Torah, *muthos* and *ethos* are bound inextricably together.

In spite of the essay's sermonic tone and tendency toward hyperbole, Sanders does raise several matters worthy of consideration, especially in his strong emphasis on the close relation between the Christian story and the

36. J. A. Sanders, "Torah and Christ," *Int* 29 (1975) 372.
37. Ibid., 373.
38. Ibid., 375.
39. Ibid., 380.
40. Ibid., 383.
41. Ibid., 386.

12

Christian lifestyle of obedience. The essay offers, however, only minimal exegetical substantiation for its central claim that "Paul's thought is rightly to be understood in terms of the narrative categories of *muthos* and *haggadah*."[42] Thus, Sanders' reading of Paul as a story-oriented thinker remains a provocative suggestion which must be explored through exegesis of the Pauline texts.

(d) William Beardslee

Another important signpost for this investigation is provided by William Beardslee in an essay entitled "Narrative Form in the New Testament and Process Theology."[43] Beardslee acknowledges that there are differences between most biblical narratives and archaic myths, because "the biblical stories of Origin and End highlight the historically concrete place of origin and the historically concrete forms of hope."[44] Nonetheless, he raises a caution against the frequently expressed view that this difference constitutes an absolute qualitative distinction. In spite of some differences, these narratives *function* in much the same way as myths.

> One must not lose sight of the way in which these stories still serve what I have been calling the function of myth, that is, to provide a paradigmatic or exemplary symbolic complex which is so raised above ordinary experience that it provides a norm and shape for it.[45]

Thus, Beardslee argues, without reference to Paul, that biblical narratives, "mythic" or not, provide paradigms which order human experience. Beardslee first brings Paul into view as an instance of "religious autobiography" in the NT, but then pushes beyond the not uncommon "autobiographical" reading of Paul.[46]

> In contrast to many modern tellers of their own story, Paul's ordering myth is not a personal one, but a universal story; his telling about himself is a

42. For instance, Sanders offers no argument in support of his interpretation of Rom 10:4 to mean "Christ is the climax of the Torah" (p. 383).
43. W. A. Beardslee, "Narrative Form in the NT and Process Theology," *Encounter* 36 (1975) 301-15.
44. Ibid., 305.
45. Ibid.
46. See, for example, J. S. Dunne, *A Search for God in Time and Memory* (London: Macmillan, 1967) 34-45: "Paul and the Story of Deeds."

way, not of inviting others to do their own thing, but of inviting his hearers to share this universal story, the story of Christ. The individual story is subordinate to the universal story; . . . the "little story" of Paul's life finds meaning by being related to the "big story" of which the organizing center is Christ.[47]

In much of this, Beardslee's interpretation closely parallels the views of Wilder and Crites as set forth above. But there is also one significant additional element in Beardslee's understanding of the function of the "big story" in relation to Paul's life. The story not only shapes and authorizes Paul's life but also calls it fundamentally into question.

> The story which orients Paul's life, the story of Christ, is one which continually challenges the continuity of Paul's own life-story, by its presenting him with the challenge of power-in-weakness through the symbol of the cross.[48]

Thus, to do justice to Paul's story, we must recognize its complex function in relation to his sense of self and world: it orders and undercuts at the same time. This question of the *function* of Paul's paradigmatic story, touched upon only very briefly by Beardslee, will be considered in the final chapter.

The fragmentary insights into Paul offered by the critics discussed here, taken together, suggest a new angle of vision, a perspective on Paul which calls for more careful elaboration. Wilder, Crites, Sanders, and Beardslee, in various ways, suggest that Paul's thinking must be understood in terms of an underlying narrative structure. This perspective is, of course, a heuristic device. (No claim is made that Paul consciously asked himself, "How can I bring my narrative paradigm into interaction with the problems in my churches?") But I propose that it is a useful heuristic device which illumines Paul's thought for us in significant ways and suggests compelling solutions to several vexing exegetical problems. The challenge that lies ahead is this: how can this interpretive intuition be carried through in a methodologically coherent manner?

---

47. Beardslee, "Narrative Form," 306-7.
48. Ibid., 306.

3. Terminological Clarifications

(a) "Story" vs. "Myth"

In the course of summarizing Beardslee's suggestions about the role of story in shaping Paul's thought, we introduced into the discussion the term "myth." This term, which has performed in the center ring of twentieth-century theological controversy, is closely related to the term "story"; in fact, there would be some arguments in favor of describing the goal of this study as an inquiry into the "mythic structure" underlying Paul's letters. This formulation would have the advantage of being concise and provocative, but it also has a number of decisive disadvantages. I have chosen *not* to refer to Paul's gospel as a mythic structure for the following reasons.

(1) The term "myth," in spite of (or perhaps *because* of) its currency in literary-religious-anthropological discussions, has become so diffuse in meaning that it is difficult to use with conceptual precision. As Wallace Douglas comments:

> The word is used by critics of many sorts; and . . . it can be expected to have almost as many meanings as critics who use it. . . . In general, "myth" seems to be less an analytical than a polemical term, calling attention rather to a critic's mood or moral attitude than to observed facts in the work under discussion.[49]

Rather than wading into the quagmire of "myth" studies and attempting to differentiate my understanding of the term from this or that view, I have chosen a less connotative and more descriptive term.[50]

(2) The term "myth," in spite of all critical efforts to purge or reform its traditional connotations, retains the meaning which it had already acquired by the time of the Pastoral Epistles, which warn Christians to

> have nothing to do with godless and silly myths. . . . For the time is coming when people will not endure sound teaching, but having itching ears will accumulate for themselves teachers to suit their own likings and will turn

49. W. Douglas, "The Meanings of 'Myth' in Modern Criticism," *Myth and Literature: Contemporary Theory and Practice* (ed. J. Vickery; Lincoln, Neb.: University of Nebraska, 1966) 119, 127.

50. Crites ("Narrative Quality of Experience," 295) also avoids using "myth," which he calls an "ambiguous term," in the hope of promoting clarity by using instead his term "sacred story." Of course, the term "story" is not unambiguous either, but it lacks some of the further complications associated with "myth," as enumerated in the following paragraphs.

away from listening to the truth and wander into myths. (1 Tim 4:7; 2 Tim 4:3-4)

It requires a sustained and disciplined effort of the will for most readers, when they hear the word "myth," to block out the overtones of "primitive," "bizarre," "false,"[51] and "antihistorical." None of these connotations is intended here in relation to Paul's gospel story. Thus, rather than fighting an uphill battle against the accumulated associations of the word "myth" in English, I have chosen a more neutral term, semantically speaking.[52] This terminological decision is especially important because I do not want to suggest that Paul's gospel story is necessarily unhistorical; indeed, Paul himself seems to want to insist in 1 Corinthians 15 that the validity of the gospel hinges upon the historical accuracy of certain central elements of the story. It lies beyond the scope of this investigation, however, either to assess the significance of this text or to discuss the historical accuracy of the texts in Galatians upon which our investigation will focus; my intention here is to avoid altogether the well-rehearsed arguments over the importance of the historical Jesus for Paul and to concentrate instead on the importance of narrative elements, as opposed to conceptual ones, in Paul's thought.

(3) The most decisive argument against using the term "myth" to describe Paul's foundational story, however, is to be found in the commonly held view of literary critics about the function of myth in determining one's perceptions of self and world. Mythic thought, in contrast to other modes of thought, is held to freeze and legitimate a static order of being, to figure forth a world which has been subjected to premature closure. This perspective is expressed in Frank Kermode's widely influential book, *The Sense of an Ending.*

> We have to distinguish between myths and fictions. Fictions can degenerate into myths whenever they are not consciously held to be fictive. In this sense anti-semitism is a degenerative fiction, a myth; and *Lear* is a fiction. Myth operates within the diagrams of ritual, which presupposes total and

51. That the term "myth" bears the connotation of falsity even among professional biblical scholars may be demonstrated by the disparaging remarks of H. D. Betz (*Galatians* [Hermeneia; Philadelphia: Fortress, 1979] xiv) concerning "the myth of Paul the nonthinker."

52. The emotional freight carried by the term "myth" was clearly demonstrated by the uproar caused in British theological circles by the publication of a collection of essays entitled *The Myth of God Incarnate* (ed. J. Hick; London: SCM, 1977). The controversy was provoked probably more by the title than by the content of the essays, which said nothing that had not been said many times before by theologians over the past two hundred years.

adequate explanations of things as they are and were; it is a sequence of radically unchangeable gestures. Fictions are for finding things out, and they change as the needs of sense-making change. Myths are the agents of stability, fictions the agents of change. Myths call for absolute, fictions for conditional assent. Myths make sense in terms of a lost order of time, *illud tempus* as Eliade calls it; fictions, if successful, make sense of the here and how, *hoc tempus.*[53]

Now it is certainly true that Paul demands absolute rather than conditional assent to his gospel "myth" (cf. Gal 1:8; 2 Cor 10:5-6), which he does take to be an explanation of things as they are and were. On the other hand, it is extremely doubtful whether Paul's gospel, rightly understood, may justly be described as an agent of stability as opposed to an agent of change. It is equally doubtful whether Paul may be said to be preoccupied with a "lost order of time"; indeed, his characteristic, near-obsessive concern is to demonstrate the urgency of living *in hoc tempore* in a manner somehow radically determined by his "myth." Hence, it is most doubtful whether the word "myth" is a helpful tool for understanding Paul's thinking. This is an especially important point because the final chapter of this study will investigate the function of Paul's paradigmatic story, asking what shape it imparts to his stance toward the world. Particularly in this final chapter, therefore, the term "myth" would prove more of a hindrance than a help in the quest for clarity.

(4) Likewise, the term "mythic structure" would be likely to cause confusion in the context of this study, because this term is used consistently in contemporary structuralist criticism to designate something rather different from the "narrative substructure" for which I am looking in Paul. The "mythic structure" (or "mythical structure"), as described by Lévi-Strauss[54] and elucidated by Daniel Patte and others, is a "deep" structure of fundamental binary symbolic oppositions which are held to underlie and generate narrative texts. To discover the "mythic structure," one must dechronologize the text and isolate the symbolic prenarrative oppositions.[55] This sort of operation has nothing in common with my inquiry, which seeks, on the contrary, to show that the "chronologized" ordering of narrative elements is visible at

53. F. Kermode, *The Sense of an Ending: Studies in the Theory of Fiction* (New York: Oxford, 1967) 39.

54. See C. Lévi-Strauss, "The Structural Study of Myth," *Structural Anthropology* (New York: Basic Books, 1963) 206-31.

55. For a description of this procedure, see D. Patte, *What Is Structural Exegesis?* (Philadelphia: Fortress, 1976) 53-83. See also D. Patte and A. Patte, *Structural Exegesis: From Theory to Practice* (Philadelphia: Fortress, 1978) 16-23.

the surface level in Paul's letters and that it plays a critical role in the formulation of Paul's thought.[56]

(5) The final consideration that weighs against using "myth" as a designation for what I am calling the "paradigmatic story" is the fact that we must in the course of the investigation reckon with Aristotle's use of the term *mythos* in the *Poetics*. For Aristotle, in the *Poetics*, *mythos* simply designates the moving plot line, the arrangement of the incidents: λέγω γὰρ μῦθον τοῦτον τὴν σύνθεσιν τῶν πραγμάτων.[57] The narrative pattern for which we are looking in Paul is actually something like what Aristotle called the *mythos* of a drama, but this meaning is so much more modest than the meanings usually associated with "myth" that confusion might easily result from using the term "myth" to translate Aristotle's *mythos*.

These five considerations together have prompted me to settle upon the word "story" as a term calculated to produce a more precise inquiry and to prevent manifold possible misunderstandings.

(b) "Story" and "Narrative"

In this study, the words "story" and "narrative" are used with some care in distinction from one another. "Narrative," as a noun, is used only to refer to explicitly articulated narrations ("performances") such as the Gospel of Luke or the Philippians hymn. "Story," on the other hand, does not necessarily refer to an actual narrated text; it can refer to the ordered series of events which forms the basis for various possible narrations. This meaning of "story" is specified by the *Oxford English Dictionary* as meaning 4: "A recital of events that have or are alleged to have happened; a series of events that are or might be narrated." Notice that, while this definition leaves room for the word "story" to denote the "recital," it points fundamentally to the sequence of events which underlies the recital. Thus, "story," for the purposes of this inquiry, designates the same thing that some critics have attempted to delineate by using the word "fabula,"[58] and it is closely related to Aristotle's use of the term μῦθος.

Unfortunately, the English language lacks an adjective derived from the word "story," and the only adjective available that means "having the form or

---

56. Note that Patte, in *What Is Structural Exegesis?*, clearly distinguishes his treatment of "mythical structures" (53-83) from his treatment of "narrative structures" (35-52).

57. Aristotle, *Poetics* 1450a.

58. See the explanation of this term in Dan O. Via, Jr., "Narrative World and Ethical Response: The Marvelous and Righteousness in Matthew 1–2," *Semeia* 12 (1978) 130.

character of a story" is the adjective "narrative." Thus, caution on the part of the reader is demanded. In terms of the ground rules established here, Paul's gospel *is* a story, and it *has* a narrative structure, but it is not *a* narrative except when it is actually narrated, as in Phil 2:6-11.

Clearly, in Paul's mind there was no sharp distinction between the "events" and the "recital" of the events. As 1 Corinthians 15 makes clear, Paul believed that the validity of the recital was contingent upon the claim that the events had actually taken place within the plane of reality rather than in some fictional "world." At the same time, however, in his typical usage, the term "gospel" refers to the recital of the events, and he is able to speak of this recital as "the power of God" and to attribute to it the saving efficacy that belongs, properly speaking, to the events themselves. All this is simply another way of saying that for Paul's gospel there was no separation between sense and reference[59] because he was supremely confident that the events recited in his gospel story were "real" events, not merely the product of a literary imagination. Thus, "story" is a particularly appropriate category for describing Paul's gospel because it participates in a parallel ambiguity: it can mean both the report and the thing reported.

4. Aims of the Investigation Contrasted to Other Approaches

Before moving on to the substance of my inquiry, it is important to clarify the aims of this study by contrasting them to some of the things that I am *not* trying to do. This purpose will be best achieved through a brief juxtaposition of my project to other interpretive approaches which might at first glance appear similar, though they are in fact very different.

Literary critics in recent years have become fond of saying that stories "render a world," that they create structures of meaning within which people can live.

> A story posits a sense of orientation and coherence. The story, the fable, the myth assume a context, an order of some kind. They impose a graph upon chaos and nescience. They carve out a lighted space, a *zu-Hause* in the darkness.[60]

59. For a discussion of the modern split between "sense" and "reference" in the reading of stories, see H. W. Frei, *The Eclipse of Biblical Narrative* (New Haven: Yale University, 1974) 1-16.

60. A. Wilder, *The New Voice: Religion Literature, Hermeneutics* (New York: Herder & Herder, 1969) 56.

But as critics have begun to speak of narrative as a means of ordering or apprehending or rendering a "world," some of them have begun to suspect that *all* ordered worlds are shaped by narrative. This view is stated in its baldest and most radical form by Stephen Crites, who claims that "the formal quality of experience through time is inherently narrative," and that all people therefore live "within" stories which give shape to their "sense of self and world."[61] Narrative is therefore not an incidental or optional type of cultural ornament but a fundamental expression of the "shape" of human consciousness. Paul Ricoeur restates this point by asserting that "this historicity of human experience can be brought to language only as narrativity,"[62] and John Dominic Crossan, in somewhat breezier fashion, says that "we live in story like fish in the sea."[63]

My attempt to discern a narrative substructure in Paul's letters must be distinguished in two important respects from the views of critics such as Crites and Crossan. First, I am making no sweeping claims about the narrative structure of human consciousness in general, nor am I arguing that we all live "within stories." Indeed, the point of my thesis is precisely that Paul's thinking is shaped by a story in a way that not all thinking is. If all discourse were rooted in story, it would be rather pointless to single out Paul as an instance of this universal truth. I propose to argue my thesis about Paul not on the basis of a phenomenology of consciousness but on the basis of an examination of the "logic" of Paul's arguments. It will be sufficient for the purposes of this inquiry to test the hypothesis that *Paul's* thinking is shaped by a particular paradigmatic story about Jesus Christ.

The second point of clarification is a corollary of the first: In depicting Paul as a thinker who lived in a "story-shaped world,"[64] I do not intend to relativize the truth-claims of his gospel, which still confront the reader with the demand for decision and commitment. Crossan is a particularly clear example of a thinker who believes that the recognition of the story-shaped quality of human cognition entails the loss of any hope for a fixed transcendent reference point for human experience. "There is no dry land," asserts Crossan. "There are only people living on rafts made from their own imaginations."[65] Paul, however, is very insistent that his gospel is not made from his own imagi-

61. Crites, "Narrative Quality of Experience," 291, 295.

62. P. Ricoeur, "The Narrative Function," *Semeia* 13 (1978) 195.

63. J. D. Crossan, *The Dark Interval: Towards a Theology of Story* (Niles, IL: Argus, 1975) 47.

64. The phrase comes from B. Wicker, *The Story Shaped World: Fiction and Metaphysics* (Notre Dame, IN: University of Notre Dame, 1975).

65. Crossan, *Dark Interval*, 44.

nation, that it is not a gospel κατὰ ἄνθρωπον (Gal 1:11). We may accept or reject this claim, but we should not be misled into supposing that the description of Paul's gospel as "story" necessarily implies that it is "only" the product of human ingenuity. Crossan's epistemological skepticism is rooted in the post-Kantian philosophical heritage, not in any inherent property of stories as a mode of grasping reality. In response to Crossan's raft metaphor, Paul might well agree that there is no dry land (at least none is yet in sight), but he would insist that his gospel story, provided by God, is the only Ark.

As a final gesture of clarification, it may prove helpful to list some other questions which this study will not address:

> What is the relation between "story" and "history"?
> What is the origin of the narrative pattern which appears in Paul's letters?
> What is Paul's relation to or knowledge of the body of oral Jesus-traditions?

All of these are important questions which arise quite naturally in relation to the subject matter of this study, but to pursue any of these paths would diffuse the focus of the work unnecessarily. These problems must be left for another time or for other inquirers.

B. Methodology and Procedure

1. The Relationship between Narrative and Reflective Discourse

The basic methodological problem which must be surmounted is this: in the case of Paul, where we encounter texts discursive in form, how is it possible to discern the shape of the narrative structure which, as we have proposed, underlies the argumentation? In order to attack this problem, it is necessary first of all to sketch a general understanding of the relationship between narrative and reflective discourse.

What does it mean to claim that a discourse has a "narrative substructure"? Does it make sense to say that a *story* can function as a constraint on the logic of an *argument*? In order for claims such as these to have validity, we must be able to show that there can be a continuity between the language of story and discursive language, that the relationship between the two can be, in at least some cases, organic rather than artificial.

21

We all know that people sometimes tell stories in order to illustrate ideas: the preacher or lecturer, in order to make a point, uses an anecdote that ornaments or emphasizes the intended message. In this case, the story belongs not to the "substructure" of the discourse, but to its "superstructure"; it could be replaced by a different illustrative story without materially altering the "meaning" of the discourse. But I want to argue that there are also instances in which an unfolding discourse is governed in decisive ways by a story that may find only allusive, fragmentary expression within the discourse. In cases such as these, the discourse would be unintelligible without the story, because the discourse exists and has meaning only as an unfolding of the meaning of the story. My thesis is that the theological portions of Paul's letters belong to this latter type of discourse.

In order to demonstrate the possibility of this kind of organic relationship between story and discourse, I shall enlist the aid of three critics from different disciplines — a literary critic, a philosopher, and a biblical scholar — who, with their different terminologies, arrive at mutually reinforcing conclusions that provide the theoretical basis for the procedures adopted in this study.

(a) Northrop Frye: Mythos and Dianoia

Northrop Frye adopts and adapts Aristotle's terminology for the constituent parts (μέρη) of tragedy in a way that is pertinent to the methodological problem that we are addressing. Of special interest for our purpose is his use of the Aristotelian terms *mythos* and *dianoia;* his distinction between these terms is most comprehensively developed in *The Anatomy of Criticism*[66] but for our purposes most concisely and suggestively explicated in *Fables of Identity*[67] and *The Stubborn Structure.*[68] Frye uses *mythos* in the sense suggested by Aristotle: the *mythos* of a literary work is its plot, the linear sequence of events depicted. But Frye deliberately extends the sense of *dianoia* well beyond Aristotle's use of it. Whereas Aristotle used it to designate the portions of dialogue in which arguments or opinions are expressly set forth,[69] Frye employs *dianoia* as a term for "theme" — "the *mythos* or plot examined as a simulta-

66. N. Frye, *Anatomy of Criticism* (Princeton: Princeton University, 1957) 77-79.
67. N. Frye, *Fables of Identity: Studies in Poetic Mythology* (New York: Harcourt, Brace & World, 1963).
68. N. Frye, *The Stubborn Structure: Essays on Criticism and Society* (Ithaca: Cornell University, 1970).
69. Aristotle, *Poetics* 1450b.

neous unity, when the entire shape of it is clear in our minds."[70] Thus, *mythos* is characterized by sequence and *dianoia* by pattern.

> The word narrative or *mythos* conveys the sense of movement caught by the ear and the word meaning or *dianoia* conveys, or at least preserves, the sense of simultaneity caught by the eye. We *listen* to the poem as it moves from beginning to end, but as soon as the whole is clear in our minds, we "see" what it means.[71]

The crucial point here is that Frye regards "theme" or "meaning" not as something abstracted from the narrative but as an organic property of the narrative. *Mythos* and *dianoia* are "the same in substance," but the latter grasps the particular narrative elements "in relation to a unity, not in relation to suspense and linear progression."[72] From a literary point of view, the meaning *(dianoia)* is not separable from the means of expression, as though the literary work were only a container for it. Because the *dianoia* is discovered in the narrative pattern, it can never be radically detached from the narrative, even though it must be distinguished from the linear articulation of narrative elements. The theme, claims Frye, is the narrative seen from a certain perspective.

> *Participation* in the continuity of narrative leads to the discovery or recognition of the theme, which *is* the narrative seen as total design. The theme is what, as we say, the story has been all about, the point of telling it.[73]

Frye is particularly interested in the perception and recollection of the theme by the critical mind, which reorders the narrative elements in a way different from the sequence in which they present themselves in the *mythos*.

> What we reach at the end of participation becomes the center of our critical attention. The elements in the narrative thereupon regroup themselves in a new way. Certain unusually vivid bits of characterization or scenes of exceptional intensity move up near the center of our memory.[74]

Thus the "scene of exceptional intensity" which dominates Paul's retrospective perception of the story of Jesus Christ is summarized in the phrase "Jesus

70. Frye, *Fables*, 24.

71. Frye, *Anatomy*, 77.

72. Frye, *Fables*, 24.

73. Frye, *Stubborn Structure*, 164. The emphasis on the word *is* is Frye's; I have added the emphasis on *participation*.

74. Ibid.

Christ crucified," and this image becomes the center of his critical attention. Nonetheless, the image receives its particular significance only because allusions to it evoke the structure of the entire story within which its meaning is rooted.

Frye, as a literary critic, is concerned with the critical process of "recalling" a narrative text, and he wants to establish that the "meaning" *(dianoia)* of a narrative text is in fact a property of the text, not an arbitrary imposition created by the critic. This study deals not with a narrative text but with Paul's letter to the Galatians. Its thesis is that in this letter we find Paul's critical re-presentation of the *dianoia* of the story of Jesus Christ. Galatians is not, of course, a piece of literary criticism, but, like a piece of literary criticism, it re-states the theme *(dianoia)* of a story "in relation to a unity, not in relation to suspense and linear progression." This investigation must be tested against the text of Galatians, but Frye's analysis provides a conceptual foundation for the claim that there is an organic continuity between a story and a non-narrative explication of the story's meaning.

(b) Paul Ricoeur: Episodic and Configurational Dimensions of Narrative

A very similar account of the relation between "sequence" and "pattern" is proposed by Paul Ricoeur in an essay, "The Narrative Function."

> All narratives combine in various proportions two dimensions, one chronological and the other non-chronological. The first may be called the episodic dimension of a narrative. . . . But . . . the activity of telling does not merely consist in piling episodes on top of one another. It also construes significant values out of scattered events. To this aspect of story-telling corresponds on the side of story-following an attempt to "grasp together" successive events. The art of telling and, accordingly, its counterpart, the art of following a story require that we be able to elicit a configuration from a succession. This "configurational" operation . . . constitutes the second dimension of narrative activity.[75]

Here, as with Frye, we see that the "configuration" of narrative elements into significant patterns is integral to the narrative itself rather than imposed upon it from outside. For this reason, Ricoeur can assert that "to tell and to follow a story is already to reflect upon events in order to encompass them in

75. Ricoeur, "Narrative Function," 183-84.

successive wholes."[76] Reflective discourse such as Paul's letters may then be understood as growing organically out of the process of narration, and, conversely, what Ricoeur has elsewhere claimed for the specific case of symbolic language may in fact be true for narrative in general.

> . . . All symbolic language calls for an interpretation. . . . The process of interpretation is not something superimposed from the outside on a self-contained expression; it is motivated by the symbolic expression itself which gives rise to thought. It belongs to the essence of a figurative expression to stand for something else, to call for a new speech-act which would paraphrase the first one without exhausting its meaningful resources.[77]

Ricoeur is concerned here with the interpretation of parables, but, as Kermode has shown persuasively in his book *The Genesis of Secrecy,* all stories, not just parables, demand interpretation.[78] Thus, to apply Ricoeur's terminology to my thesis, a Pauline letter could be understood as a "new speech act" that attempts to rearticulate in discursive language the configurational dimension of the gospel story.

(c) Robert Funk: Foundational Language and Primary Reflectivity

Both Frye and Ricoeur are working with the problems presented by texts that are narrative in form, and both, in the passages cited here, are primarily concerned to argue that a thematic or configurational dimension is inherent in narrative. In order to suggest the implications of their theories for the interpretation of Paul, I have had, so to speak, to run the film backward by suggesting that Paul's thematic expositions may be understood as reflections upon the configuration of a particular story. In the case of Robert W. Funk, however, we encounter a biblical critic who espouses a similar theory about the relation between "foundational" and reflective discourse and seeks to apply its implications specifically to Paul.

Funk posits a spectrum of "modes of discourse" and singles out "three cardinal points" on that spectrum in order to create a typology of language

---

76. Ibid., 185.
77. Ricoeur, "Biblical Hermeneutics," *Semeia* 4 (1975) 133.
78. F. Kermode, *The Genesis of Secrecy: On the Interpretation of Narrative* (Cambridge: Harvard University, 1979).

modes.[79] At one end of the spectrum, there is "primordial discourse" or "foundational language," language which founds a world or which at least "re-flects, without reflecting upon, the world."[80] Funk, following Heidegger, labels this mode the "poetical" mode, and offers no comment about the place of narrative in his scheme.[81] Nonetheless, it is clear that much biblical narrative belongs at or near this end of Funk's spectrum. At the other end of the spectrum, there is the language of "secondary reflectivity," which is defined as "reflection upon the language deposit left by previous reflection."[82] In its most extreme forms, this mode of language becomes meta-language, as in the case of linguistic analysis. Somewhere in the middle of the spectrum, we have the language of "primary reflectivity," which reflects upon "the fate of reflective language in the face of a concrete but competitive *Lebenswelt*."[83] It is to this mode of discourse that the Pauline letters belong. Funk clearly delineates the functions of the two main language forms with which he is concerned in the following aphorism.

> The parable is creating a tradition, founding a "world"; the letter is reviewing the destiny of that foundational language in relation to other "worlds," the world of the apostle, the worlds of his readers.[84]

Now, it is accurate and helpful to recognize that the letter is reviewing the destiny of (some) foundational language in relation to other worlds. The pressing question, however, is "*What* foundational language?" Funk's analysis of Paul is vitiated by his preoccupation with the attempt to demonstrate a continuity between the world founded by the parables of Jesus and the world which is "intended" in Paul's letters. Funk goes so far as to assert that Paul's language "presupposes" the parables as its "foundational language tradition."[85] He recognizes the problematical character of this assertion in an extended footnote, but still believes that his view can be defended by means of a "phenomenology of language" that will expose the "internal history of a tradition."[86]

79. R. W. Funk, *Language, Hermeneutic, and Word of God* (New York: Harper & Row, 1966) 232. Very similar projects are conceived by Crites ("Angels," 28) and Vernon Ruland ("Understanding the Rhetoric of Theologians," *Semeia* 13 [1978] 203-24).
80. Funk, *Language, Hermeneutic, and Word of God*, 232.
81. The term "poetical" is, of course, based on ποίησις, "making." Language in the poetical mode "makes" a world.
82. Funk, *Language, Hermeneutic, and Word of God*, 232.
83. Ibid., 233.
84. Ibid.
85. Ibid., 244.
86. Ibid.

I do not propose here to discuss these claims or to become entangled in debate with the "new questers." It may indeed be possible to demonstrate a congruence of some kind (at the level of "deep-structure"?) between the "world" of the parables and the "world" intended in the epistles, although it is surely very doubtful whether such a congruence, even if demonstrable, should be understood in the linear-genetic manner implied in Funk's talk about "the internal history of a tradition."

Over against all of this, however, I am proposing that Funk's insight into the *mode* of the Pauline letters may be usefully redirected if we ask ourselves this question: what is the foundational language whose destiny Paul is reviewing? It is surely not the language of the parables. The answer, already suggested here, is that Paul is reviewing the destiny of a story about Jesus Christ which is expressed most clearly in the hymnic and confessional passages of the letters. This insight must be investigated in detail. It should be understood, of course, that Paul's "reflection" and "reviewing" do not take the form of detached contemplation. Paul does not write like a literary critic analyzing the story critically; he writes as a "believer," i.e., as one whose view of reality is totally determined by the story, and he seeks to demonstrate to others the story's inexhaustible significance for shaping the life and thought of the believing community.

We should also recognize that Funk's approach to Paul yields one further crucial methodological clue about where to look for the outlines of the narrative structure.

> On the ground that the letters indicate that the message has suffered distortion or non-understanding, Paul is in the mode of recapitulation, attempting to hear again himself, and at the same time to hear with ears attuned to the auditory range of his readers.[87]

Funk expands this insight by pointing out certain texts in which Paul's "reviewing" adopts the vocabulary ("auditory range") of his readers, such as 1 Cor 2:6-16, but I see in his insight a very different implication for the present investigation. Funk suggests that Paul writes in the *mode of recapitulation;* this means that he is in effect saying, "No, no, you stupid Galatians (or Corinthians, etc.), didn't you get the point of the story? Let me explain to you what it was all about." He hammers home his interpretation of the story (= its *dianoia*) and unfolds the implications of the story for the specific issues that are at stake in the life of the community. In order to make his point, he must allude to the key events of the story, because the *dianoia* is discovered only in

---

87. Ibid., 247.

the narrative pattern. We can therefore expect that the structure (the *mythos*) of the story will appear most visibly at the points where Paul is elucidating the theme (the *dianoia*) of the story by repeating what he has already told his readers on some previous occasion. This phenomenon is most readily apparent in a text such as 1 Corinthians 15 ("Now I would remind you, brethren, in what terms I preached to you the gospel . . ."), and something closely analogous occurs when, as in Philippians 2, he quotes a hymn that is presumably already known to his readers. In both of these instances, a briefly recapitulated christological story serves as the foundation for Paul's argumentation. In 1 Corinthians 15, the story provides the basis for Paul's statement of a "doctrinal" position on resurrection of the dead, and in Philippians 2 the story undergirds an extended parenetic passage (Phil 1:27–2:18).

However, if the thesis that Paul's theology has a narrative substructure is correct, that substructure should manifest itself not only in places where Paul quotes traditional confessional material, as in 1 Corinthians 15, or hymns, as in Philippians 2, but also in a text such as Galatians, in which Paul is driven to a forceful recapitulation of the most fundamental elements of his proclamation. Thus, for the purposes of this study, the overall importance of Funk's observation that Paul writes in the "mode of recapitulation" is this: it leads us to look not only to hymnic and confessional passages but also to argumentative recapitulation for traces of Paul's foundational story.

(d) Summary

This brief discussion of insights from Frye, Ricoeur, and Funk has served to defend the credibility of a set of assumptions about the relation between stories and reflective discourse. These assumptions may be summarized briefly as follows.

(1) There can be an organic relationship between stories and reflective discourse because stories have an inherent configurational dimension *(dianoia)* which not only permits but also demands restatement and interpretation in non-narrative language.

(2) The reflective restatement does not simply repeat the plot *(mythos)* of the story; nonetheless, the story shapes and constrains the reflective process because the *dianoia* can never be entirely abstracted from the story in which it is manifested and apprehended.

(3) Hence, when we encounter this type of reflective discourse, it is legitimate and possible to inquire about the story in which it is rooted.

This inquiry may have two phases: we may first identify within the discourse allusions to the story and seek to discern its general outlines; then, in a second phase of inquiry we may ask how this story shapes the logic of argumentation in the discourse. This, in broad outline, is the procedure that will be followed in this study.

2. Galatians 3:1–4:11 as a Test Case

My hypothesis about the narrative substructure of Paul's theology will be tested through a careful analysis of Gal 3:1–4:11. This passage has been chosen for several reasons. First of all, it is necessary to test the hypothesis with reference to a block of Paul's theological prose. Philippians 2 would not be a good test passage, for example, because it is so evidently constructed upon a Christ-hymn. The central section of Galatians, however, offers a good representation of Paul the theologian at work, apart from any direct influence of hymnic language. It is both theologically substantive and brief enough to handle without undue complication. Thus it provides a good sample for analysis.

Secondly, Galatians is a letter in which Paul is clearly operating in the "mode of recapitulation," reviewing for the Galatians the basics of the gospel. Paul has learned, to his amazement, that the Galatians are coming under the influence of a "different gospel" and deserting the gospel that he had preached to them (1:6). Consequently, he feels compelled to reiterate and defend his position. In the course of this defense he alludes to his previous communication of the gospel to them (3:1: Ἰησοῦς Χριστὸς προεγράφη ἐσταυρωμένος) and employs as "clinchers" at various key points in the argument compact christological-soteriological formulations that give the appearance of being traditional or authoritative summaries of the gospel message (see 3:13-14, 22, 26-28; 4:3-6). These kerygmatic summaries will be the focal point for my analysis, because, as recapitulations of the gospel message, they express the *dianoia* of the gospel story and provide some clues to its shape. Thus Galatians, because it is evoked by a situation which Paul regards as a fundamental threat to the gospel, affords within brief compass several clear manifestations of the gospel's narrative structure.

These formulations, however, are interwoven with scriptural quotations and Paul's own exposition in a very confusing manner. Because of the dense and allusive texture of the argumentation, Galatians is a challenging text, full of exegetical puzzles, and this fact provides the third reason for working with it in this study. In the opening paragraph of his analysis of Gal 3:6-14, Hans

Dieter Betz remarks that "there is agreement among exegetes that Paul's argument in this section is extremely difficult to follow."[88] It may be hoped that a clarification of the narrative substructure will enable us to follow the logic of Paul's theological argument more readily. The long-dominant "Lutheran" interpretation of Paul has been called fundamentally into question by Krister Stendahl, Markus Barth, and others,[89] but there has not yet been any satisfying full-scale reexamination of this central section of Galatians, which was, after all, Luther's favorite epistle and the foundation stone of his teaching. Consequently, we may hope that our investigation of the narrative substructure of this text, by illuminating the internal logic of the letter, will make a significant contribution toward a better understanding of Pauline theology.

It is important to keep in mind that the narrative structure for which we are searching is the structure of the gospel story, not of Paul's personal story. This caution is necessary because among interpreters of Galatians there is a well-established tradition of referring to the autobiographical material in the first two chapters as the "narrative" portion of the letter. This designation, which dates back at least to J. B. Lightfoot's commentary,[90] has recently been reaffirmed by the rhetorical analysis of Hans Dieter Betz, who designates Gal 1:12–2:14 as the "narratio."[91] Certainly this is an appropriate description of the content of this portion of the letter, but this personal narrative about Paul must not be confused with the story which stands at the center of Paul's gospel proclamation. To discern the latter story, we must turn to the material in chapters 3 and 4, where Paul presents the substance of the gospel. Here we discover that Paul's own story is no longer the center of attention; it has been supplanted by a christological story. Our task, then, is to trace carefully the formulations in which this story appears.

---

88. Betz, *Galatians,* 137.

89. K. Stendahl, *Paul among Jews and Gentiles* (Philadelphia: Fortress, 1976); M. Barth, "The Kerygma of Galatians," *Int* 21 (1967) 131-46, idem, "St. Paul — A Good Jew," *Horizons in Biblical Theology* 1 (1979) 7-45. From a very different angle, the "Lutheran" reading of Paul is also challenged by H. Schlier's major commentary, *Der Brief an die Galater* (14th ed.; MeyerK 7; Göttingen: Vandenhoeck & Ruprecht, 1971). For polemical counterreaction to Schlier, see S. Schulz, "Katholisierende Tendenzen in Schliers Galaterkommentar," *KD* 5 (1959) 23-41, and Betz, *Galatians,* xiii.

90. J. B. Lightfoot, *St. Paul's Epistle to the Galatians* (London: Macmillan, 1865; reprinted, Grand Rapids: Zondervan, 1957) 65-67.

91. Betz, *Galatians,* 58-62.

3. Steps in the Investigation

Before turning directly to the text of Galatians, I will set my proposal in context by discussing in Chapter II several major critical approaches to narrative elements in Paul. This chapter will place these previous scholarly expositions of the narrative dimension of Paul's thought along a typological spectrum and seek to clarify some of the similarities and distinctions between their approaches and mine. The substantive contribution of the investigation will appear in Chapters III-V, in the detailed analysis of Gal 3:1–4:11. Chapter III will offer a close investigation of the narrative structure of several key christological formulations in the text. Chapter IV will focus upon the phrase πίστις Ἰησοῦ Χριστοῦ and upon the particular problem of the role of πίστις in relation to the narrative structure outlined in Chapter III. The task of Chapter V will be to demonstrate how this narrative structure informs Paul's theological argument in Galatians 3 and 4. Finally, in light of the findings of Chapters III-V, the concluding chapter will attempt to suggest some of the implications that follow from my thesis.

Chapter II

How Has the Narrative Dimension in Paul's Thought Been Handled? An Overview of Previous Interpretations

If Paul's theology is indeed rooted in a story, as I am proposing, why have Paul's interpreters not emphasized this fact? The question is a fair one. This chapter seeks to approach it by demonstrating that some interpreters of Paul have recognized that the letters contain allusions to a gospel story of some sort, though not many have used the term "story" to describe what they have recognized. While most exegetes, preoccupied with theological concerns, have turned directly to the task of constructing a Pauline theology out of the letters, there have been some whose greater sensitivity to the narrative dimension of Paul's thought has caused them to linger over the story-fragments imbedded in the letters and to ponder their significance. The resultant interpretations, though sometimes idiosyncratic, have also proved penetrating and have served as a stimulus to fresh theological appropriations of Paul's message. The work of these interpreters provides a foundation upon which the present investigation builds.

Even among those interpreters who have recognized the presence of narrative elements in Paul's letters, however, some have tended to de-emphasize these elements by proposing interpretations that do not treat the narrative quality of Paul's thought as central. Others have been preoccupied with the problem of the relation between story and history and have focused their attention on seeking to determine the historical veracity of the narrative elements. Still others have imposed upon Paul a narrative scheme derived from some other source. The present chapter, therefore, has a double task: it will review the significant contributions of various major scholars to the project of discerning the narrative character of Paul's gospel and, at the same time, it will critically assess their evaluations of the narrative elements in Paul.

Rather than attempting a comprehensive survey of critical approaches to the narrative elements in Paul, I will examine briefly the views of a few key figures whose interpretations constitute a cross-section of the various ways in which NT critics have dealt with these narrative elements. The resulting typology will provide a useful background against which to locate and assess the interpretive proposals contained in the subsequent chapters of this study.

The scholars whose views are to be considered in this chapter are Wilhelm Bousset, Albert Schweitzer, Rudolf Bultmann, Oscar Cullmann, Ernst Käsemann, C. H. Dodd, and Dan O. Via, Jr. No attempt will be made here to offer a comprehensive exposition of the way in which each of these critics interprets Paul. Instead, our attention will center on the way in which each one treats the partly submerged narrative elements in Paul's letters. For each critic, the investigation will seek to answer two closely interrelated questions: (1) how does he describe the narrative elements in Paul's thought? and (2) how does he evaluate the relation of these elements to the overall structure of Paul's thought?

A. The Identification of Narrative Elements in Paul

1. Wilhelm Bousset: Cultic Myth

Bousset's *Kyrios Christos* places Paul thoroughly within the context of a Hellenistic form of Christianity which must be, according to Bousset, sharply differentiated from the earliest Palestinian Christian movement. The language and piety of this Hellenistic Christianity are comprehensible, Bousset claims, only if we see it as the product of a religious environment characterized by a luxuriant proliferation of κύριος cults.[1] Bousset's placement of Paul in this context has significant implications for his interpretation of Pauline theology. Paul's "ideas" are always understood as outgrowths of the ecstatic worship experience of the *"heidenchristliche Urgemeinde"* from which Paul the apostle emerges.[2] But Bousset is also at pains to stress that this background is merely the "point of departure"[3] for Paul, that he builds upon and transcends this Christianized form of Hellenistic enthusiasm in at least two decisive ways.

First of all, Paul "ethicizes" and "personalizes" the gospel by expanding its implications beyond the immediate cultic experience.

1. Bousset, *Kyrios Christos,* 146-47.
2. Ibid., 135.
3. Ibid., 153.

In the Christ piety of Paul there now sounds one entirely new note, and it becomes the dominant: the intense feeling of personal belonging and of spiritual relationship with the exalted Lord. . . . For it is just his achievement to have re-formed into individual mysticism, ethicized, and transposed out of the cult into the total personal life that cultic and community mysticism. . . .[4]

One result of this "personalizing" of the communal mystical experience is that "with the apostle Paul faith . . . first appears as the inner center of the religious life."[5]

Paul's second distinctive contribution to Christianity, in Bousset's analysis, is his "unbelievably daring deed" of interpreting the Gospel within the "thought-world" of the mystery religions (with their suffering, dying, and rising divinities)[6] and, at the same time, formulating his Christology under the influence of the pervasive oriental (proto-Gnostic?) myth of "the Primal Man (Anthropos) who sinks down into matter and is again liberated from it."[7] The fusion of these mystic systems to provide a basis for Christian teaching about the significance of Jesus Christ is Paul's distinctive achievement.

Each of these two components of Bousset's description of Paul is of direct relevance for our investigation of narrative elements in Paul. To begin with, taking the second point first, one might suppose that Bousset's awareness of the close parallels between Paul's thought and the myths of the mysteries and of Gnosticism would lead him to regard these mythic stories as the key to the content of Paul's gospel. Indeed, Bousset sometimes speaks as if this were the case; for example, he remarks that through the myths "the cultic veneration of the κύριος 'Ιησοῦς Χριστός in the Hellenistic communities and the personal Christ mysticism which rests upon that veneration gain their conceptual grounding and their systematic structure."[8] However, Bousset never undertakes the exegetical task of describing that "systematic structure" in detail; he seems content to rest with pointing out various scattered parallels between Paul's letters and the myths of the Hellenistic religious environ-

---

4. Ibid., 153, 157. Bousset's opinions on this point are surely overstated. Was the early community's cultic experience really so devoid of individual and ethical dimensions as Bousset's statements seem to imply? On the other hand, even more to the point, was Paul's own "mysticism" really as individualistic as Bousset suggests?

5. Ibid., 200 (translation slightly corrected).

6. Ibid., 198.

7. Ibid., 190. Schweitzer (*Mysticism*, 32) misrepresents Bousset's position by reporting that for Bousset "Paul's only original act" is his denial of the validity of the Law.

8. *Kyrios Christos*, 198.

ment. Furthermore, having pointed out these parallels, Bousset persistently seeks to affirm that the thought of Paul somehow *transcends* the mythic thought-world.

> And yet, if we consider all this [i.e., Paul's dependence on mythic motifs], the incomparably greater moral-religious power and the spiritual originality of the apostle would emerge into a clear light. . . . Through all the mystery beliefs and mysterious speculations the ethos of the gospel is articulated.[9]

Why does Bousset stop short of the claim that Paul's gospel is itself a mythic story? The answer to this question will provide us with some useful insights.

In the first place, Bousset recognizes that his painstakingly collected parallels in the mythology of the mysteries and Gnosticism offer only rough analogies to Pauline thought, and he is careful to point out the significant differences.[10] These differences render impossible any claim that Paul's theology is, for example, simply the exposition of the Ἄνθρωπος-myth as it is found in *Poimandres*. Therefore, Bousset regards the mythic stories not as direct *sources* for Paul's theologizing, but as evidence of a cultural-religious atmosphere within which Paul lived and breathed. Thus, oriental mysticism provides the "explanatory context" for Pauline theology;[11] Bousset regards his collection of mythic parallels as samples drawn from a repository of motifs and thought-patterns from which Paul also drew in an eclectic fashion. Bousset does not discuss the possibility that Paul, rather than selectively adapting various themes from a general mythic thought-world, might be consistently reflecting upon a single story of Jesus Christ, to which the various myths offer partial parallels at particular points.[12] Certainly Bousset makes no detailed attempt to construct a single Pauline Christ-myth on the basis of the evidence found in the letters.[13]

---

9. Ibid., 194.

10. Ibid., 193, 199.

11. Ibid., 197.

12. He does insist (ibid., 154) that "the picture which Paul actually sketches of the κύριος Ἰησοῦς is not taken from the earthly life of Jesus," i.e., from the historical Jesus. But that is another matter.

13. He does occasionally offer sketchy summaries, such as the following: "The Jesus whom Paul knows is the preexistent supraterrestrial Christ who was rich and for our sake became poor, who was in the form of God and took on the form of a servant, the Son of God whom the Father gives as a sacrifice, the one who fulfills the prophecies, the one who accomplishes the promises" (154-55). This assessment is certainly correct, and it is surprising that Bousset does not pursue the point further by seeking to order and expand these elements into a great Christ-myth. His forbearance from this task is all the more surprising in view of

In the second place, Bousset is not really interested in particular cultic myths. His tendency is to think of these particular myths as adumbrations of general mythic patterns or even of a ruling monomyth.

> No more does the individual divine figure with its specific myth come so much into consideration; in all these figures is manifested the one idea which seizes Hellenistic superstitious piety with mystical power, the idea of the dying and rising, salvation-bringing deity.[14]

Furthermore, as this quotation nicely illustrates, Bousset tends to regard myths as primitive vehicles or containers of "ideas."[15] Particular myths are of interest only insofar as they illustrate ideas.

A corollary of this observation is that Bousset does not take seriously the possibility that "sacred stories" might be a valid independent mode of apprehending reality; his descriptive terminology for myths is consistently disparaging in its connotations; he calls them "fantasies," "superstitions," "speculations," and the like, and he consistently considers the process of spiritualizing abstraction which he believes Paul to have initiated as a movement to a higher and better plane.

> . . . In sublime exposition he frees that cultic experience, which had been understood only in the mood of a mystery, from its gloomy ties, reorients it to the personal, interprets it spiritually-ethically, and enlarges it. . . . It is as if here a mysticism of a more personal note struggles free and flies upward with freer strokes of the wings. But it did take its point of departure from the community's cult and sacrament.[16]

Given these intellectual predispositions, it is hardly surprising that Bousset did not seek to demonstrate that Paul's gospel could be understood as a story.

---

the alacrity with which he reconstructs myths when he is working with noncanonical sources. For example, after giving an account of the Anthropos-myth as found in *Poimandres,* he offers the following remark: "Here the myth breaks off, but its end, the story of the liberation of the Primal Man from matter and his elevation into the heavenly world, can easily be completed from the second, paraenetic half of the Tractate" (191). Might we just as "easily" use the parenetic portions of Paul's letters to "complete" a Christ-myth?

14. Ibid., 189. Bousset's approach to the mythology of Hellenistic antiquity thus anticipates, in some respects, the structuralist view that all the myths of a culture comprise a single myth.

15. Bousset's term here is *"Idee"* rather than *"Vorstellung"* (*Kyrios Christos* [3rd ed.; FRLANT N.F. 4; Göttingen: Vandenhoeck & Ruprecht, 1926] 135). His orientation is toward concepts rather than toward images.

16. *Kyrios Christos,* 157-58.

He was acutely aware of the influence of mythic patterns on the formation of Paul's theology, but, in common with most scholars of his time, he disdained myths as a naive and inferior form of thought and therefore was at pains to demonstrate that Paul had transcended the mythic mode.[17]

We may also propose, however, a third reason that Bousset does not pursue the possibility that a Christ-story might stand at the center of Paul's theological thinking. Bousset adopts the debatable opinion that the religious experience of believers precedes and precipitates the articulation of cultic myths: "If we look more closely, we find that just those speculations about the dying and rising god and his cosmic significance grew up out of the cultus and the experience of the believers in the cultus."[18] The fundamental datum at the heart of Paul's religion is not, in Bousset's view, a story or myth about Jesus but the palpable experience of the presence of the κύριος in ecstatic worship.

> Behind the Christ mysticism of the apostle stands the Kyrios who is active in the cult of the community with his miraculous powers and his fullness of life. And behind the Spirit mysticism of Paul stands the living reality of the pneumatic experiences which again are most abundantly and powerfully unfolded in the worshiping assembly.[19]

The present study presupposes a rather different understanding of the relation between language and experience; in light of Bousset's views on this matter, however, it is understandable that he tended to view the Christ-myth as a product rather than a producer of Paul's theological reflection.

Thus Bousset sees Paul's allusions to a Christ-story as fragmentary but significant pointers that help the historian locate the milieu within which Paul's theology was shaped. These story-fragments, according to Bousset, can in no way be considered the substance of Paul's gospel, however, because "everywhere the apostle pushes out above and beyond the piety of the cultus and the sacrament which surrounds and envelops him, to the purely ethical-religious, to the intellectual-personal."[20]

17. This observation is equally applicable, of course, to Bultmann, whose position will be considered more precisely below.
18. *Kyrios Christos,* 191.
19. Ibid., 163.
20. Ibid., 160.

2. Albert Schweitzer: Eschatology and "Mysticism"

Reacting vehemently against the approach to Paul taken by the *religions-geschichtliche Schule,* Albert Schweitzer insists that Paul's thought (which Schweitzer characterizes, rather dubiously, as a form of "mysticism") "cannot be reconstructed out of a patchwork of Hellenistic ideas but only becomes intelligible in the light of eschatology."[21] The Hellenistic parallels adduced by Reitzenstein, Bousset, and others are, in Schweitzer's opinion, imprecise and unilluminating.[22]

Schweitzer's fundamental thesis that Paul's thought is rooted in the world of Jewish apocalyptic enables him, he believes, to show that all of Paul's "various tenets are derived from a single fundamental conception" *(Grundvorstellung).*[23] What is this *Grundvorstellung*? It is *not* merely an idea or a body of doctrine. It is the "dramatic world-view characteristic of the late Jewish Eschatology."[24] What Schweitzer has in mind here is not some apocalyptic psychological disposition but, more precisely, the eschatological scenario of events at the turn of the ages: The Messiah will come and overthrow the evil angelic powers that exercise dominion over the world, and the Elect will rule with him in his Messianic Kingdom; after a fixed interval, the Messianic Kingdom will come to an end, and there will be a general resurrection of all people who have ever lived, followed by God's final judgment.

Schweitzer's connected picture of the apocalyptic scenario is dependent, as he acknowledges, upon 1 Enoch, the Psalms of Solomon, the Apocalypse of Baruch, and the canonical books Daniel and Revelation. Nowhere does Paul offer a narrative describing the eschatological drama from beginning to end, but Schweitzer sees numerous allusions which point to it. The letters are so occupied with other concerns that it is sometimes possible for us as readers "to forget the expectation which dominates the soul of the writer." But, whenever this happens, "suddenly, in some incidental saying, the eschatological belief stands there in all its strength as *something which always underlies the whole.*"[25]

Clearly, Schweitzer's argument is open to the criticism that he sometimes superimposes a predetermined structure on Paul's thinking even where it is not appropriate. The following two citations illustrate this difficulty.

21. Schweitzer, *Mysticism,* 138.
22. Ibid., 140.
23. Ibid., 138.
24. Ibid., 11.
25. Ibid., 52, emphasis mine. Paul's fullest descriptions of the endtime events are found in 1 Thess 4:13-18 and 1 Cor 15:20-28, 51-57.

We have from Paul no description of the Messianic Kingdom. That the conception of the Heavenly Jerusalem means something for him we learn incidentally in Galatians (iv.26). He therefore no doubt expects that this Jerusalem will in the Messianic time descend together with Paradise upon the earth, as is assumed in the Apocalypses of Ezra (4 Ezra vii.26) and of John (Rev. iii.12; xxi.2).

The general Resurrection, and the immediately following judgment upon all men and upon the defeated Angels, is not mentioned in the series of events enumerated by Paul in 1 Cor xv.23-28. All this falls for him under the general concept of 'the End' (τέλος, 1 Cor v.24), and is taken for granted as well known.[26]

Here Schweitzer invites the charge of eisegesis; his conclusions may be correct, but they surely require some weightier supporting argumentation than he in fact provides.

However, it would be inaccurate to say that Schweitzer simply reads a monolithic eschatological pattern derived from other sources *into* Paul. In the first place, he recognizes that the eschatological expectations of these other sources are not uniform. The most important discrepancy among them concerns the place of the general resurrection in the sequence of events: some texts, such as Daniel, place it at the beginning of the Messianic Kingdom,[27] whereas others, such as 4 Ezra and the Apocalypse of Baruch, place it at the *end* of the Messianic Kingdom. Schweitzer sees Paul as belonging with the second group.

The eschatology which he presupposes is, as regards its scheme and the events of the end, the same as that of the Apocalypses of Baruch and Ezra. This therefore must have been the accepted view of the Scribes among whom he was brought up.[28]

In the second place, Paul is forced, according to Schweitzer, by the fact of the death and resurrection of Jesus the Messiah to introduce some distinctive modifications of the eschatological schema: "Since the future Messiah himself lived, died, and rose again before the coming of the Kingdom, Paul can no longer hold to the traditional eschatology of the Scribes."[29] He has now to posit that the Messiah and his Elect in the Messianic Kingdom will al-

26. *Mysticism*, 66, 67-68.
27. Jesus, according to Schweitzer (ibid., 79-84), also adopted this view.
28. Ibid., 90.
29. Ibid., 95.

ready possess the resurrection mode of existence before the general resurrection at the End; hence, there must be *two* resurrections, one for the Elect who have "fallen asleep" before the return of the Lord (cf. 1 Thess 4:14) and another at the end for all humanity.[30] Furthermore, the Elect who do *not* die before the Lord's return must also be transformed into the resurrection state: "We shall not all sleep, but we shall all be changed" (1 Cor 15:51). But how is this possible? How can the Elect attain resurrection life without passing through death? Schweitzer hypothesizes that Paul invented the concept of "mystical being-in-Christ" as a way of solving this dilemma in his eschatological scheme.

> Paul's conception is that believers in mysterious fashion share the dying and rising again of Christ, and in this way are swept away out of their ordinary mode of existence, and form a special category of humanity. When the Messianic Kingdom dawns, those of them who are still in life are not natural men like others, but men who have in some way passed through death and resurrection along with Christ, and are capable of becoming partakers of the resurrection mode of existence, while other men pass under the dominion of death.[31]

Thus, in Schweitzer's account, Paul's eschatology, although rooted in an inherited ("Scribal") tradition, develops its own distinctive pattern.

It should be apparent that Schweitzer's views are of considerable importance in relation to the thesis of this inquiry. The apocalyptic drama, with its foreordained sequence of events, has a narrative shape, and Schweitzer argues that Paul's thought is rooted in this drama. Furthermore, Schweitzer observes that the shape of the eschatological drama "always underlies the whole" of Paul's thinking and exercises determinative constraint over the logic of his theological constructions. "Since Paul lives in the conceptions of the dramatic world-view characteristic of late Jewish Eschatology, he is by consequence bound to the logic of that view."[32] Thus, for example, he eschews the concept of "rebirth," so common in the religions of Hellenistic antiquity, because only "resurrection" is the appropriate category in his apocalyptic story-structure.[33]

Again, Paul knows that in the endtime drama "a resurrection of those

---

30. The scheme of two resurrections is, of course, made explicit in Revelation, but Schweitzer regards Paul as its originator.

31. Ibid., 96-97.

32. Ibid., 11.

33. Ibid., 14.

who had died was only to take place when the supernatural age had dawned."[34] But the events of Jesus' death and resurrection force Paul to a radical conclusion about where we stand in the unfolding eschatological plot.

> If Jesus has risen, that means, for those who dare to think consistently, that it is now already the supernatural age. . . . We are therefore in the Resurrection period, even though the resurrection of others is still to come. Paul draws the logical inference from the fact that Jesus, after his earthly existence, was not simply rapt away to heaven in order to return thence in glory as the Messiah but himself passed through death and resurrection.[35]

Thus, although Schweitzer never uses the term "story" to describe Paul's eschatology (and he emphatically rejects the term "myth"),[36] it is clear that he perceives the narrative fragments in Paul as consistent expressions of a single great apocalyptic story that underlies and unifies all of Paul's thought.

To say, however, that Paul's thought "has as its sole presupposition the eschatological beliefs of the primitive church" is not to devalue his creative contribution as a theological thinker, because "he draws from them [i.e., the eschatological beliefs] inferences which ordinary reflection had not arrived at."[37] It is very important to Schweitzer to defend the claim that if Paul's apparently peculiar presuppositions be granted him, his thought proceeds in a rigorously logical fashion.

> And how wrong are those who refuse to admit that Paul was a logical thinker, and proclaim as the highest outcome of their wisdom the discovery that he has no system! For he is a logical thinker and his mysticism is a complete system. In the interpretation and application of Scriptural passages he may proceed by the leaps and bounds of Rabbinic logic, but in his mysticism he proceeds with a logical consistency, which in its simplicity and clearness compels assent as a piece of thinking.[38]

The great advantage of Schweitzer's interpretation is that it accounts for the unity and coherence of Paul's thought without making him, anachronistically, into a systematic theologian; Paul's thought is seen as coherent because all his assertions proceed by inference from a single fundamental eschatological scenario.

34. Ibid., 98.
35. Ibid.
36. See, for example, *Mysticism*, 23, 167.
37. Ibid., 139.
38. Ibid.

While I would not want to press the claim of Paul's rigorous logical consistency as strongly as Schweitzer, I agree with him that Paul's argumentation should be understood as an attempt to "think through" the implications of a given story. Precisely because of this basic agreement, it will be useful here to identify some of the fundamental ways in which Schweitzer's position differs from the thesis of this investigation.

(a) First of all, the narrative foundation in Schweitzer's account is not provided by "the gospel" or by the story of Jesus Christ: it is provided instead by the eschatological worldview of "late Judaism." The Christ event intrudes upon this foundation as a dissonant element which causes Paul to rethink his eschatological schema.[39] What Schweitzer has really done is to place Paul in a different *religionsgeschichtliche* "explanatory context"; instead of emerging from Hellenistic redeemer myths, Paul's gospel now emerges from Jewish Messiah myths. But the point is this: in both cases it *emerges*. For Schweitzer, just as much as for Bousset, the gospel message is finally abstractable from the narrative systems out of which it came. This is apparent in Schweitzer's final chapter, "The Permanent Elements in Paul's Mysticism," in which he affirms that "the fact of being thought out by the aid of the conceptual apparatus of the eschatological world-view constitutes only this mysticism's outward character, not its inner."[40] Thus, although Paul's "mysticism" was "embodied in temporally conditioned conceptions to which it is impossible for us to return," we can still appropriate its "spiritual essence."[41] Over against Schweitzer's position, this study seeks to show that Paul's gospel has an irreducible story-structure; the narrative elements are not a dispensable "conceptual apparatus" but the substance of the gospel.

(b) Schweitzer's explanation of Paul begins with the eschatological drama ("the eschatological doctrine of redemption"). His exposition proceeds on this basis until he reaches the crucial point at which "the mystical doctrine of being-in-Christ" emerges as a logical inference demanded by Paul's attempt to correlate present realities with his inherited eschatology. Once this doctrine appears, however, *it* becomes the dominant theme of Schweitzer's attention, "the center of Paul's thought," whereas the eschatological story recedes to the periphery as "something occasional." This new mystical redemption doctrine, though it had its genesis in the eschatological re-

39. It might be hermeneutically fruitful to explore the idea that Paul's theology is an attempt to reconcile two different stories in collision (i.e., the apocalyptic story and the Jesus-story). But Schweitzer does not pose the matter in these terms.

40. *Mysticism*, 379-80.

41. Ibid., 384. Here, once again, we see a foreshadowing of Bultmann's demythologizing.

demption-story, is itself nonnarrative in character; instead, it "works" through the mechanism of an actual physical consubstantiality between the Messiah and his Elect.[42] Through baptism, the Elect are magically united in a single "corporeity" *(Leiblichkeit)* with the crucified and resurrected Christ. Thus, according to Schweitzer, Paul believes that the Elect are already being transformed from their mortal fleshly state into the resurrection state so that their physical bodies are actually of different composition from those of redeemed human beings:

> That what is in view in the Pauline mysticism is an actual physical union between Christ and the Elect is proved by the fact that "being in Christ" corresponds to and, as a state of existence, takes the place of the physical "being in the flesh."[43]

Schweitzer adopts this literal-physical interpretation of Paul's language about union with Christ because he wants to stress that this union for Paul is not merely a figure of speech but an experienced reality. Against the tendency to regard "dying and rising with Christ" as subjective psychological processes, Schweitzer insists that Paul the apocalyptic thinker believed that Christ's people were actually in the process of being physically transformed.

> His thought follows logical and realistic lines. Dying and rising with Christ is not for him something merely metaphorical, which could also at need be expressed in a different metaphor, but a simple reality.[44]

Two principal objections against Schweitzer's exposition of Paul's "Christ-mysticism" must be raised here.

First of all, Schweitzer's epistemology falsely dichotomizes metaphor and reality. In common with many thinkers of his generation, Schweitzer understood metaphor as a purely decorative or illustrative mode of expression rather than as a means of articulating realities which are inaccessible except

---

42. Here Schweitzer might have weighed the possibility of Gnostic influence more seriously. The doctrine of the unity of substance in one *soma* including redeemer and redeemed is one of the key motifs of Gnostic thought. Cf. the succinct description by Bultmann (*Theology,* 1.299). See also E. Käsemann's account of this motif in relation to the christology of Hebrews in *Das wandernde Gottesvolk* (FRLANT N.F. 37; Göttingen: Vandenhoeck & Ruprecht, 1939) 58-116.

43. *Mysticism,* 127. This quotation shows that Schweitzer is led astray partly by his literalistic understanding of "flesh" in Paul.

44. Ibid., 15. On the "dying and rising" motif, see R. Tannehill, *Dying and Rising with Christ* (BZNW 32; Berlin: Töpelmann, 1967).

through a particular, unique metaphor.[45] Consequently, when Schweitzer correctly sees that "dying and rising with Christ" occupies in Paul's thought a place of central and irreplaceable significance, he wrongly concludes that this dying and rising must therefore be nonmetaphorical, i.e., literal.

The second objection against Schweitzer's understanding of Paul's Christ-mysticism is that he effectually severs being-in-Christ from the apocalyptic narrative framework in which this doctrine, in Schweitzer's opinion, had its origin. Consequently, he finds it necessary to posit a literal-istic concept of physical interdependence between Christ and the Elect in order to account for a phenomenon in Paul's thinking that is better ex-plained by an understanding of the function of sacred story, which creates participation in the reality which it figures forth. The pattern "As he . . . so we" does not depend, as Schweitzer thinks, on a crudely literal belief in a shared physical substance between the Messiah and his people;[46] instead, this pattern results from Paul's lively imaginative perception of Jesus the Messiah as the protagonist in whom the destiny of the Elect is foreshad-owed and embodied.

(c) Schweitzer's position differs significantly from mine also in his treatment of "righteousness by faith," which he regards as "an unnatural con-struction," a *Nebenkrater* (in his famous phrase) within the *Hauptkrater* of Paul's Christ-mysticism.[47] He can sometimes speak of the doctrine of righ-teousness by faith as a "fragment" broken off from "the more comprehensive mystical redemption doctrine,"[48] but he more characteristically regards it as belonging to a separate and unrelated circle of ideas.[49] This evaluation stands

---

45. A literary reassessment of the function of metaphor has played an important part in theology and biblical studies in recent years, but the benefits of the resultant new perspec-tives have been reaped much more in the area of synoptic gospel criticism, especially with re-gard to the parables, than in the area of Pauline studies. For recent discussions which empha-size the power of metaphor to grasp and redefine reality, see R. W. Funk, *Language, Hermeneutic, and Word of God* (New York: Harper & Row, 1966) 133-62; J. D. Crossan, *In Parables* (New York: Harper & Row, 1973) 10-16; S. McFague TeSelle, *Speaking in Parables* (Philadelphia: Fortress, 1975) 43-65; P. Ricoeur, "The Metaphorical Process," *Semeia* 4 (1975) 75-106. All of these studies are dependent to a significant degree on the work of literary crit-ics such as Owen Barfield (*Poetic Diction* [London: Faber and Faber, 1928]) and Philip Wheelwright (*Metaphor and Reality* [Bloomington, IN: Indiana University, 1962]; *The Burning Fountain* [Bloomington, IN: Indiana University, 1968]).

46. Wrede (*Paul*, 81-82) much more accurately and circumspectly speaks of an "unde-finable coherence between the race and the individual."

47. *Mysticism*, 225.

48. Ibid., 220.

49. See, for example, *Mysticism*, 25.

in glaring contrast to Schweitzer's efforts elsewhere to demonstrate the logical coherence and interrelatedness of Paul's thought.

In dealing with "righteousness by faith," Schweitzer concludes that "considerations of linguistic and dialectical convenience" lead Paul "to express himself differently from what he actually means."[50] As Schweitzer realizes,

> That righteousness comes directly from faith cannot be meant by Paul in the strict sense, since it is in fact impossible. All the blessings of redemption which the believer possesses flow from the being-in-Christ and from this only. Faith, as such, has no effective significance. . . .[51]

If redemption is achieved through Christ's eschatological triumph and through the mystical inclusion of the Elect in his resurrection "corporeity," it is impossible, properly speaking, to attribute the attainment of righteousness/justification to the believer's activity of believing. (Schweitzer regards *der Glaube* as *"ein anders geartetes Tun,"* in contrast to the doing of the law.)[52] Thus the expression "righteousness by faith" is, according to Schweitzer, an inaccurate shorthand form of the more complete but awkward expression "righteousness, in consequence of faith, through the being-in-Christ."[53]

Schweitzer resorts to this labored explanation because he finds himself caught in a tension between his insights into the eschatological story as the basis of Paul's thought on the one hand and his acceptance of the traditional Protestant interpretation of the function of πίστις on the other. I believe that a careful reexamination of this question can resolve the tension by leading us to see the theme of "righteousness by faith" as integrally connected to the story-structure of Paul's gospel. Schweitzer himself takes an important step in this direction by affirming that in Galatians the doctrine of righteousness by faith *is* in fact developed out of Paul's eschatological drama.

> In the Epistle to the Galatians, then, as should be carefully observed, it is not a question of an atonement made to God through Christ, but of a most skillfully planned foray made by Christ against the Angel-powers, by means of which He frees those who are languishing under the Law (Gal iv.5) and so brings about "the Coming of Faith" (Gal iii.25). Thus the doctrine of righteousness by faith is developed in the Epistle to the Galatians, with the

50. Ibid., 206.

51. Ibid. (translation slightly corrected).

52. The German is quoted from *Die Mystik des Apostels Paulus* (Tübingen: J. C. B. Mohr [Paul Siebeck], 1930) 33. See the translator's footnote in *Mysticism,* 207.

53. *Mysticism,* 206-7.

aid of material drawn from the eschatological doctrine of the being-in-Christ, on strictly logical lines as a cosmico-historical speculation.[54]

We might advance Schweitzer's argument one step further, however, by suggesting that the πίστις through which righteousness comes might be, within the context of the "cosmico-historical speculation," the faith of the Messiah himself rather than that of the individual believer. If this interpretation were adopted, then "righteousness by faith" would be seen no longer as a separate doctrine of redemption but simply as one component of the eschatological story. This possibility, which Schweitzer did not entertain, will be examined in Chapter IV, below.

At any rate, the "more original" version of the righteousness-by-faith doctrine as found in Galatians, is, according to Schweitzer, supplanted in Romans by Paul's attempt to develop the doctrine independently of eschatology.[55] This opinion probably rests on a misinterpretation of Romans, but it will not be possible here to deal in detail with the problem of the relationship between Romans and Galatians. Our investigation will, however, explore the road suggested by Schweitzer's reading of Galatians as a unified exposition based on the story of Christ's "foray" against the angel-powers to rescue those under the Law. To what extent is this story ("cosmico-historical speculation") really present in Galatians? To what extent is Schweitzer correct in his assertion that Paul's argument is logically dependent on this story? These are questions that we must explore in Chapters III and V, respectively.

B. Disposing of Narrative Elements

1. Rudolf Bultmann: "Demythologizing"

Rudolf Bultmann does not belong, strictly speaking, within the confines of this chapter, because he neither identified any previously overlooked narrative elements in Paul nor contributed any new interpretive moves for reclaiming them as theologically viable. His program of "demythologizing," however, has exercised such widespread influence within and beyond the world of NT scholarship that something must be said about it in order to determine its place on the map of interpretive options which we are seeking to sketch.

54. Ibid., 212.
55. Ibid., 209. This view of Romans is rather surprising. If anything, "eschatology" is rather more prominent in Romans than in Galatians. Cf. the comments of Beker, *Paul the Apostle*, 58.

Bultmann assimilates the insights of both Bousset and Schweitzer concerning the background of Paul's thinking; he concludes that Paul emerges from Hellenistic Judaism and that his thought incorporates mythological "motifs" both from Gnostic redemption myths and from Jewish apocalyptic.[56] But Bultmann also insists more vigorously and unequivocally than his predecessors that these mythological motifs, of both types, are only the vehicles through which the *kerygma* comes to expression and that they should not be confused with the substance *(Sache)* of the proclamation. Other vehicles are not only possible but also preferable, because the objectivizing language of mythology actually hinders the clear expression of the gospel.[57] The modern critic can read through the myth to grasp its theological intention, which may then be restated more adequately in "positive language."[58] Once this restatement is achieved, the myth may be surrendered.

On the one hand, Bultmann considers it very important that the *kerygma* be understood as the proclamation of a "salvation-event" *(Heilsgeschehen)*; on the other hand, he is sure that the "objectivizing image-content" *("objektivierender Vorstellungsgehalt")* of Paul's proclamation is merely a primitive (and therefore dispensable) attempt to express the meaning of this salvation-event in mythological language.[59] The difficulty is this: if we demythologize the proclamation, what can still be said about the shape and substance of the salvation event? At this point, Bultmann's position becomes elusive.

It is easy to say what the salvation event is *not*, in Bultmann's estimation. He rigorously rejects the "Gnostic" idea that Christ was "nicht einfach ein Mensch . . . sondern ein Gottmensch" and that his death and resurrection were "ein kosmisches Geschehen . . . indas wir allen hineingezogen sind." Furthermore, the idea of Christ's preexistence is declared to be "nichtsagend" and "rational unvorstellbar."[60] Likewise, Bultmann regards the idea of an atonement wrought through Christ's sacrificial or vicarious death for the forgiveness of sins as a primitive traditional conception which does not express Paul's real intention.[61]

56. Against the more one-sided theses of Bousset and Schweitzer, this compromise position seems judicious and historically plausible.

57. Bultmann, "Neues Testament und Mythologie," 23.

58. See Boers' critique of Bultmann on this point ("Demythologizing in Reverse," 153-57).

59. Bultmann, "Neues Testament und Mythologie," 41.

60. Ibid., 21.

61. See Bultmann, *Theology,* 1.295-97. Cf. also his remarks in the essay "Jesus and Paul" (*Existence and Faith* [ed. S. M. Ogden; Cleveland: World, 1960] 197).

What, then, remains of the "salvation event"? Bultmann is willing to say that "the salvation occurrence includes the death and resurrection of Jesus."[62] But these, too, must be demythologized. Faith in the resurrection should not be understood as an affirmation that a dead man rose from his tomb: "Das Osterereignis als der Auferstehung Christi ist kein historisches Ereignis." Rather, ". . . Auferstehungsglaube ist nicht anderes als der Glaube an das Kreuz als Heilsereignis."[63] But what does it mean to believe in the cross of Christ?

> . . . An das Kreuz Christi glauben, heisst nicht, auf einen mythischen Vorgang blicken, der sich ausserhalb unser und unserer Welt vollzogen hat, auf ein objektiv anschaubares Ereignis, das Gott als uns zugute geschehen anrechnet; sondern an das Kreuz glauben, heisst das Kreuz Christi als das eigenen übernehmen, heisst sich mit Christus kreuzigen lassen.[64]

Thus, Bultmann transvalues all Paul's "mythological" language into anthropological affirmations. The salvation event is understood as an act of God which confronts us in the preached word with the possibility of a new self-understanding. This event, although it is identified with "the cross of Christ," cannot be understood in the context of the narrative or conceptual schemes which give the cross its meaning in the NT, because these schemes objectify the salvation event. Consequently, the "event" is reduced to a "Dass," a logically necessary geometrical point lacking measurable dimensions. Bultmann's insistence that it is a salvation *event* insures that it is a word which confronts us from outside ourselves rather than merely the actualization of a "natural" human potentiality. But about the shape of this event itself, very little can be said.

These features of Bultmann's program are so well known and have been so thoroughly debated that further exposition and criticism here would be superfluous. One point must be stressed, however. It is sometimes thought that Bultmann's reluctance to ascribe specifiable content to the Christ-event is a function of his skepticism about the possibility of ascertaining reliable knowledge about the historical Jesus. But this misses the point of Bultmann's real concern. Even if it were possible to give a detailed and reliable account of Jesus' life, this would be of little significance, because

> a merely "reminiscent" historical account referring to what happened in the past cannot make the salvation-occurrence visible. . . . The salvation-

62. Bultmann, *Theology*, 1.293.
63. Bultmann, "Neues Testament und Mythologie," 46-47.
64. Ibid., 42.

occurrence continues to take place in the proclamation of the word. The salvation-occurrence is eschatological occurrence just in this fact, that it does not become a fact of the past but constantly takes place anew in the present.[65]

This means that for Bultmann any attempt to *narrate* the *kerygma,* whether in historical or mythological terms, is in principle misconceived because narration necessarily objectifies the proclamation by projecting it into the plane of this-worldly events. Bultmann fears that the message, once objectified, becomes something over which we exercise control, a fixed reference point in terms of which we may falsely define ourselves rather than constantly allowing God's grace to encounter us anew. An objectified (narrated) gospel would trap God's action in the dead past, but "meaning lies always in the present."[66] Consequently, Bultmann's interpretive program, which simultaneously demythologizes and dehistoricizes the *kerygma,*[67] may most accurately be understood as an attempt to restate the meaning of the salvation-event apart from any narrative framework whatever, in order to preserve the freedom and transcendence of God. Bultmann's method really should be called not "demythologizing" but *"denarrativizing."*

What is the result of all this in Bultmann's interpretation of Paul? In his *Theology of the New Testament,* Bultmann treats the narrative elements in Paul (which he judges to be drawn mostly from the Gnostic Redeemer myth) as belonging to the "presuppositions and motifs of NT theology," specifically to the Gnostic-influenced pre-Pauline "kerygma of the Hellenistic church."[68] Bultmann then seeks the characteristic features of Pauline theology precisely where Paul diverges from or distinctively expands upon these presuppositions and motifs. The result, as Nils Dahl has observed, is that Bultmann "underestimates the degree to which the beliefs Paul shares with the early church remained important for him."[69] Thus, just as the celebrated "criterion of dissimilarity" isolates the "historical Jesus" both from Judaism and from the early church,[70] so Bultmann's presentation isolates Paul from

65. Bultmann, *Theology,* 1.302.

66. Bultmann, *The Presence of Eternity: History and Eschatology* (New York: Harper & Bros., 1957) 155.

67. This point is seen clearly by N. A. Dahl (*The Crucified Messiah* [Minneapolis: Augsburg, 1974] 117-18).

68. See Bultmann, *Theology,* 1.298-300 and esp. 175-78.

69. Dahl, *Crucified Messiah,* 122.

70. See the critical remarks of L. E. Keck concerning the negative criteria for sifting Jesus-traditions in *A Future for the Historical Jesus* (Nashville: Abingdon, 1971) 33-34.

his own time and thought-world, and this artificial isolation is created specifically by filtering out the narrative fragments in Paul as nonessential to the *Sache* of his theology.

Bultmann recognizes that Paul's letters have the character of theological reflection upon a foundational reality, but he proposes that the foundational reality upon which Paul reflects is the act of faith: "Paul's theological thinking only lifts the knowledge inherent in faith itself into the clarity of conscious knowing."[71] While Bultmann recognizes that "faith" cannot be separated from some specifiable knowledge of God, it is always primarily the act of decision, "the free deed of obedience in which the new self constitutes itself in place of the old."[72] Thus, the "knowledge inherent" in this "deed" may be most fruitfully explained as a knowledge of the human self that comes, in the decision of faith, to know itself anew. Hence, Bultmann's methodological decision that "Paul's theology can best be treated as his doctrine of man."[73]

This angle of approach decisively eliminates the possibility of understanding Paul's theology as ordered around a story about Jesus Christ. (Whether the story is understood as mythological or historical really makes no difference to Bultmann, because in either case the story is a form of objectivizing language, which is not a form of personal address and therefore cannot be regarded as *kerygma*.) If there is a narrative dimension in Bultmann's account of Pauline theology, it is to be found in the implicit story of the human self, in the movement from "Man Prior to the Revelation of Faith" to "Man under Faith."[74] Thus, Bultmann's exposition of Paul, in the effort to free God's action from mythological "objectification," inevitably tends to shift the weight of emphasis away from God's action and onto the human faith-decision. This reading of Pauline theology stands in direct antithesis to the present work, which pursues Dahl's suggestion that "precisely in their more naive and fragmentary form Paul's 'mythological' statements . . . express his true intention, and ought not to be interpreted away by the critic."[75]

---

71. *Theology,* 1.190.

72. Ibid., 1.316.

73. Ibid., 1.191.

74. These are, of course, the rubrics under which Bultmann discusses Pauline theology in his *Theology of the NT.* Cf. the famous admonition in the concluding paragraph of his Gifford Lectures (*Presence of Eternity,* 155): "Man who complains: 'I cannot see meaning in history, and therefore my life, interwoven in history, is meaningless', is to be admonished: do not look around yourself into universal history, you must look into your own personal history. Always in your present lies the meaning in history, and you cannot see it as a spectator, but only in your responsible decisions."

75. Dahl, *Crucified Messiah,* 120.

By coining the word "demythologizing," Bultmann set up a lightning rod that attracted outbursts of protest from many sides. But Bultmann's proposals, in spite of the controversy that they engendered, may be seen as nothing more than the logical culmination of a certain tendency already present in Bousset, Schweitzer and others: the tendency to regard the gospel as abstractable from the story-forms in which it finds expression in the NT. In the remainder of this chapter, we must examine a series of interpretive proposals which, in spite of significant diversity, have in common a twofold purpose: to reaffirm the centrality of narrative elements in Paul and to treat those narrative elements not as an accidental vehicle for the *kerygma* but as its constitutive structure.

C. Attempts to Reclaim Narrative Elements in Paul

1. *Oscar Cullmann:* Heilsgeschichte

At the opposite interpretive pole from Bultmann stands Oscar Cullmann's insistence that "salvation history" constitutes the kernel of Pauline theology. Cullmann intends thereby not to exclude Bultmann's concern for the existential faith-decision but to place this decision in a context, to provide a "basis" for it.[76]

As Cullmann sees it, not only for Paul but for the NT as a whole there is a "Christ-line of *Heilsgeschichte*" which is "everywhere presupposed" and which "gives the key to the understanding of all that is said."[77] There is an apparent similarity between this affirmation and the thesis of my investigation; regrettably, it is notoriously difficult to pin down exactly what Cullmann means by the term *Heilsgeschichte.*

This much, however, is clear: the term *Heilsgeschichte* for Cullmann serves two related but distinguishable purposes: (1) it articulates a claim that the biblical message of salvation is based upon factual historical *events* rather than upon myths or speculative ideas; (2) it carries a further claim that these historical events are arranged in a meaningful unified pattern — God's saving acts are not random or sporadic: they define a great continuous drama which stretches from the beginning to the end of time, from Genesis to Revelation. The strong appeal for many of Cullmann's theology of *Heilsgeschichte* is to be

---

76. See Cullmann's remarks in *Salvation in History* (New York: Harper & Row, 1967) 248.

77. *Christ and Time* (rev. ed.; Philadelphia: Westminster, 1964) 107, 109.

explained partly by the fact that this theological category allowed him to combine under one banner these twin affirmations of the Bible's patterned unity and historical factuality.[78] Unfortunately, this double valence of the term also leads into unclarity at certain points, as Cullmann blurs the distinction between these affirmations. Let us illustrate how this happens.

By employing the term *Heilsgeschichte* Cullmann intends to stress the point that early Christian theology was not abstract metaphysical speculation, that in the NT "Christology is the doctrine of an 'event,' not the doctrine of natures."[79] This observation, taken by itself, would elicit general assent from NT exegetes. The difficulty, however, is that Cullmann repeatedly makes sweeping assertions about the "historical" character of this "event," assertions that can be defended only in the most equivocal terms.

> . . . The question about Jesus was not answered by early Christianity in terms of a mythology already at hand, but in terms of a series of real facts. These facts were events which happened in the first century of our era. . . . The Christology of the New Testament was conceived on the basis of these events, and the view of Jesus' person and work from the standpoint of *Heilsgeschichte* arose out of this context. It is not a myth which was externally imposed on an essentially nonhistorical *kerygma*.[80]

It is one thing to say that the *kerygma* is "historical" in the sense that it originated as a result of actual events in the life of Jesus of Nazareth and his followers; it is quite another thing to claim that these events ("real facts") by themselves constitute a satisfactory explanation for the structure of the christology that appears subsequently in the NT. Cullmann has to acknowledge, of course, that the NT writers did draw upon mythic motifs, but he consistently downplays their importance.

> Syncretistic elements, even myths, were indeed appropriated, but they were subordinated to a Christological structure which received its character not from syncretism, not from Hellenism, not from mythology, but from the *Heilsgeschichte*. It is characteristic of this structure that from the very beginning it centers in a real history [*eine wirkliche Geschichte*].[81]

78. For a warm appreciation of Cullmann's work, see, for example, K. Löwith, *Meaning in History* (Chicago: University of Chicago, 1949) 182-90, 250 n. 1.

79. Cullmann, *The Christology of the New Testament* (rev. ed.; Philadelphia: Westminster, 1963) 9.

80. Ibid., 316-17.

81. Ibid., 322.

The difficulty with this view is that Cullmann intends the concept of *Heilsgeschichte* to encompass not only "events which happened in the first century of our era" but also "Christology as a salvation event which extends from the creation to the eschatological new creation."[82] Thus, his claim that the structure of NT christology is determined by "real history" takes on a problematical status: how can ideas about a preexistent, exalted, or returning Christ have their basis in merely "historical" first-century events? Cullmann solves this problem by including among these events "the process of arriving at Christological understanding," so that this process itself becomes part of the *Heilsgeschichte*.[83] This "solution," however, is actually a lapse into a fatal circularity that undercuts Cullmann's position. If the process of arriving at christological understanding is itself part of the *Heilsgeschichte,* there is no reason for ruling out, as Cullmann wants to, the possibility that this process may take its christological models from mythological rather than "historical" sources. One may in fact argue, employing the method of *Sachkritik* on Cullmann, that his fundamental intention (to affirm the "event" character of salvation as God's action *extra nos*) is obscured by his insistence on subsuming all of NT christology under the category of "history." His attempt to do so forces him to construe the term "history" so broadly that it becomes nebulous and virtually evacuated of meaning. As Bultmann comments, "In relation to this picture of the history of salvation, the distinction between history and myth is meaningless."[84]

Heilsgeschichte for Cullmann refers, however, not only to "real historical events in which God was at work" but also to the interpretive framework which orders all of history into a dispensational scheme. It is the latter meaning which actually seems to predominate in Cullmann's usage, and which elicited Bultmann's well-known complaint that Cullmann had replaced the kerygma with "a philosophy of history."[85] It is this second nuance of *Heilsgeschichte* that has the most immediate relevance for Cullmann's interpretation of Paul. When Cullmann discusses "Paul and Salvation History," he has in mind primarily not the question of historical factuality but the problem of the "shape" of history.[86] He portrays Paul as a thinker who con-

82. Ibid., 317.

83. Ibid.

84. "History of Salvation and History," *Existence and Faith*, 228. See Cullmann's confused discussions of history and myth in *Christ and Time* (96-104) and *Salvation in History* (136-50). Interestingly, Cullmann does recognize that history and myth have in common narrative form (*Salvation in History*, 137, 141), but he fails to develop this insight.

85. "History of Salvation and History," 233.

86. Cullmann's fullest discussion of salvation history in Paul is found in *Salvation in History* (248-68).

sistently seeks to discern the relation of the present moment to the past and future events in God's dealing with humanity. Thus, problems such as the meaning of the sacraments, the unbelief of Israel, and the validity of the Law are handled by being placed properly into the salvation-historical timeline. For example, Cullmann contends that "Paul's struggle with circumcision is ultimately a struggle for the recognition of salvation history,"[87] i.e., the recognition that God has done a new thing, that a new covenant has superseded the Law. Likewise, Cullmann rightly calls attention to the way in which "Paul fits his own calling as an apostle to the Gentiles into the entire redemptive plan."[88]

In all of this, Cullmann is able to argue with considerable plausibility that there is a *Heilsgeschichte* (= outline of events in redemptive history) which is presupposed by Paul and in which Paul understands himself to be involved. Furthermore, there is much to be said for Cullmann's opinion that this outline of events provides for Paul an explanatory context within which Christian self-understanding may be oriented: believers find their identity by recognizing their place in the great salvation-story, recognizing that they live in the peculiar interval after the coming of the Messiah and before his triumphant return, after the abrogation of the Law and before the consummation of the new creation.[89] Thus, broadly speaking, Cullmann's views are congenial with the thesis that Paul's theology has a narrative substructure.

Objections must be raised, however, against Cullmann's understanding of the shape and particular content of that substructure. His vision is so dominated by the comprehensive movement of *Heilsgeschichte* in the Bible as a whole[90] that he rarely undertakes any detailed exegetical treatment of specific Pauline texts; therefore, he fails to do justice in some cases to the actual movement of Paul's thinking. Especially telling is the criticism that Cullmann's emphasis on *Heilsgeschichte* as a process of continuous development tends to overlook Paul's penchant for dialectical antitheses, for placing the newness of the gospel in stark juxtaposition to the old covenant.

A clear illustration of Cullmann's interpretive tendency appears in his handling of Gal 3:6–4:7, which he regards as the presentation of a "salvation history of faith."

87. *Salvation in History*, 261.

88. *Christ and Time*, 110; cf. 163-66. Cf. also his earlier article, "Le caractère eschatologique du devoir missionaire et de la conscience apostolique de S. Paul" (*RHPR* 16 [1936] 210-45).

89. See *Christ and Time*, 81-93.

90. For an overall outline, see *Christ and Time*, 108-9.

Although the point of departure is the faith of those living in Paul's own present, the Pauline discussion proceeds chronologically. It begins with Abraham, to show how the descent of the people of God, as bearers of the promise, is founded upon Abraham's faith in the divine promise, and how by faith in Isaac's birth the way leads beyond the parenthesis of the Law to the One, to Christ, as the object of faith, and thence to those baptized in Christ and believing in him who become "sons." . . . Abraham is more than an "example from Scripture," more than just any example of an Old Testament witness who believed. Rather, his story is recalled as an event historically understood, the starting point for a *development* leading to the baptism of those believing in Christ.[91]

Cullmann has correctly observed that this text is concerned with a sequential (narrative) movement in history, but the fundamental problem with his interpretation is this: can this movement properly be called a "development"?[92] Cullmann's account of Galatians smooths over the tensions in Paul's thought and conveys the picture of a continuous process of *Heilsgeschichte,* originating with Abraham and developing steadily through the history of Israel, through the Christ-event, into the historical present of Christian believers. However, in a single clause (". . . the way leads beyond the parenthesis of the Law to the One, to Christ . . .") most of the history of Israel vanishes into an interpretive abyss, and along with it the problems with which Paul wrestles so tenaciously in Galatians. Is the Law a mere "parenthesis," or does it have a more significant role in the salvation-story? If the Law is a parenthesis (or perhaps a detour), how can Israel's history be regarded as *Heilsgeschichte?* Is it not rather, as Jost Eckert has suggested, *Unheilsgeschichte?*[93]

Certainly Paul does not — in Galatians, at least — speak of the historical Israel as the people of God descended from Abraham who are the "bearers of the promise." In fact, he is insistent that only Christ is Abraham's true descendant; only he is the bearer of the promise. Between Abraham and Christ there is only a time of slavery and deprivation. Thus, the story of Abraham is hardly "an event historically understood, the starting point for a develop-

91. *Salvation in History,* 129; cf. also 261-65.
92. A criticism of Cullmann on this point is raised by Bultmann ("History of Salvation and History," 233). For a vigorously polemical denial of any salvation-historical continuity in this central section of Galatians, see G. Klein, "Individualgeschichte und Weltgeschichte bei Paulus," *EvT* 24 (1964) 126-65; reprinted in Klein, *Rekonstruktion und Interpretation* (BEvT 50; Munich: Kaiser, 1969) 180-224.
93. *Die urchristliche Verkündigung,* 103.

ment"; rather, it is a story *typologically* understood which foreshadows the historically discontinuous event of God's act in Christ.

Cullmann's treatment of Gal 3:6–4:7 also glosses over a second circle of perplexing questions concerning the soteriological significance of faith. How is Christ as "object of faith" related to the faith of Abraham, who, as Cullmann points out, believed not in Christ but in the promise of Isaac's birth? What is the relation between Abraham's faith and the faith of the Christian? In spite of his assertion that this section of Galatians is a "salvation history of faith," Cullmann's exposition does little to explain *how* the line of salvation-history connects the Christ-event either with Abraham on the one hand or with Christians on the other.

Perhaps Cullmann's interpretation of the text could be defended through exegetical arguments, but Cullmann himself does not offer any such arguments. His primary concern is to show that Paul, rather than preaching a timeless message of general truths, reckons with a linear process of salvation which links past, present, and future in an orderly way. Once this point (which, stated in such general terms, is surely correct) is sufficiently demonstrated by his passing reference to Galatians, Cullmann makes no further attempt to analyze the actual structure of the story to which the text alludes or to trace the internal logic of the argument.[94]

In summary, it should be apparent that Cullmann's advocacy of *Heilsgeschichte* as the key to Paul's thought represents a counterreaction to the Bultmannian attempt to factor the narrative elements out of Paul's gospel. Cullmann seeks to resist any reduction of the gospel into a phenomenon of human subjectivity by stressing an objective sequence of events in salvation-history which comprise the core of Christian proclamation. In this regard Cullmann's intuitions and intentions are sound, but his manner of developing his position, especially in relation to Paul, leaves much to be desired. My interpretive project must be differentiated from Cullmann's in at least two important respects.

(a) Cullmann introduces confusion by his vigorous but equivocal affirmation of the historical facticity of the *Heilsgeschichte*. My study, on the other hand, seeks to bring clarity by investigating the narrative shape of the christology articulated by Paul without seeking to defend the proposition that the

---

94. This is recognized even by some of Cullmann's supporters. For an attempt to elucidate more fully the logic of the passage in terms of Cullmann's interpretation, see J. D. Hester, "The 'Heir' and Heilsgeschichte," *Oikonomia: Heilsgeschichte als Thema der Theologie, Oscar Cullmann zum 65. Geburtstag gewidmet* (ed. F. Christ; Hamburg/Bergstedt: Reich, 1967) 118-25.

structure of the christology depends upon "real facts." The distinction between historical and mythological components of this christology is bracketed out for the purposes of this inquiry.[95]

(b) Cullmann's methodology encourages, whether justly or not, the suspicion that his interpretation of Paul is shaped less by his exegesis of Pauline texts than by his impressionistic perception of the *Gestalt* of NT theology. In particular it may be doubted whether Cullmann's comprehensive scheme allows sufficient weight to the radical newness of the gospel, to the extent to which Paul sees it as a decisive break with the past. My investigation, however, seeks to avoid the danger of reading Paul through a Lukan filter, as Cullmann may be accused of doing, by focusing in a disciplined manner on a particular Pauline text, analyzing carefully the narrative structure that appears within it, and observing the logic of its argumentation. This procedure will yield a more tightly defined christological structure which, in comparison to Cullmann's *Heilsgeschichte*, lays less emphasis on a comprehensive historical development and more emphasis on a single decisive action of God in Christ.

2. Ernst Käsemann: War on Two Fronts

Ernst Käsemann sees himself as fighting a war on two fronts against the positions represented by Cullmann and Bultmann.[96] While Käsemann is fundamentally suspicious of Cullmann's attempt to objectivize the gospel in terms of a *Heilsgeschichte*, he is almost equally uneasy with the Bultmannian tendency to reduce faith to self-understanding and thus to turn the gospel into a form of gnosis that has no relation to history.[97] Käsemann's war strategy employs several different tactics; one of these is his proposal that the "historical Jesus" may and must, in spite of all attendant difficulties, func-

---

95. This is by no means to imply that the distinction between history and myth is ultimately of no theological importance.

96. Käsemann's perception of the "two fronts" is sketched with particular clarity in the essay "Justification and Salvation History in the Epistle to the Romans" (*Perspectives*, 60-78). This essay is ostensibly a response to Krister Stendahl's essay "The Apostle Paul and the Introspective Conscience of the West" (*HTR* 56 [1963] 199-215); however, Käsemann abruptly launches into an attack on the evils of "salvation history," and it soon becomes apparent that he is really reacting against Cullmann rather than Stendahl and that in fact, as Stendahl modestly replies (*Paul among Jews and Gentiles*, 129-33), Käsemann has fundamentally misconstrued Stendahl's position.

97. Käsemann, *Perspectives*, 77.

tion as a norm for Christian proclamation.[98] While this proposal need not concern us here, another of his tactics is of direct relevance for our inquiry into possible narrative roots of Paul's thought: with his insistence on the crucial role of apocalyptic in the development of early Christian theology,[99] Käsemann reopens avenues of interpretation that were previously explored by Schweitzer.

Against Schweitzer, Käsemann reaffirms strongly that the doctrine of justification is the center and substance of Paul's thought, not a minor subtheme.[100] But at the same time he suggests that this doctrine itself belongs to the world of apocalyptic thought, that the expression δικαιοσύνη θεοῦ is a technical term in apocalyptic literature. In this context, he claims, δικαιοσύνη θεοῦ refers not merely to a gift of righteousness imputed by God to individuals but to God's dynamic activity of asserting his rightful eschatological sovereignty over his creation.[101] Although Käsemann is considerably more cautious than Schweitzer in describing the specific content of Paul's eschatological scenario, his interpretive proposal has the result of setting, perhaps unintentionally, Paul's theological thinking on a narrative foundation. In another context, Käsemann stresses the *narrative* character of apocalyptic and describes it as the root both of "historical thinking" within Christianity and of the impulse to "narrate" the kerygma in the "literary form of the gospels."[102] Käsemann never explicitly carries this insight about the narrative character of apocalyptic, however, over into his attempts to show that Paul's thinking has apocalyptic roots. The outline of Paul's implied apocalyptic story is only partially sketched by Käsemann, but it includes prominently "God's victory amid the opposition of the world." Furthermore, we are told that "Christ is the new Adam because as the bearer of human destiny, he brings in the world of obedience."[103]

The narrative possibilities inherent in Käsemann's view that "Even when he became a Christian, Paul remained an apocalyptist,"[104] are lavishly

98. See the essays "The Problem of the Historical Jesus" (*Essays on New Testament Themes* [SBT 41; London: SCM, 1964] 15-47) and "Blind Alleys in the 'Jesus of History' Controversy" (*New Testament Questions of Today* [Philadelphia: Fortress, 1969] 23-65).

99. See his essays, "The Beginnings of Christian Theology" and "On the Subject of Primitive Christian Apocalyptic," *NT Questions*, 82-137.

100. See *Perspectives*, 70-78.

101. "'The Righteousness of God' in Paul," *NT Questions*, 168-82. For my evaluation of Käsemann's interpretation of δικαιοσύνη θεοῦ, see R. B. Hays, "Psalm 143 and the Logic of Romans 3," *JBL* 99 (1980) 107-15.

102. *NT Questions*, 96-97.

103. Ibid., 180.

104. Ibid., 181.

developed and illustrated by Markus Barth in an imaginative "experiment in Pauline exegesis" which treats justification as a drama unfolding in five acts ("days"), entitled as follows:

The First Day: The Last Judgment Is at Hand
The Second Day: The Mediator Is Appointed, Acts, and Dies
The Third Day: The Judge's Love and Power Reverse Death
The Fourth Day: The Verdict Is Carried Out
The Fifth Day: The Last Day Is Still to Come.[105]

While this particular sketch might fail to win Käsemann's endorsement,[106] some such drama is surely implied by his contention that δικαιοσύνη θεοῦ is an apocalyptic technical term; furthermore, Käsemann's interpretation treats this apocalyptic drama as an unelaborated presupposition which underlies and unifies Paul's thought. In this respect, his general approach to Paul is formally analogous to my thesis.

However, it should be stressed that Käsemann has no explicit interest in identifying narrative elements in Paul. In his reaction against the Bultmannian existentialist interpretation of Paul, Käsemann stresses the importance of elements — christological and apocalyptic — which lend themselves to being understood in terms of a story-structure, but, because of his counterreaction against the theology of *Heilsgeschichte*, he does not pursue this line of inquiry.

3. C. H. Dodd: The Apostolic Preaching

More clearly than any interpreter before him, C. H. Dodd emphasized the importance of distinguishing between the "Gospel" that Paul preached and "the theological superstructure of his thought."[107] In *The Apostolic Preaching and Its Developments,* when Dodd sets out in search of the primitive *kerygma,* he remarks that the Pauline epistles have the character of teaching *(didachē)* or exhortation *(paraklēsis)* rather than of proclamation. Hence, these letters pre-

---

105. M. Barth, *Justification* (Grand Rapids: Eerdmans, 1971). Does the number of "days" in Barth's drama derive from exegetical observation or from the conventions of the Western theater?

106. Indeed, he seems to regard M. Barth's work as belonging to the "salvation history" perspective (*Perspectives,* 66).

107. *The Apostolic Preaching and Its Developments* (New York: Harper & Bros., 1936) 11.

suppose the *kerygma*: "They expound and defend the implications of the Gospel rather than proclaim it."[108] On the basis of 1 Cor 1:23; 2:2-6, Dodd asserts that "Paul himself was conscious of a distinction between the fundamental content of the Gospel and the teaching that he based upon it."[109] The *locus classicus* for determining the content of the *kerygma*, according to Dodd, is 1 Corinthians 15, which presents "the facts of the death and resurrection of Christ in an eschatological setting which gives significance to the facts."[110] Not even this text sets forth the hypothetical "apostolic preaching" in its entirety, but Dodd reconstructs the outline of this preaching as follows:

(1) The prophecies are fulfilled, and the New Age is inaugurated by the coming of Christ.
(2) He was born of the seed of David.
(3) He died according to the Scriptures, to deliver us out of the present evil age.
(4) He was buried.
(5) He rose on the third day according to the Scriptures.
(6) He is exalted at the right hand of God, as Son of God and Lord of quick and dead.
(7) He will come again as Judge and Saviour of men.[111]

This outline is, of course, a composite of fragments culled from several different places in the epistles, but Dodd believes that we may fairly infer from these fragments that "there was in Paul's mind a fixed association of ideas."[112]

Dodd typically refers to the elements of this outline as "ideas" or "beliefs" or "facts,"[113] but a glance at the list will show that all of them except (1) are in fact events or crucial moments in a story. They are related to one an-

108. Ibid., 9.
109. Ibid.
110. Ibid., 13. Similarly, Conzelmann ("Zur Analyse der Bekenntnisformel I Kor. 15,3-5," *EvT* 25 [1965] 1-11) treats this passage as a confessional formula that Paul regards as authoritative in the development of his own theological reflections. For a rebuttal to Conzelmann's views, see Käsemann, "Konsequente Traditionsgeschichte?" *ZTK* 62 (1965) 137-52.
111. Dodd, *Apostolic Preaching*, 17. (I have added the numerical labels for each point in the outline.)
112. Ibid., 12.
113. W. Baird ("What Is the Kerygma? A Study of 1 Cor 15:3-8 and Gal 1:1-17," *JBL* 76 [1957] 181-91) calls them "points," a good homiletical term. Baird's article offers a lucid comparison between Dodd's understanding of the kerygma and Bultmann's.

other not through logical necessity or conceptual coherence but through narrative sequence. Thus, while Dodd does not explicitly speak of the *kerygma* as a "story," his conclusions certainly point in this direction.

Dodd emphasizes that this basic kerygmatic outline was not a Pauline creation but that Paul held it in common with the earliest church as a whole; indeed, Paul "received" (παρέλαβον) its content as traditional material authenticated by apostolic testimony (1 Cor 15:1-7).[114] Dodd finds Paul's claim to share this Gospel with the other apostles corroborated by an analysis of other NT writings, especially the speeches in Acts, in which he discerns the same fundamental kerygmatic pattern.

In *The Apostolic Preaching*, Dodd regards the *kerygma* as the foundation upon which Paul's theological superstructure is directly built, but in his later work, *According to the Scriptures*, Dodd proposes a more complicated version of this metaphor: the *kerygma* is the "ground plan," but between this ground plan and the "theological edifice" constructed by Paul, there is an intermediate structure, a "substructure" that Paul shares with John, the writer of the Epistle to the Hebrews, and other NT writers.[115] This substructure consists of a collection of "passages of OT scripture with their application to the gospel facts." This body of material "is the substructure of all Christian theology and contains already its chief regulative ideas."[116]

In his detailed analysis of the OT texts which comprise this substructure, Dodd discovers three basic thematic groupings: "Apocalyptic-eschatological Scriptures," "Scriptures of the New Israel," and "Scriptures of the Servant of the Lord and the Righteous Sufferer."[117] In all three groups, Dodd discerns a common pattern, and in describing this pattern he slips involuntarily (but significantly) into the language of literary criticism.

> If we now survey this group of scriptures as a whole, we observe that a single "plot" runs all through. The "hero" suffers shame, ignominy, torment, disaster, and then by sheer grace of God is delivered, raised up, glorified.[118]

In some of these scriptures the "hero" is the sinful Israel whose disaster is God's judgment and whose deliverance is God's pardon. In others, the "hero"

---

114. Dodd, *Apostolic Preaching*, 13-16. Baird ("What Is the Kerygma?" 186) urges against Dodd the criticism that he fails to reckon sufficiently with Paul's vehement denial in Gal 1:11-12 that he "received" his gospel through human tradition.

115. Dodd, *Scriptures*, 12-13.

116. Ibid., 127.

117. Ibid., 62-103.

118. Ibid., 102.

is a righteous sufferer whose disaster is persecution by the enemies of God and whose deliverance is vindication. Dodd finds the hermeneutical link between these patterns in the picture of the Suffering Servant in Isa 52:13–53:12, who bears vicariously the sins of others. This servant is identified with Christ.

> It is thus possible to recognize Christ as the "hero" of the drama of disaster and triumph in all three groups alike. . . . In his triumph over death and disaster is enacted the promised renovation of the Israel of God, whose sins had brought disaster.[119]

Thus, to restate Dodd's view in different terminology, there is a narrative structure common to this body of OT texts, and this common narrative structure allows all of them to be drawn together in order to elaborate the theological significance of the "facts" enumerated in the *kerygma*. This assembling of texts was already accomplished in the tradition that Paul received.[120] "Upon this fundamental material he sets reason and imagination to work . . . and so brings forth his massive theology."[121]

The similarities of my thesis to Dodd's views are considerable, and it is necessary to draw some careful distinctions in order to clarify the difference. Although in *The Apostolic Preaching* he regards Paul's letters as attempts to draw out the "implications" of the "fundamental beliefs"[122] stated in the *kerygma* (a formulation which I would accept as basically correct), Dodd clutters the picture by insisting in *According to the Scriptures* that the "setting which displays the significance"[123] of the events recited in the *kerygma* is given only by a preformed grouping of OT texts. I would argue, however, that the pattern of the Christ-story (= the gospel) governs the selection and interpretation of OT texts rather than vice versa. A careful examination of Galatians 3 and 4 will show that Dodd's OT texts which embody the pattern of "the drama of disaster and triumph" are altogether absent, and that the christological formulations which constitute the fundamental warrants in Paul's argument are not dependent on any such texts. Instead, Paul's theological "superstructure" (to use Dodd's term) is constructed directly on the basis

---

119. Ibid., 103. For arguments against the view that Isaiah 53 provides the organizing center for NT christology, see M. D. Hooker, *Jesus and the Servant* (London: SPCK, 1959); S. K. Williams, *Jesus' Death as Saving Event* (HDR 2; Missoula: Scholars, 1975) 221-29.

120. Indeed, Dodd dares to suggest (*Scriptures*, 109-10) that Jesus himself was the creative exegetical mind responsible for the "intellectual feat" of bringing together these OT texts.

121. Ibid., 135.

122. *Apostolic Preaching*, 10.

123. *Scriptures*, 11.

of the christological story, and the OT texts that Paul draws into the discussion, rather than determining the shape of the theological development, are used in a highly eclectic fashion and reinterpreted in light of the story. This angle of vision eludes Dodd because of his oddly positivistic tendency to regard the elements in the *kerygma* as "facts" in search of an interpretation,[124] or as points in a catechetical outline. My alternative proposal seeks to reflect the character of the *kerygma* more faithfully by treating its elements not as atomized facts but as moments in a story, as the highlights of a *mythos* which by its nature embodies its own *dianoia*.

On the whole, however, in spite of these differences, my approach to interpreting Paul remains formally very close to Dodd's in attempting to distinguish between a gospel foundation and its theological developments. The difference of emphasis is to be found above all in the narrowing of scope that I am imposing upon this project: rather than attempting to reconstruct an outline of a primitive common-denominator *kerygma* that underlies not only the Pauline letters but also the NT as a whole, I am seeking to trace the narrative structure of the gospel as it appears in one particular letter and to show in detail *how* Paul draws out the implications of that structure. The choice of Galatians, with its strong disavowal of dependence on human tradition, for this purpose offers an interesting counterpoint to Dodd, who establishes his kerygmatic outline on the basis of texts where Paul's dependence on tradition is evident, making practically no use of Galatians.

4. Dan O. Via, Jr.: Paul and the Comic Structure

In *Kerygma and Comedy in the New Testament,* Dan O. Via, Jr. undertakes a highly original approach to the narrative elements in Paul's thought. Via's interpretation of Paul has neither won a wide following nor even stimulated

---

124. Dodd's effort to establish such a fixed set of "facts" as the fundamental outline of NT preaching has recently received harsh criticism from J. I. H. McDonald (*Kerygma and Didache* [SNTSMS 37; Cambridge: Cambridge University, 1980] 3), who charges that Dodd's work "had the unfortunate effect of encouraging an inflexible understanding of the *kerygma* in terms of supposedly primitive and relatively stereotyped confessional formulae. . . . The consequence of the inherent rigidity of this position was that the dynamic and fluid activity of preaching was caught and stopped as by a still camera." McDonald's criticism of Dodd is probably unfair. Though McDonald may prefer the cinema, there is nothing inherently evil about still photographs. Dodd never intended to freeze the *kerygma* or to limit or deny its dynamic character; he was attempting to carry out an analytic procedure, to see whether it was possible to identify a fundamental unity amidst the diversity of the forms of NT proclamation.

much discussion among Pauline scholars,[125] but his description of the "comic structure" of Paul's letters is a creative attempt to recognize and come to grips with an aspect of Paul's thought that I have designated as the "narrative substructure."

Via describes his interpretive project as an attempt to employ the category of comedy as a device for interpreting Paul's kerygma.[126] "My purpose," he affirms, "is to construct a nonconventional version of the comic (or tragicomic) genre-structure into which New Testament texts may be placed and hence better understood."[127] This approach to Paul differs radically from a historical approach which seeks to "explain" Paul's ideas by tracing their causal-genetic derivation from other ideas and environmental factors. For example, the dispute (illustrated by the contrasting positions of Bousset and Schweitzer) over whether Paul's christology has its historical roots in Palestinian or Hellenistic systems of thought is of no concern to Via, who chooses the vehicle of Greek drama as a device for elucidating the Pauline letters because he finds in this drama an analogous *structure*. Via explicitly disclaims any intention of demonstrating a historical dependence of Paul on Greek comedy; instead, his point is that the writings of Aristophanes and of Paul are performance manifestations "generated" by a comic genre-structure whose underlying pattern of death and resurrection is imbedded in human consciousness at a level deeper than the surface differences between Greek and Jewish culture.[128] Hence, an analysis of the genre-structure of Greek comedy, in which the structural pattern is more clearly manifested, will, Via believes, illuminate the structure and meaning of Paul's thought.

Via's procedure for describing the comic genre is inspired by Francis Cornford's classic study, *The Origin of Attic Comedy*,[129] which argued that Aristophanic comedy had its roots in ancient fertility rituals, and that its schematic plot-structure could be described as follows:

(1) The first major episode is the agon in which the agonist-hero engages in a struggle or contest with an antagonist and wins a victory.

125. Unlike most of the other interpretations discussed in this chapter, Via's work does not purport to be a major study of Paul; the bulk of the book deals with Mark, and only thirty pages are devoted to Paul.

126. D. O. Via, Jr., *Kerygma and Comedy in the New Testament* (Philadelphia: Fortress, 1975) xi.

127. Ibid., 15.

128. Ibid., 49.

129. F. M. Cornford, *The Origins of Attic Comedy* (Cambridge: Cambridge University, 1934).

(2) Then he enjoys the fruits of his victory while offering a sacrifice and cel-
ebrating a feast.
(3) Finally the hero leads a victory procession — *komos* — and enters into
some kind of marriage and experiences a resurrection of some sort.[130]

Following the general outlines of Cornford's schema, Via creates a grid on
which he is able to illustrate the sequential (syntagmatic) ordering of events
in each individual drama or Pauline text and, at the same time, the structural
(paradigmatic) analogies among events occurring in the different texts. Thus,
in Pauline texts such as Rom 5:12-18, Phil 2:5-11, 1 Cor 1:7–2:5, and Rom
9:30–10:21, Via discerns a *syntagm* (sequence of events in a plot-structure)
which corresponds to the pattern of Attic comedy.

One crucial aspect of Via's interpretive project is his tacit assumption
that the Pauline letters, which are nonnarrative texts, somehow contain or
presuppose a narrative structure. To cite a single example, Via remarks that
"in 1 Cor 1:18ff. the narrative form is comic, ending on the note of life and
justification, while in Rom 9:30ff. the narrative form is tragic, the last word
being Israel's disobedience."[131] The fact that the texts to which he refers are
not actually in narrative form gives Via little pause; he simply *assumes* that he
can describe a narrative structure in them, and he proceeds to do so, as illustrated by the following retelling of 1 Cor 1:18ff., in which Via employs
Cornford's terms for the stereotypical comic roles.

> God identifies himself with the lowly and despised — the crucified Christ
> and the Church — and thus becomes an eiron, and the world (son) is a
> boastful alazon. The alazon is shown that his wisdom is really a foolish illu-
> sion (that he can dispose of his own existence). . . . The irony of God is that
> he enters into (he saves through the foolish kerygma) the suffering and hu-
> miliation (the cross) caused by man's illusion (that he runs the world) and
> thereby shatters that illusion. But God's victory, which is the defeat of the
> alazon-world, ironically is the victory of man as freedom for a new life.
> Thus the eiron-hero-God does not simply win a victory for himself over
> the alazon and chase the latter away. . . . For "Pauline comedy" the ironical
> action of the hero affects a radical change in the alazon.[132]

130. Via, *Kerygma and Comedy*, 45.
131. Ibid., 50.
132. Ibid., 48. The "eiron" is an "ironical man" who often is cast in the role of hero,
though he "feigns stupidity and makes himself out to be less than he is." The "alazon" is a
boastful, foolish imposter.

This example illustrates how Via can use the analogy of Greek comedy to discern a comic structure in Paul's thought and at the same time to point out distinctive features of the Pauline narrative structure.

However, Via leaves himself open to the criticism that he is insufficiently reflective about the problems involved in his recasting of Paul's text into a narrative structure. Is this structure really present in 1 Corinthians, or is it Via's own imaginative construction based on the raw material of symbolic elements provided by Paul? Does the attempt to fit Paul's discourse into a comic dramatic structure in the end distort Paul's message? For example, in Via's analysis of this passage, "Christ's death" appears early in the syntagmatic sequence, whereas near the end of the sequence we find the following entry: "agon: eiron-god shatters alazon-world."[133] This event must appear here in the grid because in Aristophanic comedy the hero's defeat of the alazon occurs near the end of the play's action (as an entirely separate event from the hero's conquest of the antagonist, which occurs earlier), and it immediately precedes the *komos*. Thus Via's identification of the world with the alazon-figure forces him to place God's shattering of the alazon-world toward the end of the sequence as an event separate from and subsequent to death. But surely the whole burden of Paul's argument in the passage under examination is that it is precisely in Christ's death on the cross that the world's pretensions are shattered. This shattering is not a separate event in a narrative sequence; rather, it is Paul's *interpretation* of the event of the cross. Via's scheme has forced him to factor out elements which are for Paul aspects of a single event and to project these elements into a narrative syntagm as separate events.

No one would deny that Via's retelling of 1 Cor 1:18–2:5 is clever, illuminating, and perhaps even homiletically serviceable. But many will question whether the Pauline text on which the retelling is based actually has a narrative structure, particularly in light of Via's omission of any methodological justification for his translation of a nonnarrative text into a narrative mode. Only once does Via drop a hint about the theoretical basis for such a transformation, when — again following Cornford — he asserts that "while myth is dominant in tragedy it is logos — theme or idea — which is most prominent in comedy. Thus a comic view is more amenable than tragedy to a representation which is only semi-narrative."[134] Does Via mean to suggest here that Paul's letters manifest the comic structure in a "semi-narrative" form? If so, the suggestion is not developed further.

---

133. Ibid., 47, fig. 4.
134. Ibid., 41. Note that this distinction between "myth" and "logos" corresponds closely to Frye's distinction between *mythos* and *dianoia*.

This unclarity about the distinction between narrative and nonnarrative texts points also to an equally puzzling latitude in Via's use of the term "genre." His exposition seems to require us to accept the proposition that Romans and *The Frogs* both belong to the same genre, the genre of "comedy." But surely this use of "genre" violates the normal and permissible meaning of the term in literary criticism. A genre is constituted not merely by a plot-structure but by a complex configuration of formal and material considerations (which often remain maddeningly elusive).[135]

Via, however, uses the term "genre" much more expansively. When he speaks of the "comic genre," he seems to have in mind some sort of super-genre, encompassing texts from a wide range of genres, texts which somehow manifest the death/resurrection (or upset/recovery) pattern. In this very broad sense, the Pauline letters do indeed participate in the "comic genre," or, as Via puts it in terms of the structuralist conceptuality, "the comic genre . . . generates Paul's performance texts."[136]

This broad use of the term *genre* runs the risk, however, of obscuring the particular character of the Pauline letters, which, regarded as literary works, belong, after all, not to the genre of comic drama but to the "pastoral letter" genre. Therefore, I would prefer to formulate the matter as follows: we may discern as a substructure in Paul's letters a Christ-story that has certain structural analogies to the plot-structure characteristic of Attic comedy. Paul's creative act of interpretation may then consist partly in the elucidation of the meaning of this story through the medium of a new genre, i.e., the pastoral letter. The structural isomorphism between Paul's gospel story and the plot-structure of Attic comedy is an arresting phenomenon which the critic may explore, as Via has done, but the pastoral-letter genre displays this story in a new context, a different structure of expectation, and thus disposes the reader differently toward it, creating new meanings. One task of the critic is to describe the meanings which arise from the placement of a particular story-pattern into a different genre-structure, but this task is hindered by Via's sweeping assimilation of the Pauline letters into the "comic genre."

135. Via's understanding of "genre" seems to be derived primarily from T. Todorov, "Poétique," *Qu'est-ce que le structuralisme?* (ed. F. Wahl; Paris: Seuil, 1968) 150-57. For discussion of the problem of defining "genre" and for further references on this issue, see Kermode, *Genesis of Secrecy,* 162-63 n. 20; C. H. Talbert, *What Is a Gospel?* (Philadelphia: Fortress, 1977) 1-16; M. J. Buss, "Principles for Morphological Criticism," *Orientation by Disorientation: Studies in Literary Criticism and Biblical Literary Criticism Presented in Honor of William A. Beardslee* (ed. R. A. Spencer; PTMS 35; Pittsburgh: Pickwick, 1980) 71-86.

136. *Kerygma and Comedy,* 57.

Another matter of central importance for our purposes here is that Via's reconstructed narrative syntagms are imprecise about identifying the characters who occupy the key roles in the Pauline comic drama. Nowhere in Via's grids do we learn the identity of the antagonist, for example. The most crucial question, however, concerns the identity of the protagonist-hero. In Via's actual exposition, the hero is identified only as God, but in the syntagmatic grids, the "agon" square is filled, for Pauline texts, only by references to "*Christ's* obedient struggle," "*Christ's* humble obedience," and "*Christ's* death to sin."[137] This surely suggests that Via's analysis should require us to see Christ as the protagonist-hero of the "comedy of justification." Via, however, neither calls attention to this point nor offers any reflections on its significance. Here is a clue that must be further examined as we analyze the narrative structures in Galatians in Chapter III, below.

Finally, we may conclude our observations about Via's work on a positive note by concurring strongly with his opinion that the self-understanding of faith receives its norm and shape from the narrative structure of the gospel.

> The Pauline Christian does not know himself in relation to God and the world by having what he already latently knows brought to light, but by choosing a paradigm which comes to him out of his trans-personal history as a model for his life. Thus he knows and becomes himself by deciding for a model outside of himself. . . . The new self of the Pauline Christian does not lose its irreducible individuality, but that individuality is projected into the paradigm of the death and resurrection of Jesus, the story which is continuous with other comic syntagms. . . .[138]

In spite of the emphasis on "decision," the contrast to Bultmann's position is striking, because according to Via the believer's faith-decision is a decision to identify himself with a syntagmatic pattern (story) and thus to discover his own life "projected" into that story. The life of the believer becomes determined by participation in the "paradigm" of Jesus' story, which serves as a model for the new life of faith. What this "model" might look like remains somewhat unclear, though we hope to sketch its outline in the following

---

137. Ibid., 42, fig. 2. The quotations refer to, respectively, Rom 5:12-18, Phil 2:5-11, and Rom 6:3-10.

138. Ibid., 66. Apparently, Via here slips out of using "paradigm" as a structuralist technical term and uses it instead in its ordinary English meaning. This unannounced shift, if not recognized, might cause considerable confusion in the attempt to perform an exegesis of Via's sentences.

chapters. Via's insight here is a particularly promising one, because it offers a hope of bridging the notorious gap between Paul's theology and ethics. This bridge will be tested in the final chapter of this study as we ask what kind of stance toward self and world the gospel story embodies and promotes.

In summary, Via's unorthodox approach to Paul, in spite of the methodological objections raised against it here, is an illuminating one which highlights the narrative elements in Paul's letters. Perhaps the most important contribution of Via's study is his effort to identify these narrative elements and outline their syntagmatic structure without getting drawn into the problem of their historical facticity. He undertakes a *literary* analysis of the story-pattern as it actually appears in Paul's letters; this approach enables him to reclaim this pattern as a central and meaningful component of Paul's thought. Interestingly, nowhere in his analysis does Via deal with any passages from Galatians. The task of the next chapter will be to see whether it is possible to identify a similar narrative pattern in Galatians and to examine its shape and meaning.

D. Conclusions

We have now completed our brief study of critical treatments of narrative elements in Paul's letters. Once again, it must be emphasized that this survey makes no pretense of being comprehensive; its intention is not to review a historical development but to sketch a spectrum of interpretive possibilities.

The spectrum may be divided broadly in half. On one end are those interpreters (Bousset, Schweitzer, Bultmann) who, while recognizing that Paul drew upon narrative patterns (whether Gnostic or apocalyptic), nonetheless believe that the gospel is capable of being restated in ways that minimize its narrative elements and thus make its real meaning more apparent. These critics see the narrative *Vorstellungen* in Paul's thought-world as imperfect gropings toward articulating a nonmythological, nonnarrative *kerygma*. At the other end of the spectrum are those interpreters (Cullmann, Dodd, Via) who think that a narrative pattern is integral to the gospel message, though each of them defines this narrative pattern in a different way. My interpretive project is in sympathy with this half of the spectrum, but it must be differentiated from the work of these critics in various ways which have been explained in each particular case.

In spite of their diverse approaches to describing and evaluating the narrative elements in the letters, all of the critics considered in this chapter, including Bultmann, concur in recognizing the *presence* of a narrative substructure in Paul's theology.[139] Some of them like it, some of them dislike it, and some (particularly Käsemann) appear highly ambivalent about it. But all sense and acknowledge its presence. The task before us is to describe and evaluate it more exactly.

---

139. None of them, of course, employs precisely this terminology.

Chapter III

Analysis of Narrative Christological Formulations in Galatians

Our analysis of the narrative substructure of Paul's theology will center upon the third and fourth chapters of the letter to the Galatians. The reasons for this choice of focal point have already been indicated in Chapter I, above: Galatians is evoked by a situation that Paul regards as a fundamental threat to the gospel; therefore, in this letter, Paul is forced to operate in a "mode of recapitulation," restating and defending the basic content of his message.

This argumentative recapitulation employs several pithy kerygmatic formulations, some of which appear to be relatively fixed units of tradition that would have been known already to the Galatians and accepted by them as authoritative. There is a growing consensus among scholars that these kerygmatic statements, which take the form of christological confessional formulae, are not original Pauline compositions but that they are units of tradition that emerge from the pre-Pauline Christian communities.[1] My investi-

---

1. That Paul employs traditional confessional formulae in his letters has long been widely assumed by NT scholarship. Most of the discussion of these formulae has centered on passages such as 1 Cor 15:3ff., in which Paul explicitly appeals to tradition. For recent attempts, however, to discern units of traditional material in the central section of Galatians, see W. Kramer, *Christ, Lord, Son of God* (SBT 50; London: SCM, 1966) 111-14, 187-89; E. Schweizer, "Zum religionsgeschichtlichen Hintergrund der 'Sendungsformel' Gal 4:4f. Rm 8:3f. Joh 3:16f. I Joh 4:9," *ZNW* 51 (1966) 199-210; idem, "υἱός, κτλ.," *TDNT* 8.374-76; J. C. O'Neill, *The Recovery of Paul's Letter to the Galatians* (London: SPCK, 1972) 58-59; N. A. Dahl, *Studies in Paul* (Minneapolis: Augsburg, 1977) 130-36, 171-72; M. Wilcox, "Upon the Tree: Deut 21.22-23 in the NT," *JBL* 96 (1977) 85-99; H.-J. van der Minde, *Schrift und Tradition bei Paulus* (Paderborner Theologische Studien 3; Munich: Schöningh, 1976) 128-30; P. Stuhlmacher, "Zur paulinischen Christologie," *ZTK* 74 (1977) 449-63; H. D. Betz, *Galatians,* 26-28 *et passim.*

gation does not depend, however, on any particular theory about the origin of these christological formulations, nor does it require them to be pre-Pauline. The important observation is that Paul introduces them as authoritative statements upon which his argumentation rests. Werner Kramer summarizes the matter as follows.

> Evidently the primary consideration in Paul's mind when he adopted any formula was that his church would be bound to assent to it, simply because it represented a piece of tradition which was generally acknowledged. That is why he often uses formulae, either as the point of departure for his train of thought, or as the decisive argument in it, or as its climax.[2]

Kramer is speaking of pre-Pauline formulae, but even if the formulations in question were of Paul's own coinage, the point stands that these condensed christological statements function as the warrants on the basis of which Paul argues other points. There is no question here of a debate between Paul and his opponents over christological dogma; the dispute concerns the proper soteriological consequences that follow from accepted christological premises.

Chapter V, below, will attempt to analyze with some care the way in which Paul's argument in Galatians 3 and 4 builds upon these christological formulations; the task of the present chapter is to analyze the formulations themselves with a view to discerning in them a narrative structure. For the sake of clarity, the discussion will concentrate initially on Gal 4:3-6 and 3:13-14, two passages that are widely recognized as having a formalized character and as standing in some sort of close, albeit puzzling relationship to one another. It will be argued that these formulations, in spite of surface differences, share a common narrative structure and that they illuminate the center of Paul's gospel story. Once the narrative structure of these formulations has been described, it will be possible to examine other statements in Galatians and to determine their relationship to this structure.

A. The Relationship Between Galatians 4:3-6 and 3:13-14: The Problem

How the two passages relate to one another doctrinally and historically is difficult to say.

H. D. Betz[3]

2. Kramer, *Christ, Lord, Son of God,* 186.
3. *Galatians,* 207 n. 51. Betz's comment refers to the relationship between 3:13-14 and

Commentators on Galatians usually point out the striking parallelism between Gal 4:4-5 and 3:13-14, but opinions differ widely on the question of how to understand the relationship between these two passages. Hans Dieter Betz, for example, speaks of a "discrepancy" between the two formulations and insists that they "cannot be harmonized."[4] Josef Blank, on the other hand, thinks that "die Strukturähnlichkeit der beiden Aussagen fällt so stark in den Blick, dass sie nicht weiter bewiesen zu werden braucht," and he attempts to show that the correspondence between them is one not only of form but also of content.[5] In order to grasp the basis for these differing judgments, it will be useful to set forth the similarities and differences between the two formulations and then to review briefly the different theories about their origins.

1. Similarities

Both formulations correspond broadly to a formal-grammatical pattern which Nils Dahl, in his essay "Form-Critical Observations on Early Christian Preaching," has described as "the teleological pattern." Furthermore, Dahl includes both under the subtype of teleological preaching pattern, which he characterizes as follows: "Christ . . . for us — so that we. . . ."[6] It will be observed that Gal 4:4-5 actually fails, strictly speaking, to correspond to this pattern in several respects which we must consider below; it is true, however, that both passages conclude with parallel double ἵνα-clauses that express the soteriological implications of the action described in the main clause.[7]

Blank attempts to demonstrate the parallelism between the texts in greater detail by outlining their components *(Glieder)* as follows.[8]

4:4-5. Most critics pose the comparison in this way. I have widened the comparison to include Gal 4:3-6 for reasons which will appear in the study; see part D below.

4. Ibid., 144 n. 57, 207 n. 51.

5. J. Blank, *Paulus und Jesus* (SANT 18; Munich: Kösel, 1968) 262. J. Eckert (*Die urchristliche Verkündigung,* 89) cites Blank's discussion as persuasive and adopts the same view. See also F. Mussner, *Der Galaterbrief* (HTKNT 9; Freiburg: Herder, 1974) 271-74.

6. N. A. Dahl, *Jesus in the Memory of the Early Church* (Minneapolis: Augsburg, 1976) 35.

7. This point is noted by Betz (*Galatians,* 208).

8. The outlines reproduced together here are introduced separately by Blank (*Paulus und Jesus,* 260-61 and 262).

Gal 4:4-5	*Gal 3:13-14*
a) ἐξαπέστειλεν ὁ θεὸς τὸν υἱὸν αὑτοῦ	a) Χριστὸς ἡμᾶς ἐξηγόρασεν ἐκ τῆς κατάρας τοῦ νόμου
b¹) γενόμενον ἐκ γυναικός b²) γενόμενον ὑπὸ νόμον	b) γενόμενος ὑπὲρ ἡμῶν κατάρα
c¹) ἵνα τοὺς ὑπὸ νόμον ἐξαγοράσῃ	c¹) ἵνα εἰς τὰ ἔθνη ἡ εὐλογία τοῦ Ἀβραὰμ γένηται ἐν Χριστῷ Ἰησοῦ
c²) ἵνα τὴν υἱοθεσίαν ἀπολάβωμεν	c²) ἵνα τὴν ἐπαγγελίαν τοῦ πνεύματος λάβωμεν διὰ τῆς πίστεως

Some of the similarities may be listed briefly. Both passages employ the verb ἐξαγοράζω,[9] which occurs elsewhere in the NT only at Eph 5:16 (= Col 4:5), there with a somewhat different meaning. In both cases, the second component of the formulation (b) is constructed with the participle γενόμενος and points out "die irdisch-geschichtliche Ereignishaftigkeit des Heilsgeschehens, dass es im Raume menschlicher Geschichte stattfand."[10] Blank also calls attention to the fact that the verbs λάβωμεν/ἀπολάβωμεν occur in the second ἵνα-clause (c²) of the two formulations. One further similarity that is not revealed by Blank's outline is that both passages build toward and culminate in the gift of the Spirit; in 3:14 the Spirit is received by us, and in 4:6 it is sent by God.

Blank also attempts to show that the parallelism between the two passages is material as well as formal. His final summary of the parallelism of thought-progression between the two formulations is worth quoting in full.

> Das Glied a) stellt in kerygmatisch-satzhafter Formulierung ohne dies weiter zu begründen, das Heilsgeschehen in seiner vom Menschen unabhängigen Gültigkeit heraus, als Handeln Christi bzw. Gottes, als ein Geschehen "extra nos." Glied b) untermauert jeweils die Geschichtlichkeit des Heilsgeschehens im Kreuz bzw. in der "Menschenwerdung" zugleich mit seiner soteriologischen Bedeutung. Glied c¹ stellt die vorgängige universale Bedeutung des Heilsgeschehens, seine allgemein-Menschliche

9. It should be noted, however, that, whereas this verb occurs in 3:13 as the verb of the main clause, it appears in 4:5 in the ἵνα-clause. The significance of this fact must be explored further below. On the meaning of the verb, see S. Lyonnet, "L'emploi paulinien de ἐξαγοράζειν au sens de 'redimere' est-il attesté dans la littérature grecque?" *Bib* 42 (1961) 85-89; C. Andresen, "Erlösung," *RAC* 6.59.

10. Blank, *Paulus und Jesus*, 263.

Tragweite heraus. Glied c² endlich führt die soteriologische Gültigkeit zum "pro nobis" bzw. "pro me" durch — und hier erst, hier aber dann auch berechtigterweise, ist der Ort, wo die Existenz des einzelnen getroffen wird.[11]

This might pass as a very general summary of the "drift" of the two passages, but it is necessary to inquire whether this summary reckons sufficiently with the numerous differences in detail, many of which Blank glosses over with a casual *"bzw."* Does Blank's statement in fact paper over some fairly major discrepancies between the texts in view?

2. Differences

Although Gal 4:4-5 corresponds in a general way to the teleological preaching pattern described by Dahl, it also differs formally from this pattern (and specifically from Gal 3:13-14) in several ways. First of all, instead of the title "Christ," we find in Gal 4:4-5 the title "his [= God's] Son." Secondly, the grammatical subject in the first purpose clause in the formula (4-5a) is "he" (God's Son) rather than "we," as Dahl's categorization of this passage would suggest; thus, 4:4-5 appears to be a mixed type, manifesting characteristics of two of Dahl's subtypes: subtype a ("Christ . . . for us — so that we . . .") and subtype b ("Christ . . . for us — so that he . . .").[12] Thirdly, Christ's action of redemption (ἐξαγοράζειν), which in 3:13 constitutes the main clause of the formulation, appears instead in a purpose clause in 4:4-5. Finally, in contrast not only to 3:13-14 but also to all of the other examples adduced by Dahl, Gal 4:4 presents the Son of God (= Christ) as the object rather than the subject of the main clause.[13] Thus, this formulation portrays God as the active

11. Ibid. Blank's summary is partly intended to illustrate certain difficulties with the "existentialist" interpretation of Paul. It seems odd, however, that he is willing to concede that the final component of both formulations (c²) concerns "die Existenz des einzelnen." In fact, both of these clauses use the first person *plural* form of the verb and arguably have in view a corporate soteriology. Paul does *not* say ". . . in order that *I* might receive adoption . . ." or ". . . in order that each one of us individually might receive adoption." Instead, he envisions the adoption of believers (Gentiles in particular) corporately.

12. Dahl, *Jesus in Memory,* 35. For a clear example of subtype b, see Gal 1:4.

13. Rom 8:3, which Dahl presents for comparison, does parallel Gal 4:4 both in using the title "Son" and in making the Son the direct object of God's sending action, but in other respects it is not a close *formal* parallel to the pattern that Dahl is attempting to identify. Undeniably, however, there are significant *material* similarities between Rom 8:3 and Gal 4:4 on the one hand and Dahl's other examples on the other. This observation encourages the hy-

agent who "sent" his Son into the world, whereas this motif is absent from 3:13-14.

The last point also directs our attention to the possibility that these formal differences between the two passages may signal material differences as well. We may mention two of these here.

(1) The blessings of salvation are achieved, according to 3:13, through Christ's death on a cross, but 4:4-5 says nothing about Christ's death. This point is emphasized strongly by both Betz and E. Lohse, who think that 4:4-5 reflects a christology which views redemption as effected through Christ's incarnation rather than through his atoning death. "Hier heisst es," comments Lohse, "dass seine Menschwerdung und Unterworfenheit unter das Gesetz den Loskauf vom Gesetz bewirkten."[14] If Lohse is right about this, the two christologies are flatly incompatible, and as Betz insists, they "cannot be harmonized."[15] But then we must ask how and why Paul has incorporated them both in Galatians. Was he oblivious to the discrepancy? Or is there some other explanation?[16]

(2) Gal 3:13-14a draws a sharp distinction between "the Gentiles" and "us" (= Jews); thus, this formulation views and explains the significance of the Christ-event from a clearly Jewish perspective. The formulation in 4:5, however, with its distancing reference to τοὺς ὑπὸ νόμον, seems to reflect a non-Jewish point of view. In light of these observations, the following assertion by Blank is open to question: "Glied c¹ stellt die vorgängige universale Bedeutung des Heilsgeschehens, seine allgemein-menschliche Tragweite heraus."[17] Rather, it appears that Blank's component c¹ expresses in one instance the meaning of the salvation-event for Gentiles and in the other instance its meaning for Jews.[18]

---

pothesis that all of these passages are united not by a "formula" pattern which may be discerned by form-critical methods, but by some other kind of pattern, which we will seek to outline in this chapter.

14. E. Lohse, *Märtyrer und Gottesknecht* (FRLANT, N.F. 46; Göttingen: Vandenhoeck & Ruprecht, 1955) 156 n. 2. See also Betz, *Galatians,* 150 n. 119.

15. Betz, *Galatians,* 207 n. 51.

16. O'Neill solves this problem (and all other problems of logical continuity in Galatians) with an interpolation theory. In this case, he asserts that this whole section has been "glossed heavily by two different hands, one responsible for verses 1-3, 8-10, and the other responsible for verses 4f." (*Recovery,* 59). This chapter will seek to provide another explanation that will render such speculative proposals unnecessary.

17. Blank, *Paulus und Jesus,* 263.

18. Schlier (*Galater,* 136-37), representing a long-cherished interpretive tradition, universalizes the meaning of νόμος in 3:13 and of τοὺς ὑπὸ νόμον in 4:5, so that being "under the law" is metaphorized and the Jew is treated as a "type" that represents the universal unre-

3. Origins

Critics who emphasize these differences tend to think that they are attributable to the origin of one or both formulations in different pre-Pauline christological traditions which "were not smoothed out by the Apostle."[19] There is widespread agreement that Gal 3:13 preserves a Jewish-Christian christological tradition. According to Betz, this tradition interpreted Jesus' death "by means of the Jewish concept of the meritorious death of the righteous and its atoning benefits."[20] Dahl has proposed that 3:13-14a is a fragment of "an old Jewish Christian midrash which understood the crucifixion in light of Genesis 22,"[21] and a similar argument has recently been advanced by M. Wilcox, who thinks that "behind the present context in Galatians 3 there is an earlier midrashic link between Gen 22:6-9 and Deut 21:22-23 by way of the common term עץ (ξύλον, קיסא)."[22] While these hypotheses differ slightly in detail, they concur essentially in the opinion that in 3:13 Paul has drawn upon a source of christological tradition that emerges from the early Jewish-Christian community.

Likewise, several scholars have argued that 4:4-5 contains a pre-Pauline *Sendungsformel* of some sort, probably emerging from a Hellenistic environment, though there are disagreements in detail about what exactly the pre-Pauline formula would have included. Kramer, for example, thinks that he can reconstruct the "original structure of the formula" as follows: "God sent forth his Son, so that we might receive adoption as sons." According to Kramer, it was Paul himself who inserted the words "born under the law in order to redeem those who were under the law" in order to serve the purposes of his argument.[23] Ulrich Luz is in general agreement with this position, but

---

deemed human condition with particular vividness. Another well-established line of interpretation, most recently joined by Betz (*Galatians*, 148 n. 101), insists that the Jew-Gentile distinction must maintain its historical specificity for Paul, and that ἡμᾶς in 3:13 and τοὺς ὑπὸ νόμον in 4:5 must refer to Jews. It is not possible to pursue this matter in detail here, but it seems clear that a passage such as 3:13, in which ἡμᾶς is immediately set in juxtaposition to τὰ ἔθνη, tips the balance in favor of the latter interpretation, which is adopted for the purposes of the analysis which will follow in this chapter. For a lengthy roll-call of distinguished scholars on both sides of this question, see Eckert (*Die urchristliche Verkündigung*, 78 n. 3).

19. Betz, *Galatians*, 144 n. 57.

20. Ibid., 151. For a detailed exposition of this concept, see Williams, *Jesus' Death.*

21. Dahl, *Studies in Paul*, 171. See also idem, *Crucified Messiah*, 154.

22. Wilcox, "Upon the Tree," 98.

23. Kramer, *Christ, Lord, Son of God*, 113. One problem with the reconstruction is that it makes it difficult to see why Paul should have quoted the formula at all. If, as Kramer thinks, Paul quotes formulas in order to authorize his arguments, would it really serve his

he thinks that the content of the ἵνα-clause may already be influenced by the ideas of 4:6, so that it is no longer possible to reconstruct the original conclusion of the *Sendungsformel*.[24]

On the other hand, other scholars deny that there is any pre-Pauline formulation underlying 4:4-5. Klaus Wengst, for example, offers a refutation of Kramer's reconstruction on the grounds that the evidence does not even fit Kramer's own criteria for the existence of a formula: Kramer says that a formula is present where there are "fixed key words and clear formal patterns."[25] Wengst denies that these features can be demonstrated for Gal 4:4-5.[26] Blank takes a different tack; working on the assumption that 3:13-14 is Paul's own language, he takes the structural similarity of 4:4-5 to it as presumptive evidence that there are no non-Pauline origins for the latter, that in both cases we encounter simply Paul's own theological thought-structure.[27]

A more nuanced position is taken by E. Schweizer, who discerns in 4:4-5 not a fixed formula but a traditional thought-schema — the sending of the Son of God into the world — derived from the realm of Hellenistic Jewish Wisdom and Logos-speculation.[28] According to Schweizer, Paul has employed the thought pattern of this tradition, but fully reinterpreted it in light of the crucifixion, so that the meaning of Gal 4:4 is determined by its relation to 3:13: ". . . was im ursprünglichen, schon verchristlichten Schema eine Aussage über die Inkarnation des Präexistenten war, bei Paulus eindeutig zur Verkündigung des Kreuzes Jesu wird."[29]

---

purpose to cite a formula into which he must interpolate something in order to make it say what he wants it to say? If the formula (without Paul's interpolation) were already recognized by the Galatians as authoritative, would this strategy not weaken, rather than strengthen, Paul's position?

24. U. Luz, *Das Geschichtsverständnis des Paulus* (BEvT 49; Munich: Kaiser, 1968) 282-83. Others who accept the hypothesis of a pre-Pauline formula include Mussner (*Galaterbrief*, 271-74) and M. Hengel (*The Son of God* [Philadelphia: Fortress, 1976] 10-11). The first to propose this theory seems to have been J. M. Robinson (*Kerygma und historischer Jesus* [Zürich: Zwingli, 1960] 69 n. 2).

25. Kramer, *Christ, Lord, Son of God*, 112.

26. K. Wengst, *Christologische Formeln und Lieder des Urchristentums* (SNT 7; Gütersloh: Gerd Mohn, 1972) 59. Wengst's view is explicitly rejected by Betz (*Galatians*, 206 n. 40) and Hengel (*Son of God*, 11). See, however, J. D. G. Dunn, *Christology in the Making* (Philadelphia: Westminster, 1980) 38-44. Dunn's denial that Gal 4:4-5 incorporates a pre-Pauline formula is part of a larger argument against the view that Paul presupposed or taught a clear doctrine of preexistence and "incarnation" of Christ.

27. Blank, *Paulus und Jesus*, 262-63.

28. Schweizer, "Sendungsformel," 206-8.

29. Ibid., 209.

4. The Relation between the Texts: A Hypothesis

Schweizer's argument follows the path which has often been taken by commentators on Galatians who, without raising as Schweizer does the question of different origins for the two formulations, have traditionally taken them as complementary and used them to elucidate one another. So, for example, H. Schlier explains 4:4 by saying that "was dieser Unterwerfung unter das Gesetz für den Sohn bedeutete war schon 3:13 gesagt."[30] Even Betz, who insists that "Gal 3:13 and 4:4-5 must be kept separate,"[31] finds himself explaining the meaning of ἐξηγόρασεν in 3:13 by appealing to 4:4-5.[32] And again, in relation to 4:4, he affirms that "this sending, of course, includes Christ's death and resurrection," appealing for evidence to 3:13, among other texts.[33] This sort of interpretive procedure has always seemed natural (indeed, as Betz's failure to keep the texts "separate" attests, almost inevitable)[34] for one very simple reason: even though these formulations may have different historical origins and even though they may appear to us to contain certain discrepancies if they are considered in isolation from one another, Paul himself did not seem to see any discrepancies, and *he* has brought the formulations into close relation with one another in the course of his discussion. Was Paul merely careless, or was he operating (unconsciously) on the basis of some larger principle of coherence which enabled him to see these formulations as compatible or even equivalent? In my opinion, the latter alternative is the correct one. It will be proposed here that, unlike modern form-critics who seek scrupulously to separate christological ideas that come from different "ranges" or "circles" or "contexts,"[35] Paul was able to assimilate and synthesize varying christological formulations because he saw them as expressions and interpre-

---

30. Schlier, *Galater*, 196. This inclination to treat these texts as complementary may be observed in commentaries ranging from J. B. Lightfoot (*Galatians,* 168) to D. Lührmann (*Der Brief an die Galater* [Zürcher Bibelkommentare NT 7; Zürich: TVZ, 1978] 56, 59). Cf. Bultmann, *Theology,* 1.297.

31. Betz, *Galatians,* 150 n. 119.

32. Ibid., 149.

33. Ibid., 176 n. 123.

34. To be entirely fair to Betz's position, it should be acknowledged that when he insists that the formulations "must be kept separate," he probably means, though he does not say explicitly, that they must be kept separate in a history-of-traditions analysis. However, in light of his strong statement that the formulations "cannot be harmonized," his interpretations in the passages cited in nn. 32 and 33 appear, without further explanation, surprising.

35. This tendency is carried to an instructive extreme by Kramer, who assumes throughout that even slight variations in christological formulae signal different "contexts" or historical origins for the formulae in question.

tations of a single foundational story. Gal 4:3-6 and 3:13-14 provide us with an excellent place to begin our investigation of the structure of this story. We will attempt to describe the narrative structure that is manifested in these two formulations and to show that the apparent discrepancies between them disappear when they are understood in terms of this structure. Before we can proceed to an analysis of these texts, however, we must sketch the method that will be used for identifying and describing narrative structure.

B. A Model for Analyzing Narrative Structure

In order to describe the structure of Paul's gospel story with some methodological precision, it is necessary to adopt a particular model for narrative analysis. For the purposes of this study, we will employ a model based upon A. J. Greimas' theoretical research on narrative structures.[36] The following discussion, while it will illustrate the usefulness of the model, will not seek to present an apology or theoretical justification for it.[37] My goal is neither to defend nor to refine the model, but to understand Paul. The model is of interest only insofar as it serves that end.

36. Greimas' fundamental studies are contained in two works: *Sémantique structurale* (Paris: Librairie Larousse, 1966) and *Du Sens* (Paris: Seuil, 1970). Helpful summaries of Greimas' method are offered by D. Patte *(What Is Structural Exegesis?)* and J. Calloud (*Structural Analysis of Narrative* [Semeia Supp 4; Philadelphia: Fortress, 1976 and Missoula: Scholars, 1976]). While Greimas has been the most widely influential theorist in the field of structuralist narrative analysis, there have been other significant attempts to develop models for narrative structure; see, for example, C. Bremond, "The Narrative Message," *Semeia* 10 (1978) 5-55. It is beyond the scope of this project, however, to undertake an assessment of the relative merits of these other proposals. The past decade has witnessed such an awesome proliferation of structuralist scholarship that the nonspecialist may advisedly despair of any attempt at a comprehensive assessment of it. (For one helpful selective bibliography, see A. M. Johnson [ed.], *Structuralism and Biblical Hermeneutics* [PTMS 22; Pittsburgh: Pickwick, 1979] 209-24.) For the purpose of the present chapter, a rudimentary model adapted from the basic work of Greimas will prove sufficient. The exposition which follows here, therefore, will depend almost entirely upon Greimas, Patte, and Calloud. The English terminology follows the usage of Patte.

37. For a lucid historical overview of the development of structuralism, see R. Scholes, *Structuralism in Literature* (New Haven: Yale University, 1974). See also H. C. White, "Structural Analysis of the Old Testament Narrative," *Encounter with the Text* (ed. M. J. Buss; Semeia Supp 8; Philadelphia: Fortress, 1979 and Missoula: Scholars, 1979) 45-66.

1. Theoretical Presuppositions

A fundamental presupposition of Greimas' technique for narrative analysis is that narrative texts, like individual sentences, are governed by laws of syntax. At the level of the sentence, we learn to distinguish, out of the infinite variety of possible sentence elements, syntactical units (subject, predicate, object, etc.) that are related to one another in fixed recurring patterns. Speakers or writers may generate a theoretically infinite number of actual sentences, but only within a set of constraints imposed by the syntactical laws of their language. Thus, as every schoolchild learns, whether with delight or dismay, it is possible to "diagram" the syntactical structure of all possible sentences in terms of a fixed schema that classifies sentence elements into a limited inventory of syntactical units and displays their relation to one another. Greimas seeks to elucidate a "narrative grammar" which would, in a similar fashion, enable us to "diagram" the "narrative syntax" of all possible stories by isolating a limited inventory of *narrative* syntactical units and discovering invariant principles that govern their relation to one another in narrative texts.[38]

Some critics have declared this task to be a priori impossible, on the grounds that laws of syntax operate only at the level of the sentence, and that the flexibility and variety of larger units of discourse render them unsuited to syntactical analysis.[39] According to this view, it would be impossible to formulate a universally applicable narrative grammar. The present study does not seek, however, to grapple with this problem. The claim is made here only that the model developed by Greimas does in fact aptly describe the structure of *some* narrative texts, particularly folk tales and mythic or epic texts, and that Paul's gospel story lends itself readily to analysis in terms of this structure. My use of this model should not be taken to imply an endorsement of any claims for its universality; still less should it be taken to imply any acceptance of the wide-ranging ideological claims of orthodox "structuralism."[40]

The description that follows represents my attempt to distill and restate the essential components of Greimas' model for the analysis of the *morpho-*

38. It should be noted that the term "narrative syntax" is metaphorical or, more precisely, analogical in character.

39. A particularly significant spokesman for this view is R. Barthes (*S/Z* [Paris: Seuil, 1970]), who is a defector from the structuralist movement. See also Scholes (*Structuralism in Literature*, 94-95) and S. Santiago, "Ouroboros," *MLN* 86 (1971) 790-92.

40. See the judicious assessments of structuralism's ideological tendencies by R. Detweiler ("Generative Poetics as Science and Fiction," *Semeia* 10 [1978] 137-50) and Scholes (*Structuralism in Literature*, 1-12), who observes that structuralism "is seeking nothing less than the unification of all the sciences into a new system of belief" (p. 2).

syntactic structure of narrative texts. No effort is made here to employ any of Greimas' methods for analyzing *semantic* structures.[41] I have sought instead to digest, simplify, and clarify some of his insights about narrative syntax in order to produce a workable model of narrative structure that may be applied to the analysis of narrative elements in Galatians.

2. Narrative Sequences

At least since Aristotle, people have been sagely observing that every story must have a beginning, a middle, and an end.[42] This conventional wisdom has been incorporated by Greimas, who proposes that the fundamental narrative structure is composed of three "sequences," which he designates as the "initial sequence," the "topical sequence," and the "final sequence." The initial and final sequences are called "correlated sequences," because they are related to one another in a very specific way: the final sequence represents the completion of a task that was somehow stymied in the initial sequence or the reestablishing of an order that was disrupted in the initial sequence. The "topical" sequence is so called because it forms the center of attention ("topic") of the story. A single story may have several topical sequences (the more complex the story, the more of these are likely to appear),[43] but it need have only one. Thus we may begin to describe our model for narrative structure with the very simple diagram in Figure 1.

41. The methodologies between which I am distinguishing here (analysis of the "morpho-syntactic structures of narrative" and analysis of "semantic contents") are logically separable; in fact, one of the most difficult problems for structuralist criticism has been the lack of clear coordination between these aspects of analysis. This methodological cleavage is a result of the different and perhaps incompatible approaches of the founders of the two types of methodology, V. Propp and Lévi-Strauss. For an attempt at synthesis, see Patte and Patte, *Structural Exegesis: From Theory to Practice.* In this study, I, like Kermode (*Genesis of Secrecy,* 80-81), "allow myself some use of neo-formalist terminology to say things that its inventors and proponents would certainly disapprove of." I employ, among other tools, the methods of Greimas et al. in order to render a descriptive account of the structure of Paul's gospel story, but the actual task of interpreting this structure at the semantic level is carried out within the more traditional categories of literary and theological exegesis.

42. Aristotle, *Poetics* 1450b.

43. On narrative sequence, see A. J. Greimas, "Narrative Grammar: Units and Levels," *MLN* 86 (1971) 802. For Greimas' development and application of the theory, see especially *Du Sens* (185-230). Cf. also Patte, *What Is Structural Exegesis?*, 37-39, 50-51. For the sake of simplicity, the following exposition will treat the case of stories with a single topical sequence.

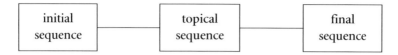

Figure 1

3. Narrative Syntagms

What constitutes a "sequence"? A sequence, according to Greimas, contains and is determined by three fixed elements, which he calls "narrative syntagms."[44] ("Syntagm" is simply a term which means "syntactical unit.") There is the "contract syntagm" (in which the protagonist is charged with a task to perform), the "disjunction/conjunction syntagm" (in which the protagonist sets out on the quest to carry out the "contract"), and the "performance syntagm" (in which the protagonist carries out or fails to carry out the task).[45] These syntagms logically must occur in the order described here, although a given text may not necessarily manifest them in this order.[46] Let us introduce these subdivisions into the model in Figure 2. In this diagram, C stands for contract syntagm, D for disjunction/conjunction syntagm, and P for performance syntagm.

initial sequence			topical sequence			final sequence		
C	D	P	C	D	P	C	D	P

Figure 2

4. Canonical Functions

Each of the syntagms is made up of "narrative statements," which Greimas divides into two classes: "qualifications" (state-of-being descriptions, such as "the dragon was fierce") and "functions" (action-descriptions, such as "St.

44. Greimas, *Du Sens*, 191; idem, "Narrative Grammar," 803; cf. Patte, *What Is Structural Exegesis?*, 39-40.

45. See Patte, *What Is Structural Exegesis?*, 44-45.

46. Devices such as flashback allow a narrator to tell the events of a story in an order different from their bare chronological succession.

George slew the dragon"). In Greimas' system, the functions may be "re-duced" (i.e., classified) into a limited number of basic general categories, which are called "canonical functions."[47] These canonical functions occur in fixed ("canonical") places within the narrative sequence; in other words, the various functions are linked to particular syntagms. To take an obvious ex-ample, a narrative statement such as "St. George slew the dragon," which Greimas would classify as a manifestation of a canonical function called "domination/submission," can belong only to the performance syntagm of a story-sequence, never to the contract syntagm. The implication of this is that each syntagm may be further subdivided according to the canonical func-tions of which it is characteristically composed.

There are two canonical functions which comprise the contract syn-tagm. Greimas refers to these as "contractual statements"; they are designated as CS1 and CS2. The first contractual statement (CS1) manifests the function "mandating/acceptance"; here the protagonist receives a mandate to carry out a given task.[48] This task entails overcoming an opponent or removing an

---

47. See Greimas, *Sémantique structurale*, 192-203. The canonical functions are conve-niently summarized in Calloud, *Structural Analysis of Narrative*, 17-18.

48. If the protagonist should refuse the mandate, then the narrative may take several courses.

(a) The narrative could simply abort, as in the following "story": "Now the word of the Lord came to Jonah the son of Amittai, saying, 'Arise, go to Nineveh, that great city, and cry against it; for their wickedness has come up before me.' But Jonah rose to flee to Tarshish from the presence of the Lord. He went down to Joppa and found a ship going to Tarshish; so he paid the fare, and went on board, to go with them to Tarshish, away from the presence of the Lord" (Jonah 1:1-3). If the book of Jonah ended here, we would have an aborted story. Some modern stories are indeed of this aborted type. Their impact derives, however, pre-cisely from their iconoclastic violation of our expectations for how a story "ought to go." See T. L. Estess, "The Inenarrable Contraption: Reflections on the Metaphor of Story," *JAAR* 42 (1974) 415-34; D. Cannon, "Ruminations on the Claim of Inenarrability," *JAAR* 43 (1975) 560-85.

(b) The mandate may be given to a new protagonist, who then becomes, by definition, the Subject of the narrative sequence. A classic example of this pattern is the Saul/David story.

(c) The narrative may introduce an extended development (subsequence) whose pur-pose is to induce the protagonist to accept the mandate after all. This is the pattern in fact manifested in the book of Jonah. The whole subsequence in which Jonah is swallowed by a fish merely serves to persuade Jonah to accept the initial mandate (= his role as Subject) so that the story can begin. The preoccupation of Christian interpreters with this subsequence is at least partly attributable to the fact that patristic exegetes saw in it a typological foreshad-owing of the topical sequence of the Christ-story; indeed, this development is already visible within the NT in Matt 12:39-40.

obstacle so that an object or value can be communicated to someone. According to Greimas' theory, the establishment of a contract is the essential presupposition for all stories: "The *contract* is an essential element of a narrative. It is presupposed in any endeavor even if it is not explicitly mentioned."[49] The second contractual statement (CS2) manifests the function "communication/ reception"; here the protagonist (= "Subject") receives various aids (knowledge, powers, companions, etc.) that will enable him to carry out his mandate.[50] This function is sometimes presupposed rather than actually manifested in the narrative. In any case, however, the contract syntagm is crucial for providing the shape of the narrative sequence because it determines the agenda that the rest of the story must somehow carry through. The disjunction/conjunction syntagm is easy to recognize, because it appears wherever we find the function "arrival/departure" or "departure/return." Whenever a movement is narrated, this function is manifested.

The performance syntagm is composed of three "performance statements."[51] The first of these is the "confrontation" function (PS1), in which the protagonist encounters an adversary. The second performance statement (PS2) manifests the function "domination/submission," in which either the protagonist or the adversary triumphs over the other. Finally, the third performance statement (PS3) manifests the function of "attribution"; the protagonist's victory allows the contract to be fulfilled and some object or value to be attributed (given) to a "receiver." When this attribution, which is the goal of the sequence's action, is achieved, the sequence ends. Thus, a narrative sequence contains, according to this model, six canonical functions, as illustrated in Figure 3.

CS1: mandating/ acceptance	CS2: communication/ reception	DS: disjunction/ conjunction	PS1: confrontation	PS2: domination/ submission	PS3: attribution/ deprivation

Figure 3: The ordering of canonical functions in a narrative sequence

How does this theoretical model apply to an actual story? Let us use part of the Exodus story to demonstrate briefly.

49. Calloud, *Structural Analysis of Narrative*, 25; see Greimas, *Sémantique structurale*, 195-96.
50. See Patte, *What Is Structural Exegesis?*, 44.
51. Greimas, "Narrative Grammar," 803-4; Patte, *What Is Structural Exegesis?*, 45-46.

CS1 (mandating/acceptance) —
God appears to Moses in burning bush and commissions him to lead Israel out of Egypt.

CS2 (communication/reception) —
Moses receives helpers: miraculous signs, Aaron as spokesman.

DS (disjunction/conjunction) —
Moses leaves Midian and goes to Egypt, where he rejoins his people.

PS1 (confrontation) —
Conflict with Pharaoh, series of plagues.

PS2 (domination/submission) —
Passover; Israel crosses the Red Sea and Pharaoh's army is destroyed.[52]

PS3 (attribution) —
Israel receives freedom from bondage.

Of course, this is not the end of the story that Exodus tells. We have illustrated here only one sequence within the story. Israel's wandering in the wilderness and ultimate entry into the promised land constitute another sequence which contains many subsequences, and the story as a whole is a long and complicated one. The above sketch does show, however, what the theoretical skeleton of a narrative sequence looks like when some flesh is put upon it. In theory, each of the three fundamental sequences (initial, topical, and final) could be fleshed out analogously, so that the complete narrative structure would appear as diagrammed in Figure 4.

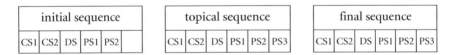

Figure 4: The ordering of canonical functions in the complete narrative structure

It should be noted that there cannot be an "attribution" function in the initial sequence. The initial sequence is necessarily an incomplete sequence, whose failure creates the "situation of lack" which the topical sequence must remedy. This incompleteness is symbolized in Figure 4 by the blank box in place of

52. In this complex story, the "domination" function appears in more than one narrative statement. The Passover, as the culmination of the plagues, brings about a partial victory, but the "domination" is not complete until Pharaoh's chariots disappear beneath the waters.

PS3 in the initial sequence. Another way of making this same point is to call the function associated with PS3 "attribution/deprivation," so that it corresponds to the binary structure of most of the other functions. If this terminology is adopted, then we see that the initial sequence must always conclude in a deprivation function; otherwise there would be no story.[53]

The complete narrative structure depicted in Figure 4 is by no means fully actualized in every narrative. The initial and final sequences are often only hinted at or allusively treated. For example, in Patte's analysis of the Good Samaritan story, the entire initial sequence is represented by a single sentence: "A man was going down from Jerusalem to Jericho and he fell among robbers who stripped him and beat him and departed, leaving him half dead."[54] The final sequence, moreover, is not manifested in the narrative at all, as the storyteller leaves the victim convalescing in the inn; presumably, he will recover and go on to Jericho to fulfill his "contract" (whatever it may have been — we are not told *why* he was going to Jericho), but all of that is left to our imagination rather than narrated in the text. Thus, Luke's Good Samaritan narrative, like many narratives, concentrates on the topical sequence and leaves us with a sense that there must be more to the story than our narrator has chosen to tell. Because this is such a common pattern in story telling, the fully articulated model that is presented in Figure 4 is actually too detailed and unwieldy for the analysis of most stories. Consequently, in the analysis that follows we will use a somewhat simplified version of the model, which is adapted here from Patte.[55] This simplified model, shown in Figure 5 (on p. 90), eliminates subdivisions within the correlated sequences and also within the syntagms of the topical sequence, except that it maintains, within the performance syntagm, a separate status for the attribution function.[56] Thus, Figure 5 portrays graphically the proportionately greater

---

53. This is a particularly useful way of describing stories in which the "problem" is caused by the intervention of a malevolent character or force (example: a dragon kidnaps the king's daughter). This is what V. Propp (*Morphology of the Folktale* [2nd ed. rev.; ed. L. A. Wagner; Austin: University of Texas, 1968] 30-35) terms the "villainy."

54. Patte, *What Is Structural Exegesis?*, 39. For his full analysis of the Good Samaritan story, see his "An Analysis of Narrative Structure and the Good Samaritan," *Semeia* 2 (1974) 1-26.

55. See Patte's diagram in *What Is Structural Exegesis?*, 51; cf. Greimas, *Du Sens*, 198.

56. The fact that Greimas and Patte set the model up this way reinforces my personal inclination to think of the attribution function as defining a syntagm in its own right, separate from and subsequent to the performance syntagm. Since, however, we are not attempting here to refine the theoretical model, we need not pause over this problem of definition. The model as set forth is entirely suitable to illuminate the substantive issues with which we will be concerned.

initial sequence	topical sequence				final sequence
	contract	disjunction/ conjunction	performance	attribution	

Figure 5: A simplified model of narrative structure

detail with which the topical sequence is usually manifested in the actual telling of stories.

5. The Actantial Model

Throughout the discussion so far, we have referred to agents, or characters, in the narrative model in terms of stereotyped role-designations: protagonist, adversary, and so forth. At this point, we will introduce a formal schema for classifying these narrative elements. One of Greimas' most important contributions to the study of narrative texts is his exposition of the "actantial model," which attempts to define a constant network of relations among the "actants" (agents and objects) of the story.[57] According to this theory, any narrative sequence presupposes or manifests six actantial roles or positions. These may be occupied by human characters, but objects or abstract values or qualities may also fill actantial positions. The actantial roles may be described briefly as follows.

(a) The *Sender* is the figure who establishes the mandate in the contract syntagm.
(b) The *Subject* is the figure who receives the mandate. (The Subject is usually called, in the language of literary criticism, the hero or protagonist.)
(c) The *Object* is the thing or quality that the Sender wants to communicate to someone.
(d) The *Receiver* is the figure to whom the Sender wants to communicate the object.
(e) The *Opponent* is the figure or force that seeks to prevent the Subject from carrying out the mandate.

57. See *Sémantique structurale*, 173-82, and *Du Sens*, 249-70.

(f) The *Helper* is the figure or force that aids the Subject in carrying out the mandate.

The interrelation of these actants is represented diagrammatically in Figure 6.

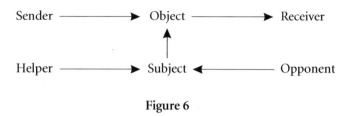

Figure 6

In this arrangement, the top line (Subject→Object→Receiver) is called the "axis of communication," because it represents the Sender's act of communication of the object to the Receiver. The bottom line (Helper→Subject←Opponent) is called the "axis of power"; it represents the story's conflict, played out in the performance syntagm, in which the success or failure of the Subject is determined by the relative power of the Helper and the opponent. If the opponent is too strong, the Subject will fail to carry out the mission, and the communication of the Object to the Receiver will not occur. If, on the other hand, the Helper is stronger than the Opponent, the Subject will succeed in his task, and the attribution function (the communication of the Object to the Receiver) will be carried out.

It must be emphasized that the actantial model presents not a cross-section of the action at any particular point within the narrative sequence but a *stereoscopic* view of the sequence as a whole. Since the actantial model diagrams the relations among the actants within a narrative sequence, it follows that for each narrative sequence there is one and only one investment of the actantial structure. When different characters occupy the actantial positions (for example, if we encounter a new Subject), this is a sign that a new sequence has begun.

Greimas offers as one illustration of the actantial model the story of the quest for the Holy Grail.[58] Here the Subject is "heros" and the Object is the Holy Grail. The Sender is God and the Receiver is Humanity. Within this complex legend there are various Helpers and Opponents. This is a use-

---

58. *Sémantique structurale,* 178. Scholes (*Structuralism in Literature,* 105-6) raises some theoretical questions about this illustration.

ful example because it illustrates the fact that the Receiver need not be a particular character in the story but can be instead a corporate entity such as "humanity."

The actantial model is, of course, only one aspect of the narrative structure, but it can serve as a useful analytical tool for exposing the network of relations manifested in a sequence. Consider the following two actantial structures in Figure 7, one based on the Exodus sequence already described above and the other based on Shakespeare's *Hamlet*.

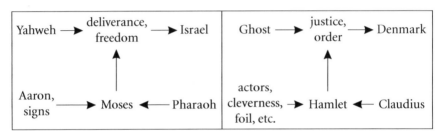

Figure 7: Actantial structures based on Exodus and *Hamlet*

These illustrations call to our attention a number of significant matters. First of all, in both cases the Object is not a concrete "thing" manifested in the story but a value or state of being which might be described in various ways; that is why I have suggested in each case two different terms to characterize it. Secondly, in each case there are multiple Helpers. In the case of *Hamlet*, the identification of the Helpers is a complex matter, because, as in most complex stories, there are many of them. The Helpers that I have singled out here serve to illustrate the point that, in terms of Greimas' analysis, the Helper can appear in the form of other characters (acting troupe), inanimate objects (the foil), or even qualities of the Subject (Hamlet's cleverness).[59] Finally, these illustrations demonstrate how even very elaborate narrative sequences can be allusively summarized by simple references to the figures that occupy these fundamental actantial roles. The actantial model provides a synchronic picture of action which is manifested diachronically in the telling of a story; this means that the actantial structure of a sequence is closely akin to the *dianoia* described by Northrop Frye, because it offers a retrospective overview of the sequence seen as a unity. Thus, if my hypothesis is correct, we should find

59. See Calloud, *Structural Analysis of Narrative*, 31; cf. Patte, *What Is Structural Exegesis?*, 42-43.

Paul, in his argumentative recapitulations of the gospel story, writing summary sentences that manifest an obvious actantial structure.

6. Interrelation of the Model's Components

We have now sketched the essential components of our model for narrative structure. Before starting to apply it, however, we must point out some important aspects of the model which are not always sufficiently emphasized and which will be crucial for our understanding of Galatians.

First, we must emphasize the relation of the topical sequence to the correlated sequences. In a coherent story, the topical sequence is not an unrelated tale arbitrarily sandwiched as an interlude between two other sequences that express frustration and fulfillment; on the contrary, it serves a definite purpose in advancing the movement and *logic* of the story. The purpose of the topical sequence is to reestablish the possibility that the unfulfilled contract of the initial sequence be carried to completion.[60]

Secondly, it is necessary to grasp clearly the relationship between the actantial model and the structure of the narrative sequences. Each sequence presents one and only one actualization of the actantial model. Thus, the basic narrative structure could be diagrammed as a succession of three actantial structures, as in Figure 8.

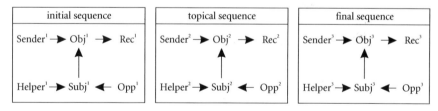

Figure 8: The basic narrative structure as a succession of three actantial structures

This depiction, however, is somewhat misleading because it fails to represent the fact that the final sequence is always the fulfillment of an aborted initial sequence. This means that the initial and final sequences (the correlated sequences) will always manifest (with one important exception which we must discuss in a moment) the *same* actualization of the actantial positions: the

---

60. See Patte, *What Is Structural Exegesis?*, 50.

same Subject who was unable to fulfill the "contract" of the initial sequence is now enabled, as a result of the transactions effected in the topical sequence, to succeed, so that the intended Object can now be communicated to the originally designated Receiver.

How does the topical sequence accomplish this purpose? What change is effected in order to enable the Subject of the initial sequence to fulfill the initial contract? In many stories, the answer is that this Subject must receive a new Helper. The initial contract was thwarted because the Subject had no Helper adequate to counteract the power of the Opponent. Thus, in this type of story pattern, the *purpose* of the topical sequence is to communicate to the initial Subject an Object which can become an adequate Helper.[61]

This can be diagrammed through some modifications of the structure presented in Figure 8. Notice, in Figure 9, that the Subject of the correlated sequences (here designated as X) is the same as the Receiver of the topical sequence. The Object of the topical sequence (Y) becomes the Helper of the final sequence. The resultant interlocking network of relations may be illustrated as follows.

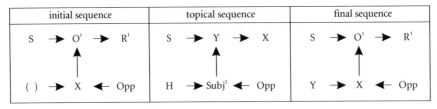

initial sequence	topical sequence	final sequence
S → O¹ → R¹	S → Y → X	S → O¹ → R¹
( ) → X ← Opp	H → Subj² ← Opp	Y → X ← Opp

Figure 9

The Sender and Opponent may or may not be the same in the topical sequence as in the correlated sequences.

Does the structure sketched in Figure 9 apply to all narratives? Though some might wish to argue that it does apply universally, we may be content with the observation that this structure is an exceedingly common one and that it provides a readily discernible narrative "logic" which relates the sequences in a coherent manner. In stories of this type (i.e., stories in which the initial sequence is interrupted because of the lack of a Helper), if we know how the actantial roles are filled in the topical sequence, we already know a good deal about the structure of the final sequence. The logic of the narrative

61. Ibid., 50-51. Cf. Calloud, *Structural Analysis of Narrative*, 33.

structure requires the Receiver of the topical sequence to become the Subject of the final sequence. This fact has never particularly engaged the attention of structuralist critics, but it will prove to be of considerable importance for our analysis of the logic of Paul's argumentation.

It must be reiterated that the narrative model described here is not necessarily applicable to all stories. It will serve us only insofar as it aptly renders an account of the narrative elements in the Pauline text. We must now return to the text of Galatians and see whether the model applies.

C. Analysis of the Narrative Structure of Gal 4:3-6 and 3:13-14

1. Gal 4:3-6

The formulation in Gal 4:3-6, which has frequently been singled out as a confessional formula (as we have already indicated), has been a hotly contested interpretive battleground. Critics who stress the centrality of mythic components in Paul's thought point to the sending of a preexistent Son of God into the world as a thoroughly mythological motif;[62] on the other hand, tenacious proponents of *Heilsgeschichte* have argued that precisely this text demonstrates the centrality of historical events in Paul's thinking, because this "Son of God" was "born of woman, born under law."[63] We do not propose here to become involved in this argument. The important point for our present purpose is that both of these critical approaches recognize in these few verses a formulation that tells a story, or a piece of one.

Throughout the discussion that follows, the reader must bear in mind the considerations developed in Chapter I about the relationship between story and reflective discourse. The necessary presuppositions of our investigation are that a reflective discourse may be rooted in and shaped by a story and that an author's attempt to expound the *dianoia* of a story will necessarily include allusions to and manifestations of its mythos. Thus, the task of the present investigation is to identify allusions and manifestations of this sort in the text of Galatians and to map them coherently within the framework of the narrative model.

---

62. Bousset, *Kyrios Christos*, 206-10; Bultmann, "Neues Testament und Mythologie," 15; cf. idem, *Theology*, 1.175-76, 295, 304-5.

63. See, for example, Mussner (*Galaterbrief*, 269). This argument is developed to its fullest extent by Dunn (*Christology in the Making*, 42-44), who then, however, shies away from affirming it unequivocally.

When we start looking for the narrative structure of Gal 4:3-6, we can see at once that the initial sequence is clearly though briefly manifested in verse 3: οὕτως καὶ ἡμεῖς, ὅτε ἦμεν νήπιοι, ὑπὸ τὰ στοιχεῖα τοῦ κόσμου ἤμεθα δεδουλωμένοι. The story opens at a point at which the initial sequence has already been suspended. The Subject (ἡμεῖς) has already been enslaved by the Opponent (τὰ στοιχεῖα), and the contract (the receiving of our inheritance? cf. 3:15-18 and 3:29–4:2) remains unfulfilled. Thus a "situation of lack" is created, necessitating a topical sequence, which begins with 4:4.

> ὅτε δὲ ἦλθεν τὸ πλήρωμα τοῦ χρόνου
> ἐξαπέστειλεν ὁ θεὸς τὸν υἱὸν αὐτοῦ

This is the contract syntagm of the topical sequence. God is manifested in the actantial position of Sender, and "his Son," as the one who is sent, accepts a mandate and assumes the role of Subject. The nature and purpose of his mission will be explained presently. First, however, we must consider the function of the paired participial phrases in 4:4b.

> γενόμενον ἐκ γυναικός
> γενόμενον ὑπὸ νόμον

There are two ways to understand the function of these phrases in the narrative structure, depending on the meaning that is assigned to the participle γενόμενον. They could be taken merely as "qualifications" of the Subject, i.e., statements that describe a state of being rather than an action. In this case, they would simply provide additional information about the Subject. On the other hand, if the participle expresses a narrative action, a change in the Subject's circumstances ("being born of a woman, becoming subject to the Law"), these phrases could be taken as the disjunction/conjunction syntagm of the topical sequence: the Son of God leaves his heavenly environment (disjunction) and enters the network of earthly relations (conjunction). In this case, the participial phrases should be understood to be structurally analogous to Phil 2:7.

> ἀλλὰ ἑαυτὸν ἐκένωσεν
> μορφὴν δούλου λαβών
> ἐν ὁμοιώματι ἀνθρώπων γενόμενος

This is surely the more satisfactory way of construing the text, because it accounts for the use of γενόμενον rather than ὄντα.[64] In Gal 4:4b, just as in

64. E. DeW. Burton (*A Critical and Exegetical Commentary on the Epistle to the*

Phil 2:7, the participle γενόμενος indicates movement rather than state of being; it narrates the entry of the Son of God into human affairs.

Next, in two ἵνα clauses, the nature of the mission (= substance of the topical contract) is spelled out.

ἵνα τοὺς ὑπὸ νόμον ἐξαγοράσῃ
ἵνα τὴν υἱοθεσίαν ἀπολάβωμεν

It is important to notice that, formally speaking, these purpose clauses, with their verbs in the subjunctive mood, do not actually manifest the performance syntagm. They describe the purpose of the Son of God's mission rather than narrating his fulfillment of the task, and therefore they actually belong to the contract syntagm rather than to the performance syntagm. This fact may help to explain why there is no reference here to Christ's death, which belongs to the performance syntagm of the sequence. Paul certainly knows/assumes that the mission (= the contract of the topical sequence) has been fulfilled by Christ, but he does not explicitly say so in Gal 4:5. We must remember that Paul is recapitulating the story by means of allusion, not narrating it anew. His readers already know the story.[65] Thus, Paul omits the performance syntagm here, though we may (indeed, *must*) infer its successful issue because 4:6 presupposes it.

In any case, 4:5 provides a good deal of information about the actants of the topical sequence. In 4:5a, we find that the object communicated is redemption (= freedom; cf. 5:1) and the Receivers[66] are τοὺς ὑπὸ νόμον. This way of describing the Receivers implies that the opponent is νόμος and that, furthermore, νόμος may somehow be equated with τὰ στοιχεῖα τοῦ κόσμου (4:3).[67] In 4:5b, "we" are the Receivers, and the Object is ἡ υἱοθεσία. If we as-

---

Galatians [ICC; Edinburgh: T. & T. Clark, 1920] 218-19) opts for an "attributive" interpretation of the participial phrases, so that they are taken to characterize the Son's nature. On the other hand, Schlier (*Galater,* 196) and A. Oepke (*Der Brief des Paulus an die Galater* [3rd ed.; THKNT 9; Berlin: Evangelische Verlagsanstalt, 1973] 132) offer interpretations which give to γενόμενον its due weight and thus support the interpretation offered here. The parallel to the use of γενόμενος in Phil 2:7 is strangely overlooked by the commentaries, with the exception of M.-J. Lagrange (*Saint Paul Épître aux Galates* [2nd ed.; Paris; Gabalda, 1925] 102).

65. Cf. Gal 3:1: Ὦ ἀνόητοι Γαλάται . . . οἷς κατ' ὀφθαλμοὺς Ἰησοῦς Χριστὸς προεγράφη ἐσταυρωμένος.

66. Technically, the structuralists would require us to say, "the Receiver *is* τοὺς ὑπὸ νόμον," since "Receiver" is not a character, but an actant, i.e., a syntactical value. I nonetheless use the plural here and in similar sentences in the interest of felicitous English expression.

67. This equation provokes, of course, a notorious interpretive problem, which we can only acknowledge here, leaving a discussion of it for Chapter V. Paul's attitude toward the

sume, with the majority of commentators, that the ἵνα-clauses are coordinate, both dependent on the verb ἐξαπέστειλεν, we are still left with the question of whether Paul means to describe a single transaction in two different ways (so that redemption = adoption and τοὺς ὑπὸ νόμον = "we") or whether he has in mind two different attributions that are to result from the Son of God's action. The surprising but clear distinction between "those under law" and "we" favors the latter interpretation, and we shall adopt it as a working hypothesis.

We can now diagram the actantial structure of the topical sequence, as shown in Figure 10.

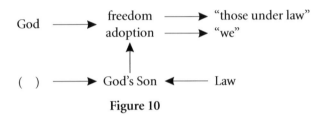

Figure 10

The actantial position of Helper is left unfilled because no Helper is mentioned in Paul's brief summary. Again, this omission may be partly attributable to the fact that he does not "tell" the performance syntagm explicitly in these verses.

But now we must consider the relation of verse 6 to the narrative structure: ὅτι δέ ἐστε υἱοί, ἐξαπέστειλεν ὁ θεὸς τὸ πνεῦμα τοῦ υἱοῦ αὐτοῦ εἰς τὰς καρδίας ἡμῶν. . . .[68] Is this the final sequence of the story, or is it the culminating narrative statement in the "attribution" phase of the topical sequence's performance syntagm?

Actually, this is a new way of asking an old question. Commentators have long debated whether Paul means to describe the sending of the Spirit as a second action of God subsequent to redemption and adoption, or whether the sending of the Spirit is part of a single "package" along with redemption

---

Law is far from unambiguous. For the moment, however, restricting ourselves to an analysis of the narrative structure as manifested in Gal 4:3-6, we may designate Law the Opponent, while recognizing that further consideration of this problem will be necessary later on.

68. There is, of course, a textual problem here; some later manuscripts read ὑμῶν in place of ἡμῶν, "thus conforming the person of the pronoun to the earlier ἐστε" (B. M. Metzger, *A Textual Commentary on the Greek New Testament* [New York: United Bible Societies, 1971] 595). The strange variation between first and second person pronouns in this passage may be further evidence that Paul is here quoting traditional material.

and adoption. The issue sometimes gets blurry in the course of the various critical attempts — many of which are pursuing particular dogmatic agendas — to solve this problem, but the opposite poles are clear enough. Some exegetes, such as Schlier and Oepke, come out unequivocally in favor of a two-step process: first we receive "sonship," then, subsequently, the Spirit is given. "Seine zweite Liebestat grundet in der ersten und setzt sie fort."[69] On the other hand, some exegetes, in an effort to avoid this sort of interpretation, appeal to parallels in Rom 8:9, 15 and produce a labored translation which renders ὅτι as "that" and treats the rest of the sentence as elliptical: "But that you are sons (you can see from this fact): God sent forth the Spirit of his Son. . . ."[70] Burton rightly judges that this sort of rendering "introduces unwarranted complication into a sentence which is on its face complete and simple."[71]

John Calvin achieved a more balanced exegetical result with less violence to the text simply by observing that here Paul reasons from the effect to the cause: "(Why did God send the Spirit?) God sent the Spirit because you are sons." Thus Calvin takes ὅτι in its most obvious sense here, as meaning "because," and acknowledges that "adoption by God precedes the testimony of adoption given by the Holy Spirit." At the same time, however, he is able to recognize that the *purpose* of Paul's argument is to convince the Galatians, on the basis of their indisputable experience of the Holy Spirit, that they really *are* God's sons: "Therefore it is certain that you are the sons of God."[72] This interpretation ties in nicely with Gal 3:2-5, because in both cases Paul appeals to the Galatians' experience of the Spirit as the fundamental datum on the basis of which he seeks to draw inferences. Calvin's line of interpretation, which has been followed also by Lightfoot, Burton, and Betz,[73] thus does justice to the text and to the fundamental concerns of the opposed exegetical positions described above.

But the narrative model can now provide further reinforcement for Calvin's position by posing the question in different terms. Is the Spirit the Object of the final sequence or of the topical sequence? On the basis of the principles articulated above and summarized in Figure 9, we already know that

69. Schlier, *Galater*, 197; cf. Oepke, *Galater*, 133.

70. This interpretation is offered by H. Lietzmann (*An die Galater* (3rd ed.; HNT 10; Tübingen: J. C. B. Mohr (Paul Siebeck), 1932] 27) and by Lagrange (*Galates*, 103-4).

71. Burton, *Galatians*, 222.

72. J. Calvin, *The Epistles of Paul the Apostle to the Galatians, Ephesians, Philippians and Colossians* (Calvin's Commentaries; Edinburgh: Oliver and Boyd, 1965) 75.

73. Lightfoot, *Galatians*, 169; Burton, *Galatians*, 221-22; Betz, *Galatians*, 209-10. Interestingly none of them cites Calvin in support of his position.

the Subject of the final sequence must be "we," because "we" occupied the role of Subject in the initial sequence (4:3) and the role of Receiver in the topical sequence (4:5). That means that, if the Spirit is the Object of the final sequence, the purpose of the topical sequence must have been to enable us — now having received adoption — to obtain the Spirit for ourselves. In other words, if 4:6 manifests the final sequence of the story, then "we" must occupy the roles both of Subject and of Receiver in the actantial structure of this sequence. Diagrammatically this structure would be represented by Figure 11.

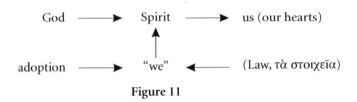

Figure 11

In terms of the narrative grammar, this is not an "ungrammatical" construction; it belongs to the set of theoretically possible sequences, because the same personage can sometimes be both Subject and Receiver.[74] However, it is highly questionable whether such a sequence is thinkable for *Paul*, for whom the Spirit is conceived as a gift rather than as a prize acquired through human volition and action (cf. 3:2). The fact that Gal 4:6 presents "us" in the role of Receiver surely creates a strong presumption that we are still dealing here with PS3 of the topical sequence: the sign and culmination of the gifts (Objects!) communicated to us through Christ's action is the Spirit. If this interpretation is correct, our representation of the actantial structure of the topical sequence may be completed as shown in Figure 12.

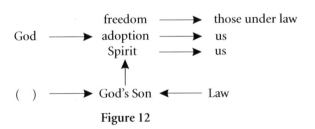

Figure 12

74. Calloud, *Structural Analysis of Narrative*, 33-34.

This means, however, that we come to the end of Paul's recapitulation of the story without encountering any actualization of the final sequence. This should not surprise us, for several reasons. First of all, we have already pointed out that it is not unusual for a narration to leave the final sequence of the narrative structure implied rather than articulated. Secondly, Paul is alluding to and commenting upon the story rather than telling it to people who are unfamiliar with it; hence, we do not expect his remarks to retell the whole story. Finally, Paul has not yet reached the point in his argument where he wants to elaborate on the final sequence; this phase of the argument will begin in Galatians 5.

We can, however, on the basis of the transformational principles sketched above, propose that Paul's gospel story must move toward a final sequence in which the following actantial structure will appear.

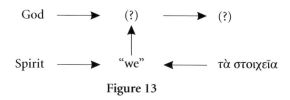

Figure 13

Caution is demanded here: this diagram, which is full of unknowns in any case, is purely an extrapolation, based on the narrative model developed in the earlier part of this chapter. We have not yet encountered any statements in the text of Galatians that actualize this structure. But *if* Paul's thinking is indeed shaped by or based upon a story, and *if* our narrative model is applicable to this story, then we should find some evidence in the text of Galatians that the story does indeed move toward a conclusion that will correspond to the actantial configuration of Figure 13, toward a conclusion, in other words, in which believers become the Subject of the story's action with the Spirit as their Helper.

We may now summarize our analysis of the narrative structure that is manifested in Gal 4:3-6. The initial sequence is briefly evoked in verse 3: "we" were enslaved by the στοιχεῖα; thus, the initial contract (the precise nature of which we have not yet been able to determine) remained unfulfilled. But God dealt with this predicament in the story's central action (topical sequence) by sending forth his Son to bring redemption to those under the Law (= Jews), adoption to "us" = Gentiles) and the gift of the Spirit to all who are "sons" (= Jews and Gentiles together). (In Gal 4:3-6 we are not told *how* the Son accomplishes this mission.) This structure implies but does not articulate a final sequence in which those who have received the Spirit become protagonists in their own story, overcoming the Opponent that once enslaved them. The findings of our analysis are represented in Figure 14 (on p. 103).

2. Gal 3:13-14

When we begin an analysis of the christological formulation that appears in Gal 3:13-14, we discover that we have plunged directly into the topical sequence of the gospel story-structure: Χριστὸς ἡμᾶς ἐξηγόρασεν ἐκ τῆς κατάρας τοῦ νόμου. Unlike the parallel formulation in Gal 4:5, this is not couched as a contract statement; with the aorist indicative verb ἐξηγόρασεν, this is a "performance statement" summarizing the successfully completed action of the performance syntagm. Whereas ὁ υἱός appears as the direct object of the main verb's action (i.e., God's action) in 4:4, Paul here uses Χριστὸς as the subject of the verb in the main clause of the formulation; this difference is due to the fact that the narrative statement of 3:13 expresses a different "canonical function" in the topical sequence of the narrative structure: while 4:4 manifests the "mandating/acceptance" function (CS1: the Subject is given a mission), 3:13 manifests the logically subsequent "domination/submission" function (PS2: the Subject acts and overcomes the Opponent). The difference between the titles "Son of God" and "Christ," whatever their historical origin, is of no importance for our analysis of the story-structure, because Paul uses them synonymously, as different names for the same person.

The participial phrase γενόμενος ὑπὲρ ἡμῶν κατάρα, unlike the formally parallel phrases in 4:4, is not a disjunction/conjunction syntagm. Paul's parenthetical citation (or, rather, paraphrase) of Deut 21:23 shows that Christ "became a curse" not through leaving his preexistent blessedness and entering the network of human relations but very specifically through and in his crucifixion. If one follows the RSV in ascribing temporal force to the 2nd aorist participle ("Christ redeemed us from the curse of the law, *having become a curse for us. . . .*") so that its action is conceived as chronologically prior to the action of the main verb (ἐξηγόρασεν), then the phrase could be understood as a manifestation of the "confrontation" function (PS1: the Subject encounters the Opponent). Theologically, it may be attractive to think of the cross as the point at which the decisive confrontation occurs between Christ and the curse, or power, of the Law, but grammatically the aorist participle need not have the significance of expressing an action temporally antecedent

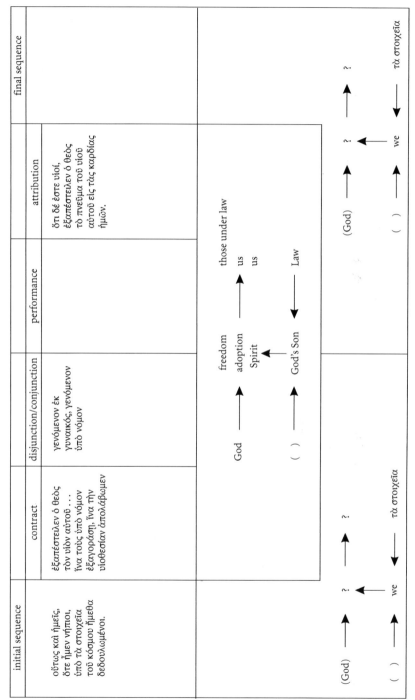

Figure 14: The narrative structure of Gal 4:3-6

103

to the main verb.[75] In this particular case, it should probably be taken in a modal sense, explaining *how* Christ achieved the result described in the main clause of the sentence: "Christ redeemed us from the curse of the Law by becoming a curse for us. . . ."[76] Thus, 3:13 does not relate discrete events in chronological succession (first Christ became a curse for us, then he redeemed us from the curse of the law); instead it summarizes the action of the performance syntagm, seen as a whole. In Frye's terminology, we can say that 3:13 presents the *dianoia* of the Christ-story rather than recounting its *mythos*.

The ἵνα-clauses in 3:14 manifest the "attribution" function that concludes the performance syntagm of the topical sequence.

ἵνα εἰς τὰ ἔθνη ἡ εὐλογία τοῦ Ἀβραὰμ γένηται ἐν Χριστῷ Ἰησοῦ.
ἵνα τὴν ἐπαγγελίαν τοῦ πνεύματος λάβωμεν διὰ τῆς πίστεως.

Strictly speaking, since these clauses state the *purpose* of the main action, they are not statements which narrate the completion of the contract; however, just as in 4:4-6, the entire context compels us to infer that the sequence was a successful one.

As in the case of 4:4-6, we are able to construct a virtually complete actantial model for the sequence that is manifested in 3:13-14. Christ is the Subject, and the Opponent is "the curse of the Law." In 3:13 the Object is redemption (= freedom) and the Receivers are "us." In 3:14a the object is "the blessing of Abraham" and the Receivers are "the Gentiles." In 3:14b the object is "the promise of the Spirit" (= the Spirit) and the Receivers are "we." Thus, just as in 4:5-6, we have three objects and three Receivers.

God ⟶ freedom ⟶ us (= Jews)
God ⟶ blessing of Abraham ⟶ Gentiles
God ⟶ Spirit ⟶ us

Here, as in 4:5-6, the final "us" includes Jews and Gentiles together.[77] There is no explicit manifestation of the actantial role of Sender in Gal 3:13-14, but

75. See *BDF* §339, pp. 174-75. Cf. A. T. Robertson, *A Grammar of the Greek New Testament in the Light of Historical Research* (Nashville: Broadman, 1934) 1113-14.

76. Cf. *NEB*: "Christ bought us freedom from the curse of the law by becoming for our sake an accursed thing."

77. If, as Dahl suggests, vv. 13-14a are a unit of traditional material quoted here by Paul, then v. 14b is Paul's own explanatory summary.

clearly, for Paul, God remains in this role. It is *God* who sends the blessing of Abraham upon the Gentiles (cf. 3:8) and God who gives the Spirit (cf. 3:5 and 4:6). All of this is exhibited in Figure 15.

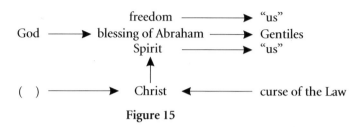

Figure 15

But this sketch of the actants leaves out one very important element that appears in 3:14. Here we find a phrase that is of central importance in Paul's gospel, a phrase which has no parallel in 4:4-6: διὰ τῆς πίστεως. Now we must ask a crucial question: what role does πίστις play within the narrative structure that we have described so far? To pose the question in these terms is already to suggest the answer: πίστις fills the heretofore vacant actantial role of Helper. (It is important to remember that according to the narrative model the Helper need not be a person or character but can be an inanimate thing or even a quality of the Subject.) "Christ redeemed us from the curse of the Law . . . in order that we might receive the Spirit διὰ τῆς πίστεως." Christ's mission of delivering freedom, blessing, and the Spirit to humanity is achieved through the aid of πίστις; thus, πίστις fills the role of Helper. This bare statement leaves many questions unanswered. What does πίστις mean? *How* does it help in the fulfillment of the narrative program? These questions cannot be answered on the basis of Gal 3:13-14 alone, and they will have to be pursued in Chapter IV below. At this point in our analysis of the narrative structure, πίστις appears as an allusion whose function is clear but whose content and meaning remain to be elucidated. We may now complete our depiction of the actantial structure of Gal 3:13-14 in Figure 16.

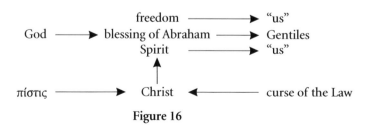

Figure 16

What conclusions are yielded by our analysis of the narrative structure manifested in Gal 3:13-14? Gal 3:13 picks up the thread of the gospel story precisely at its climactic point, alluding to and summarizing Christ's completion of his mission. In terms of the narrative model, this action comprises the performance syntagm of the topical sequence. Gal 3:14 then spells out in some detail the attribution functions that follow from Christ's faithful execution of the "contract": the "blessing of Abraham" accrues to the Gentiles, and Jews and Gentiles together receive the Spirit, with πίστις somehow functioning as the facilitator of this consummation. The formulation in verses 13-14, taken by itself, does not manifest either an initial or a final sequence; all the attention here is focused on the topical sequence. Thus, we may sketch these findings into the narrative model in Figure 17.

initial sequence	topical sequence				final sequence
	contract	disjunction/ conjunction	performance	attribution	
			Χριστὸς ἡμᾶς ἐξηγόρασεν ἐκ τῆς κατάρας τοῦ νόμου γενόμενος ὑπὲρ ἡμῶν κατάρα.	ἵνα εἰς τὰ ἔθνη ἡ εὐλογία τοῦ Ἀβραὰμ γένηται ἐν Χριστῷ Ἰησοῦ, ἵνα τὴν ἐπαγγελίαν τοῦ πνεύματος λάβωμεν διὰ τῆς πίστεως.	

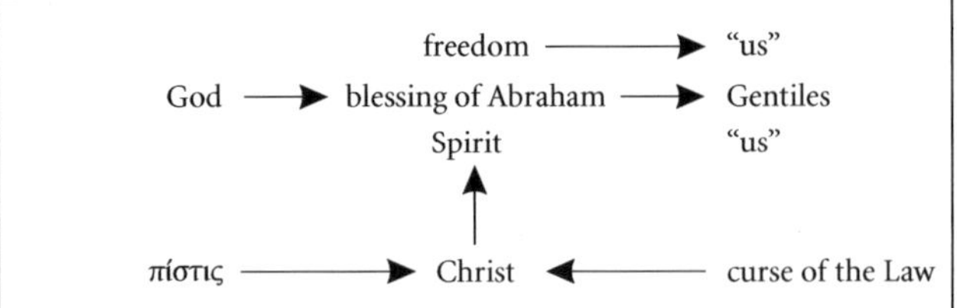

freedom ────────► "us"

God ──► blessing of Abraham ──► Gentiles

Spirit "us"

↑

πίστις ────────► Christ ◄──────── curse of the Law

Figure 17: The narrative structure of Gal 3:13-14

D. The Relationship between Gal 4:3-6 and 3:13-14: Some Conclusions

Having analyzed the narrative structure of the two christological formulations in Gal 4:3-6 and 3:13-14, we may now draw some conclusions about their relationship to one another. Clearly, 4:3-6 offers a somewhat fuller actualization of the narrative structure. But, once we realize that 3:13-14 manifests only part of the topical sequence of the gospel story, we are enabled to correlate the parallels between the texts appropriately and to recognize their striking similarity. The correspondence between them may readily be demonstrated by reproducing together (in Fig. 18) the two topical-sequence actantial models already derived separately for the two formulations in Figures 12 and 16.

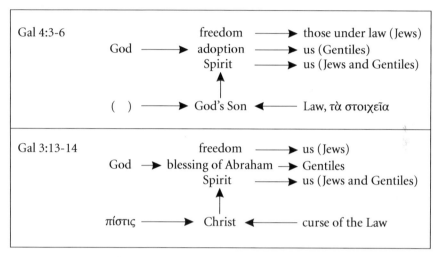

Figure 18: Topical sequence actantial structures of Gal 4:3-6 and 3:13-14

It would be belaboring the obvious to demonstrate point by point that we are dealing here with two tellings ("performance manifestations") of the same story. Two matters of particular interest may, however, be emphasized in the comparison of these actantial structures. First of all, the parallelism suggests that "the blessing of Abraham" is equivalent to "adoption." This is an observation that will prove useful in our efforts to trace the logic of Paul's argumentation in Chapter V below. Secondly, we may note that in both formulations the Receivers appear in the following order: (1) Jews, (2) Gentiles, (3) "us" (Jews and Gentiles together). However, the two formulations tell the story from different points of view: in Gal 4:5 "we" means the Gentiles, whereas in 3:13 "us" means the Jews. This observation might indeed lend support to the view that Paul is here citing traditional formulations that come from Gentile and Jewish-Christian communities, respectively. But we might equally well suppose that Paul for rhetorical purposes alternately identifies himself with these two different constituencies;[78] this possibility should be taken seriously, especially in light of Paul's explicit statement in 1 Cor 9:20-21 that he was indeed self-consciously capable of such switches in identification.[79] It is impossible to decide between these two possibilities on the basis of narrative structure alone. We can only say that one formulation tells the story from a Gentile point of view and that the other tells it from a Jewish point of view. The important thing to be stressed is that the different points of view entail no contradiction or "discrepancy." The pattern is the same in both cases: Christ's action enables the Jews to receive redemption, the Gentiles to receive blessing/adoption, and Jews and Gentiles alike to receive the Spirit. Furthermore, in both cases the formulation moves from an initial division between "us" and "them" toward a final inclusive "we" which makes no distinction between Jew and Gentile, and in both cases this movement is associated with the gift of the Spirit. Clearly, the "logic" of this narrative pattern is closely interrelated with the overall logic of Paul's argument in the letter.

At this point we may reassess Blank's attempt to demonstrate the parallelism between the two passages (see part A.1 above). In light of our analysis, we may now conclude that Blank, along with those who have accepted his arguments, is misled by a surface-level syntactical parallelism into matching up the elements of the formulations in a semantically inappropriate manner, with the result that his attempt to outline the material parallelism between the two passages turns out to be very general and somewhat forced. Actually, the content of the formulations demands that their components be outlined as in the diagram on page 109. This way of setting forth the comparison between the two passages not only clarifies the narrative logic which binds them together but also provides a basis for dealing with the most significant discrepancy that is alleged to exist between them. We have already seen that critics such as Betz and Lohse interpret the absence of any reference to Christ's death in 4:4-5 to mean that this formulation embodies a christology in which Christ's death is of no soteriological import. If, however, both formulations serve for Paul as al-

---

78. Betz's commentary opens up vast new fields for inquiry concerning the relationship between Paul's letters and the rhetorical conventions of his time. Cf. also W. Wuellner, "Paul's Rhetoric of Argumentation in Romans," *The Romans Debate*, 152-74. The case under consideration in this paragraph illustrates in an interesting way the need for carefully controlled comparative studies, because the same evidence here may be construed either as evidence of "traditional" formulae or as evidence of rhetorical artifice. One recent study which makes an attempt to begin sorting out problems of this kind is S. K. Stowers (*The Diatribe and Paul's Letter to the Romans* [SBLDS 57; Chico: Scholars, 1981]).

79. Of particular interest here is Paul's remark that he himself is not ὑπὸ νόμον. Indeed, 1 Cor 9:20 offers an extremely interesting parallel to Gal 4:4d-5a.

Gal 4:3-6	Gal 3:13-14
a) ἐξαπέστειλεν ὁ θεὸς τὸν υἱὸν αὐτοῦ	a)
b¹) γενόμενον ἐκ γυναικός	b¹)
b²) γενόμενον ὑπὸ νόμον	b²)
c) ἵνα τοὺς ὑπὸ νόμον ἐξαγοράσῃ	c) Χριστὸς ἡμᾶς ἐξηγόρασεν ἐκ τῆς κατάρας τοῦ νόμου
d)	d) γενόμενος ὑπὲρ ἡμῶν κατάρα
e) ἵνα τὴν υἱοθεσίαν ἀπολάβωμεν	e) ἵνα εἰς τὰ ἔθνη ἡ εὐλογία τοῦ Ἀβραὰμ γένηται ἐν Χριστῷ Ἰησοῦ
f) ἐξαπέστειλεν ὁ θεὸς τὸ πνεῦμα τοῦ υἱοῦ αὐτοῦ εἰς τὰς καρδίας ἡμῶν	f) ἵνα τὴν ἐπαγγελίαν τοῦ πνεύματος λάβωμεν διὰ τῆς πίστεως

lusions to the narrative pattern that we have described here, then the absence of an explicit reference to Christ's crucifixion and death (component d in the above outline) in Gal 4:3-6 is of no particular importance, because any allusion to a part of the story presupposes the story as a whole. This point may be illustrated by projecting the two formulations together into a single actualization of the narrative structure model (Fig. 19 on p. 110). That this projection is not an arbitrary "harmonization" is demonstrated clearly by the close correspondence between the content of the contract syntagm, derived from 4:4-5, and the content of the performance and attribution syntagms, derived primarily from 3:13-14, as well as from 4:6. The two formulations fit together like pieces of a jigsaw puzzle to form a single coherent story outline. Thus, in the context of Galatians, in which 4:4-5 is preceded not only by 3:13-14 but also by references to Christ's crucifixion and/or death in 1:1, 1:4, 2:20, 2:21, and 3:1, it is unthinkable to read the christological formulation in 4:4-5 without recognizing that here also Paul certainly presupposes Christ's death as the central action in the gospel story, although he does not explicitly mention it.

My claim must be carefully defined. Nothing in this analysis necessarily precludes the theory that 4:4-5 might originally have been a piece of independent tradition, and it is even conceivable that this tradition in its pre-Pauline form might have served as an expression of a christology (or, perhaps more aptly, a way of telling the Christ-story) that did not emphasize the salvific efficacy of Christ's death.[80] If so, however, Paul has placed it within a new setting,

---

80. I began this study under the assumption that Gal 4:4-5 was in fact a fragment of

initial sequence	topical sequence				final sequence
	contract	disjunction/ conjunction	performance	attribution	
οὕτως καὶ ἡμεῖς, ὅτε ἦμεν νήπιοι, ὑπὸ τὰ στοιχεῖα τοῦ κόσμου ἤμεθα δεδουλωμένοι (4:3)	ἐξαπέστειλεν ὁ θεὸς τὸν υἱὸν αὐτοῦ . . . ἵνα τοὺς ὑπὸ νόμον ἐξαγοράσῃ ἵνα τὴν υἱοθεσίαν ἀπολάβωμεν (4:4-5)	γενόμενον ἐκ γυναικός, γενόμενον ὑπὸ νόμον (4:4)	Χριστὸς ἡμᾶς ἐξηγόρασεν ἐκ τῆς κατάρας τοῦ νόμου γενόμενος ὑπὲρ ἡμῶν κατάρα (3:13)	ἵνα εἰς τὰ ἔθνη ἡ εὐλογία τοῦ ᾿Αβραὰμ γένηται ἐν Χριστῷ ᾿Ιησοῦ, ἵνα τὴν ἐπαγγελίαν τοῦ πνεύματος λάβωμεν διὰ τῆς πίστεως (3:14) --- ὅτι δέ ἐστε υἱοί, ἐξαπέστειλεν ὁ θεος τὸ πνεῦμα τοῦ υἱοῦ αὐτοῦ εἰς τὰς παρδίας ἡμῶν . . . (4:6)	

Figure 19: A simultaneous projection of Gal 4:3-6 and 3:13-14
into the narrative model

the setting of the gospel story that we have sketched here.[81] Thus, Paul sees no discrepancy between this formulation and the formulation in 3:13-14 because he plots both of them onto the map provided by the structure of the gospel story.

Thus, at least in this case, the narrative structure of the gospel provides the principle of coherence that accounts for the compatibility of theological

---

pre-Pauline tradition; this investigation has substantially undermined my confidence in this assumption, as most of the features which have been thought to mark it off from the "grain" of Paul's thought have been shown to be capable of explanation in other ways.

81. My conclusion here approaches Schweizer's ("Sendungsformel," 209-10), but there is this significant difference: against Schweizer, I would resist the reduction of the meaning and message of Gal 4:4-5 "eindeutig zur Verkündigung des Kreuzes Jesu." I am more nearly in agreement with Burton (*Galatians*, 219), who believes that this text implies that Jesus' "human birth and subjection to law were contributory to the achievement of redemption," and with Kramer (*Christ, Lord, Son of God*, 114), who affirms that "What is envisaged here is neither the death nor the resurrection, nor even simply the birth, but the 'coming' of Jesus, his life viewed as a whole."

formulations which, taken in isolation from one another, might be seen as incompatible. It remains to be seen whether the proposed structure is unique to the formulations from which we have derived it here or whether it is also manifested elsewhere in Galatians.

One further word of clarification might be in order at this point. I do not claim to have discovered some unprecedented interpretation of these texts by applying the esoteric technology of Greimas' narrative model. As I already indicated in the earlier part of this chapter, NT critics have long read the two passages as complementary and mutually illuminating, and, if it is thus with NT critics, how much more for communities of believers from Paul's time to the present! The point is this: commentators and believers alike (and most commentators have been, after all, believers) could read the text this way because they, too, knew the story, because they approached the text as readers whose understanding and expectation were formed by the structure of the gospel story. Thus, they took it for granted that "Christ" was the same person as "God's Son," and that God's sending him forth into the world certainly included, above all else, his crucifixion and resurrection.[82] Given the existence of this organic, living mode of reading the text, what purpose is served by the relatively pedantic exercise of analyzing the text in terms of a theoretical narrative model? Just this: it provides a degree of methodological control, a criterion by which we can assess the intuitive perception that Paul's exposition presupposes a gospel story.

In this chapter, we have sought to test this intuitive perception by examining one particular problem, using the model as an instrument to assess the claim that 4:4-5 presupposes 3:13 (and vice-versa). The analysis has shown that Paul has not artlessly spliced together contradictory christologies, that the two formulations do cohere fitly in the structure of the narrative model. Thus we can demonstrate that, even if these christological formulations have their origins in hypothetical pre-Pauline traditions, they are united, *at the level of Paul's usage of them*, in a single story-structure. To read them in terms of this story, therefore, is not an illegitimate harmonization of fragmentary elements; if there is any harmonization in operation here, it has already occurred *within* the text of Galatians. Hence, contrary to Betz's dictum, our two passages must not be "kept separate"; if we are to understand Paul's meaning they must be kept together as allusions to, or manifestations of, the same gospel story.

---

82. It is interesting that neither formulation mentions the resurrection of Jesus. Should we suppose, then, that both formulations embody traditional christologies for which the resurrection was of no importance?

E. Analysis of the Narrative Structure of Gal 3:21-22

Before leaving our analysis of the narrative structure of the gospel as it is manifested in Galatians 3 and 4, we must consider one more text, which establishes a link between the narrative pattern that we have already discerned and the theological vocabulary of justification.

Gal 3:21b poses a contrary-to-fact condition which plays a crucial role in Paul's argument: εἰ γὰρ ἐδόθη νόμος ὁ δυνάμενος ζῳοποιῆσαι, ὄντως ἐκ νόμου ἂν ἦν ἡ δικαιοσύνη. This sentence sketches concisely a hypothetical alternative gospel,[83] which also may be understood in terms of the narrative structure. In order to understand the structure of this "other gospel," it will be useful to introduce some further theoretical reflections about the actantial model.

Since any narrative, according to Greimas' scheme, embodies a power-clash between two opposing forces, a value decision — or at least an alignment of sympathies[84] — is already implied in the decision to call one the "Subject" and the other the "Opponent."[85] Theoretically, any story could be retold from the opposite orientation. But here some subtlety is required. The Opponent is not simply to be equated with the figure that would become the Subject in such a hypothetical repolarized narrative. Rather, the Opponent is "the 'figuration' of the 'negative power' of a second Subject that Greimas also calls the *anti-subject*."[86] Or, to put it another way, the Opponent is actually the Helper of the anti-Subject. This is spelled out clearly by Calloud.

> If the Opponent is nothing more than the figuration of the inverse power of a symmetrical Subject, it is because the actantial model should be viewed as twofold. A specific model in which the Subject is characterized by the Helper presupposes an anti-model in which the Subject (an anti-Subject) is characterized by the Opponent. It is often useful to reconstitute as in a mirror this inverse model in which each of the actantial positions receives an inverse sign.[87]

Now, if we analyze Gal 3:21 with the aid of the actantial model, we will see that Paul has, in effect, done precisely what Calloud suggests here. He has reconstituted, as in a mirror, the antithesis of the gospel story by raising for rhe-

---

83. Cf. Gal 1:6: ἕτερον εὐαγγέλιον.
84. Greimas uses the term "orientation"; see *Du Sens*, 165.
85. See Greimas' discussion of this point (*Du Sens*, 172-73).
86. Calloud, *Structural Analysis of Narrative*, 31.
87. Ibid., 31-32.

torical purposes the possibility that a life-giving Law might have been provided by God. If this were the case, says Paul, then δικαιοσύνη would be ἐκ νόμου. In this schema, "life" and "righteousness" are virtually equated, as they are pervasively in Paul's thought, and both occupy the actantial role of Object.[88] Νόμος, as the power-source[89] in this hypothetical anti-gospel, functions as the Helper, which is precisely what we should expect on the basis of our newly introduced theoretical considerations, since νόμος occupies the role of Opponent in Paul's "positive" gospel story. Thus we may diagram in Figure 20 (on p. 114) the actantial structure manifested in Gal 3:21b. Neither God nor humanity is explicitly mentioned in the text of 3:21b, of course, but this structure is clearly implied. The passive verb (in this case ἐδόθη) as a circumlocution for divine action is a well-known mannerism of Jewish piety, and it is clear that only God could be the giver of this hypothetical, life-giving law. Likewise, if we ask ourselves "To whom would this law have been given?"

88. Paul's assertion here has about it the ring of a statement that is regarded as self-evident: "If the Law could give life, then righteousness would be (by definition) ἐκ νόμου." This statement seems to belong to the class of statements that Wittgenstein calls "class-two grammatical utterances," i.e., statements which constitute, in Wittgenstein's metaphor, "the scaffolding of our thoughts." See A. Thiselton (*The Two Horizons* [Grand Rapids: Eerdmans, 1980] 392-401) for a discussion of class-two grammatical utterances in the Pauline letters.

89. Notice that the text does *not* say, "If a law had been given which offered a possible means to life. . . ." Instead, it says, "If a law had been given which had the *power to give life*, then δικαιοσύνη would indeed come from the law (ἐκ νόμου)." Righteousness would be ἐκ νόμου if (and only if?) νόμος were an active life-giving power. Cf. Rom 8:3, which also proclaims the "weakness" of the Law, its inability to produce the fulfillment to which it points. This observation suggests an alternative interpretation of Gal 3:21. Is it possible that this "anti-gospel" is also to be equated with the initial sequence of the gospel story? On this view, the Law would be the Helper in the initial sequence, and this sequence would have failed precisely because of the Law's inadequacy, thus necessitating the topical sequence, in which faith achieves what Law could not. This interpretation would comport well with the traditional understanding of Paul's pre-Christian experience as a time of frustrated and futile striving for righteousness under the Law. This understanding has, however, been decisively exploded by the work of K. Stendahl and E. P. Sanders, among others. To their observations we may now add a further argument based on the properties of the narrative structure. The topical sequence does *not* accomplish the unfulfilled goal (contract) of the initial sequence; instead it removes barriers to fulfillment or communicates to the original Subject a new and more adequate Helper. Thus, if the structure that I have designated as an anti-gospel is taken instead to be the initial sequence, this would carry the implication that Christ's work in the topical sequence has not secured life and righteousness for us but only made them a possibility which we still must achieve for ourselves. Clearly, this is not what Paul thought. It does seem to me, however, that the structure which I have sketched for Gal 3:21b could be construed, particularly in light of Rom 8:3, as an *aborted topical sequence*. This approach might prove to be hermeneutically fruitful.

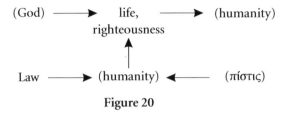

Figure 20

the answer is obviously "humanity," or perhaps "the Jews." This "giving" of a life-empowering Law would then correspond to CS2 (communication/reception), that element in the contract syntagm in which the Subject receives the Helper as empowerment for the task.

All of this is, of course, flatly rejected by Paul, who insists that the Law cannot give life (cf. Rom 8:3ff.) and was never intended to do so. Against the structure of this anti-gospel, Paul juxtaposes in 3:22 another allusive summary of the gospel story's *dianoia*: ἀλλὰ συνέκλεισεν ἡ γραφὴ τὰ πάντα ὑπὸ ἁμαρτίαν ἵνα ἡ ἐπαγγελία ἐκ πίστεως Ἰησοῦ Χριστοῦ δοθῇ τοῖς πιστεύουσιν. The main clause of this sentence corresponds to Gal 4:3 and evokes the initial sequence of the gospel story, in which humanity was powerless, imprisoned, and enslaved.[90] The purpose clause, which is closely parallel to Gal 3:14b, then functions as a concise summary of the topical sequence, whose actantial structure we may diagram as in Figure 21.

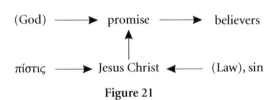

Figure 21

A comparison of this figure to Figure 18 will readily demonstrate that this actantial structure corresponds closely to the structure that has already been described in 3:13-14 and 4:3-6.

90. The role of ἡ γραφή here is paradoxical. Is it Helper or Opponent? This ambiguity is a tipoff to a characteristic feature of Paul's gospel story: God is not only the Sender *in* the story but also the author *of* the story. He is sovereign even over the failed initial sequence, and the enslavement of humanity is a necessary part of the story of its deliverance. Cf. Rom 11:32.

Several points here call for attention. First, Paul this time specifically characterizes the Receivers as "believers" rather than simply as "we." This makes explicit something that was implicit in the formulations previously analyzed.

Second, the "promise," which is equated with the Spirit in 3:14, is here, by its immediate connection with 3:21, linked with life and righteousness.[91] This shows that Paul is very flexible in his choice of terms for designating the Object in his gospel story. Spirit, promise, blessing, life, righteousness: all these seem to function as virtually interchangeable terms for the benefits of salvation.[92] This multiplicity of designations for the Object may appear strange in view of the relatively consistent designations of the other actants in the gospel story; however, this multiplicity is a natural result of the character of the Object itself, for in this case it is neither a person nor a thing, but a "value." In such cases, as Calloud points out, "it is difficult to know what is communicated."[93] Paul's various specifications of the Object thus reflect his attempts to define and articulate "what is communicated, transmitted, . . . given back, asked for"[94] through the action of Jesus Christ. In any event, in Gal 3:21-22, δικαιοσύνη appears in the actantial role of Object. Thus, in this passage at least, δικαιοσύνη does *not* function as a salvation-creating power, as Käsemann has proposed with reference to certain texts in Romans; instead, it is the Object communicated to humanity through Christ's redemptive action.[95] If we may speak of a "salvation-creating power" in this sequence of the gospel story, it is to be identified with πίστις, not with δικαιοσύνη.

But this leads to a third very important point that is raised by an actantial analysis of Gal 3:22: this analysis, in agreement with the above analyses of 3:13-14 and 4:3-6, places Jesus Christ in the role of Subject, with πίστις as the power or quality which enables him to carry out his mandate. If this is

91. The sense of the argument goes like this: "If Law had the power to give life, then δικαιοσύνη would be ἐκ νόμου. But the Law has no such power. Therefore δικαιοσύνη (= life = the promise) must come some other way; it is given ἐκ πίστεως Ἰησοῦ Χριστοῦ."

92. "Redemption" and "adoption" do not seem, however, to be interchangeable in the texts considered here. The former relates specifically to Jews, the latter to Gentiles.

93. Calloud, *Structural Analysis of Narrative*, 30.

94. Ibid., 29.

95. Δικαιοσύνη is the object in the topical sequence, but that means it may become the Helper in the *final* sequence. Does this provide a new angle of vision on the Bultmann-Käsemann debate over the meaning of δικαιοσύνη θεοῦ? Is it possible that Bultmann centers his arguments on texts which manifest (or reflect upon) the topical sequence of the gospel story, whereas Käsemann — with his interest in apocalyptic — emphasizes texts which manifest or reflect upon the role of δικαιοσύνη θεοῦ in the final sequence?

correct, Gal 3:22 must not be interpreted to mean that believers receive the promise by the subjective act of placing their faith in Jesus Christ;[96] instead, it must mean that Jesus Christ, by the power of faith, has performed an act which allows believers to receive the promise.[97] The interpretive problem may be stated the other way around: if Gal 3:22 means solely that believers receive the promise by placing their faith in Jesus Christ as "object of faith," then the proffered analysis of the narrative structure of this verse is erroneous. This problem establishes the agenda for Chapter IV of this study: what does πίστις Ἰησοῦ Χριστοῦ mean for Paul? Are we required to render it as "faith in Jesus Christ? and if not, what other options exist? Grammatically, lexically, and contextually, can this expression bear the meaning that I have suggested for it here? If so, the narrative analysis, which demonstrates clear parallels between 3:22 and the texts previously considered, strongly favors the interpretation that I have proposed.

F. Summary and Preview

Let us review what has been accomplished in this chapter. Through the use of Greimas' narrative model, we were able to offer a reasonably detailed analysis of the narrative structure of two key christological formulations in Galatians, 4:3-6 and 3:13-14. Although these formulations are sometimes regarded as contradictory, we were able to show them to be consistent and complementary manifestations of a single story-pattern. Then, more briefly, we sketched out the structure of a third passage, Gal 3:21b-22, which manifests the same pattern. This passage is particularly important because it links the story-structure with the term δικαιοσύνη and thus provides some important clues about the relation of the gospel story-structure to Paul's theological language about "justification." Furthermore, our consideration of actantial roles in Gal 3:22 introduced a crucial problem, which must be explored in Chapter IV, about the meaning of the phrase ἐκ πίστεως Ἰησοῦ Χριστοῦ.

The goal of the present chapter has been to establish the presence and shape of a gospel story to which Paul alludes and appeals in Galatians. The allusive christological formulations discussed in this chapter give us a glimpse

---

96. The *RSV* translation, which is in any case a very odd rendering of the Greek in this verse, reflects the interpretation that I am rejecting here: "But the scripture consigned all things to sin, that what was promised *to* (!) faith in Jesus Christ might be given to those who believe."

97. "Receive the promise" means, of course, "receive that which was promised."

into the "foundational language" of Paul's gospel. Two major questions remain to be considered. (1) Does the recognition of this narrative pattern in any way materially affect our understanding of the theological formulations in which we have discerned allusions to the gospel story? Chapter IV will be devoted to one of the most striking material implications that may emerge from the narrative analysis. (2) How does this narrative pattern inform or constrain the logic of Paul's argument in Galatians? This question will be taken up in Chapter V.

Chapter IV

The Function of Πίστις in the
Narrative Structure of Paul's Gospel

*The Reformers' understanding of faith had no effect on the
formation of Christology — not, at least, in normal church
dogmatics. . . . Hence the difficulty . . . of maintaining the strict
inner connexion between Christology and the doctrine of
justification. The Christology mostly does not lead by any
compelling necessity to the doctrine of justification, and the latter
in turn usually leaves it an open question how far Christology is
really needed as its ground.*

GERHARD EBELING[1]

*Suppose one man to rely on his own faith and another to rely on
his own works, then the faith of the one and the works of the
other are equally the same worthless filthy rags.*

WILLIAM LAW[2]

Our analysis of the narrative structure of the christological formulations in
Gal 3:13-14 and 3:22 has raised sharply the question of the meaning and
function of πίστις in Galatians. This is a question which takes us to the roots
of Pauline thought and forces us to reevaluate the meaning of several key
statements that are usually taken to be the quintessential expressions of Paul's
doctrine of justification by faith.

Since Luther's time, Protestant theology has found in Galatians the
classic prooftexts for the doctrine that individuals are saved not by perform-

---

1. G. Ebeling, *Word and Faith* (Philadelphia: Fortress, 1963) 203.
2. Cited in A. G. Hebert, "'Faithfulness' and 'Faith,'" *Theology* 58 (1955) 379.

ing works but by believing in Jesus Christ. As popularly understood, however, this doctrine has always carried with it the risk of turning faith into another kind of work,[3] a human achievement. In pietistic-enthusiastic circles, this justifying "faith" has often been understood as a psychological disposition; in scholastic circles "faith" has been equated with intellectual assent to propositionally formulated dogma. Bultmann attempted to escape these pitfalls by speaking of faith as "the free deed of obedience in which the new self constitutes itself in place of the old."[4] But in all these cases, including Bultmann, "faith" is understood as an activity of the human individual,[5] a means (putatively alternative to "works") of securing our acceptance before God. Against this understanding of justification by faith, G. M. Taylor raises a cogent protest.

3. It is perhaps unfair to lay the responsibility for the so-called "Lutheran" interpretation of Paul entirely at Luther's door. Luther protested against the Anabaptist practice of "believers' baptism" precisely on the ground that it turned "faith" into a "work," the assiduous cultivation of a particular interior disposition: "There is . . . a *Werkteufel* among them. . . . He uses the name and guise of faith to lead the poor people to rely on a work" ("Concerning Rebaptism: A Letter of Martin Luther to Two Pastors," p. 248 in *Luther's Works* 40 [trans. and ed. C. Bergendorff; Philadelphia: Muhlenberg, 1958]). In Luther's view, the remedy for this error was to understand faith as a response to the grace of God objectively given as *verbum visibile* in preaching and the sacraments. He spells this view out in a passage that illustrates in illuminating fashion how Luther's own theology differs from the post-Kantian interpretation of it which has been popularized by Bultmann and his followers: "But these leaders of the blind are unwilling to see that faith must have something to believe — something to which it may cling and upon which it may stand. . . . These people are so foolish as to separate faith from the object to which faith is attached and bound on the ground that the object is something external. Yes, it must be external so that it can be perceived and grasped by the senses and thus brought into the heart, just as the entire Gospel is an external, oral proclamation. In short, whatever God effects in us, he does through such external ordinances" ("Large Catechism," p. 440 in *The Book of Concord* [trans. and ed. T. G. Tappert; Philadelphia: Fortress, 1959]).

4. Bultmann, *Theology*, 1.316. Bultmann then attempts to render this definition tenable as interpretation of Paul by introducing a distinction between a "deed" *(Tat)* and a "work" (ἔργον): "In a true deed the doer himself is inseparable from it, while in a 'work' he stands side by side with what he does." This distinction, which is questionable in any case, is certainly incorrect as an interpretation of Paul, for whom one problem with "works" is precisely that they *do* come to constitute the self in such a way that the doers (ὅσοι ἐξ ἔργων νόμου, Gal 3:10) become inseparable from them. See H. Hübner, "Identitätsverlust und paulinische Theologie," *KD* 24 (1978) 183.

5. This understanding may be illustrated by a remark of P. R. Jones ("Exegesis of Galatians 3 and 4," *RevExp* 69 [1972] 478): "Faith in the context of Galatians means primarily 'faithing.'"

... It simply substitutes the mental act of having faith for the bodily one of being circumcised as a precondition of salvation, and (so far as the mechanism of justification is concerned) leaves Christ in the passive role of being the object of our justifying faith.[6]

Sensitive exegetes have always recognized the difficulty that Taylor emphasizes here, and various proposals have been made to circumvent it. Most typically it has been argued that faith is not the product of human will but of divine agency, that it is a gift planted in the human heart by God. Adolf Schlatter was an eloquent spokesman for this view.

Die Überzeugung tritt überall hervor, dass das Glauben nicht durch den Menschen gemacht werde, vielmehr ihm als ein Erlebnis widerfahre, das sein eigenes persönliches Wollen, aber nicht seine eigene Schöpfung, sondern eine Wirkung von oben sei, eine Gabe, die Gott in die Seele legt. Paulus heisst den Glaubenden "den aus Glauben," ὁ ἐκ πίστεως, weil nicht die Person ihr Glauben produziert und gestaltet, sondern das Glauben die Person formt, bewegt und regiert; denn es ist "geschenkt."[7]

As a phenomenological description of "faith" as experienced by the believer, Schlatter's statement is exemplary, and it relieves the theological problem of making justification contingent upon a human "work" of faith, because, according to Schlatter, "der Glaube ist Jesu Werk in uns."[8] We must ask, how-

---

6. G. M. Taylor, "The Function of ΠΙΣΤΙΣ ΧΡΙΣΤΟΥ in Galatians," *JBL* 85 (1966) 75. (For an evaluation of Taylor's alternative proposal, see Chapter V below.) Cf. the remarks of H.-J. Schoeps (*Paul: The Theology of the Apostle in the Light of Jewish Religious History* [Philadelphia: Westminster, 1961] 204-5): "With Paul the faith of the pious believer (in the Messianic status of Christ) replaces the Jew's fidelity to the law and becomes the sum of all truth and wisdom. The next stage in the development is that Paul postulated of this new kind of believing a righteousness proper to it.... Many texts speak of faith as though it had the character of a meritorious achievement."

7. A. Schlatter, *Der Glaube im Neuen Testament* (Stuttgart: Calwer, 1963) 262-63. For a sampling of similar opinions, see the following: A. Deissmann, *Paul*, 169-70; D. E. H. Whiteley, *The Theology of St. Paul* (Philadelphia: Fortress, 1966) 161-65; P. Stuhlmacher, *Gottes Gerechtigkeit*, 83; K. Kertelge, "Zur Deutung des Rechtfertigungsbegriffs im Galaterbrief," *BZ* 12 (1968) 218. One very interesting voice in this chorus is that of J. Haussleiter ("Was versteht Paulus unter christlichem Glauben?" *Griefswalder Studien* [Gütersloh: Bertelsmann, 1895] 177-78). On the significance of Haussleiter for our topic, see part C.1 of this chapter.

8. Schlatter, *Der Glaube*, 382. It should be pointed out that a precisely parallel argument could be mounted in defense of "works" as a means of justification: good works are not our creation, but they are God's work in us. Indeed, just such an affirmation may be found in

ever, whether this sort of explanation may be read into our texts in Galatians. Do these passages speak of πίστις as a gift placed by God in the human soul? Is faith described here as an experience ("Erlebnis") that encounters us from above? What is the connection between faith and Christ? When Paul writes of πίστις Χριστοῦ does he mean to refer to a human act of "believing" *(das Glauben)* which has Christ for its object as well as its author? The answers to such questions are by no means as clear as the Protestant tradition has sometimes assumed.

As we saw in Chapter III, when we become aware of the narrative pattern of Paul's christological formulations, the usual understanding of πίστις becomes at once problematical. Two of these narrative summaries (3:14, 22) seem to speak of πίστις as the power or quality which enables Christ to carry out his mission of deliverance. Is such an interpretation tenable? How would this way of reading the text affect our understanding of Paul's teaching about justification ἐκ πίστεως? These are the questions that we must address in this chapter.

Many treatments of the problems with which I am dealing here take Gal 2:16 as their point of departure. It is often argued that the expression εἰς Χριστὸν Ἰησοῦν ἐπιστεύσαμεν provides a definitive determination of the sense of πίστις Ἰησοῦ Χριστοῦ, since both expressions occur in this verse.[9] This approach, however, fails to reckon sufficiently with the extreme, almost epigrammatic, concision of this sentence and its place within the literary structure of the letter.

Betz's rhetorical analysis, which identifies 2:15-21 as the *propositio* of Paul's argument, has reconfirmed a point that has long been grasped intuitively by commentators on this letter: Gal 2:15-21 provides a highly condensed summary of the "thesis" that Paul intends to argue in the subsequent chapters.[10] Because of its programmatic character, "the *propositio* is extremely concise and consists largely of dogmatic abbreviations, i.e., very short

Eph 2:10. If the Qumran texts have taught us anything, they have shown us vividly how a rigorous religion of law-observance may coincide with a theological emphasis on human unworthiness and God's grace.

9. See, for example, W. Mundle, *Der Glaubensbegriff des Paulus* (Leipzig: Heinsius, 1932; repr. Darmstadt: Wissenschaftliche Buchgesellschaft, 1977) 76; Burton, *Galatians*, 121, 140; F. Neugebauer, *In Christus: Eine Untersuchung zum Paulinischen Glaubensverständnis* (Göttingen: Vandenhoeck & Ruprecht, 1961) 168 n. 69; Betz, *Galatians*, 118; D. Lührmann, *Glaube im frühen Christentum* (Gütersloh: Gerd Mohn, 1976) 48.

10. Betz, *Galatians*, 113-14. See also Schlier, *Galater*, 87-88; G. S. Duncan, *The Epistle of Paul to the Galatians* (MNTC; New York: Harper & Bros., 1934) 75; K. Berger, "Abraham in den paulinischen Hauptbriefen," *MTZ* 17 (1966) 47.

formulaic summaries of doctrines."[11] These summaries, furthermore, are not new doctrines invented by Paul, but they represent commonly acknowledged confessional traditions of the early church, including Jewish Christianity.[12] They therefore can serve as an agreed-upon presuppositional basis *from which* Paul can argue his case. There is a sense in which all of Galatians 3 and 4 can be read as Paul's "exegesis" of the concise authoritative formulations of 2:16. If it is true that phrases such as ἐκ πίστεως Χριστοῦ are "formulaic summaries," then we must seek to unfold their meaning by seeing how Paul uses them in his exposition. Otherwise, we run the risk of merely reading our preconceptions into them.

This much must be said, however, at the beginning of our inquiry: Gal 2:16 speaks clearly and unambiguously of faith *in* Christ (εἰς Χριστὸν Ἰησοῦν ἐπιστεύσαμεν), of an act of believing/trusting directed toward Christ as "object." As we shall see, a few critics have made attempts to deny this unmistakable fact,[13] but all such attempts are necessarily tendentious and unconvincing. Paul does in fact speak of Jesus Christ as the object of faith. The question is whether this observation determines the meaning of Paul's expression πίστις Ἰησοῦ Χριστοῦ so that it must be read as equivalent to πίστις εἰς Ἰησοῦν Χριστόν. Is there any significance to the fact that Paul uses a different grammatical construction here? Is it possible that some distinction is intended? Is it possible that in Paul's thought the faith *of* Jesus Christ may play some role as well as our faith *in* Christ Jesus? D. W. B. Robinson offers the following interpretation of Gal 2:16.

> The whole verse may be taken as relating Paul's believing to Christ's firm adherence to the will of God in the work of atonement and redemption: "a man is not justified by performing the law, but only by means of the faithfulness of Christ. So even we Jews believed on Jesus Christ so that we might be justified in Christ, i.e., as a result of his faithfulness to God's will, and not as a result of our lawkeeping.[14]

11. Betz, *Galatians,* 114. We will leave aside for the moment the question of whether "doctrines" is the best characterization for whatever it is that Paul is summarizing.

12. Ibid., 116-19. See also Dahl, "The Doctrine of Justification: Its Social Function and Implications," *Studies in Paul,* 95-120, esp. 100, 109. D. W. B. Robinson ("'Faith of Jesus Christ' — A New Testament Debate," *Reformed Theological Review* 29 [1970] 79) remarks that Gal 2:16 "introduces us to an already-formulated doctrine of justification in which *pistis Christou* has a thought-out place."

13. For example, G. Kittel, "πίστις Ἰησοῦ Χριστοῦ bei Paulus," *TSK* 79 (1906) 419-36; G. Schläger, "Bemerkungen zu πίστις Ἰησοῦ Χριστοῦ," *ZNW* 7 (1906) 356-58.

14. Robinson, "Faith of Jesus Christ," 79-80. The view that the different grammatical construction must signal some distinction in meaning between πιστεύειν εἰς Χριστόν, and

Is this paraphrase exegetically justifiable?

In order to answer this question, we must examine Paul's use of πίστις in Galatians 3. This examination will be carried out in some detail in relation to three key passages: Gal 3:2, 3:11, and 3:22. In each case, we will ask what πίστις means and how it functions in the thought of the passage. Two controversial theses will be advanced about these texts.

1. In none of these passages does Paul's emphasis lie upon the salvific efficacy of the individual activity of "believing."
2. Nowhere in Galatians 3 does Paul speak of Jesus Christ as the object toward which human faith is to be directed.

If these theses can be sustained through exegetical investigation, the way will be open for a comprehensive reinterpretation of Galatians 3 in accordance with my claim that the logic of Paul's argument depends upon a story in which Jesus Christ acts by the power of faith to bring salvation to humanity. Finally, after our investigation of Galatians 3, the last part of the chapter will examine the important parallel passages in Gal 2:20, 3:26, and Rom 3:21-26 to see whether my suggested interpretation of πίστις Ἰησοῦ Χριστοῦ also makes sense there.

A. The Message of Faith (Gal 3:2-5)

Beginning in Gal 3:1, Paul gets to work in earnest on the central argumentative section of his letter.[15] Gal 3:2 (along with its parallel in 3:5) is actually the linchpin of Paul's argument, because he appeals here to evidence that he considers irrefutable: the Galatians' own experience of having received the Spirit.[16] "Let me ask you only this," he says: "Did you receive the Spirit ἐξ

πίστις Ἰησοῦ Χριστοῦ is championed by G. Howard, "On the 'Faith of Christ,'" *HTR* 60 (1967) 460, and supported now also by S. K. Williams, "The 'Righteousness of God' in Romans," *JBL* 99 (1980) 274.

15. Betz's rhetorical analysis designates this part of the letter as the *probatio;* again, this serves to lend support to well-established critical views. J. B. Lightfoot (*Galatians*, 65), for example, had already divided the letter "into three sections of two chapters each, the first couplet (i, ii) containing the personal or narrative portion, the second (iii, iv) the argumentative or doctrinal, and the third (v, vi) the hortatory or practical."

16. Here I am in agreement with Betz (*Galatians*, 310, 132) over against Schlier (*Galater*, 126) and Mussner (*Galaterbrief*, 211), who consider the appeal to experience relatively insubstantial and unsatisfactory. However, precisely the observation that Paul appeals

ἔργων νόμου or ἐξ ἀκοῆς πίστεως?" Paul appears willing to rest his case on this one item of evidence. If the Galatians fail to concede Paul's point here, then the argument is lost; if, however, they grant him this point by answering "ἐξ ἀκοῆς πίστεως of course," then the outcome of the argument is clinched. Thus Paul's assumption that the Galatians received the Spirit ἐξ ἀκοῆς πίστεως is of central importance in the argumentative logic of Galatians.

1. Possible Meanings of ἐξ ἀκοῆς πίστεως

The exegetical difficulty lies, however, in knowing what Paul *means* by the phrase ἐξ ἀκοῆς πίστεως. The problem is caused not only by the ambiguity of the genitive case but also by the fact that both ἀκοή and πίστις have at least two possible meanings. Ἀκοή can mean either "the action (or sense) of hearing" or "that which is heard" (= report, message); πίστις can mean either "the act (or state?) of believing/trusting" or "that which is believed" (= the gospel).[17] Various further nuances within these meanings are possible to distinguish, but this general categorization enables us to distinguish four possible meanings for the phrase as a whole.[18]

to the Galatians' experience of the Spirit as a premise *from which* he can argue deals a serious blow to Betz's theory that Galatians is an apology written "in defense of the Spirit" (25). This thesis is discussed at greater length in Betz's essay, "In Defense of the Spirit: Paul's Letter to the Galatians as a Document of Early Christian Apologetics," pp. 99-114 in *Aspects of Religious Propaganda in Judaism and Early Christianity* (ed. E. Schüssler-Fiorenza; Notre Dame: University of Notre Dame, 1976). It would seem that Betz's hypothesis about the purpose of the letter contradicts his exegetical observations about 3:1-5.

17. πίστις has other possible meanings, of course: reliability, pledge, proof, etc. None of these meanings, however, would seem to be possible in Gal 3:2, 5. The much discussed distinction between ("Greek") faith and ("Hebrew") faithfulness is often overstressed; cf. the accurate appraisal of J. Haussleiter ("Der Glaube Jesu Christi und der christliche Glaube," *NKZ* 2 [1891] 136), who recognizes that for Paul "die Spaltung des Begriffes πίστις in die Bedeutungen 'Treue' und 'Glaube,' zu der uns die deutsche Sprache nötigt, nicht in den Sinn gekommen ist."

18. The translation ". . . by believing the gospel message," which is found in Duncan (*Galatians,* 79), Whiteley (*Theology of St. Paul,* 164-65), and *NEB,* is an interpretive paraphrase which is impossible to justify as an actual translation of Paul's words. This would require us to take πίστεως as the object of the preposition ἐξ, with ἀκοῆς understood to mean "the (gospel-) message" and taken as an objective genitive dependent on πίστεως. Because of the word order, however, such a construction is awkward and farfetched. The point may be illustrated by comparing the parallel expression διὰ νόμου πίστεως in Rom 3:27. Would anyone want to suggest that Paul means to say here that boasting is excluded "through believing the Law"?

— If ἀκοή means "hearing":
  (a) (πίστις = "believing") "by hearing with faith"
  (b) (πίστις = "the faith") "by hearing 'the faith'"
          = "by hearing the gospel."

— If ἀκοή means "message, proclamation":
  (c) (πίστις = "believing") "from the message that enables faith"
  (d) (πίστις = "the faith") "from the message of 'the faith'" =
          "the gospel-message."

Let us examine each of these possibilities in turn.

(a) "... *by hearing with faith.*" This translation, which has been advocated by a long line of interpreters[19] and adopted by the *RSV*, would lay stress upon human *response* to the gospel as a necessary means of receiving the Spirit. Lightfoot paraphrases ἐξ ἀκοῆς πίστις as "... the willing hearing that comes of faith,"[20] and Burton explains, somewhat more precisely, that "ἀκοὴ πίστεως is a hearing (of the gospel) accompanied by faith, ... in other words, a believing-hearing, acceptance of the gospel."[21] It is probably fair to say that this translation/interpretation of Gal 3:2 accurately reflects the general "Protestant" understanding of Paul's message. The apparent strength of this interpretation lies in the fact that it seems to offer a clear antithesis to the parallel expression ἐξ ἔργων νόμου, so that the two expressions describe "two contrasted principles of religious life,"[22] two different modes of human response to God. The juxtaposition is emphasized sharply by J. B. Tyson, who translates ἐξ ἀκοῆς πίστεως as "... on the basis of a believing *act* of hearing."[23] Most critics who *defend* this interpretation (as opposed to assuming it to be self-evident) do so explicitly on the basis of the assumption that since ἐξ ἔργων νόμου describes one type of human action, ἐξ ἀκοῆς πίστεως must describe some alternative type of human action.[24] To put the matter baldly and

19. For example: Lightfoot, *Galatians,* 134; Burton, *Galatians,* 147; Schlatter, *Der Glaube,* 611-12; Lagrange, *Galates,* 59; H. Ridderbos, *The Epistle of Paul to the Churches of Galatia* (NICNT; Grand Rapids: Eerdmans, 1953) 113; D. Guthrie, *Galatians* (2nd ed.; New Century Bible; London: Oliphants, 1974) 92-93.

20. Lightfoot, *Galatians,* 134. Strangely, Lightfoot seems to suppose here, contrary to Rom 10:17, that hearing comes from faith.

21. Burton, *Galatians,* 147. Cf. Lagrange, *Galates,* 59: "L'audition conduit à la foi, elle est même accompagnée de la foi."

22. Burton, *Galatians,* 147.

23. J. B. Tyson, "'Works of Law' in Galatians," *JBL* 92 (1973) 427.

24. This line of argument is explicitly articulated by Lightfoot, Burton, Schlatter, and Ridderbos.

schematically, this interpretation attributes to Paul the thought: "You received the Spirit not because you did X (= performed works) but because you did Y (= heard and believed)." In spite of its widespread acceptance, this interpretation is, for reasons that we shall see, problematical, and it has not gone uncontested.[25]

(b) "*. . . by hearing the gospel.*" This is the interpretation of Calvin, who remarks simply, "faith is here put by metonymy for the Gospel."[26] The same interpretation is advocated by J. Bligh, who points to Gal 1:23 as evidence that πίστις can mean for Paul "that which is believed."[27] This interpretation has not received much attention from modern interpreters, most of whom are convinced, like Lagrange, that "πίστις n'a pas jamais pour Paul le sens de 'doctrine de la foi.'"[28] A. Oepke likewise insists that "der Sinn wäre dann aber kaum: Hören der Glaubensbotschaft (Gen. obj.). So stark ist die πίστις bei Paulus nicht verobjektiviert."[29] It is difficult to see, however, what evidence can be adduced to support such assertions. This meaning of πίστις, which appears unmistakably in 1:23, and perhaps in 3:23, 25 as well, should also be considered as a legitimate possibility here. F. Mussner, who goes so far as to suggest that πίστις in 3:2 could refer to a fixed formulated "Glaubensüberlieferung" (as in 1 Cor 15:1-5), also finds in ἀκοή the nuance of "obedient hearing" (cf. Rom 1:5: ὑπακοὴ πίστεως), so that he renders the whole phrase "aufgrund der gehorsamen Annahme der Glaubenspredigt."[30]

(c) "*. . . from the message that aims at (or enables) faith.*" This interpretation has gained fairly widespread acceptance among interpreters, many of whom have recognized, on the basis of Rom 10:16-17, that ἀκοή for Paul probably means "report, proclamation, preaching, message." πίστις is then taken to designate the human response to the preached message, although the precise way in which this "faith" is related to the proclamation is variously understood, as may be illustrated by listing a few of the translations that have been put forward: "the preaching which aims at faith" (Hatch),[31] "the preaching which demands faith or . . . opens up the possibility of faith" (Bult-

---

25. For a recent protest against this interpretation of faith in Paul, see J. L. Martyn [review of Leander Keck, *Paul and His Letters*], *Reflection* 77/3 (1980) 20.

26. Calvin, *Galatians*, 48.

27. J. Bligh, *Galatians in Greek* (Detroit: University of Detroit, 1966) 127.

28. Lagrange, *Galates*, 59.

29. Oepke, *Galater*, 100.

30. Mussner, *Galaterbrief*, 207.

31. W. H. P. Hatch, *The Pauline Idea of Faith in Its Relation to Jewish and Hellenistic Religion* (HTS 2; Cambridge: Harvard University, 1917) 33 n. 1. Cf. Oepke (*Galater*, 101): "Heilskunde, die auf Glauben abzielt."

mann),[32] "la prédication qui produit la foi" (Bonnard),[33] "die Verkündigung, mit der der Glaube heraustritt" (Schlier).[34] All of these interpretations are plausible, and the differences among them are the result not of any substantive argument over the meaning of the expression ἐξ ἀκοῆς πίστεως in itself but of subtle differences in the way in which these critics understand the overall relationship between preaching and faith in Paul. Does preaching "demand" faith or does it "produce" faith? Answers to such questions clearly cannot be extracted from the single enigmatic phrase ἐξ ἀκοῆς πίστεως.

(d) "... from the gospel-message." A rendering of this sort is supported by Lietzmann, who simply notes that πίστις means here "Glaubensbotschaft."[35] W. Schenk argues at some length that πίστις in this case, as well as elsewhere in Paul, must be understood as "Terminus zur Bezeichnung der Verkündigung."[36] Betz's commentary seems to follow this line of interpretation: he translates Gal 3:2 as follows: "This only I want to learn from you: did you receive the Spirit by 'works of the law' or by [the] 'proclamation of [the] faith'?" This interpretation is similar to (b) above, but, as Betz remarks, it "unavoidably shifts the emphasis from the hearing to the preaching of the message."[37]

2. The Meaning of ἀκοή

Since all of these interpretations are "dictionary" possibilities (i.e., the words ἐξ ἀκοῆς πίστεως could, without undue strain, bear any of these meanings), what conclusions may be drawn? It seems reasonably clear that the weight of the evidence based on Paul's usage tells strongly *against* translations (a) and (b), which understand ἀκοή to mean "hearing." In the parallel text in Rom 10:16-17, ἀκοή enters the discussion through Paul's citation of Isa 53:1: κύριε, τίς ἐπίστευσεν τῇ ἀκοῇ ἡμῶν; here ἀκοή unambiguously means "report, proclamation."[38] Thus when Paul comments on this text in Rom 10:17,

32. R. Bultmann, "πίστις, πιστεύω, κτλ.," *TDNT* 6.213.

33. P. Bonnard, *L'Épître de Saint Paul aux Galates* (CNT 9; Neuchâtel-Paris: Delachaux & Niestle, 1953) 63.

34. Schlier, *Galater,* 122.

35. Lietzmann, *An die Galater,* 18.

36. W. Schenk, "Die Gerechtigkeit Gottes und der Glaube Christi," *TLZ* 97 (1972) 161-74, see esp. 166.

37. Betz, *Galatians,* 128 n. 3. Betz does not, however, offer any discussion of his translation of πίστις as "(the) faith."

38. Cf. E. Käsemann, *An die Römer* (HNT 8a; Tübingen: J. C. B. Mohr [Paul Siebeck], 1973) 282.

ἄρα ἡ πίστις ἐξ ἀκοῆς, he must mean "therefore, faith comes from the proclamation."

C. K. Barrett thinks that in Rom 10:17 Paul "uses the word 'hearing' in the sense it commonly has in his writings, though the same word is differently employed [as 'report,' i.e., 'what they heard'] in the previous verse, where Paul's usage is determined by the Old Testament."[39] Thus Paul's "exegesis"[40] of Isa 53:1 would amount to a play on words. This kind of wordplay would be by no means uncharacteristic of Paul, but Barrett's assertion that ἀκοή "commonly" means "hearing" in Paul's writings is surely open to serious doubt. Apart from the passages presently under consideration (Rom 10:16-17; Gal 3:2-5), the word occurs only twice in the generally acknowledged Pauline letters. In one of these instances (1 Cor 12:17), ἀκοή means the *sense* of hearing (not, note, the *act* of hearing). In the other instance (1 Thess 2:13), the word occurs in a somewhat awkward construction, the meaning of which seems to be "... you received God's 'word of proclamation' from us...." In this passage, which is really much closer than 1 Corinthians 12:16-17 to the conceptual field of Rom 10:17 and Gal 3:2, 5, the translation of ἀκοή as "hearing" seems entirely inappropriate. Thus, Barrett's appeal to the way Paul "commonly" uses ἀκοή breaks down both because there is an insufficient body of evidence and because the existing evidence does not support Barrett's assertion.[41]

Thus, on the basis of the evidence provided by Rom 10:16-17 and 1 Thess 2:13, it seems likely that ἀκοὴ πίστεως in Gal 3:2 means "the message of faith" (i.e., either meaning c or meaning d above). But what of the argument that ἐξ ἀκοῆς πίστεως must be interpreted in antithetical parallelism to ἐξ ἔργων νόμου and must therefore refer to a human activity of "hearing"?[42]

It is indisputable that Paul sets up these two phrases as parallel and mutually exclusive alternatives. It is *not* clear, however, that ἀκοὴ πίστεως must therefore refer to some kind of human activity. In the first place, the detailed

39. C. K. Barrett, *The Epistle to the Romans* (HNTC; New York: Harper & Row, 1957) 205.

40. Martyn (review, *Reflection* 77/3 [1980] 20) rightly so describes Rom 10:17.

41. Schlatter, who insists that the train of thought in Galatians allows for ἀκοή no interpretation other than "hearing," goes a step further than Barrett by supposing that Paul already interprets his understanding of ἀκοή *into* the text of Isa 53:1: "Er findet auch dort nicht eine Predigt, sondern ein Hören geweissagt" (*Der Glaube,* 612). Unfortunately Schlatter neglects to explain what the resulting apparently unintelligible sentence ("Lord, who has believed our hearing?") would have been understood by Paul to mean.

42. Lightfoot, for example, clearly recognizes the force of the parallel in Rom 10:16-17, but he takes this second argument to have overriding weight in the interpretation of Gal 3:2.

parallelism is not as neat as it is often alleged to be. "Works" do not stand in the same relation to "Law" as does "hearing" to "faith." Whereas faith comes ἐξ ἀκοῆς (Rom 10:17), Law does not come ἐξ ἔργων; the relation is the reverse.[43] The truth of the matter is that the juxtaposed phrases must be taken as indivisible meaning-units: "Did you receive the Spirit from ⊠ or from ⊻?" To argue that the individual elements within each phrase must be precisely parallel is to stand on shaky ground. Betz's translation captures the proper sense of the matter by placing each phrase in quotation marks so that it becomes clear that each one is a catchphrase or slogan.

In the second place, the whole passage makes better sense if we suppose that Paul's primary intention is not at all to juxtapose one type of human activity ("works") to another ("believing-hearing") but rather to juxtapose human activity to God's activity, as revealed in the "proclamation." The antithesis would then lie between human "works" and God's ἀκοή (= message), which comes *extra nos* (cf. 1 Thess 2:13). This contrast is even clearer in 3:5, because the syntax of the sentence, though elliptical, makes it clear that the prepositional phrases are intended as modifiers of God's action: "He who supplies the Spirit to you and works miracles among you — (does he do it) ἐξ ἔργων νόμου ἢ ἐξ ἀκοῆς πίστεως?" Paul's formulation here has a facetious tone; it would be ridiculous to say that God supplies the Spirit and works miracles ἐξ ἔργων νόμου. That is precisely the point, but it would be equally ridiculous to say (as the *RSV* does) that God works miracles "through hearing with faith." Thus, ἀκοὴ πίστεως in Gal 3:5 is best understood as a designation for the proclamation of the gospel, a proclamation which has *power* and thus becomes the instrument through which God gives the Spirit and works miracles. This understanding of the proclamation as a manifestation of God's power is characteristic of Paul, and it is well attested elsewhere in his letters (cf. 1 Thess 1:5; Rom 1:16).[44] Consequently, Gal 3:5 should be translated as follows: "He who supplies the Spirit to you and works miracles among you — (does he do it) through works of the Law or through the proclamation of the

43. O'Neill (*Recovery*, 46-47), with characteristic acuity, perceives the awkwardness of the alleged antithetical parallelism. Then, with characteristic obtuseness, he "solves" the problem by deleting (with no manuscript support) ἀκοῆς from the text and amending ἐξ to ἐκ in order to produce the reading ἐξ ἔργων νόμου τὸ πνεῦμα ἐλάβετε ἢ ἐκ πίστεως. Thus, by resorting to arbitrary textual emendation, O'Neill makes Paul say what modern interpreters have usually understood him to mean.

44. For discussion of this aspect of Paul's thought, see P. Bormann, *Die Heilswirksamkeit der Verkündigung nach dem Apostel Paulus* (Paderborn: Bonifacius, 1965); also J. Schütz, *Paul and the Anatomy of Apostolic Authority* (SNTSMS 26; Cambridge: Cambridge University, 1975) 35-53.

gospel?" (or, ". . . through the proclamation which evokes faith"). This would not, of course, preclude a concern for human receptivity to the message; it would simply mean that the point of the contrast would be located differently from the way in which Lightfoot et al. locate it.

In view of all these considerations, it seems that we are justified in translating ἀκοή as "message" rather than as "hearing," and thus narrowing our consideration to translations (c) and (d) above. But what about πίστις? Is it possible to determine whether it means "believing" or "the faith (= the gospel)" and thus to choose between the two remaining possibilities?

3. The Meaning of πίστις

At first sight, the evidence appears to stand in favor of meaning (c), once again largely on the basis of Rom 10:17: ἡ πίστις ἐξ ἀκοῆς. No one would argue that Paul means here "'the faith' comes from the message." Clearly, as an explication of Isa 53:1, Paul's sentence means "Faith (= believing) comes from the message." Thus, a significant presumption is created in favor of the view that ἀκοὴ πίστεως in Gal 3:2 means "the message that evokes faith."[45]

It is not possible, however, to rule the other possibility (that πίστις = "the faith") entirely out of consideration. In Gal 1:23, we find πίστις "objectified" as the direct object of a verb of proclaiming: ὁ διώκων ἡμᾶς ποτε νῦν εὐαγγελίζεται τὴν πίστιν ἥν ποτε ἐπόρθει. Likewise, in Gal 3:23-26, "the faith" which has now "come" is not the faith of an individual but the historical phenomenon of "the faith" (= Christianity).[46] Finally, in Gal 6:10, ἡ πίστις appears as "the common name for the Christian movement."[47] In light of these other usages in Galatians, it is certainly possible to defend the translation of ἀκοὴ πίστεως in Gal 3:2, 5 as "the message of faith (= the gospel-message)."

Perhaps the truth of the matter is that Paul's compressed language will not answer all the questions that we would like to put to it and that he did not intend a clear distinction: ἀκοὴ πίστεως means simply "the faith-message," and the attempt to distinguish between "the message that evokes faith" and "the message of 'the faith'" is our problem rather than Paul's. Even the

45. "Evokes" is my own preferred word (as opposed to "produces," "demands," etc.) for expressing the relation between the message and faith.

46. Lietzmann, *An die Galater*, 23; Betz, *Galatians*, 176 n. 120; this point was acknowledged also by Bultmann (*Theology*, 1.319; *TDNT* 6.213). O'Neill (*Recovery*, 53) makes the same observation but concludes that 3:23-25 must therefore be an interpolation!

47. Betz, *Galatians*, 311. His footnote 201 on this page seems to imply that he regards 3:2 as another instance of this same usage of πίστις.

staunchest defenders of interpretation (d) above would join Schenk in acknowledging this point: "πίστις heisst das Evangelium . . . als die das Glauben eröffnende und ermöglichende Nachricht."[48] Thus even if πίστις is a quasi-technical term for "the gospel," the implication of some human response is scarcely thereby excluded.

4. Conclusions

For our present purposes, three conclusions should be emphasized in relation to Gal 3:2.

(a) Even if πίστις here means "believing" *(das Glauben),* no object of faith is specified.[49]

(b) Even if πίστις here means "believing," Paul's emphasis lies not upon the individual act of *believing* as the means of receiving the Spirit, but upon the proclaimed *message* (ἀκοή), which calls forth faith, as the means by which the Spirit is given.[50]

(c) It is at least possible that πίστις here, as in other texts in Galatians, functions as a collective designation for "that which is believed" and does not refer explicitly to the Galatians' act or attitude of faith.

B. The Righteous One Will Live ἐκ πίστεως (Gal 3:11)

The rather odd elliptical expression ἐκ πίστεως appears repeatedly in Galatians 3 (vv. 7, 8, 9, 11, 12, 22, 24). In order to grasp the thrust of Paul's argument, we must try to discern the meaning of this phrase. The place to begin this investigation is with Paul's citation of Hab 2:4, because this prophetic word appears to be the source from which Paul draws the phrase;[51] Paul's fondness for this particular expression is explained by the fact that it provides a link to an authoritative scriptural text in which he finds his understanding of "justification" foreshadowed. Indeed, most if not all of the other occur-

---

48. Schenk, "Gerechtigkeit Gottes und Glaube Christi," 166.

49. Contra Lagrange (*Galates,* 59), who thinks that "il va sans dire que cette foi a pour objet le Christ."

50. This point is emphasized by D. J. Lull (*The Spirit in Galatia: Paul's Interpretation of Pneuma as Divine Power* [SBLDS 49; Chico: Scholars, 1980] 54-59), who stresses the "cultic" activity of missionary preaching as the *"Sitz im Leben"* for the Galatians' reception of the Spirit.

51. Cf. Rom 1:17.

rences of ἐκ πίστεως in this chapter may be understood as "catchword" allusions to the full Habakkuk citation.[52]

1. What Does ἐκ πίστεως Modify?

Much of the discussion of Gal 3:11 (and of its parallel in Rom 1:17) has centered on the problem of whether Paul understands the Habakkuk quotation to mean "the righteous [one] shall live by faith" or "the one-who-is-righteous-by-faith shall live."[53] In other words, does the phrase ἐκ πίστεως modify δίκαιος, thus explaining how one becomes "righteous" (= justified), or does it modify the verb ζήσεται, thus explaining the manner in which the one who is righteous shall "live"? With all due respect to the careful labors of conscientious exegetes, it is difficult to see what is really at stake in this question, for no one seriously supposes that Paul reckons with the possibility of some hypothetical person who is δίκαιος *apart from* faith.

The key to a proper understanding of the words ὁ δίκαιος ἐκ πίστεως ζήσεται lies in the recognition that the word ζήσεται carried for Paul eschatological connotations and that it is used in 3:11b as a virtual synonym of δικαιοῦται in 3:11a.[54] Thus, ἐκ πίστεως should be taken as an adverbial modifier of ζήσεται, functionally parallel (and materially antithetical) to ἐν νόμῳ in 3:11a, which is clearly a modifier of δικαιοῦται, not of οὐδείς.[55] This syn-

52. Cf. the observation of W. R. Schoedel ("Pauline Thought: Some Basic Issues," p. 284 in *Transitions in Biblical Scholarship* [ed. J. C. Rylaarsdam; Essays in Divinity 6; Chicago: University of Chicago, 1968]): "The term 'faith' . . . tends to be used as an abbreviation for a more complex formula." Betz (*Galatians*, 27-28) lists ἐκ πίστεως in his catalogue of "theological abbreviations" in the letter. Dahl (*Studies in Paul*, 169) points out that this sort of catchword allusion to a scriptural text is a characteristically rabbinic mode of expression.

53. For a summary of the problem and a survey of the critical literature, see H. C. C. Cavallin, "The Righteous Shall Live by Faith: A Decisive Argument for the Traditional Interpretation," *ST* 32 (1978) 33-43. The most thorough and judicious summary of the exegetical problems is provided by D. Moody Smith ("Ο ΔΕ ΔΙΚΑΙΟΣ ΕΚ ΠΙΣΤΕΩΣ ΖΗΣΕΤΑΙ," pp. 13-25 in *Studies in the History and Text of the New Testament in Honor of Kenneth Willis Clark* [ed. B. L. Daniels and M. J. Suggs; SD 29; Salt Lake City: University of Utah, 1967]). Both Cavallin and Smith support the "traditional" translation: "The righteous shall live by faith."

54. Cf. Gal 3:21b: εἰ γὰρ ἐδόθη νόμος ὁ δυνάμενος ζῳοποιῆσαι, ὄντως ἐκ νόμου ἂν ἦν ἡ δικαιοσύνη. The power to give life is the same thing as the power to confer justification. Paul never feels the need to argue in favor of this equation between "life" and "righteousness/justification"; it is axiomatic for him.

55. The parallelism between 3:11a and 3:11b is noted by Williams ("Righteousness of

tactical parallelism is further reinforced by the following quotation from Lev 18:5, in which ἐν αὐτοῖς modifies ζήσεται.[56] The parallelism may be laid out as follows.

3:11a	οὐδεὶς	δικαιοῦται	ἐν νόμῳ
3:11b	ὁ δίκαιος	ζήσεται	ἐκ πίστεως
3:12b	ὁ ποιήσας αὐτὰ	ζήσεται	ἐν αὐτοῖς

Consequently, Gal 3:11b should be translated "the righteous one shall live [= be justified] by faith." But the *meaning* of this statement is substantially identical to the affirmation that "the one who is righteous [= justified] by faith shall live." If there is any material distinction to be found between these statements, it lies in a realm of theological nuances far subtler than Paul could have imagined. In either case, the phrase ἐκ πίστεως specifies the manner in which ὁ δίκαιος shall find life (= be justified).[57]

2. Who Is ὁ δίκαιος?

Far more crucial and interesting is a question that has less often been posed by exegetes: who is "the righteous one" to whom the Habakkuk citation refers? Typically, the singular adjective δίκαιος is taken to have a generic significance, so that the prophecy would mean, "anyone who is righteous shall live by faith" (or, for those who insist on taking ἐκ πίστεως as a modifier of ὁ δίκαιος, "anyone who is righteous through faith shall live"). This interpretation was emphatically encouraged by the *KJV*, which reads "the just shall live by faith," as if the Greek text had οἱ δίκαιοι. Actually, this is probably a correct interpretation of the sentence in its original context in Habakkuk.[58]

However, another interpretation has been put forward by A. T. Hanson, who suggests that ὁ δίκαιος is read by Paul as a designation, if not a formal title, for the Messiah.[59] This hypothesis deserves serious consideration, not only be-

God," 257 n. 49), who then draws the surprising conclusion that "*ek pisteos* goes with *ho dikaios,* just as *en nomou* [*sic*] must go with *dikaioutai.*"

56. This parallelism between 3:11b and 3:12 is pointed out by Lightfoot (*Galatians,* 251) and by Smith ("ΔΙΚΑΙΟΣ," 19); it also is the basis for the "decisive argument" promised by Cavallin in the title of his article.

57. This interpretation agrees materially with that of Burton (*Galatians,* 166).

58. The text is explicitly so interpreted in 1QpHab 8:1-3.

59. A. T. Hanson, *Paul's Understanding of Jesus* (Hull: University of Hull, 1963) 6-9; idem, *Studies in Paul's Technique and Theology* (London: SPCK, 1974) 42-45. Hanson's pro-

cause other (non-Pauline) NT texts explicitly apply the designation ὁ δίκαιος to Jesus (Acts 3:14, 7:52, 22:14, 1 Pet 3:18, 1 John 2:1; cf. also 1 Enoch 38:2, and especially Isa 53:11) but also because, as Hanson indicates, the LXX rendering of Hab 2:3-4 would have appeared to Paul as unmistakably messianic.

διότι ἔτι ὅρασις εἰς καιρὸν
καὶ ἀνατελεῖ εἰς πέρας καὶ οὐκ εἰς κενόν.
ἐὰν ὑστερήσῃ ὑπομεῖνον αὐτόν
ὅτι ἐρχόμενος ἥξει καὶ οὐ μὴ χρονίσῃ
ἐὰν ὑποστείληται, οὐκ εὐδοκεῖ ἡ ψυχή μου ἐν αὐτῷ
ὁ δὲ δίκαιος ἐκ πίστεώς μου ζήσεται.

Because the vision still awaits its time,
and will rise to its fulfillment and not be in vain.
If he delays, wait for him,
because a Coming One will arrive and will not linger;
if he draws back, my soul will have no pleasure in him;
but the Righteous One shall live by my faith.[60]

The masculine pronoun αὐτόν in 2:3b cannot refer to "the vision" (ἡ ὅρασις); likewise the masculine participle ἐρχόμενος cannot refer back to the "vision" and must therefore mean "a Coming One." (This nuance is further clarified by the citation of this same passage in Heb 10:37, which adds the definite article: ὁ ἐρχόμενος.) It is possible that the LXX reading could have arisen simply through inept translation, since חזון, a masculine noun, is followed by a masculine form of the pronoun and participle in the Hebrew text.[61] But whether the LXX translators intended it or not, they produced a text that is readily susceptible to messianic interpretation.

This point is recognized by Dodd, who suggests that Paul may have drawn upon "a tradition which already recognized the passage from Habakkuk as a *testimonium* to the coming of Christ." Furthermore, Dodd points out that Paul's argument in Galatians "would be far more effective with his Jewish-Christian antagonists if it was already common ground between

---

posal seems to have been advanced independently of J. Haussleiter, who had made the same suggestion in relation to Rom 1:17 more than seventy years earlier ("Der Glaube Jesu Christi," 212-13).

60. Hanson, *Paul's Technique*, 42.

61. This point is noted neither by Hanson nor by T. W. Manson, who observes that "the LXX interpretation of Habakkuk 2:3b-4 is through and through Messianic" ("The Argument from Prophecy," *JTS* 46 [1945] 134). Manson assumes, however, that Paul took the prophecy to apply not to the Messiah but to individual believers.

them that when the Coming One should come, ὁ δίκαιος ἐκ πίστεως ζήσεται. The exact exegesis of these words would then be legitimate matter for discussion."[62] Thus Dodd contends that Hab 2:3-4 was understood by Paul as a messianic prophecy, but he stops cautiously short of the further inference drawn by Hanson that ὁ δίκαιος should be identified with (ὁ) ἐρχόμενος, so that the sentence ὁ δίκαιος ἐκ πίστεως ζήσεται would apply to the Messiah himself. This inference is, however, by no means an unreasonable one, as will appear in the light of Gal 3:16, with its messianic exegesis of Gen 17:8.

Paul insists that the promise was made to Abraham and to his (singular) seed (σπέρμα), a single individual who was destined to be the heir of "the blessing of Abraham." Dahl has pointed out that Paul's exegesis of σπέρμα is not entirely arbitrary, that it rests upon "an exegetical inference by analogy"[63] to the promise made to David in 2 Sam 7:12-14.

> καὶ ἀναστήσω τὸ σπέρμα σου μετὰ σέ . . .
> καὶ ἀνορθώσω τὸν θρόνον αὐτοῦ ἕως εἰς τὸν αἰῶνα.
> Ἐγὼ ἔσομαι αὐτῷ εἰς πατέρα
> καὶ αὐτὸς ἔσται μοι εἰς υἱόν

In this promise, which was already understood as a messianic prophecy in pre-Christian Judaism,[64] σπέρμα is properly and unambiguously singular; the inference that σπέρμα in Genesis 17 must also be understood as referring to a single individual was an easy one to make. M. Wilcox has now assembled further evidence to show that this exegetical linkage between the "seed of Abraham" and the "seed of David," both understood in messianic terms, was "a pre-NT midrashic development."[65]

The importance of Gal 3:16 in the development of Paul's argument is not always fully appreciated: Paul insists that the Messiah (Χριστός) is the one and only heir of the promise to Abraham and that others participate in this inheritance only "in Christ Jesus" (Gal 3:14).[66] How does this bear upon the

---

62. Dodd, *Scriptures*, 51.

63. Dahl, *Studies in Paul*, 130-31.

64. See the evidence cited by Dahl (*Studies in Paul*, 130 n. 12). Cf. D. Daube, "The Interpretation of a Generic Singular in Galatians 3:16," *JQR* 35 (1944-45) 227-30; E. Lucchesi, "Nouveau Parallele entre Saint Paul (Gal iii.16) et Philon d'Alexandrie (*Quaestiones in Genesim*)?" *NovT* 21 (1979) 150-55.

65. M. Wilcox, "The Promise of the 'Seed' in the New Testament and the Targumim," *JSNT* 5 (1979) 2-20. Wilcox also calls attention to Gen 3:15 and 4:25 as other important texts in the chain of messianic "seed" prophecies.

66. Cf. Dahl, *Studies in Paul*, 131. For fuller discussion of the development of the argument, see Chap. V below.

interpretation of ὁ δίκαιος ἐκ πίστεως ζήσεται? We have already seen that the Habakkuk citation is taken from a context in the LXX that Paul would very likely have understood as a messianic prophecy; furthermore, we have also seen that the whole thrust of Paul's argument in this section of the letter is dependent upon the assertion that the Messiah is the one destined recipient of "the promises" (3:16), which Paul interprets to include blessing, righteousness, life, and the Spirit. The conclusion lies close at hand that the Messiah is ὁ δίκαιος, the Righteous One who shall live ἐκ πίστεως, whose faith becomes the means whereby others may live (cf. Gal 2:20).[67] We can easily imagine Paul explaining Hab 2:4, on the analogy of Gal 3:16, by saying οὐ λέγει· οἱ δίκαιοι, ὡς ἐπὶ πολλῶν, ἀλλ' ὡς ἐφ' ἑνός· ὁ δίκαιος, ὅς ἐστιν Χριστός.

The probability that Paul identifies ὁ δίκαιος with the messianic σπέρμα is strengthened still further by a consideration of the LXX of Isa 53:10b-12a.

> ἡ ψυχὴ ὑμῶν ὄψεται <u>σπέρμα</u> μακρόβιον.
> καὶ βούλεται κύριος ἀφελεῖν ἀπὸ τοῦ πόνου τῆς ψυχῆς αὐτοῦ,
> δεῖξαι αὐτῷ φῶς, καὶ πλάσαι τῇ συνέσει,
> δικαιῶσαι <u>δίκαιον</u> εὖ δουλεύοντα πολλοῖς,
> καὶ τὰς ἁμαρτίας αὐτῶν αὐτὸς ἀνοίσει.
> Διὰ τοῦτο αὐτὸς <u>κληρονομήσει</u> πολλούς. . . .

Here, of course, the LXX text does not *intend* to identify the "seed" with the "Righteous One" who "will bear their sins," but anyone approaching this text with Paul's presupposition that the σπέρμα is the Messiah could very easily read the passage that way simply by taking σπέρμα as the antecedent of the pronouns αὐτοῦ and αὐτῷ in 53:11. This reading of the text would be especially natural for Paul, because 53:12 declares that the Righteous One "will *inherit* many," an affirmation that fits neatly into Paul's argument that the σπέρμα is the heir of the promises. Paul does not, of course, quote from Isaiah 53 in Galatians 3, but it seems likely that he is drawing upon a traditional as-

---

67. Independently of Hanson, this interpretation of Gal 3:11 is supported in various ways by J. Bligh, "Did Jesus Live by Faith?" *HeyJ* 9 (1968) 414-19; M. Barth, "The Faith of the Messiah," *HeyJ* 10 (1969) 363-70; H. Ljungman, *Pistis: A Study of Its Presuppositions and Its Meaning in Pauline Use* (Lund: Gleerup, 1964) 39. Close at hand lies the tradition of the *Akedah* (the binding of Isaac), according to which Abraham's faith-obedience in offering up his son is regarded as having vicarious soteriological consequences for all of Israel. The relation of this tradition to Paul's christological thought has been developed in various ways by Schoeps (*Paul*, 141-49), G. Vermes (*Scripture and Tradition in Judaism* [Leiden: Brill, 1961] 193-227), and Dahl (*Crucified Messiah*, 146-60), among others. For a recent review of the discussion, see R. J. Daly, "The Soteriological Significance of the Sacrifice of Isaac," *CBQ* 39 (1977) 45-75.

sociation of messianic themes (Righteous One, seed, inheritance) for which Isaiah 53 is one source among others. What Paul has done in Gal 3:6-18 is to bring this cluster of messianic themes into conjunction with Hab 2:4, interpreted messianically, so that the Messiah's faith becomes the key to his inheritance of life and the promises. If this interpretation is correct, then οἱ ἐκ πίστεως (Gal 3:7, 9) must be those who "live" on the basis of the faith of the Messiah, or perhaps those who share the faith of the Messiah (cf. Rom 4:16, ἐκ πίστεως Ἀβραάμ).[68]

Hanson cautiously acknowledges that "it cannot be taken as proved that Hab 2:4 is regarded by Paul as a prophecy of the Messiah," but it is certainly, as he claims, "at least a reasonable suggestion,"[69] and it yields a very good sense in this passage. This interpretation offers the possibility of establishing greater coherence in Paul's rather confusing argumentation in Galatians 3, by identifying "the Righteous One" who will live by faith (3:11) with "the seed" who inherits the promises (3:16). Furthermore, this reading of the passage corresponds harmoniously to the narrative structure identified in Chapter III, in which Christ is the hero/subject in the drama of justification. From this point of view, Paul's repeated allusions in Galatians 3 to Hab 2:4 (in the catchphrase ἐκ πίστεως) would serve as references not primarily to the individual believer's justifying faith but to the faith of Christ. But this leads to the final question that we must raise about Gal 3:11.

3. By Whose Faith Shall the Righteous One Live?

Paul's citation of Hab 2:4 differs both from all extant LXX manuscripts and from the MT. The manuscript evidence presents basically four different readings.[70]

(a) וצדיק באמונתו יחיה
   "The righteous one shall live by his faith(fulness)."
   — MT, 1QpHab (vid.).

---

68. In any case, the claim that Paul understood Hab 2:4 to apply "first and foremost to Christ" (Bligh, "Did Jesus Live by Faith?" 418) should by no means be understood to exclude its simultaneous secondary application to believers (οἱ πιστεύοντες).

69. Hanson, Paul's Technique, 45.

70. For discussion of the manuscript evidence, see Smith, "ΔΙΚΑΙΟΣ," 15-16; G. Howard, Crisis in Galatia, 62; B. Lindars, New Testament Apologetic (London: SCM, 1961) 230-31.

(b) ὁ δὲ δίκαιος ἐκ πίστεώς μου ζήσεται.

"The righteous one shall live by my faith(fulness)."

— most LXX manuscripts.

(c) ὁ δὲ δίκαιός μου ἐκ πίστεως ζήσεται.

"My righteous one shall live by faith."

— LXX^{A,C}, Heb 10:38.

(d) ὁ (δὲ) δίκαιος ἐκ πίστεως ζήσεται.

"The righteous one shall live by faith."

— Rom 1:17, Gal 3:11 (the latter omits δὲ).

As has often been noted, the divergence between the MT and the LXX is readily explicable because י and ו are easily confused: hence a Hebrew text reading באמונתו ("by his faithfulness") could easily be read as באמונתי ("by my faithfulness") or vice-versa. The text represented by Heb 10:38 could easily be explained as an alteration intended to underline the messianic significance of ὁ δίκαιος[71] or, as Barnabas Lindars thinks, to stress the importance of individual faith, rather than God's faithfulness.[72] The two LXX manuscripts that also have ὁ δίκαιός μου possibly result from assimilation to the text of Hebrews.[73]

Paul's citation differs from all the others in omitting the personal pronoun altogether. How is this circumstance to be explained? Was Paul working from an LXX manuscript that lacked the pronoun? Was he simply offering an approximate citation from memory? Was he aware of the textual problems and seeking to compromise by dropping the pronoun? Did he omit μου from an LXX text reading ἐκ πίστεώς μου because he wanted to interpret the passage to mean "the righteous one shall live by [his own] faith"?[74] These questions are impossible to answer, but some conclusions can be drawn. The LXX text (with ἐκ πίστεώς μου) provides unmistakable evidence for the currency of the idea in Hellenistic Judaism that Yahweh's own faithfulness was salvific, an idea which Paul echoes in Rom 3:3. If, however, Paul had intended unambiguously to affirm this interpretation of πίστις as God's own lifegiving faithfulness, he certainly missed his chance to do so in Gal 3:11. The text in the form given by Paul is ambiguous: πίστις, like the Hebrew אמונה, is a term that

71. Hanson, *Paul's Technique*, 45.

72. Lindars, *NT Apologetic*, 231.

73. Manson ("Argument from Prophecy," 134) regards this reading as the original LXX text.

74. Lindars (*NT Apologetic*, 231) thinks that ἐκ πίστεώς μου is "undoubtedly the true Septuagint text" and that Paul deliberately omits μου, "leaving the text free for his own interpretation."

139

may with equal aptness be used to describe either God's steadfast faithfulness to his people or the trusting and faithful response of people to God.[75] The textual history of Hab 2:4 shows that it was understood at different times in each of these two ways. Paul, whatever his reasons, has cited the text in a form that makes no explicit choice between the LXX and MT readings. Thus, whether intentionally or not, Paul has left room for πίστις to assume multivalent significance.

In fact, there are at least three possible interpretations of πίστις in Paul's version of Hab 2:4.

— God's faithfulness
— the faith(fulness) of the Messiah
— the faith of people in God.

There is no explicit discussion in Galatians (unlike Romans) of *God's* faithfulness, and there is therefore no reason to think that Paul intends to emphasize this meaning here. In fact, Paul's omission of μου from the citation may well mean that he was intentionally avoiding this interpretation of the text. There is every reason to think, however, that the remaining ambiguity of ἐκ πίστεως (= the faith of the Messiah/the faith of the believer) serves Paul's purposes very well. Thus, three possible interpretations of Gal 3:11 (= Hab 2:4 as employed by Paul) remain:

(a) The Messiah will live by (his own) faith(fulness).
(b) The righteous person will live as a result of the Messiah's faith(fulness).
(c) The righteous person will live by (his own) faith (in the Messiah).

Paul's thought is rendered wholly intelligible only if all three of these interpretations are held together and affirmed as correct. The ambiguity of Paul's formulation allows him to draw multiple implications out of the Habakkuk text.[76]

Paul's gospel is founded upon the story of a Messiah who is vindicated (= "justified") by God through faith. This Messiah (Jesus Christ) is not, how-

75. Hebert ("'Faithfulness' and 'Faith,'" 374) incorrectly maintains that "the Hebrew word denoting steadfastness and firmness applies properly to God and not to man"; thus he sets himself up for the criticism of James Barr (*The Semantics of Biblical Language* [London: Oxford University, 1961] 162-63). See the discussion of this debate in part C.1 of this chapter.

76. For a brief discussion of the proposition that Paul's language might have this multivalent character, see Chap. VI, part E, below.

140

ever, a solitary individual whose triumph accrues only to his own benefit; he is a representative figure in whom the destiny of all God's elect is embodied.[77] Thus, all are justified through *his* faith. Their response to him, however, is also one of faith. Consequently, the statement ὁ δίκαιος ἐκ πίστεως ζήσεται can function for Paul on all three levels at once. Level (b) is logically dependent on level (a) for its validity. While level (c), which has usually been taken to represent Paul's entire meaning, is not logically dependent on level (a), it may be regarded as more readily intelligible if level (a) is also affirmed as true.

4. Conclusions

The result of this discussion has been to open up interpretive possibilities beyond those considered in the standard commentaries. Two concluding observations about Gal 3:11 are in order.

(a) Once again, it is clear that the passage in view — not just 3:11, but the whole section 3:6-18 — does not explicitly point to Christ as the object of faith.[78] Gal 3:11 specifies neither object nor "subject" of faith; thus the phrase ἐκ πίστεως is capable of being understood in several different ways, some of which lead to a closer connection between christology and justification by pointing to Christ himself as the Righteous One who is justified ἐκ πίστεως.

(b) The exegetical considerations advanced here have pointed toward a reading of Gal 3:11 which places the primary emphasis upon Christ's faith, rather than upon the faith of the individual Christian as a means of attaining life. This point must now be explored further in our examination of Gal 3:22. Does Paul really speak of the faith *of* Jesus Christ?

C. The Faith of Jesus Christ (Gal 3:22)

Galatians 3:22 poses significant difficulties for the usual interpretation of πίστις Ἰησοῦ Χριστοῦ as "faith in Jesus Christ." The *RSV* translation, which is an impossible distortion of Paul's Greek, reflects the awkwardness that results from attempting to make the text say what Paul is usually supposed to mean:

77. See the discussion of "Jesus as Representative Man" offered by J. D. G. Dunn ("Paul's Understanding of the Death of Jesus," *Reconciliation and Hope* [ed. R. Banks; Grand Rapids: Eerdmans, 1974] 125-41). Interestingly, Dunn does not deal with any texts from Galatians. See also C. K. Barrett, *From First Adam to Last* (New York: Charles Scribner's Sons, 1962) 68-91.

78. This is pointed out also by Howard (*Crisis in Galatia*, 63).

"But the Scripture consigned all things to sin, that what was promised *to* faith in Jesus Christ might be given to those who believe." The preposition ἐκ cannot bear the meaning that *RSV* here forces upon it. Furthermore, the phrase ἐκ πίστεως ᾽Ιησοῦ Χριστοῦ should, on the analogy of Paul's usage in 2:16; 3:8, 11, 14, 24, almost certainly be understood to modify the verb δοθῇ rather than the noun ἐπαγγελία. Both of these difficulties are avoided in Burton's rendering: ". . . that, on the ground of faith in Jesus, the promise might be given to those who believe."[79] But two important problems remain.

First of all, the sentence, when so translated, is redundant. Paul could have omitted either ἐκ πίστεως ᾽Ιησοῦ Χριστοῦ or τοῖς πιστεύουσιν without changing the meaning.[80] Secondly, it is necessary to ask whether the genitive construction πίστις ᾽Ιησοῦ Χριστοῦ can in fact legitimately be translated as "faith *in* Jesus Christ." Here we plunge into the heart of the matter.

1. A Brief History of the Question

The possibility that Paul's expression πίστις ᾽Ιησοῦ Χριστοῦ should be interpreted as "the faith of Jesus Christ" was introduced into modern NT scholarship in 1891 by Johannes Haussleiter,[81] whose argument took its point of departure from the expression ἐκ πίστεως ᾽Ιησοῦ (Rom 3:26), which he saw as a clear reference to Jesus' own personal faith, because of Paul's use of the name ᾽Ιησοῦς with no further title. Haussleiter placed a great deal of weight on the

79. Burton, *Galatians*, 196. Cf. Betz, *Galatians*, 175. A more felicitous rendering that preserves this same sense is offered by *NEB:* ". . . so that faith in Jesus Christ may be the ground on which the promised blessing is given, and given to those who have such faith."

80. This is pointed out also by Williams ("Righteousness of God," 274), who concludes on this basis alone that "the apostle is making a deliberate distinction between the faith of Christ and the faith of Christians." Although I happen to agree with Williams, it is only fair to point out that he (and I) might be accused of overinterpreting the evidence. Redundancy would not in itself necessarily constitute a decisive objection against Burton's translation; one could easily enough point out other places where Paul's writing would benefit from the judicious application of a red pencil. Schlier (*Galater,* 165) attempts to explain Paul's intention in a way that minimizes the redundancy: "πίστις ist . . . in seiner Verbindung mit ἐκ und ohne Artikel das objective Heilsgut des Glaubens. Deshalb fügt Paulus auch noch ein τοῖς πιστεύουσιν hinzu. Der Glaube als das neue Heilsprinzip aktualisiert sich im jeweiligen Glaubensakt des Einzelnen." This interpretation, however, seems contrived; could Paul have expected his readers to make such a distinction between *Heilsprinzip* and *Glaubensakt?*

81. J. Haussleiter, "Der Glaube Jesu Christi und der christliche Glaube," *NKZ* 2 (1891) 109-45, 205-30. A list of earlier advocates of this interpretation has been compiled by G. Howard ("The Faith of Christ," *ExpTim* 85 [1974] 212-15 esp. 213).

distinction between the names Ἰησοῦς (the historical Jesus) and Χριστός (the glorified Lord, the object of religious faith) and upon the *order* in which they appear in Paul's formulations. He contended, for example, that whereas a hypothetical διὰ πίστεως Χριστοῦ Ἰησοῦ might be translated as "durch Glauben an Christum Jesum," the actual reading in Rom 3:22, διὰ πίστεως Ἰησοῦ Χριστοῦ, could only mean "durch Glauben Jesu Christi."[82] In spite of this overschematization of Paul's usage, and in spite of occasional lapses into melodramatic prose and the tendency to inquire into "das Seelenleben Jesu," Haussleiter's argument is actually conducted with considerable exegetical sophistication, as Sanday and Headlam recognized.[83] Haussleiter was not attempting to deny that Paul proclaimed faith in Christ; he was only seeking to determine the precise meaning of Paul's various expressions. Indeed, in a second essay, published in 1895, he studied the same problem in relation to the phrase πίστις Χριστοῦ in Galatians and concluded that it meant neither "the faith of Christ" nor "faith in Christ" but "der von Christus gewirkte, in ihm ruhende Glaube," thus coming into substantial agreement with Schlatter, without surrendering his earlier interpretation of πίστις Ἰησοῦ Χριστοῦ.[84] While Haussleiter's interpretation is still frequently mentioned (and dismissed) in commentaries on Romans,[85] few critics since Sanday and Headlam seem actually to have read and weighed his arguments,[86] some of which have been subsequently revived or independently recapitulated by other scholars.

In 1906, Gerhard Kittel, noting that Haussleiter's proposals had been roundly ignored, reopened the question in his article "πίστις Ἰησοῦ Χριστοῦ bei Paulus." With regard to Romans, Kittel advanced some substantial arguments, some of which we shall mention in part D, below, but, in dealing with Galatians, he unfortunately fell into a tendentious attempt to deny that εἰς

82. Haussleiter, "Der Glaube Jesu Christi," 127. See the excellent critique by O. Schmitz (*Die Christusgemeinschaft des Paulus im Lichte seines Genetivgebrauchs* [NTF 1/2; Gütersloh: Bertelsmann, 1924] .117). Schmitz charges Haussleiter with oversystematizing Paul and rightly insists that for Paul there was no distinction between the historical Jesus and the present living Lord. Haussleiter's sharp division between the two imposes an anachronistic scheme on Paul's thought.

83. W. Sanday and A. C. Headlam, *A Critical and Exegetical Commentary on the Epistle to the Romans* (ICC; New York: Charles Scribner's Sons, 1913) 83-84, 86-87. Sanday and Headlam, in spite of their kind words, rejected Haussleiter's exegesis.

84. Haussleiter, "Was versteht Paulus . . . ?" 178.

85. See, most recently, Käsemann (*An die Römer*, 87) and C. E. B. Cranfield (*A Critical and Exegetical Commentary on the Epistle to the Romans* [ICC; Edinburgh: T. & T. Clark, 1975] 1.203).

86. An exception to this judgment is Schmitz.

Χριστὸν Ἰησοῦν ἐπιστεύσαμεν (2:16) means "we believed in Jesus Christ." He tried to argue that εἰς here is equivalent to κατά.[87] Unlike Haussleiter, Kittel was undertaking a systematic attempt to argue that Paul did not regard Christ as the object of religious faith; because his position was overstated, it failed, not surprisingly, to win much acceptance.[88]

Deissmann also argued against the view that πίστις Ἰησοῦ Χριστοῦ should be translated as "Glaube an Jesum Christum," but he proposed that the genitive construction should be understood as a "genitive of fellowship" or "mystical genitive," so that πίστις Χριστοῦ = πίστις ἐν Χριστῷ: "'The faith of Jesus Christ' is 'faith in Christ,' the faith which the Christian has in fellowship with Christ."[89] Deissmann's views, in distinction from those of Haussleiter, were based less on detailed exegetical observation than upon an overall assessment of Paul's theology, which he understood as Paul's attempt to express the experience of spiritual union with Christ.

The proposals of Haussleiter, Kittel, and Deissmann precipitated a flurry of answering studies that investigated the role of "faith" in Paul's thought: we may mention in particular the monographs of W. H. P. Hatch, O. Schmitz, E. Wissmann, and W. Mundle.[90] Of this grouping, the work of Schmitz is the most thorough and cautious. He accepts as valid the arguments of Haussleiter and Kittel against the "objective genitive" interpretation of πίστις Ἰησοῦ Χριστοῦ, but he rejects their positive expositions of the genitive as subjective. While his own view is fairly close to that of Deissmann, he also rejects as unnecessary Deissmann's positing of a new grammatical category ("mystical genitive") to explain Paul's usage. According to Schmitz, πίστις Χριστοῦ belongs to the "Klasse der allgemein charakterisierenden Genetive" and should simply be translated as "Christus-Glaube" ("Christ-faith").[91] Hatch, Wissmann, and Mundle, on the other hand, emphatically rejected the arguments against an "objective genitive" interpretation. Their rebuttals, based primarily on Col 2:5 and Gal 2:16, seemed to win the field so thoroughly that Bultmann, in his *TDNT* article on "πίστις, πιστεύω, κτλ.," does

87. Kittel, "πίστις Ἰησοῦ Χριστοῦ," 428-29.

88. Schläger ("Bemerkungen zu πίστις Ἰησοῦ Χριστοῦ") did agree with Kittel's theological contention, but he achieved this result by arguing tendentiously that all the passages in Paul which speak of Jesus Christ as object of faith — not only the allegedly "objective genitive" constructions but also texts such as Gal 2:16 — should be regarded as interpolations.

89. Deissmann, *Paul*, 161-65.

90. Hatch, *Pauline Idea of Faith*; Schmitz, *Christusgemeinschaft*; Wissmann, *Das Verhältnis von ΠΙΣΤΙΣ und Christusfrommigkeit bei Paulus* (FRLANT N.F. 23; Göttingen: Vandenhoeck & Ruprecht, 1926); Mundle, *Glaubensbegriff*.

91. Schmitz, *Christusgemeinschaft*, 230, 134.

not even consider the problem. A single footnote states, without supporting argumentation, that the genitives following πίστις in Rom 3:22, 26; Gal 2:16, 3:22; Phil 1:27, 3:9; Col 2:12; Eph 3:12; and 2 Thess 2:13 are to be taken as objective genitives.[92] Thus the view that prevailed was substantially identical to that of Bousset, who spoke emphatically and without hesitation of πίστις εἰς Χριστὸν 'Ιησοῦν as the characteristic feature of Paul's piety.[93] Views of this sort were almost universally accepted in NT scholarship, and the issue seemed to disappear from consideration for a time.

However, in the 1950s A. G. Hebert and Thomas Torrance, apparently without any knowledge of the earlier discussion provoked by Haussleiter and Kittel in the world of German scholarship, raised once again the possibility that πίστις 'Ιησοῦ Χριστοῦ in Paul should be translated "faith of Jesus Christ."[94] Unlike Haussleiter and Kittel, who had based their arguments on contextual considerations, Hebert and Torrance appealed primarily to the fact that the word πίστις is the Greek equivalent of the Hebrew אֱמוּנָה. For them, the question was, as Hebert posed it, "whether the word 'faith,' as St. Paul uses it, carried a Hebrew rather than a Greek meaning,"[95] the meaning, that is, of "faithfulness" as opposed to "believing." This understanding of πίστις was important because both men wanted to interpret πίστις Χριστοῦ to mean "the faithfulness of God manifested in Christ's human faithfulness,"[96] an interpretation which is possible only if πίστις does not mean primarily "believing." In Torrance's case, at least, this exegesis took its inspiration from the christology of Karl Barth, who, in his Romans commentary, translates διὰ πίστεως 'Ιησοῦ Χριστοῦ (Rom 3:22) as "through his [i.e., God's] faithfulness in Jesus Christ."[97] Though Torrance appeals to the argument that πίστις has a "Hebrew" meaning, the real thesis of his article is to be found in his assertion that Paul presents Jesus as "the incarnate faithfulness of God." According to this interpretation, "He is the truth of God actualized in our midst — that is the faithfulness of Christ Jesus *(pistis Christou Iēsou)* of which St. Paul speaks so often."[98]

92. Bultmann, *TDNT* 6.204 n. 230.

93. "For the Christian, faith, the πίστις εἰς Χριστὸν 'Ιησοῦν, becomes the organ with which he grasps the present reality of the πνεῦμα-κύριος" (Bousset, *Kyrios Christos*, 205). This in spite of the fact that Paul nowhere uses the phrase πίστις εἰς Χριστὸν 'Ιησοῦν.

94. Hebert, "'Faithfulness' and 'Faith'"; T. Torrance, "One Aspect of the Biblical Conception of Faith," *ExpTim* 68 (1957) 111-14.

95. Hebert, "'Faithfulness' and 'Faith,'" 373.

96. Ibid., 376.

97. K. Barth, *The Epistle to the Romans* (London: Oxford, 1933) 96. Barth makes no effort to justify this rather problematical translation.

98. Torrance, "Biblical Conception of Faith," 112.

Neither one of these scholars wanted to deny the reality or importance of human faith in Christ. The place of "faith in Christ" in Torrance's understanding is spelled out in his conclusions.

> In most of these passages the *pistis Iesou Christou* does not refer only either to the faithfulness of Christ or to the answering faithfulness of man, but is essentially a polarized expression denoting the faithfulness of Christ as its main ingredient but also involving or at least suggesting the answering faithfulness of man, and so his belief in Christ, but even within itself the faithfulness of Christ involves both the faithfulness of God and the faithfulness of the man Jesus. . . . Jesus Christ is not only the incarnation of the divine *pistis,* but he is the embodiment and actualization of man's *pistis* in covenant with God.[99]

Here the influence of Barthian christology is unmistakable. The question that we must pursue here concerns the extent to which Torrance's theological assertions are justifiable as exegesis of the texts to which he refers.

The suggestions of Hebert and Torrance were immediately subjected to criticism by C. F. D. Moule[100] and by John Murray,[101] but the truly crushing rejoinder was delivered by James Barr. In his widely influential book, *The Semantics of Biblical Language,* Barr attacked the linguistically naive assumptions that the Greek πίστις could have a fundamental "Hebrew meaning" which it would carry regardless of context or usage and that a single word could carry the freightload of theological concepts that are attached to πίστις by Hebert and Torrance.[102] Barr's urbane critique builds inexorably toward the conclusion that "the linguistic portions of the essays by Hebert and Torrance contain practically no facts which are not used or presented in extremely misleading ways."[103]

Anyone who reads Barr's criticisms will necessarily acknowledge their force; Hebert and Torrance argued their case badly and on illegitimate grounds.[104] Nonetheless, the twenty years since the publication of Barr's

99. Ibid., 113.

100. C. F. D. Moule, [letter to the editor in response to Torrance's article], *ExpTim* 68 (1957) 157.

101. J. Murray, *The Epistle to the Romans* (NICNT; 2 vols.; Grand Rapids: Eerdmans, 1959) 1.363-74: "Appendix B: From Faith to Faith."

102. Barr, *Semantics of Biblical Language,* 161-205.

103. Ibid., 205.

104. It is significant that Barr's criticisms, as he himself indicates, do not invalidate the theological position advanced by Torrance and Hebert; his critique merely undercuts the linguistic arguments employed. Our intent here will be to show that a very similar interpreta-

withering refutation of the Hebert-Torrance position have witnessed a profuse upspringing of new advocates for the claim that πίστις Ἰησοῦ Χριστοῦ in Paul means "the faith of Jesus Christ."[105] Even many who do not accept this particular interpretation have called for a reopening of the question.[106] Why should this be so? I would suggest that the nature of the evidence requires it: "Faith *in* Jesus Christ" is not the most natural translation of πίστις Ἰησοῦ Χριστοῦ; once the question has been raised, it is understandable that critics should seek a more satisfying interpretation. Particularly in a time when the fundamental contours of Pauline thought are being reassessed, it is not surprising that the meaning of this expression should be under discussion; Schenk has rightly noted, for example, that a reconsideration of "faith" in Paul is a corollary of the reconsideration of "righteousness" that was stimulated by Ernst Käsemann.[107]

In the following pages, our brief consideration of the meaning of

tion of πίστις Ἰησοῦ Χριστοῦ can be advanced without recourse to the fallacious modes of argumentation employed by Torrance and Hebert.

105. Some of the scholars who have argued in favor of this interpretation are as follows: P. Vallotton, *Le Christ et la Foi* (Geneva: Labor et Fides, 1960); H. W. Schmidt, *Der Brief des Paulus an die Römer* (THKNT 6; Berlin: Evangelische Verlagsanstalt, 1966) 64-66; R. N. Longenecker, "The Obedience of Christ in the Theology of the Early Church," *Reconciliation and Hope*, 142-52; Taylor, "Function of ΠΙΣΤΙΣ ΧΡΙΣΤΟΥ in Galatians"; G. Howard, "On the 'Faith of Christ'"; idem, "Romans 3:21-31 and the Inclusion of the Gentiles," *HTR* 63 (1970) 223-33; idem, "The Faith of Christ"; idem, *Crisis in Galatia*, 46-65; E. R. Goodenough, "Paul and the Hellenization of Christianity," *Religions in Antiquity: Essays in Memory of Erwin Ramsdell Goodenough* (ed. J. Neusner; Leiden: Brill, 1968) 23-68; J. Bligh, "Did Jesus Live by Faith?"; M. Barth, "The Faith of the Messiah"; H. Ljungmann, *Pistis,* 38-40; D. W. B. Robinson, "Faith of Jesus Christ"; Hanson, *Paul's Understanding of Jesus,* 4-10; idem, *Paul's Technique,* 39-51; S. K. Williams, "Righteousness of God," 265-80; L. Gaston, "Abraham and the Righteousness of God," *Horizons in Biblical Theology* 2 (1980) 54-55; T. E. Pollard, "Exit the Alexandrian Christ: Some Reflections on Contemporary Christology in the Light of New Testament Studies," *Colloquium* 13 (1980-81) 16-23; L. T. Johnson, "Romans 3:21-26 and the Faith of Jesus," *CBQ* 44 (1982) 77-90.

106. For example: H. Binder, *Der Glaube bei Paulus* (Berlin: Evangelische Verlagsanstalt, 1968); Stuhlmacher, *Gottes Gerechtigkeit,* 81-84; Schenk, "Gerechtigkeit Gottes und Glaube Christi," 161-74. The problem has also been summarized by Neugebauer (*In Christus,* 150-56) and by K. Kertelge (*"Rechtfertigung" bei Paulus* [NTAbh N.F. 3; Münster: Aschendorff, 1 1967] 162-66). The article of A. Hultgren ("The *Pistis Christou* Formulation in Paul," *NovT* 22 [1980] 248-63), which became available to me only after the completion of this chapter, in no way necessitates any modification of the position argued here. Hultgren tries to argue on syntactical grounds that the subjective genitive interpretation of πίστις Ἰησοῦ Χριστοῦ is "excluded" (p. 258). His arguments are, however, refuted by Johnson ("Romans 3:21-26 and the Faith of Jesus").

107. Schenk, "Gerechtigkeit Gottes und Glaube Christi," 161-63.

πίστις Ἰησοῦ Χριστοῦ will be divided into three parts: first we shall examine the grammatical issue; secondly, we shall explore issues related to the theological interpretation of πίστις Ἰησοῦ Χριστοῦ; finally, we shall examine other relevant texts in Galatians to see whether they might shed any light on our problem.

2. The Grammatical Issue

We have already pointed out that Gal 3:22 describes πίστις Ἰησοῦ Χριστοῦ as the source or ground *out of* which the promise is given to those who believe. Clearly, the concept πίστις/πιστεύειν is used in this verse with a double directionality; it characterizes both the recipients (οἱ πιστεύοντες) and the source from which the promise is given (ἐκ πίστεως Ἰησοῦ Χριστοῦ). With regard to the phrase Ἰησοῦ Χριστοῦ, the fundamental grammatical question is whether πίστις followed by a proper noun in the genitive case should be understood to mean "faith *in* X" (objective genitive) or "faith *of* X" (subjective genitive). With regard to Gal 3:22, Kittel comments rightly: "Jeder unbefangene Leser wird auch hier in erster Linie den fraglichen Genetiv subjektiv verstehen und nur dann darauf verzichten, wenn gewichtige Gründe im Kontexte dazu zwingen."[108] It has been argued, of course, that Gal 2:16 does provide precisely what Kittel demands, a compelling reason in the context to read Ἰησοῦ Χριστοῦ as an objective genitive. As we have seen in our consideration of this passage above, however, this sentence is not as perspicuous as many interpreters have supposed. For the moment let us set it aside and examine the grammatical evidence that can be assembled from Paul's other uses of πίστις followed by a name or a pronoun.

Apart from the disputed cases in which the genitive is Χριστοῦ or its equivalent, George Howard tabulates twenty-four such instances,[109] of which twenty refer to the faith of Christians, two to the faith of Abraham (Rom 4:12, 16), one to the faith of anyone who believes (Rom 4:5), and one to the faithfulness of God (Rom 3:3).[110] Thus in every instance in which πίστις is followed by a proper noun or pronoun in the genitive case, the genitive is unmistakably subjective. While this fact is not conclusive in itself, it must be weighed seriously.

---

108. Kittel, "πίστις Ἰησοῦ Χριστοῦ," 431.
109. Howard, "On the 'Faith of Christ,'" 459.
110. For a fuller elucidation of the meaning of πίστις θεοῦ in Rom 3:3, see R. B. Hays, "Psalm 143 and the Logic of Romans 3," *JBL* 99 (1980) 107-15.

In a more recent article, Howard extends his survey to the LXX and the literature of Hellenistic Judaism in general, and he arrives at the same result, which he is bold enough to state as a general principle.

> It was inappropriate to the Hellenistic Jewish mentality to express the object of faith by means of the objective genitive. Though a textbook case can be made for it, in actual practice it does not appear. Characteristically the writers use the preposition when they wish to express the object.[111]

For what it may be worth, D. W. B. Robinson contributes the observation that the ninth edition of Liddell and Scott cites no instance of πίστις followed by an objective genitive.[112] Against this sort of evidence, however, it may be argued that the NT itself supplies a few instances of πίστιν with an objective genitive, the clearest of which is probably Mark 11:22: ἔχετε πίστιν θεοῦ.[113] Robinson attempts to explain this usage away,[114] but it is probably wisest to accept that the objective genitive construction after πίστις is possible, though rare, in NT Greek. The really significant point, however, is that this construction cannot be demonstrated in the Pauline corpus. Against the evidence collected by Howard, the objective genitive "parallels" provided by Murray from non-Pauline texts weigh lightly indeed.[115]

Finally, the most telling piece of evidence from a grammatical point of view is the fact, already noticed by Haussleiter,[116] that the expression ἐκ πίστεως Ἰησοῦ (Χριστοῦ) (Rom 3:26; Gal 3:22) has a precise parallel in Rom 4:16, ἐκ πίστεως Ἀβραάμ. Kittel comments: "Will man nicht behaupten, dass Paulus von einem Glauben an Abraham redet, so muss man auch zugeben, dass er bei dem Korrelaten Ausdruck von einem Glauben an Christus nicht hat reden wollen."[117]

---

111. Howard, "The Faith of Christ," 213. Howard's observation applies to constructions with the noun πίστις. It should be added that the LXX often uses the *dative* case without a preposition to express the object of the verb πιστεύω. We have an instance of this in Gal 3:6 (quoting Gen 15:6): Ἀβραὰμ ἐπίστευσεν τῷ θεῷ. This is perhaps best translated not as "Abraham believed in God," but as "Abraham trusted God."

112. Robinson, "Faith of Jesus Christ," 78.

113. Cf. also Acts 3:16, ἐπὶ τῇ πίστει τοῦ ὀνόματος αὐτοῦ. In Jas 2:1, Rev 2:13, 14:12, however, πίστις, as in Gal 1:23, means "the [Christian] faith," and the genitive is, as Robinson rightly judges ("Faith of Jesus Christ," 79), "broadly adjectival."

114. Robinson, "Faith of Jesus Christ," 102-3.

115. Murray, *Romans*, 1.368-70. A similar criticism of Murray's position is cogently advanced by Williams ("Righteousness of God," 272-74).

116. Haussleiter, "Der Glaube Jesu Christi," 110-11.

117. Kittel, "πίστις Ἰησοῦ Χριστοῦ," 424. Murray (*Romans*, 1.366), interestingly, seizes

Thus, the balance of the grammatical evidence favors the view that πίστις Ἰησοῦ Χριστοῦ means "faith of Jesus Christ," however that might be interpreted. The case on grammatical grounds for the translation "faith in Jesus Christ" is really very weak. The latter rendering has nonetheless won widespread acceptance on the assumption that it makes more sense theologically. This assumption must now be evaluated.

3. The Theological Issue

The basic theological issue is this: what would it mean for Paul to speak of Jesus Christ's own faith as the basis upon which "the promise" is given to those who believe? Does such a conception make sense and does it fit intelligibly into the overall structure of Paul's thought?

We would do well to begin by asking whether it is more intelligible to suppose that "believing in Jesus Christ" is the basis upon which "the promise" is given to those who believe.[118] Is this traditional view entirely satisfactory as an account of Paul's thought? If this is the correct reading of Paul, what sense does it make for him to invoke the example of Abraham, whose faith was, after all, not directed toward Jesus? Indeed the apparent appeal to Abraham as the prototype of the justified believer has always created considerable difficulties for Christian exegesis and theology precisely because his faith was *not* directed toward Christ as object: Ἀβραὰμ ἐπίστευσεν τῷ θεῷ καὶ ἐλογίσθη αὐτῷ εἰς δικαιοσύνην (Gal 3:6, quoting Gen 15:6).[119] This is one of the causes of the difficulty described by G. Ebeling, that the doctrine of justification by faith, as usually understood, is not integrally linked with christology. If we are justified by believing in Jesus Christ, in what sense is Abraham's theocentric

---

upon this same text to prove, contra Torrance, that the expression ἐκ πίστεως can only refer to human faith directed toward God, not God's own faithfulness. But Murray fails to see the implications of his claim for the meaning of the phrase ἐκ πίστεως Ἰησοῦ (Χριστοῦ).

118. The theological inadequacy of this interpretation has been widely acknowledged. Whiteley (*Theology of St. Paul,* 165), for example, comments: "Faith is not the reason why God justifies some and not others, but the 'response' of those who are justified." Critics have been slower, however, to draw the consequent conclusion that ἐκ πίστεως Ἰησοῦ Χριστοῦ in Gal 3:22 *must* mean something other than "by believing in Jesus Christ."

119. For a discussion of this problem, see H. Boers, *Theology out of the Ghetto: A New Testament Exegetical Study concerning Religious Exclusiveness* (Leiden: Brill, 1972) 74-104, "The Significance of Abraham for the Christian Faith." Cf. E. Käsemann, "The Faith of Abraham in Romans 4," *Perspectives,* 79-101. It is not appropriate to read into Paul the Johannine idea (see John 8:56) that Abraham saw and believed in Jesus.

faith a precedent for ours, or in what sense is our christocentric faith analogous to his? If Abraham could be justified by trusting God, why should we need to believe in *Christ* to be justified? Why not simply put our trust in God, as Abraham did?

Paul's entire discussion makes much better sense if he is interpreted as presupposing that Jesus Christ, like Abraham, is justified ἐκ πίστεως and that we, as a consequence, are justified *in* him (cf. Gal 2:17, δικαιωθῆναι ἐν Χριστῷ), as a result of his faith(fulness). This position is argued forcefully by Markus Barth.

> The justification of man cannot take place upon the ground of an immediate relationship between the believer and God. . . . The means of justification is Jesus Christ himself in *his* relationship to God and to man. He alone brings us into the right with God . . . ; by his faithfulness he is the true representative of all men. . . . When [Paul] elaborates on justification, the faith of Christ is the means and the faith of men in Christ is the purpose and response.[120]

This kind of representative christology is clearly present elsewhere in the NT, especially in Hebrews, which depicts Jesus as τὸν τῆς πίστεως ἀρχηγὸν καὶ τελειωτὴν Ἰησοῦν (Heb 12:2). Likewise, Eph 3:11-12 (a very interesting text for our present purposes) speaks of "Christ Jesus our Lord, ἐν ᾧ ἔχομεν τὴν παρρησίαν καὶ προσαγωγὴν ἐν πεποιθήσει διὰ τῆς πίστεως αὐτοῦ."

The *RSV* translates διὰ τῆς πίστεως αὐτοῦ as "through our faith in him." Surely, however, this is a very strained translation; the more natural rendering would be "through his faith(fulness)," and the meaning would be that we who are "in" Christ Jesus have access to God as a result of Christ's faithful execution of God's eternal purpose (πρόθεσις). Christ is here, as in Hebrews, portrayed as the ἀρχηγός, the representative figure in whom the drama of salvation is enacted, in whose destiny the destiny of all is carried.

Is it possible that the kind of representative christology that appears in Hebrews and Ephesians might provide some decisive clues for understanding Paul's christology also? Is it possible that Eph 3:12, as interpreted here, might provide a new angle of vision into the meaning of Paul's expressions such as διὰ πίστεως Ἰησοῦ Χριστοῦ and ἐκ πίστεως Ἰησοῦ Χριστοῦ? We may compare to Eph 3:12 the close parallel in Rom 5:1-2: Δικαιωθέντες οὖν ἐκ πίστεως εἰρήνην ἔχομεν πρὸς τὸν θεὸν διὰ τοῦ κυρίου ἡμῶν Ἰησοῦ Χριστοῦ δι' οὗ καὶ τὴν προσαγωγὴν ἐσχήκαμεν τῇ πίστει εἰς τὴν χάριν ταύτην ἐν ᾗ ἑστήκαμεν.

---

120. M. Barth, "Faith of the Messiah," 366, 367, 369. Barth presents a series of seven arguments in favor of translating πίστις Χριστοῦ as "faith of the Messiah."

Murray also notes this parallel and uses it to argue that, since the faith mentioned in Rom 5:2 is "undoubtedly our faith in Christ," πίστις αὐτοῦ in Eph 3:12 must also mean "our faith in him."[121] Is it possible, however, for the inference to be drawn in the opposite direction, so that the meaning of ἐκ πίστεως and τῇ πίστει in Rom 5:1-2 (which, after all, are presented absolutely, with no specification of object of "subject") might be open to more doubt than Murray supposes?

Is it really so odd to think that Paul might attribute soteriological significance to Jesus' faith? It is universally acknowledged that Paul speaks at least twice in his letters of Jesus' obedience[122] and attributes to this obedience saving significance. This is said most unmistakably in Rom 5:19: ὥσπερ γὰρ διὰ τῆς παρακοῆς τοῦ ἑνὸς ἀνθρώπου ἁμαρτωλοὶ κατεστάθησαν οἱ πολλοί, οὕτως καὶ διὰ τῆς ὑπακοῆς τοῦ ἑνὸς δίκαιοι κατασταθήσονται οἱ πολλοί. Christ's obedience is here presented (in juxtaposition to Adam's disobedience) as a representative action, vicariously effective on behalf of "the many": the destiny of the many is enacted in the one. A clearer articulation of a representative christology could hardly be demanded.[123] Furthermore, as Bultmann properly insisted, obedience and faith belong in the closest possible relation to one another, as the expression ὑπακοὴ πίστεως (Rom 1:5) indicates.[124] If Paul can speak so compellingly in Rom 5:19 of the soteriological consequences of Christ's ὑπακοή, there is no a priori reason to deny that Paul could intend the expression πίστις Ἰησοῦ Χριστοῦ to refer to Christ's soteriologically efficacious faith(fulness).[125]

---

121. Murray, *Romans*, 1.370.

122. Rom 5:19; Phil 2:8. This fact is pointed out by V. P. Furnish, *Theology and Ethics in Paul* (Nashville: Abingdon, 1968) 186. Furnish also calls attention to Gal 1:4 with regard to this motif.

123. For expositions of this type of christology in Paul, see the following: K. Barth, *Christus und Adam nach Römer 5* (Theologische Studien 35; Zollikon-Zürich: Evangelischer Verlag, 1952); Barrett, *First Adam;* E. G. Edwards, *Christ, A Curse and the Cross: An Interpretive Study of Galatians 3:13* (Th.D. diss., Princeton Theological Seminary; Ann Arbor: University Microfilms, 1972) 316-21; Dunn, "Paul's Understanding of the Death of Jesus"; Longenecker, "The Obedience of Christ." An intriguing parallel to this reading of Paul is found in Hans Frei's analysis of the "identity" of Jesus as portrayed in the Gospels: "In the New Testament story, Jesus is seen to enact the good of men on their behalf — or their salvation — in perfect obedience to God" (*The Identity of Jesus Christ* [Philadelphia: Fortress, 1975] 102).

124. Bultmann, *Theology*, 1.314. Bultmann interprets the expression to mean "the obedience which faith is"; cf. Furnish, *Theology and Ethics*, 184-85.

125. Hanson (*Paul's Understanding of Jesus*, 11-13) adds to the discussion another Pauline passage that is not usually considered in connection with these questions: 2 Cor 4:13-14. Ἔχοντες δὲ τὸ αὐτὸ πνεῦμα τῆς πίστεως κατὰ τὸ γεγραμμένον· ἐπίστευσα διὸ ἐλάλησα,

We may conclude that it is indeed theologically intelligible to interpret πίστις Ἰησοῦ Χριστοῦ as "the faith of Jesus Christ." Such a conception can be understood to manifest a representative christology attested not only elsewhere in the NT but also elsewhere in Paul's letters. To read Gal 3:22 in this way will require a significant shift in our understanding of the shape of Paul's thought, but this new reading can be shown to yield a configuration which is coherent — more coherent, as Chapter V will argue, than the conventional way of understanding Paul.

Gal 3:22b, then, may be interpreted to mean that the promise (= the Spirit; cf. 3:14) is given (by God) to believers as a result of Jesus Christ's faithfulness. This is precisely the interpretation that resulted from an application of our model for narrative analysis in Chapter III. It should be stressed that none of the arguments advanced here in favor of this interpretation has probative force, but taken together they offer an interpretation of Gal 3:22 that gives a clear meaning to an expression which would otherwise be a redundancy and which is more coherent with other basic christological assertions of Paul than any other interpretation. We must now consider whether this interpretation of πίστις Ἰησοῦ Χριστοῦ will yield equally satisfactory results in the other cases where analogous expressions occur in Galatians.

4. Other Texts

(a) Gal 2:20b: ὃ δὲ νῦν ζῶ ἐν σαρκί ἐν πίστει ζῶ τῇ τοῦ υἱοῦ τοῦ θεοῦ. It may be regarded as a matter for some amazement that English translations (with

---

καὶ ἡμεῖς πιστεύομεν, διὸ καὶ λαλοῦμεν, εἰδότες ὅτι ὁ ἐγείρας τὸν κύριον Ἰησοῦν καὶ ἡμᾶς σὺν Ἰησοῦ ἐγερεῖ. . . . "Having the same spirit of faith (as it is written, 'I believed; therefore I spoke'), we also believe and therefore we also speak, knowing that the one who raised the Lord Jesus will also raise us with Jesus." Hanson asks simply, "Paul has the same spirit of faith as who?" (*RSV* supplies an answer by pointing to the psalmist: ". . . the same spirit of faith [as he had who wrote]: . . . .") Hanson suggests plausibly that Psalm 116 (LXX 115), which Paul quotes here, would have been read by Paul as a messianic psalm, in which Christ himself is the speaker. Thus, "if we go back to the Septuagint and read it with Paul's eyes, there can be only one answer: Paul is claiming the same spirit of faith as Christ." Hanson's interpretation is almost surely correct, because the whole thrust of the passage depends upon a series of parallels that Paul is drawing between himself and Christ. The verses quoted here say in effect, "Jesus believed and spoke, and God raised him; therefore, we also believe and speak, knowing that God will raise us too along with him." This pattern of correspondence between Jesus and those who are in or with him will be considered at greater length in Chap. VI. Here we may merely note that this text lends further support to the hypothesis that Paul may have thought of Jesus as one who "believed."

the exception of the *KJV*) invariably interpret this sentence to mean "The life I now live in the flesh I live by faith *in* the Son of God." Once we have admitted even the bare possibility that πίστις for Paul may designate not only a phenomenon within the consciousness of the individual subject but also a source of life-giving power external to the individual, it becomes immediately clear that Gal 2:20 makes much better sense if we take the genitive τοῦ υἱοῦ τοῦ θεοῦ either as a subjective genitive or as a "genitivus auctoris,"[126] producing the following sense: "The life that I now live in the flesh I live by faith, i.e., by the faith of the Son of God. . . ," or ". . . by the faith which comes from the Son of God."[127]

A very illuminating parallel to Paul's usage in Gal 2:20 of an extended genitive construction as if it were an adjective in the attributive position is found in Rom 5:15: πολλῷ μᾶλλον ἡ χάρις τοῦ θεοῦ καὶ ἡ δωρεὰ ἐν χάριτι τῇ τοῦ ἑνὸς ἀνθρώπου Ἰησοῦ Χριστοῦ εἰς τοὺς πολλοὺς ἐπερίσσευσεν. It would never occur to anyone to translate τοῦ ἑνὸς ἀνθρώπου Ἰησοῦ Χριστοῦ here as an objective genitive. Yet the only real difference is that here the phrase is appended as a modifier of χάρις, whereas in Gal 2:20 the precisely parallel phrase functions as a modifier of πίστις. Laid out schematically, the parallel looks like this:

Rom 5:15 ἐν χάριτι τῇ [τοῦ ἑνὸς ἀνθρώπου Ἰησοῦ Χριστοῦ.]
Gal 2:20 ἐν πίστει τῇ [τοῦ υἱοῦ τοῦ θεοῦ.]

In Rom 5:15, the grace of God is manifested "in the grace *of* the one man Jesus Christ."[128] In Gal 2:20, Paul is provocatively denying his own role as the acting "subject" of his own life and claiming that he has been supplanted in this capacity by Christ: "the faith of the Son of God" is now the governing power in Paul's existence.

This interpretation treats the conjunction δέ in 2:20b in a continuative rather than adversative sense. Usually the verse is read as though Paul in 2:20a

---

126. This observation runs directly counter to Wissmann's assessment of the same verse: "Gibt doch bereits Gal 2.20 den zwingenden Hinweis darauf, dass auch die übrigen Stellen nur einen 'Glauben an Christus' meinen. . . ." (*ΠΙΣΤΙΣ und Christusfrömmigkeit*, 69). This surprising assertion is unsupported by any further argumentation. A similar opinion is expressed by Schmitz (*Christusgemeinschaft*, 108).

127. These two translations differ in meaning, of course; Paul's language will admit either interpretation. Either one is a far more natural rendering of the Greek than the conventional objective genitive translation.

128. This affirmation, of course, occurs in the context of the same exposition of representative christology already discussed in relation to Rom 5:19.

makes a hyperbolic claim, then stops himself and offers in 2:20b a dialectical correction to the first half of the verse. I am suggesting that all three occurrences of δέ in 2:20 might merely serve as connectives that keep the sense flowing continuously from Χριστῷ συνεσταύρωμαι (2:19b). It is clear that the first two occurrences of δέ (2:20a) function in precisely this way; if Paul did intend a sudden sharp turnabout in 2:20b, would it not be necessary for him to use ἀλλά or some more clearly adversative expression?

The fact that the Son of God is viewed as the acting subject of the "faith" mentioned in Gal 2:20 is confirmed not only by Paul's immediately preceding claim that "it is no longer I who live, but Christ who lives in me," but also by the immediately following participial modifier: τοῦ υἱοῦ θεοῦ τοῦ ἀγαπήσαντός με καὶ παραδόντος ἑαυτὸν ὑπὲρ ἐμοῦ. The whole context portrays Christ as the active agent and Paul as the instrument through which and/or for whom Christ's activity comes to expression. Indeed, this unrelenting emphasis on the priority of Christ's (or God's) willing and doing over any human will or action is the theological keynote of the whole letter. Thus, a strong case can be made for taking τοῦ υἱοῦ τοῦ θεοῦ in 2:20 as a subjective genitive or at least as a genitive of author. This fits the context more satisfactorily than the objective genitive interpretation, "faith in the Son of God."

(b) Gal 3:26: πάντες γὰρ υἱοὶ θεοῦ ἐστε διὰ τῆς πίστεως ἐν Χριστῷ Ἰησοῦ. This text requires only brief consideration, because, although some of the older commentators seized upon it as evidence for the "objective genitive" interpretation of πίστις Χριστοῦ,[129] there is now virtually universal critical agreement that ἐν Χριστῷ Ἰησοῦ neither modifies πίστις nor expresses the object toward which faith is directed. Instead, we find here an instance of Paul's characteristic formula ἐν Χριστῷ, as the parallelism with 3:28d makes clear.

(3:26) πάντες γὰρ υἱοὶ θεοῦ ἐστε διὰ τῆς πίστεως ἐν Χριστῷ Ἰησοῦ.
(3:28d) πάντες γὰρ ὑμεῖς εἷς ἐστε   ἐν Χριστῷ Ἰησοῦ.

Betz suggests plausibly that διὰ τῆς πίστεως in 3:26 might be a Pauline addition to a traditional baptismal formulation.[130] In any case, in its present context πίστις in 3:26 might be understood in light of 3:23, 25, where ἡ πίστις, used absolutely, designates the new era or principle or power which has now "come."[131] The connection is clearly spelled out by Schlier, who paraphrases 3:25-26 as follows.

129. For example, Mundle, *Glaubensbegriff*, 74 n. 1; Lagrange, *Galates*, 92.
130. Betz, *Galatians*, 181.
131. These passages constitute the point of departure for Binder, who maintains that

Nachdem aber der Glaube gekommen ist, stehen wir nicht mehr unter dem Paidagogos. Denn ihr alle seid Söhne Gottes. Das hat der eben erwähnte Glaube vermittelt. Ihr seid es aber in Christus Jesus.[132]

Thus, the fact that ἐν Χριστῷ ᾽Ιησοῦ follows διὰ τῆς πίστεως in the word order of Paul's sentence is of no particular consequence; he does not intend to speak of a πίστις ἐν Χριστῷ ᾽Ιησοῦ. Even the *RSV,* which otherwise leans strongly, as we have seen, to interpretations which stress "believing in Christ," renders this sentence, clearly and correctly, in accordance with the interpretation set forth here: ". . . for in Christ Jesus you are all sons of God, through faith." Thus Gal 3:26 (along with 3:23, 25) offers neither confirmation nor disconfirmation with regard to the thesis that πίστις ᾽Ιησοῦ Χριστοῦ might be interpreted in the framework of a narrative christology as "the faith of Jesus Christ." This verse, like 3:14, names πίστις as the principle or power through which salvation is actualized, but it tells us neither whose faith is meant nor how this faith accomplishes the result ascribed to it.

D. "The Faith of Jesus Christ" in Rom 3:21-26

In the course of this investigation of "the faith of Jesus Christ" in Galatians, there have necessarily been numerous sidelong glances into closely parallel texts in Romans, but there has been no systematic effort to evaluate the meaning of Rom 3:21-26, where Paul twice speaks, in the very center of his exposition of the gospel, of πίστις ᾽Ιησοῦ (Χριστοῦ). A full-scale examination of this crucial text is not possible here, but we may indicate briefly how it relates to the interpretation of Paul that is proposed in this study.

In point of fact, by working with Galatians, I have been considering the most difficult case for my proposed interpretation; Romans has always proved more hospitable territory than Galatians for advocates of the "faith of Jesus Christ" interpretation. The evidence of Romans 3 fits very neatly into the narrative pattern that has been developed in the foregoing discussion. Consider the following points of evidence.

(a) First of all, it should be noted that Romans is from start to finish thoroughly theocentric. Nowhere is there any statement comparable to Gal 2:16 that unambiguously presents Christ as an object of faith. In Romans,

---

πίστις in Pauline usage always means "das von Gott herkommende Geschehen im Neuen Bund, das den Charakter einer transsubjektiven Grösse, einer göttlichen Geschehenswirklichkeit hat" (*Glaube bei Paulus,* 5).

132. Schlier, *Galater,* 171.

righteousness is reckoned "to those who believe in *the One who raised Jesus our Lord from the dead*" (τοῖς πιστεύουσιν ἐπὶ τὸν ἐγείραντα ᾽Ιησοῦν τὸν κύριον ἡμῶν ἐκ νεκρῶν, 4:24).

(b) Second, as Kittel noted, the references to πίστις ᾽Ιησοῦ (Χριστοῦ) in Rom 3:22, 26 are sandwiched between unmistakably "subjective genitive" references to πίστις θεοῦ (3:3) and πίστις ᾽Αβραάμ (4:12, 16).[133] Furthermore, there is no indication anywhere in the surrounding context that Jesus Christ is to be considered the object of faith. Consequently,

> der Apostel würde sich für den Leser geradezu unverständlich ausgedrückt haben, wenn er den Glauben an Jesum gemeint hätte. Denn weder durch die Ausführungen in den vorangegangenen noch durch diejenigen in den nachfolgenden Kapiteln hat er ihm ein solches Verständnis nahegelegt. Nirgends hat er in dem ganzen Briefe in unmissverständlicher Weise ausgesprochen, dass man an Jesum glauben müsse, um gerecht zu werden.[134]

This argument carries a particular cogency precisely in the case of Romans, since Paul was writing to a congregation where he had never visited in person; thus, fewer things could be taken for granted.

(c) Closely related to the previous point is the fact that ἐκ πίστεως ᾽Αβραάμ (4:16) forms a precise formal parallel to the phrase ἐκ πίστεως ᾽Ιησοῦ in 3:26. This observation was also emphasized by E. R. Goodenough, in his posthumously published essay, "Paul and the Hellenization of Christianity."

---

133. It is interesting to note that although both of these expressions are subjective genitive constructions, the meaning of πίστις is not the same in both cases. Cf. Williams, "Righteousness of God," 275: "When Paul speaks of the *pistis tou theou* (Rom 3:3), he means that God is trustworthy because he is true to his promises, the program and purpose announced to Abraham. But when he talks about the *pistis Abraam* (Rom 4:12, 16), he does not mean that Abraham was trustworthy, but that he trusted God, relying totally on him who was able to do what he had promised (4:21)." This observation serves to demonstrate once again that our strict distinction between "faith" and "faithfulness" is not applicable to the Greek word πίστις, which contains both ideas. This is a point of considerable importance for us in our attempts to determine the meaning of πίστις ᾽Ιησοῦ Χριστοῦ. Torrance may not have expressed himself in the most felicitous manner when he argued that πίστις ᾽Ιησοῦ Χριστοῦ is a "polarized expression," but his fundamental insight was correct: the word πίστις contains semantic potentialities that cannot be adequately reproduced by a single English word. Thus, an expression such as πίστις ᾽Ιησοῦ Χριστοῦ is inherently multivalent.

134. Kittel, "πίστις ᾽Ιησοῦ Χριστοῦ," 424. Cranfield (*Romans*, 1.203), observing the same facts, draws a very different conclusion: "Here for the first time in the epistle, Christ is explicitly referred to as the object of faith."

There have been many attempts to make this phrase conform to the traditional idea of Christian faith; I see no possible way to do so. Rather, as the parallels between the faith of Abraham and the faith of Christ in the next chapter will make clear, the faith of Christ is simply his trusting that the cross would not be the end. . . .[135]

These observations so far deal with parallels and with the larger context of 3:21-26, but closer exegetical examination of 3:22 also supports the hypothesis that πίστις 'Ιησοῦ Χριστοῦ does not mean "believing in Jesus Christ."

(d) Just as in Gal 3:22, there is a ponderous redundancy in Rom 3:22 if πίστις 'Ιησοῦ Χριστοῦ means "faith in Jesus Christ." Why then would Paul need to add εἰς πάντας τοὺς πιστεύοντας?

(e) In 3:22 the righteousness of God is said to be "revealed" (πεφανέρωται) διὰ πίστεως 'Ιησοῦ Χριστοῦ. It is very difficult to see what possible sense this could make if the phrase is translated as "through believing in Jesus Christ." On the other hand, it makes very good sense to say that the righteousness of God is manifested "through the faithfulness of Jesus Christ."[136] This also gives a reasonable explanation for Paul's use of the perfect tense: "The righteousness of God has been manifested in the past, in the faith/obedience of the crucified one."[137]

All of the above considerations have been advanced at various times in piecemeal fashion by various scholars, but there have been few attempts to relate these observations together in a constructive account of the flow and sense of Paul's argument in this section of Romans.[138] In my article "Psalm

135. Goodenough, "Paul and Hellenization," 45. Goodenough seems to regard the "faith of Christ" as a sort of infused virtue by means of which we participate in Christ's hope: "As we identify with Christ, become one with him, we ourselves are given the faith *of* Christ. . . . By this faith of Christ, transferred to us, we have hope of immortality ourselves" (ibid.). Thus, for Goodenough, Paul's "faith of Christ" cashes out to mean that we are enabled to have a faith like Christ's faith. This interpretation drastically downplays Paul's insistent proclamation that a decisive event took place in Christ's death and resurrection which has now transformed the human situation. I would want to insist that the "faith of Christ" in Paul must always be understood in the context of the gospel story, in which Christ's faith enables him obediently to carry out his mission of deliverance. We are saved by Christ's faith(fulness), not by having a faith like his. Parenthetically, it is also interesting to note that Goodenough substitutes for Paul's resurrection-hope the "hope of immortality."

136. This is noted by H. W. Schmidt, *Der Brief des Paulus an die Römer* (2nd ed.; THKNT 6; Berlin: Evangelische Verlagsanstalt, 1966) 66.

137. Williams, "Righteousness of God," 276; cf. Kittel, "πίστις 'Ιησοῦ Χριστοῦ," 424-25.

138. Williams' article is a welcome attempt in this direction. His views and mine,

143 and the Logic of Romans 3," I have attempted to sketch the general structure of Paul's argument in Romans 3.[139] The following discussion will seek to suggest briefly how πίστις 'Ιησοῦ Χριστοῦ fits into that structure.

In Romans 3, Paul's fundamental concern is to assert the integrity of God. In the early part of the chapter, God's faithfulness (πίστις θεοῦ, 3:3) and righteousness/justice (θεοῦ δικαιοσύνη, 3:5) are called into question, at least for rhetorical purposes. After a crushing indictment of humanity's injustice (vv. 9-20), Paul sets forth his positive affirmation of the faithfulness and righteousness of God; God, he asserts, has now revealed his righteousness in a new way, overcoming human unfaithfulness by his own power and proving himself faithful and just. We discover, furthermore, that this demonstration of God's righteousness (ἔνδειξις τῆς δικαιοσύνης αὐτοῦ, 3:25) has something to do with Jesus, that this righteousness is manifested διὰ πίστεως 'Ιησοῦ Χριστοῦ (3:22).

Does it make sense to say that our faith in Jesus Christ somehow manifests the righteousness of God or proves God's integrity? Once the question is asked in these terms, it is immediately clear that for Paul God's integrity is made manifest not in our believing (or at least not primarily there) but in Jesus Christ[140] whom God "put forward" (προέθετο, 3:25) as an answer to the problem of humanity's unfaithfulness. God's righteousness *has been* manifested, claims Paul. Where and how? Through the faithfulness of Jesus Christ, the one who "became a servant of circumcision for the sake of the truthfulness of God (ὑπὲρ ἀληθείας θεοῦ)[141] in order to confirm the promises given to the fathers . . ." (Rom 15:8), the one in whom "all the promises of God find their Yes" (2 Cor 1:20).

But how is "the faithfulness of Jesus Christ" enacted so that it becomes effectual and visible? S. K. Williams has advanced the argument that the phrase διὰ τῆς πίστεως in Rom 3:25 also refers to Jesus' faith, and that the verse means that God regarded "Christ crucified as a means of expiation by virtue of faith [i.e., his faith] at the cost of his blood," *or* ". . . as a means of expiation due to [his] faith, on account of his blood."[142] Williams' proposal,

---

though developed independently of one another, are closely parallel, as may be seen by comparing pp. 265-80 of his article to my article in the immediately preceding issue of *JBL*.

139. Hays, "Logic of Romans 3," 109, 113-15.

140. Cf. Goodenough, "Paul and Hellenization," 44.

141. On the functional equivalence of ἀλήθεια, πίστις, and δικαιοσύνη in Rom 3:3-7, see Hays, "Logic of Romans 3," 110-11.

142. Williams, *Jesus' Death*, 47, 51. In this study, Williams was cautious about placing weight on this interpretation, but his recent article ("Righteousness of God," 277 n. 113) reaffirms it. This article has also moved decisively in the direction of accepting "faith of Jesus Christ" as the proper translation of πίστις 'Ιησοῦ Χριστοῦ.

which interprets Rom 3:25 on the analogy of the understanding of martyrdom found in 4 Maccabees, would allow this verse to fit smoothly into the logic of Romans 3 as I have traced it here. Jesus' faithful endurance and obedience even to an undeserved death on the cross (cf. Phil 2:8) has saving significance for all humanity; this is the "righteous act" (δικαίωμα) of obedience (ὑπακοή) by which "the many" are constituted as righteous, i.e., set in right relation to God (Rom 5:18-19). The unfaithfulness of fallen humanity is counteracted and overcome by the representative faithfulness of Christ.

But does it make sense to regard this "faith of Jesus Christ" as a demonstration of *God's* righteousness? Clearly, this is precisely how Paul regards it: God "put him forward"[143] in his act of justifying τὸν ἐκ πίστεως Ἰησοῦ, i.e., the beneficiary of Jesus' faithfulness.[144]

The redemption is accomplished by God's grace (τῇ αὐτοῦ χάριτι, 3:24). This means that God is the one ultimately responsible for setting things right, so that πίστις θεοῦ and δικαιοσύνη θεοῦ are demonstrated through Jesus' faithfulness (διὰ πίστεως Ἰησοῦ Χριστοῦ). This idea is paralleled precisely by Paul's remarkable statement that ἡ χάρις τοῦ θεοῦ abounds to many ἐν χάριτι τῇ τοῦ ἑνὸς ἀνθρώπου Ἰησοῦ Χριστοῦ (Rom 5:15) — the grace of *God* is manifested and made effectual by the grace of the *one man* Jesus Christ.

We hardly need to draw actantial diagrams to recognize that in statements such as these we encounter another encapsulated telling of the same story that was analyzed in Chapter III. God is the Sender whose purpose to convey blessing to humanity is carried out through the action of a single "Subject," Jesus Christ. In Romans, Paul highlights different implications of this story from the ones that he dwells upon in Galatians because his purpose is different. In Galatians 3, he uses the story to show that the promise is a gift

143. Cf. Gal 4:4: "God sent forth his Son. . . ."

144. A little-noted variant reading here (D, L, Ψ, 33, etc.) has Ἰησοῦν instead of Ἰησοῦ. This would yield the meaning ". . . in order that he might be just precisely by justifying Jesus on the basis of faith." Although this reading would fit nicely with some aspects of my interpretation, it is not to be defended as the original text; the earlier and better witnesses tell against it, as does the context. (Notice, however, that the UBS *Greek NT* gives to the reading Ἰησοῦ only a "C" degree of certainty.) One can find traces elsewhere in the NT of the idea that Jesus was "justified" (= vindicated) through the resurrection (cf. 1 Tim 3:16), an idea that could naturally arise through the church's penchant for reading the Psalms as messianic prophecies. See Hanson's discussion of "The Reproach and Vindication of the Messiah" (*Paul's Technique*, 13-51). All of this may explain the context in which the reading Ἰησοῦν could arise and be regarded as theologically sound. Probably, however, Rom 3:26 should be understood to mean that God justifies "the person who lives on the basis of Jesus' faith." This interpretation assumes that ἐκ πίστεως here as elsewhere is an allusion to Hab 2:4, interpreted messianically.

given through the faith of Jesus Christ. In Romans 3, he uses it to prove that God's integrity is still intact, that he has not abandoned his promises, because he has overcome humanity's unfaithfulness through the faithfulness of Jesus Christ.

This broad overview of Romans 3 allows us to see that the whole argument becomes more cohesive if πίστις 'Ιησοῦ Χριστοῦ is understood to mean the faith *of* Jesus Christ. The faith(fulness) of Jesus was manifested in his death on the cross, which, as a representative action of human faith, brought about redemption and which at the same time manifested the faithfulness of God.[145]

E. Conclusions

Now we must draw together the results of this chapter and assess their cumulative significance. First of all, it should be clear that πίστις is not a univocal concept for Paul. His use of it is extensive and flexible, and its meaning in any particular sentence must be determined in view of a whole range of considerations.[146] To take a clear example, πίστις in Gal 1:23 (εὐαγγελίζεται τὴν πίστιν) demands a different interpretation from πίστις in 3:11 (ὁ δίκαιος ἐκ πίστεως ζήσεται). Some studies, such as Binder's, suffer from a tendency to seek a single comprehensive definition that will account for every instance in which the word πίστις occurs. This has the result of leveling out Paul's uneven usage and suppressing the connotative diversity inherent in Paul's language. We should be willing to recognize that Paul's language may sometimes be ambiguous by design, allowing him to speak in one breath of Christ's faith and our faith.

We have argued in this chapter that the phrase πίστις 'Ιησοῦ Χριστοῦ may be understood as a reference to the faithfulness of "the one man Jesus Christ" whose act of obedient self-giving on the cross became the means by which "the promise" of God was fulfilled. (This interpretation should not be understood to abolish or preclude human faith directed toward Christ, which is also an important component of Paul's thought.) In the nature of the case,

---

145. It will be apparent that this exegesis has arrived, by a different path, at a conclusion very close to Torrance's position; while Torrance's methods are subject to criticism, his interpretive intuition was fundamentally correct.

146. Thiselton (*Two Horizons,* 409) declares that "faith in the New Testament is a polymorphous concept, and therefore questions about faith must not be answered 'outside a particular language-game.'" I take this declaration to be roughly equivalent to the common-sense rule that the interpreter must attend to context and usage.

161

it is not possible to prove this interpretation in such a way that all others are excluded, but the investigations set forth in this chapter have shown that in every case except Gal 2:16 "the faith of Jesus Christ" provides a better and more satisfying sense than the traditional translation of "faith in Jesus Christ." In the case of Gal 2:16, the sentence is so compact that it is difficult to decide what διὰ πίστεως Ἰησοῦ Χριστοῦ and ἐκ πίστεως Χριστοῦ might mean. The exegetical observations advanced in this chapter entitle us to claim, however, that an interpretation such as Robinson's (p. 123 above) is at least as defensible as the traditional exegesis which interprets the verse as though it meant εἰς Χριστὸν Ἰησοῦν ἐπιστεύσαμεν ἵνα δικαιωθῶμεν ἐκ τοῦ πιστεύειν εἰς Χριστόν. Against this view, it is justifiable to maintain that the text means ". . . we placed our trust in Christ Jesus in order that we might be justified on the basis of Christ's faithfulness." This way of reading 2:16 should be taken seriously as an interpretive option, especially since the parallels in Gal 3:22 and Rom 3:22, 26 seem clearly to favor such an interpretation.

This understanding of πίστις Ἰησοῦ Χριστοῦ allows us to reaffirm the narrative analysis of Gal 3:22 that was sketched near the end of Chapter III above, in which this verse was seen to manifest the same narrative structure already discerned in 3:13-14 and 4:3-6. At the conclusion of part E in Chapter III, I suggested that the narrative analysis pointed toward interpreting πίστις Ἰησοῦ Χριστοῦ to mean "the faith of Jesus Christ" *if* the phrase could bear such a meaning on lexical, grammatical, and contextual grounds. The investigations carried through in this chapter have shown that such an interpretation is not only possible but also preferable, totally apart from any appeal to techniques of narrative analysis. Thus, the conclusions of Chapters III and IV are mutually reinforcing. Using very different methodologies, both chapters point to the conclusion that Paul's gospel presents Jesus Christ as the protagonist sent by God whose faithful action brings deliverance and blessing to humanity.

Up to this point, my case has been argued by examining brief formulations excerpted from Galatians. The task that remains in Chapter V is to demonstrate the way in which these formulations fit together with their context: how is the narrative pattern that we have discerned in these formulations related to the overall logic of Paul's argument in Gal 3:1–4:11? Part D of the chapter just concluded outlines the way in which an awareness of the narrative shape of Paul's representative christology contributes to a coherent reading of Romans 3. Can it be shown that the proposed gospel story-structure will also provide a basis for a more cohesive and clear understanding of the central argumentative section of Galatians?

162

Chapter V

The Logic of Argumentation
in Galatians 3:1–4:11

In Galatians, a series of scriptural testimonies about Jesus the Messiah forms a partially concealed substructure for the whole argument concerning the promise and the law.[1]

NILS DAHL

A. The Problem: Internal Coherence of the Argument

In spite of its historic importance for Protestant dogmatics, the central "theological" section of Galatians remains a vexing exegetical puzzle. Although there is general agreement that this section of the letter is intended as Paul's exposition and defense of his doctrine of justification by faith, it is not at all easy to follow the logic of the argument that Paul has constructed. This problem was partly obscured by the tendency of many older commentaries to read Paul within the grid of a predetermined dogmatic-confessional system and/or to work through the text verse by verse with little attempt to grasp the function of larger sense-units. But as critical exegetes have sought to trace the line of thought within Galatians 3 and 4 and to discern the rhetorical structure of the letter, the difficulties have become increasingly apparent.

Some have despaired of the task of discovering any argumentative coherence in the letter. Alfred Loisy described Paul's exegetical argument as a "mirage de mots et de confusion d'idees."[2] A psychological explanation for this state of affairs is offered by W. Schneidermeyer.

1. Dahl, *Studies in Paul,* 130.
2. Cited in A. Goffinet, "La prédication de l'Évangile et de la croix dans l'Épître aux Galates," *ETL* 41 (1965) 435.

So frustrated is Paul that he cites authority without explaining its relevance (the story of Abraham); he introduces new thoughts before completing earlier ones. Words tumble out in such confusion that structure and pattern are lost. . . . His intensity of thought bursts the bonds of conventional language.[3]

Thus, concludes Schneidermeyer, Galatians should be read as "a model of purely emotive prose."[4] Few biblical critics, however, have been willing to yield to such extreme counsels of despair. Paul certainly intended to say something intelligible, and he has long been perceived within the Christian tradition as having done so; consequently, it must be possible to give some sort of account of the coherence of his argument, even if its "logic" is not of a propositional or philosophical sort.

Why is the argument of this central section of Galatians difficult to follow? A concise diagnosis of the difficulty is offered by Klaus Berger: "Die Bindung der Erfüllung der Abrahamsverheissung einerseits an den Glauben, anderseits an die Person Jesu Christi ist das theologische Kernproblem von Gal 3."[5] In Gal 3:6-9 Paul seems to say that all who believe are ipso facto Abraham's children and heirs of the promise, but in 3:16-19 he clearly argues that Christ is the one "seed," the exclusive heir. How are these claims to be reconciled? Any attempt to demonstrate the coherence of Paul's argument must meet this problem squarely.

A somewhat more intricate analysis of the problem of logical coherence in the central section of the letter is presented by J. C. Beker, who, while attempting to account for Paul's discussion as a purposeful whole, also explicitly recognizes the presence of "peculiar shifts in the argument."[6] According to Beker, the argument has three phases that manifest distinct soteriologies.

(1) In Gal 3:6-9, all who believe are, like Abraham, justified: they are "sons of Abraham" because, like him, they believe (cf. Rom 4:11-12, 16). Christ seems to have no role here at all.

---

3. W. Schneidermeyer, "Galatians as Literature," *JRT* 28 (1971) 137. For quite a different evaluation, see P. Haeuser (*Anlass und Zweck des Galaterbriefes: Seine logische Gedankentwicklung* [NTAbh 11/3; Münster: Aschendorff, 1925] v), who contends "dass der Galaterbrief trotz der Eigenheiten einer Gelegenheitsschrift ein wohl geordnetes Ganzes ist, in dem ein Schriftseller [*sic*] von nicht nur tiefem Gemüte, sondern auch klarem Verstande logisch Gedanke an Gedanke reiht."

4. Schneidermeyer, "Galatians as Literature," 138; cf. Schoeps, *Paul,* 176.

5. "Abraham in den paulinischen Hauptbriefen," *MTZ* 17 (1966) 47.

6. *Paul the Apostle,* 51.

(2) In Gal 3:10-14, Christ is "the enabler of the blessing . . . because he enables the prior promise to Abraham to flow" to the Gentiles by removing the curse of the law.

(3) In Gal 3:16-29, Christ is represented as "the sole recipient and content of the promise. . . . Paul now states that faith did not become a reality until Christ came (vv. 23-25), and he seemingly ignores both the case of Abraham (vv. 6-9) and the function of Christ as the enabler of the promise (vv. 10-14)."[7]

These three soteriologies are in fact, in Beker's view, dissonant. Their presence side by side in Galatians 3 is an indicator of the contingent (i.e., situationally determined) character of Paul's argumentation.

> Paul bends the Abraham story — which the opposition used for its benefit — to his own purpose. . . . The peculiar logic of the argument shows that the salvation-historical thrust of the Abraham story can be used by Paul against the Judaizers only if he centers the story Christocentrically (Christ as the exclusive seed) and therefore discontinuously.[8]

Beker has performed a valuable service by focusing attention upon these apparent shifts in Paul's argument; Protestant exegesis has tended to treat this material carelessly, assuming that the basic sense of the passage is contained in 3:6-9 and the rest of the argument must somehow conform to the idea presumably expressed there: just as Abraham was justified by believing in God, so also we are justified by believing in Christ. From this point of view, it has always been difficult to comprehend Paul's argument about Christ as the singular "seed" in verses 16 and 19, and there has been a strong tendency to disregard this latter conception as a peculiar and inessential quirk in Paul's thinking. Beker rightly perceives, however, that the idea of Christ as the one "seed" who is the sole heir of the promise governs verses 16-29, and that it is in fact the "center" of Paul's treatment of the Abraham story.[9] The difficulty is then that verses 6-9 and 10-14 seem to stand as unintegrated remnants of other theological positions.[10] Beker's somewhat unclear references to

---

7. Ibid., 50. For a similar analysis of the composition of the argument, see H. Hübner, "Pauli Theologiae Proprium," *NTS* 26 (1979-80) 452-53. In contrast to Beker, however, Hübner regards vv. 6-9 as the real center of Paul's argument.

8. Beker, *Paul the Apostle*, 51.

9. This point has also been made in various ways by other critics. See Boers, *Ghetto*, 78-82; Barrett, *First Adam*, 76-79; E. P. Sanders, *Paul and Palestinian Judaism*, 457.

10. Cf. the widespread opinion that Gal 3:13-14 must represent a pre-Pauline tradition. See the discussion of this point in Chap. III above.

Paul's "discontinuous hermeneutic" fail to provide a fully satisfactory means of finding coherence in the passage, but he has delineated the problem clearly and rightly observed that its solution must somehow be found in Paul's surprising use of the Abraham story.

The task of this chapter will be to address this problem by offering an explanation of the overall development of Paul's argument in Gal 3:1–4:11. Are there really three distinct sections in 3:6-29 that manifest clashing soteriologies? Or does the whole chapter, contrary to Beker's view, somehow express a single coherent soteriology?

In the analysis that follows, I will make two closely interrelated proposals.

(1) Our difficulty in grasping the argumentative coherence of the central section of Galatians is attributable in large part to a deeply entrenched but mistaken interpretation of the first half of Galatians 3.

(2) The "logic" of the text is a narrative logic, founded upon the narrative substructure identified in Chapters III and IV above.

These two proposals will determine the structure of the discussion. First it will be necessary to undertake a detailed investigation of Gal 3:1-14 in order to clear away numerous obstacles to a unified reading of the text. Only after this part of the task has been accomplished will it be possible to take the further step of analyzing the patterns of narrative logic that inform the argument.

The positive thesis toward which this investigation leads may be summarized briefly as follows: Christians are justified/redeemed not by virtue of their own faith but because they participate in Jesus Christ, who enacted the obedience of faith on their behalf. Abraham is understood by Paul not as an exemplar of faith in Christ but as a typological foreshadowing of Christ himself, a representative figure whose faithfulness secures blessing and salvation vicariously for others. With this hypothesis in mind, let us turn to the text.

B. A Reinterpretation of Gal 3:1-14

1. Gal 3:1-5

With a rhetorical flourish ("O foolish Galatians, who has bewitched you?"), Paul launches into the central theological argument of his letter. For our purposes we may accept Betz's account of the rhetorical architecture, i.e., that 2:15-21 functions as the letter's *propositio*, a capsule statement of the position to be defended in the body of the argument, which begins with 3:1.

It is highly significant that Paul places front and center, in the first sentence of this major section, an allusion to the content of the gospel already proclaimed to the Galatians in the past: Ἰησοῦς Χριστὸς προεγράφη ἐσταυρωμένος.[11] This shows that Paul is operating "in the mode of recapitulation," elucidating the significance of something that is already so familiar to his readers that he need not recount it in detail. Furthermore, the impatient tone of his recapitulation betrays his incredulity that such recapitulation should be necessary at all.[12] It seems to Paul that anyone to whom Jesus Christ has been portrayed as crucified should not need to be dragged along to see the implications of that portrayal; he takes it as a sign of the Galatians' incorrigible dullness that they fail to understand the point. To Paul, the message of Christ's death carries with it as a corollary the negation of the Law: "for if righteousness is through Law, then Christ died gratuitously" (2:21b).

To put the matter another way, we can have recourse to Northrop Frye's terminology.[13] The *dianoia* of the gospel story is embodied in the phrase "Jesus Christ crucified." This summary phrase recalls the "scene of exceptional intensity" that stands at the center of Paul's recollection of the story of Jesus Christ. The allusion, therefore, which would be meaningless outside the frame of reference provided by the gospel story, stands for the whole story and distills its meaning.

Paul's opening question in 3:1 strongly implies that the image of Christ crucified, rightly understood, *ought* to make the Galatians immune to bewitchment and wandering from "the truth of the gospel" (2:14). In this single image, the *dianoia* of the gospel is so fully comprehended that Paul finds it astonishing that he is now forced to go back and spell out for the Galatians what the image signifies. But that is exactly what he must now do. Thus Gal 3:1–

11. P. G. Bretscher ("Light from Galatians 3:1 on Pauline Theology," *CTM* 34 (1963) 77-97) thinks that Paul is referring to the OT prophecies of Christ. He points to Paul's use of προεγράφη in Rom 15:4, where clearly it refers to things "written previously" in Scripture; the meaning of Gal 3:1 would then be: "You foolish Galatians, do you not remember that you read with your own eyes the scriptures that portray the crucified Christ?" This suggestion cannot be dismissed altogether, but see the discussions of Lightfoot (*Galatians,* 134), G. Milligan (*Here and There among the Papyri* [London: Hodder and Stoughton, 1922] 78-79), and Betz (*Galatians,* 131-32).

12. Whether Paul's impatience and incredulity are genuine or feigned for rhetorical purposes makes no difference for our purposes; the logic of the argument remains the same either way. My own view is that Paul is genuinely exasperated with the Galatians and that he plays upon his own exasperation to good rhetorical effect.

13. See Chap. I.B.1.a above.

4:11 may be read as an extended explication of the implications of the gospel story within which the phrase "Christ crucified" finds its meaning.

Gal 3:1-5 is often described as an appeal to the Galatians' own experience;[14] it is certainly that, with its reference to the fact that they "saw," as it were, with their own eyes Christ crucified (presumably through Paul's vivid proclamation — or narration — of the gospel);[15] with its references to the Galatians' experience of receiving the Spirit and witnessing miracles (3:5) in their midst; with its plaintive rhetorical question, "Did you experience such things in vain?" (3:4). It is equally important to recognize, however, that the *purpose* of Paul's appeal to experience is to establish his claim that the foundation for this experience was the gospel message (ἀκοή).[16] The Galatians were enabled to have these experiences because of one and only one thing: Paul's proclamation of the gospel message, whose content is precisely the story to which 3:1b alludes: Jesus Christ crucified. Thus the real thrust of this opening argument (vv. 1-5) is to establish the efficacy and sufficiency of the gospel message as the basis for beginning (3:2) and sustaining (3:5) Christian existence.[17]

2. Gal 3:6-9

With verses 6-9, Abraham enters the discussion, and complications arrive along with him. Traditionally, this treatment of the significance of Abraham is understood in the light of Romans 4, in which Abraham is portrayed as the exemplification of the faith that justifies. This "Romans 4" interpretation of verses 6-9 is then taken as the central message of Galatians 3, with the result that the latter half of the chapter appears peculiar and incongruous. The idea that only Christ is the heir of the promises to Abraham (3:16) clashes with the idea that all who believe are Abraham's sons (3:7). Likewise, the mystical-sacramental language of verses 26-29 appears to comport oddly with the "justification by faith" teaching found in verses 6-9. Bousset was particularly conscious of this latter difficulty.

14. See, for example, Mussner, *Galaterbrief*, 205-6.
15. Goffinet ("La prédication de l'Évangile," 429), commenting on Gal 3:1, remarks that this verse shows that Paul's proclamation of the gospel must have included "une narration de l'événement de la croix." Cf. Betz, *Galatians*, 131: "One of the goals of the ancient orator was to deliver his speech so vividly and impressively that his listeners imagined the matter to have happened right before their eyes."
16. See Chap. IV.A.2 above.
17. Note in 3:5 the present participles ἐπιχορηγῶν and ἐνεργῶν, implying ongoing phenomena in the life of the community.

How curiously this brief allusion stands out in contrast with the surrounding thought-world in the Galatian epistle! Elsewhere the statements of the apostle about sonship and servanthood, about the inheritance of Abraham, about God's free gracious will, his relation to the law, and his acceptance through faith are almost dominated by a sober judicial rigor. Now here suddenly a mystic note sounds: sonship through the miracle of the sacrament, and the sacramental union with Christ! This is indeed a sound from another world. But the cultic mysticism which is present here is again interwoven in peculiarly free fashion with the purely intellectual ideas of the apostle about faith and divine sonship. . . .[18]

Is Gal 3:26-27 a sudden and jarring sound from another world, or is the world of Galatians 3 less soberly "judicial" and "purely intellectual" than Bousset supposes? Is it possible to read this text as a unity in such a way that its "world" is from start to finish the "world" which Paul's Christ-story establishes?

In the following pages, I would like to advocate a different approach: Gal 3:6-9 must be read and interpreted in light of the discussion that *follows* it, which culminates in verses 26-29. To read this passage through the lens of Romans 4 is to misread it. Instead, the central section of Galatians (3:1–4:11) may and must be read as a coherent whole on its own terms. Only then can comparisons to Romans be drawn validly.

(a) The Function of Gal 3:6 in the Argument

Verse 6 poses an immediate interpretive problem because it is an elliptical sentence: καθὼς Ἀβραὰμ ἐπίστευσεν τῷ θεῷ καὶ ἐλογίσθη αὐτῷ εἰς δικαιοσύνην. The conjunction καθώς indicates some kind of comparison, but the question is to *what* the comparison is drawn. Should we understand Paul to mean, "Just as Abraham believed God and it was reckoned to him as righteousness, (so also we believe and it is reckoned to us as righteousness)"? Lightfoot achieved essentially this interpretation by stressing the connection of καθώς to verse 5: "The answer to the question asked in the former verse is assumed, 'surely of faith,' and so it was with Abraham."[19] This interpretation finds support in the much more explicitly worked-out parallel in Rom 4:22-24.[20]

18. Bousset, *Kyrios Christos,* 158.
19. Lightfoot, *Galatians,* 136, followed by Burton, *Galatians,* 153.
20. For the sake of argument I concede the traditional interpretation of these verses. In point of fact, however, the text might equally well be interpreted to mean that Abraham's

Although it might appear attractive to read Gal 3:6 in light of this parallel, this solution presents one serious difficulty: for the comparison to be drawn as Lightfoot suggests, verse 5 would have to be interpreted in a way that emphasizes the human act of "hearing with faith." For reasons already explained in Chapter IV, however, this interpretation of ἐκ ἀκοῆς πίστεως is to be rejected. The accent in verse 5 falls heavily upon the action of God, who "supplies the Spirit and works miracles," and ἐξ ἀκοῆς πίστεως must therefore be understood to mean "through the proclamation of [the] faith." Thus, if καθώς refers back to verse 5, the primary point of comparison must be God's working in both cases, rather than the faith of Abraham and the Galatians.[21]

Betz suggests that καθώς is an abbreviated citation formula, equivalent to καθὼς γέγραπται.[22] This interpretation, which has much to be said for it as a way of minimizing the syntactical difficulty, also slightly weakens the connection to verse 5, since it takes καθώς not strictly as a comparative conjunction but as a way of introducing a scripture quotation which will serve as the topic for the next phase of the argument. The logic of the argument would then progress in the following manner. Verse 5 asks what kind of God it is with whom we have to do:[23] does he operate ἐξ ἔργων νόμου or ἐξ ἀκοῆς πίστεως? Verse 6 sets about answering this question by posing for consideration a scriptural text which explains how God dealt with Abraham.

(b) The Meaning of οἱ ἐκ πίστεως

On the basis of this scriptural text (Gen 15:6), Paul advances a bold thesis: οἱ ἐκ πίστεως are the sons of Abraham.[24] This assertion hardly follows self-evidently from Gen 15:6, and Paul must set about defending it in the ensuing discussion. In order to make sense of this claim, however, we must pause for a moment over the phrase οἱ ἐκ πίστεως. It occurs in Paul *only* here and in verse 9, a fact whose significance we would do well to ponder.[25] Why has Paul

---

faith is reckoned not only to him as righteousness but also vicariously to those who (now) trust in the God who raised Jesus from the dead. See the discussion of Gal 3:8 below.

21. This point is worked out as fully as possible by L. Gaston, "Abraham and the Righteousness of God," 39-68. See especially pp. 44, 49, 54-55.

22. Betz, *Galatians*, 140; cf. Schlier, *Galater*, 127.

23. Boers, *Ghetto*, 74-75.

24. Betz (*Galatians*, 141-42) regards this verse as the statement of an exegetical thesis which is then supported in vv. 8-13 by five separate "proofs" from scripture.

25. Cf., however, Rom 3:26, 4:16, where an analogous expression occurs in the singular.

formulated (or adopted) this rather awkward expression? Is it conditioned by something in the surrounding context? Does it function in some special way in his argument?

Usually, the phrase is read as though it were equivalent to οἱ πιστεύοντες ("the believers") or ὅσοι πιστεύουσιν ("those who believe"), and the thought of verses 6-9 is consequently treated as a condensed version of Romans 4: Christian believers are justified, like Abraham, because, like Abraham, they believe.[26] Schlier, observing the unusual character of the expression οἱ ἐκ πίστεως, attempts to offer a somewhat richer explanation of Paul's meaning.

> Οἱ ἐκ πίστεως hat einen umfassenden Sinn: es sind die Menschen, die in der πίστις die Grundweise ihres Lebens haben, deren Lebensprinzip die Pistis ist.[27]

This explanation is certainly correct, as far as it goes. Even so, "faith" is still understood as the religious disposition (opposed — according to the inclinations of the interpreter — to "works-righteousness" or to "guilt" or to "boasting") which enables a person to stand in a right relationship to God. As we have repeatedly emphasized, it is not entirely clear what role Christ might play in relation to this justifying faith, and the soteriological schema that results from this interpretation of verses 6-9 stands in apparent contradiction to the latter half of Galatians 3.

We may begin to glimpse a solution to this problem only when we recognize that verses 7-9 already anticipate Paul's citation of Hab 2:4 in Gal 3:11, and that the phrase οἱ ἐκ πίστεως is best understood in the context of Galatians 3 as an ad hoc formulation based upon this prophetic text. This would explain why Paul does not use the expression elsewhere in his letters. The phrase οἱ ἐκ πίστεως serves for Paul as a deliberate catchword allusion to the scriptural dictum: ὁ δίκαιος ἐκ πίστεως ζήσεται.[28]

If this analysis is correct, what are its implications for the interpretation of Gal 3:7? At the very least it suggests that 3:7 should be understood to mean, "Those [who live] ἐκ πίστεως are sons of Abraham."[29] However, we can trace the implications farther than this. We have already contended in the previous

---

26. See Berger ("Abraham," 51), to cite just one example.

27. Schlier, *Galater*, 128. Boers (*Ghetto*, 80) protests that this interpretation still places too much emphasis on the "structure" of individual faith.

28. Dahl, *Studies in Paul*, 166-69. See also the discussion of this expression in Howard (*Crisis in Galatia*, 57).

29. For the interpretation of Gal 3:11, see Chap. IV.B above.

chapter that Paul understands Hab 2:4 as a messianic text that proclaims that the Messiah (ὁ δίκαιος) will live by faith; furthermore, the Messiah's faith is deemed to have redemptive consequences for his people (see 3:13-14 and especially 3:22), who, as a result of his faithful obedience which led to death on the cross, are redeemed from the curse and given "the promise of the Spirit." This is clearest in 3:22, in which, as we have seen, the promise is given "out of Jesus Christ's faith" (ἐκ πίστεως Ἰησοῦ Χριστοῦ) to those who believe (τοῖς πιστεύουσιν). As a result of Christ's faith, his people are given life. This, as we have seen in the previous chapter, is precisely the meaning of Gal 2:20b: ". . . I live by (ἐν instrumental) the faith of the Son of God, who loved me and gave himself for me." In view of all these considerations, we may suggest that οἱ ἐκ πίστεως carries not primarily the connotation of "those who have faith" but rather the connotation of "those who are given life on the basis of [Christ's] faith."[30]

Caution is demanded: Paul's language here is by no means as unambiguous as my interpretive paraphrase might suggest. Paul, as we have repeatedly emphasized, does regard Christ's people as "believers"; those who receive life "out of" Christ's faith in turn trust in him (cf. 3:22) and live their lives also in a manner characterized by faith (cf. 2 Cor 5:7 — διὰ πίστεως γὰρ περιπατοῦμεν). Thus, οἱ ἐκ πίστεως is a phrase capable of sustaining several interpretations. It would be a mistake to attempt to exclude "those who believe" as one part of Paul's meaning. However, this is not the exclusive or even primary meaning demanded by the context; Paul is not concerned here with developing the parallelism between Abraham's faith and the faith of Christians. Instead, he wants to argue that a particular group of people — for whom he invents the designation οἱ ἐκ πίστεως — are Abraham's "sons" and therefore share in the blessing that Abraham received. As the discussion unfolds, it becomes clear, as Hendrikus Boers has observed, that these people share the blessing *not* because their faith imitates Abraham's faith, but because they participate in Christ, who is Abraham's "seed."[31] Boers reads 3:6-9 in light of 3:29 and thus preserves the unity of Paul's argument.

> His reasoning in Gal. is in terms of the Christian believers' participation in Christ (3:26f., 29), the one seed of Abraham in whom the promise went into fulfilment (3:16), as had been intended already at the announcement of the promise (3:8, cf. 3:29). Christians, thus, have no direct relationship to Abraham. Their relationship to him is dependent on their belonging to

30. Cf. Howard, *Crisis in Galatia,* 57.
31. See Boers, *Ghetto,* 79-81.

Christ (3:29). . . . He is the mediating point between Abraham and the peoples that are blessed in him.[32]

Boers still maintains, however, that "Abraham's faith was, in a sense, faith in Christ, since the one seed in which the promise to him went into fulfilment was Christ."[33] By contrast, my proposal suggests a very different relation between Abraham and Christ. Christ is not the object of Abraham's faith; rather, Abraham's faith is a foreshadowing of Christ's (see the discussion that follows below). This interpretation hinges upon the claim that ἐκ πίστεως in verses 7 and 9 should be understood as an allusion to Hab 2:4, understood messianically. The value of this suggestion may be tested by its fruits: will it enable us to discern more adequately the coherence of the chapter?

(c) The Function of the Genesis Quotation in Gal 3:8

Taken by itself, verse 7 is a stark and obviously controversial assertion. Paul now sets about supporting it, and the way in which he does so sheds much light on the logic of the argument. Rather than discussing the salvific efficacy of faith as a mode of relationship to God, he appeals again to Genesis, this time producing a mixed quotation from Gen 12:3 and 18:18.

Gen 12.3	<u>ἐνευλογηθήσονται ἐν σοὶ</u> πᾶσαι αἱ φυλαὶ τῆς γῆς
Gen 18:18	<u>ἐνευλογηθήσονται</u> ἐν αὐτῷ <u>πάντα τὰ ἔθνη</u> τῆς γῆς
Gal 3:8	<u>ἐνευλογηθήσονται ἐν σοὶ πάντα τὰ ἔθνη</u>

Paul uses this quotation to underscore three key points in his argument.

(1) First of all, the text serves Paul well as a proof for his contention that the *Gentiles* (τὰ ἔθνη) are included in the blessing of Abraham, a point which Paul nails down firmly in 3:9, with the significant substitution of οἱ ἐκ πίστεως for τὰ ἔθνη.[34] The verb προευηγγελίσατο indicates that Paul virtually equates "the gospel" with the proclamation that the Gentiles are to be blessed and included among God's people.[35]

(2) Secondly, it is very important to recognize that the blessing is given to the Gentiles not in consequence of *their* faith, but in consequence of *Abra-*

---

32. Ibid., 81.

33. Ibid., 79.

34. Cf. Rom 4:16, in which Abraham's "whole seed" is said to include ὁ ἐκ τοῦ νόμου (the Jew) as well as ὁ ἐκ πίστεως (the Gentile).

35. See Käsemann, *Perspectives,* 90; Howard, *Crisis in Galatia,* 46-65.

ham's; the blessing that God confers upon Abraham is extended vicariously to all nations. The Gentiles are blessed not on the analogy of Abraham, but "in" him.[36] This point is made clearly by Käsemann in his remarks on the figure of Abraham in Rom 4:17ff., and these remarks are equally appropriate, if not more so, with regard to Gal 3:8.

> ... The patriarch no longer counts merely as an example of the believing person; he has the Jewish meaning of being the bearer of the promise *per se,* who is replaceable by no other figure. . . . He has not merely representative significance but, since he is the ancestor of the believing Gentiles as well, universal significance also. Like Moses [*sic* — surely Käsemann means Adam?] in Rom 5.12ff., he is the bearer of destiny, though not in antithesis to eschatological reality but in anticipation of it.[37]

There are obvious similarities between this understanding of the Abraham story and the much-discussed Jewish "doctrine" of "the merits of the fathers."[38] Various misunderstandings of this idea are corrected in E. P. Sanders'

36. On the interpretation of Abraham in the Genesis stories as a representative figure, see J. Van Seters, *Abraham in History and Tradition* (New Haven: Yale University, 1975) 272-78. Commenting on Gen 26:3-5, Van Seters points out that "Abraham's past obedience effects a blessing for the following generations as well. This is certainly a concept of the 'merits of the fathers' that insures the destiny of the people as a whole." Van Seters hypothesizes that this attribution of a "dynastic principle" to Abraham is the result of the transference of originally royal motifs (cf. Ps 72:17) onto the Abraham tradition during the exilic period. Although Van Seters does not address the question of Paul's use of the Abraham stories, his remarks provide a significant background for understanding the way in which Paul deals with this material. Cf. Gaston, "Abraham and the Righteousness of God," 53-56. Several interpreters of Paul have emphasized that he treats Abraham as a representative figure. See especially Barrett, *First Adam,* 22-45. Cf. Howard, *Crisis in Galatia,* 55: "The idea is that the Gentiles are blessed not simply like Abraham but because of Abraham." Mussner (*Galaterbrief,* 222) tries to explain this state of affairs in terms of the idea of "corporate personality" ("korporativen Persönlichkeit"). Against this view, Betz (*Galatians,* 143 n. 41) objects that Paul employs the concept of "corporate personality" only with reference to Adam and Christ. But this response begs the question. Mussner has in fact identified an important aspect of Paul's thought that has eluded many commentators, but "corporate personality" is probably an unfortunate conceptual category for describing it. Paul's logic depends not on the idea of "corporate personality" but on the idea of vicariously efficacious representative action.

37. Käsemann, *Perspectives,* 98. In this quotation, Käsemann uses the word "representative" as a synonym for "exemplary" rather than in the more pregnant sense in which I have been using it through this discussion.

38. For the older understanding of this idea, see A. Marmorstein, *The Doctrine of Merits in Old Rabbinical Literature* (New York: KTAV, 1968 [originally published in 1920]).

helpful treatment,[39] which allows the central idea to emerge with greater clarity: for the sake of the fathers, God intervenes to help Israel in various historical situations or suspends otherwise deserved punishment for the nation. This idea is closely associated with the idea of God's faithfulness to his promises and with the motif of covenant election, as we can see in Psalm 105.

> He is mindful of his covenant for ever,
> Of the word that he commanded for a thousand generations,
> The covenant which he made with Abraham,
> His sworn promise to Isaac.
> . . . .
> He opened the rock, and water gushed forth;
> It flowed through the desert like a river.
> For he remembered his holy promise,
> And Abraham his servant. (vv. 8-9, 41-42)

This is also the wider context in which the *Akedah* (the binding of Isaac) should be understood: it is a particular, and highly dramatic, instance of a meritorious deed which accrues to the benefit of subsequent generations because God remembers Abraham and therefore looks upon his descendants with favor. Paul has introduced a crucial new emphasis into this traditional way of thinking by claiming, on the basis of the scriptural text, that Abraham's faithfulness was "reckoned" by God to the benefit not only of Israel (as in the Jewish exegetical tradition) but also of the Gentiles.[40]

The interpretation of the Abraham story proposed here is expressed with complete clarity in Gen 22:18, another passage which is, as we shall see, of considerable importance for understanding Paul's reasoning in Galatians 3.

> καὶ ἐνευλογηθήσονται ἐν τῷ σπέρματί σου
> πάντα τὰ ἔθνη (τῆς γῆς)
> ἀνθ᾽ ὧν ὑπήκουσας τῆς ἐμῆς φωνῆς.

We shall have occasion to refer back to this text; for the moment, we may simply note that it affirms that all the nations (τὰ ἔθνη) are to be blessed *because*

---

39. E. P. Sanders, *Paul and Palestinian Judaism*, 183-98.

40. Barrett (*First Adam*, 34) follows J. Bonsirven (*Le Judaïsme palestinien au temps de Jésus Christ* [2 vols.; Paris: Beauchesne, 1934-35] 1.76) in thinking that "this universalist promise was neglected in the Jewish treatment of Abraham." This way of putting the matter is, however, slightly anachronistic; it would be more accurate to say that Paul forged an interpretive innovation by emphasizing the "universalist promise" as the essential content of the promise to Abraham.

of Abraham's obedience. Paul does not quote this text in 3:6-9, but, as the subsequent exposition will show, he surely has it in mind. "The faithful Abraham" (3:9) receives from God a blessing that carries with it a promise that the Gentiles will be blessed "in" Abraham and/or "in his seed." This blessing is not said to be contingent upon anything that the Gentiles might do in the future. If it can be said to be contingent upon anything at all, other than God's grace, it is contingent, in the Genesis story, upon Abraham's obedient faith. That is why the Gentiles are to be blessed, in the words of the promise that Paul quotes, "in you."[41]

(3) Paul uses the Genesis citation in support of his argument that God justifies the Gentiles ἐκ πίστεως (3:8a). The action of justification is portrayed in this formulation as *God's* action done *to* the Gentiles. The crucial exegetical question concerns the meaning of ἐκ πίστεως. Does the sentence mean that God justifies the Gentiles on the basis of *their* faith? Or does it mean that God, out of *his* faithfulness, justifies the Gentiles?[42] Or does it mean that God justifies the Gentiles on the basis of Abraham's faith? The first of these interpretations is by all accounts the least likely. The most natural reading, from a syntactical point of view, would be to interpret ἐκ πίστεως as an adverbial modifier expressing the manner in which God performs his act of justifying the Gentiles, rather than the condition they must fulfill in order for him to perform it. Furthermore, as the citation in 3:8b shows, Paul equates the justification of the Gentiles ἐκ πίστεως with the fact that they are blessed (by God) in Abraham, long before and apart from any "believing" on their part.

Thus, Paul's use of a (composite) citation from Genesis in Gal 3:8 establishes three important points.

(1) The Gentiles are included in God's blessing of Abraham.
(2) They are included not on the ground of their own faith, but on the ground of Abraham's faith, which is deemed to have a vicarious soteriological effect.
(3) This blessing is equated with justification.

---

41. It remains to be considered how Paul can equate the blessing "in" Abraham with the blessing "in" his seed.

42. For an interesting example of bipolar wordplay on πίστις, cf. Philo, *De Abr.* 273: ὃς τῆς πρὸς αὐτὸν πίστεως ἀγάμενος τὸν ἄνδρα πίστιν ἀντιδίδωσιν αὐτῷ, τὴν δι' ὅρκου βεβαίωσιν ὧν ὑπέσχετο δωρεῶν, "[God] marvelling at Abraham's faith in Him repaid him with faithfulness by confirming with an oath the gifts which He had promised" (*Philo,* trans. F. H. Colson [LCL; 10 vols.; Cambridge: Harvard University, 1935; London: Heinemann, 1935] 6.133).

We have now concluded our investigation of Gal 3:6-9. The traditional interpretation of these verses (according to which οἱ ἐκ πίστεως = ὅσοι πιστεύουσιν and Christians are justified because their faith is structurally analogous to Abraham's faith) clashes not only with the latter part of Galatians 3 but also with verse 8, which depicts Abraham not as an exemplary paradigm for faith but as a representative figure in and through whom others are blessed. This observation has led us to suggest that the curious expression οἱ ἐκ πίστεως (vv. 7, 9) must be reinterpreted in light of the rest of the chapter, especially verses 14, 16, 22, and 29.

3. Gal 3:10-14

With verse 10, Paul counterattacks.[43] Having stated positively his claim that the blessing of Abraham encompasses οἱ ἐκ πίστεως, he now propounds the polemical thesis that ὅσοι ἐξ ἔργων νόμου εἰσίν are under a curse. The blessing-curse polarity is already suggested by Gen 12:3, from which Paul had quoted in verse 8.

> καὶ εὐλογήσω τοὺς εὐλογοῦντάς σε
> καὶ τοὺς καταρωμένους σε καταράσομαι
> καὶ ἐνευλογηθήσονται ἐν σοὶ πᾶσαι αἱ φυλαὶ τῆς γῆς.

Paul does not, however, pursue the line of argument that might be developed from this text, i.e., that those who seek to be justified by the law (cf. Gal 5:4) thereby nullify the grace of God (cf. 2:21) and in effect curse Abraham, thus incurring God's curse. Instead, quoting Deut 27:26, he seeks to demonstrate that the Torah itself imposes a curse upon all who fail to abide scrupulously by its provisions.

(a) Why Is No One Justified ἐν νόμῳ?

Generations of exegetes have debated whether Paul's argument here requires the tacit assumption that no one can possibly obey "all the things that are written in the book of the Law."[44] It is hard to escape the impression that the

---

43. Barrett, *First Adam*, 40.
44. Burton (*Galatians*, 164) says, "The unexpressed premise of the argument . . . is that no one does, in fact, continue in all the things that are written in the book of the law to do them." Schoeps (*Paul*, 175-77) agrees: "Paul's intention is to demonstrate the 'unfulfillability'

long-prevailing scholarly consensus in support of such an assumption was conditioned heavily by the "Lutheran" reading of Paul that has been forcefully challenged in recent years by, among others, Krister Stendahl.[45] Of particular weight in Stendahl's argument that Paul had a "robust conscience" (rather than a terrified one) is the evidence of Phil 3:6, in which Paul makes the claim — so astounding to most Protestant ears — that during his career as a Pharisee he was κατὰ δικαιοσύνην τὴν ἐν νόμῳ ἄμεμπτος: "in legal rectitude — faultless" *(NEB)*. A statement such as this should certainly cause us to reexamine carefully any interpretation of Galatians 3:10-14 that requires us to supply the unexpressed idea that it is impossible to obey the Law.

More fundamental, however, is the simple observation that Paul is explicitly making an entirely different point in this passage. Whether it is possible to keep all the commandments of the Law is beside the point, because in any case keeping the commandments cannot produce justification and life.[46] How does Paul know this? It is clear (δῆλον), he asserts, because ὁ δίκαιος ἐκ πίστεως ζήσεται. The interpretation of this text has already been discussed in Chapter IV above, and we may now apply the conclusions drawn there. The Messiah himself (ὁ δίκαιος) attains life and vindication not through the Law but ἐκ πίστεως; the same principle must therefore apply also to the Messiah's people. The Messiah defines the "pattern" for justification and life; consequently, since *he* lived and died and was raised ἐκ πίστεως, justification through keeping the commandments must be *in principle* (not merely de facto) impossible.

This interpretation of Galatians accords in many respects with the views of E. P. Sanders, whose work *Paul and Palestinian Judaism,* while not considering the messianic interpretation of Gal 3:11, does insist that Paul's rejection of the Law comes about through a process of inference from the gospel proclamation.[47] The chain of reasoning may be reconstructed as follows.

If a Law had been given which could give life,
righteousness would be through the Law (3:21).

If righteousness were attainable through the Law,
Christ died for no purpose (2:21).

---

of the law as its intrinsic meaning." On the other side of the question, see, e.g., Betz (*Galatians,* 145): "Paul not only fails to say what Schoeps thinks is self-evident, but in fact he says the opposite."

45. See his essay, "The Apostle Paul and the Introspective Conscience of the West" (*HTR* 56 [1963] 199-215), now reprinted in *Paul among Jews and Gentiles,* 78-96.

46. Notice that this is the same point that Paul makes in Philippians 3.

47. E. P. Sanders, *Paul and Palestinian Judaism,* 484.

But we know that Christ died for us (3:13, 2:20).

Thus, righteousness must not be attainable through the Law.

Thus, the Law has no power to give life.

Paul rejects the Law not because of an empirical observation that no one can do what it requires but because its claim to give life, explicitly articulated in Lev 18:5 (ὁ ποιήσας αὐτὰ ζήσεται ἐν αὐτοῖς [Gal 3:12]), is incompatible with the gospel story, which says that Christ had to die in order to give life to us (3:13-14; cf. 2:21). Up to this point, my interpretation runs parallel to Sanders'.

(b) Christ as the Agent of Redemption

Beyond this, however, we must reaffirm the observations already made in Chapter IV, which demonstrate the likelihood that Hab 2:4 would have been read by Paul as a messianic text. This interpretation is reinforced by the way that Paul develops the discussion in 3:13-14, in which Χριστός appears as the active agent in the center of the argument. These verses have sometimes been regarded as a fragment of traditional material, dropped in a curious, unmediated fashion into the discussion at this point. If, however, Χριστός = ὁ δίκαιος, the connection is a much smoother one.

In 3:13 Christ acts as a representative figure, taking the curse upon himself in order to set his people free from it. The "logic" of this transaction may appear puzzling to us, but it is central to Paul's understanding of the Christ-event. A clear parallel is to be found in 2 Cor 5:21: "[God] made him who knew no sin to be sin for us, in order that we might become the righteousness of God in him." The logic of such a transformation must be a narrative logic: it depends upon a "pattern of exchange," to use Hans Frei's phrase,[48] which can be made intelligible only in terms of a sequence of events in which a hero/protagonist acts on behalf of others. As we have seen in a detailed examination of this passage in Chapter III of this study, this is precisely the type of logic that is operative in Gal 3:13. Christ assumes the curse on behalf of "those under the law." But is there anything here that corresponds to 2 Cor 5:21b, in which *benefits* are also received vicariously (ἐν αὐτῷ)? There is indeed a precise correspondence in Gal 3:14a, which affirms that the Gentiles receive the blessing of Abraham ἐν Χριστῷ Ἰησοῦ.

48. Frei, *Identity,* 74-84.

The failure to recognize this last point is one of the flaws in Beker's analysis of the logic of the argument. Beker thinks that verses 10-14 portray Christ as an "enabler" who enables the blessing to "flow" to the Gentiles by removing the curse of the law. It is evident, however, from 3:14 that Christ is not just an enabler who removes an obstruction; instead, he is the indispensable means through whom the blessing is mediated. It is only through *participation* in him that the Gentiles receive the blessing.

Dahl has perceptively noted that "Gal 3:14a already presupposes the messianic interpretation of 'the offspring of Abraham.'"[49] The formulation of 3:14a (ἐν Χριστῷ Ἰησοῦ) anticipates the assertion of verse 16 that Christ is the one heir of the promise. On the basis of this assertion, Paul is enabled (or required) to say that the Gentiles inherit the promise "in Christ Jesus." According to Dahl, the link between 3:14a and 3:16 is supplied by Gen 22:18: καὶ ἐνευλογηθήσονται ἐν τῷ σπέρματί σου πάντα τὰ ἔθνη. This text restates the promise to Abraham (Gen 12:3; cf. 18:18) in such a way that the Gentiles are said to be blessed in Abraham's seed. Given an already established exegetical tradition that interpreted these "seed" texts as messianic promises,[50] the way was clear for Paul to affirm, as he does in verse 14, that the promise to Abraham was really a promise that the Gentiles would be blessed "in Christ Jesus." This is apparently a step forward from the position that Paul had argued in verse 8, that the Gentiles are blessed "in" Abraham; for Paul, however, it is a small step forward, since the Genesis texts, as he points out in verse 16, address the blessing to Abraham καὶ τῷ σπέρματί σου. Paul then takes the blessing of Abraham himself as a prefiguration of the blessing which will be fulfilled, as Gen 22:18 indicates, only in the "seed."[51] Thus, although Paul's exegesis could never pass historical-critical muster, it is internally consistent and compelling, once one grants his premise that σπέρμα is to be understood as a reference to the Messiah.

If Gal 3:11 is also understood as a messianic text, then a unified picture begins to emerge in this section of the argument. The Messiah, in obedience to God's will,[52] bears the curse and dies vicariously on behalf of others (3:13).

---

49. Dahl, *Studies in Paul*, 131.

50. See Wilcox, "The Promise of the 'Seed'"; D. C. Duling, "The Promises to David and Their Entrance into Christianity," *NTS* 20 (1973-74) 55-77.

51. Abraham is thus a "type" or "figure" of Christ. See the discussion of "figural interpretation" by H. Frei (*The Eclipse of Biblical Narrative* [New Haven: Yale University, 1974] 27-30), which draws heavily upon E. Auerbach (*Mimesis* (Princeton: Princeton University, 1968]). Cf. Auerbach, "Figura," *Scenes from the Drama of European Literature* (New York: Meridian, 1959) 11-26. See also the discussion of Pauline typology in Käsemann, *Perspectives*, 95-99.

52. See the discussion of this point in Edwards, *Christ, a Curse, and the Cross*, 316-21.

Because of his faithfulness, however, he is vindicated by God and given life (3:11) and the inheritance of God's blessing, which had been promised to Abraham (3:16). In receiving this blessing/promise, he remains a representative figure: just as others received the benefits of his death, so also they participate with him in the inheritance, which they have "in" him (3:14).

(c) The Spirit as Fulfillment of the Promise

But this still leaves one major question unanswered, a question rarely raised by commentators and, even when raised, never answered clearly. Even if we grant Paul his argument that the promise to Abraham is fulfilled in Christ, what authorizes his further inference that the *Spirit* is the fulfillment of this promise? In Gal 3:14 it is clear that "the blessing of Abraham" is somehow equated with "the promise of the Spirit." But how can Paul pose this equation? Nowhere in the OT does the promise to Abraham have anything to do with the Spirit. The content of the promise is clear: the land, descendants, and an eternal covenant. There is no reference to the *Spirit* at all. Yet Paul speaks of the presence of the Spirit as an obvious evidence that the promise is now fulfilled. Is this a purely arbitrary assertion?

A survey of the commentaries on this question produces very little illumination. Many do not address the problem at all.[53] Some attempt to explain the phrase ἡ ἐπαγγελία τοῦ πνεύματος by pointing to Luke's use of the phrase ἡ ἐπαγγελία τοῦ πατρός to describe the Holy Spirit in Luke 24:49 and Acts 1:4.[54] Schlier also refers to Acts 2:33 as a "commentary" on this text.[55] These Lukan passages, however, provide no help in relation to our question, not only because they come from texts written later than Paul's letter but, more pertinently, because the "promise" in these passages is still in no way related to Abraham. The most embarrassing explanation of all is offered by H. Ridderbos: "The gift of the Spirit is now designated as the content of the promise to Abraham. It is the guarantee or pledge of the perfected redemption which Abraham was promised."[56] Was Abraham promised "perfected redemption"?

---

53. This may be said of Lightfoot, Zahn, Lietzmann, Bonnard, Oepke, Bligh, and Lührmann.

54. Typical is the interpretation of Duncan (*Galatians*, 103): ". . . Though no mention of 'the Spirit' had been made in the promise given to Abraham, Paul is only bringing out a latent truth when he speaks of the promised Spirit — a phrase which is doubtless also meant to recall certain words of Jesus (cf. Luke xxiv.49; Acts i.4)." Cf. Guthrie, *Galatians*, 100.

55. Schlier, *Galater*, 141.

56. Ridderbos, *Epistle to Churches of Galatia*, 128.

Ridderbos' tendency to read Reformed dogmatics into the text of Galatians stands in contrast to Calvin's perspicacious grasp of the difficulty at this point. Calvin solved it by concluding that Paul did *not* mean to refer to the gift of the Holy Spirit, as in the Acts parallels, but that the phrase ἡ ἐπαγγελία τοῦ πνεύματος should be translated as "the spiritual promise."[57] This solution would eliminate the difficulty, but, unfortunately, it fails to take into account the wider context: Gal 3:14 must be read within the framework provided by 3:2-5 and 4:6, in which the gift of the Spirit is unmistakably under discussion.

Lagrange and Betz both recognize the problem and conclude that Paul's identification of the gift of the Spirit with the promise to Abraham must be an inference based solely on experience.[58] As Lagrange puts the matter concisely, "Ce don n'était pas annoncé à Abraham en termes exprès, mais sa nature est constatée par l'experience des Galates à laquelle Paul a fait appel au début du chapitre." Burton, without mentioning anything about the Galatians' spiritual experiences, simply notes that "the apostle refers to the promise to Abraham and has learned to interpret this as having reference to the gift of the Spirit."[59] The question is, *how* did Paul learn to interpret the promise to Abraham in this way? Is there something that bridges the gulf between the content of the promise and the content of that which Paul now claims as the fulfillment of that promise?

Schlier offers the seemingly inevitable conclusion that for Paul "nur das Dass einer verheissenen κληρονομία und nicht ihr Was von Bedeutung war."[60] Can we be satisfied with this explanation? Dahl, even while emphasizing Paul's desire to maintain continuity with Scripture and with the God who made the promises, acknowledges that "Paul has, by the standards of Jewish expectations, dissipated the promise's objective content."[61] Another way of posing our question is this: was there something within the realm of Jewish expectations that *did* associate the Spirit with the promises to Abraham?

A partial answer might be found once again in Paul's use of scriptural testimonies concerning the messianic seed. The key text is Isa 44:3: ἐπιθήσω τὸ πνεῦμά μου ἐπὶ τὸ σπέρμα σου καὶ τὰς εὐλογίας μου ἐπὶ τὰ τέκνα σου. This promise is addressed, to be sure, not to Abraham but to "my servant Jacob and my beloved Israel whom I have chosen" (Isa 44:2). Nonetheless, the parallelism between this passage and Gal 3:14 is very striking, and the association

---

57. Calvin, *Galatians*, 56.
58. Lagrange, *Galates*, 74; Betz, *Galatians*, 152-53.
59. Burton, *Galatians*, 177.
60. Schlier, *Galater*, 145.
61. Dahl, *Studies in Paul*, 136.

of τὸ πνεῦμα and αἱ εὐλογίαι with τὸ σπέρμα might be of significance for understanding Paul's thinking. Gal 3:16 and 3:19 show that Paul understood certain scriptural promises to the seed of Abraham as messianic prophecies. As we have already seen, there is strong evidence to indicate that this interpretation rests upon an established exegetical tradition which also read such texts as Gen 3:15 and 2 Sam 7:12-14 as promises of a coming messianic "seed." Isa 44:3 might well have been grouped with these other passages as a testimonium concerning the messianic σπέρμα; if so, it would provide the basis for Paul's inference that the Spirit now given to Christians constituted a fulfillment of the promised blessing, particularly since the reference to εὐλογίαι in Isa 44:3 provides another verbal link to the Abraham texts.

But we may also consider a second way of approaching the problem. We have already observed that Paul tends to build his arguments upon concise christological formulations that manifest a narrative structure, and in our analysis of this structure we have observed that its topical sequence culminates in the communication of the Spirit to God's "sons." Is it possible, then, that this foundational Christ-story creates for Paul the link between the experience of the Spirit in the community and the Abraham story? As the story is proclaimed, the Spirit is given to the community (3:1-5), and the story itself portrays Christ as the agent in and through whom the Spirit is given (3:14; 4:6). At the same time, the story also identifies Christ as Abraham's messianic "seed," in whom the promise of blessing to the nations is to be fulfilled. The conclusion lies readily at hand, within the framework defined by this story, that the experienced Spirit, given to the Gentiles, must be equated with the promised fulfillment. Thus the "logic" of the story would inform Paul's exegesis of the Genesis text.

In any case, once we see that Paul assumes an identification between the Spirit and the blessing of Abraham, we are enabled to grasp more clearly the coherence of Gal 3:1-14. In particular, the transition between verses 1-5 and 6-9 becomes clearer in light of this assumption, and we can see that verse 14 closes the circle of ideas that began in verse 2.[62] The Spirit that the Galatians have received is not just a self-authenticating religious experience; rather, the experience is significant for Paul's argument because he interprets it, in light of scripture, as the fulfillment of God's promise to Abraham.

62. Cf. Eckert, *Die urchristliche Verkündigung,* 78-79; van der Minde, *Schrift und Tradition,* 133.

C. Narrative Logic in the Argument

The foregoing analysis has laid the groundwork for a unified reading of the central section of Galatians. Contrary to Beker's outline of the structure of the argument in Galatians 3, which posited differing soteriologies in verses 6-9, 10-14, and 16-29, I have proposed that verses 6-9 and 10-14 are best interpreted as expressions of the "participationist" soteriology that is found in the last half of the chapter. Furthermore, I have suggested that the "logic" of this participationist soteriology is a *narrative* logic, i.e., that Paul understands salvation as a sharing in the destiny of a representative figure whose story is the enactment of God's salvific purpose. This suggestion must now be developed and tested in the final part of this chapter. Three steps will be necessary. First we must give some attention to three other innovative proposals concerning the "logic" that gives coherence to Paul's argument in the central section of Galatians, seeking to determine how these proposals relate to the thesis argued here. Secondly, we must define more precisely what is meant by "narrative logic." Finally, we must focus directly upon the texts in Gal 3:16–4:11 in which salvation is described in terms of participation in Christ and trace the ways in which the narrative pattern shapes the logic of Paul's discussion.

1. The Nature of Paul's Logic: Other Proposals

(a) Greer M. Taylor: Juristic Logic

One original explanation of the internal logic of Galatians was offered in 1966 by Greer M. Taylor in an article entitled "The Function of ΠΙΣΤΙΣ ΧΡΙΣΤΟΥ in Galatians."[63] Taylor insists that it makes no sense to regard justification as a benefit which can be acquired "simply by having a certain state of mind."[64] Instead, in Taylor's view, the substance of Paul's teaching is

> that man is saved by Christ's work and by Christ's work alone, and circumcision or any other work of the law is theologically objectionable because it implies that Christ's work is insufficient and needs to be complemented. From this point of view a system of justification simply by faith in Christ is also objectionable, as assigning to man too much of a function and to

63. Greer M. Taylor, "The Function of ΠΙΣΤΙΣ ΧΡΙΣΤΟΥ in Galatians," *JBL* 85 (1966) 58-76.
64. Ibid., 75.

Christ too little: it simply substitutes the mental act of having faith for the bodily one of being circumcised as a precondition of salvation, and (so far as the mechanism of justification is concerned) leaves Christ in the passive role of being the object of our justifying faith.[65]

Against this unsatisfactory standard interpretation, Taylor offers a new suggestion which he believes will account for the coherence of Paul's argument in a comprehensive and much more satisfactory manner: πίστις refers not to our act or attribute of "faith" but the Roman legal institution of *fidei commissum,* a device whereby a testator could leave property "in trust" under the care of a "testamentary heir" with the stipulation that the testamentary heir should transmit it to a third party or parties. By the use of this legal procedure a Roman testator could "name national aliens as beneficiaries of his testament" and "adopt strangers as his sons." As a result of this transaction, the adopted person "lost his previous juristic personality and acquired an entirely new and different juristic personality," i.e., "he was exonerated from the various civil liabilities and obligations he had acquired prior to this adoption." This was possible, however, only because the testamentary heir was required to "pay the cost of the exoneration."[66]

According to Taylor, Paul has employed this legal institution as a "conceptual analogy" to explain his gospel to the Galatians. God is the testator, Abraham and Christ are successive testamentary heirs, and the Gentiles are the ultimate beneficiaries, aliens who are adopted and constituted as new persons entirely apart from any action on their part. Christ, as a faithful trustee, distributes the inheritance to the Gentiles and sets them free from past liabilities and obligations by taking these liabilities upon himself. Crucial to Taylor's argument is his proposal that πίστις can mean *fidei commissum* and that the phrase πίστις Ἰησοῦ Χριστοῦ thus refers to "Christ's reliability as a trustee."[67]

Taylor's innovative hypothesis has been greeted among Pauline scholars with benign neglect: neither has it exercised any discernible influence on major recent interpretations of Paul,[68] nor has there been, so far as

65. Ibid.

66. Ibid., 65-67. Taylor's account of *fidei commissum* is based on Gaius (*The Institutes* [ed. and trans. F. de Zulueta; 2 vols.; Oxford: Clarendon, 1946-53] 1.138-49).

67. Taylor, "Function of ΠΙΣΤΙΣ ΧΡΙΣΤΟΥ," 72.

68. See the casual dismissal in Betz (*Galatians,* 118 n. 45). Taylor's proposal is not mentioned at all in most recent surveys of Pauline theology, but it is sometimes cited with qualified approval by advocates of the "faith of Jesus" interpretation of πίστις Ἰησοῦ Χριστοῦ. For example, Williams ("Righteousness of God," 274-75) calls Taylor's article "an

I am able to determine, any published refutation of it. The hypothesis deserves more thorough consideration because, if it is correct, it provides a thoroughgoing explanation for the unity of the argument in Gal 3:6–4:7, all of which could then be read as an explication of the conceptual analogy of the *fidei commissum*. If the hypothesis is wrong, it nonetheless deserves a careful critique. The following examination of Taylor's essay will show that, in spite of some important insights, his argument cannot withstand detailed scrutiny.

Criticisms may be raised against Taylor's position at two crucial points: (1) he places a great deal of weight on spurious arguments to show that πίστις is for Paul a "juristic" concept; (2) his usage of parallels from the papyri is loose and misleading. Let us take each of these matters in turn.

(1) The foundation of Taylor's argument is his claim that "in Galatians πίστις plays an integral part in an elaborate transaction which is *explicitly juristic*."[69] In support of this view he marshals two arguments.

First of all, he observes that the incidence of the word πίστις in the Pauline epistles is heaviest in Romans and Galatians and indeed precisely in the sections of these letters which are concerned "with the relation between the Christian and the Mosaic Law."[70] While he acknowledges that πίστις occurs throughout Paul's letters in all sorts of contexts, Taylor still wants to argue that "the very irregular incidence of the word indicates that Paul does not ascribe to πίστις a sort of undifferentiated power for salvation; its usefulness to him lies in the answer it provides to the problem of the law."[71]

We may let pass Taylor's debatable judgment that the incidence of πίστις is "very irregular" (as though we ought to expect to find it sprinkled in an even layer across Paul's letters) and grant the point that it occurs prominently in contexts where it is juxtaposed to νόμος. The question is what this observation proves. Taylor thinks that he can use it to prove that πίστις must be a juridical concept.

> The direct contrast of any two concepts necessarily implies their common membership in a single conceptual system in terms of which they can be contrasted: we can contrast sweet and sour, good and evil, peace and war, but not sweet and red or peace and youth. If in Galatians Paul can directly

---

important essay largely ignored by Pauline scholars" and judges it "essentially sound," but he then argues that Paul modifies the Roman juristic concept to suit his own needs. Williams thus broadens his interpretation of πίστις Χριστοῦ beyond the scope of Taylor's hypothesis.

69. Taylor, "Function of ΠΙΣΤΙΣ ΧΡΙΣΤΟΥ," 58.
70. Ibid., 59.
71. Ibid., 60.

contrast πίστις with the specifically juridical νόμος and its works, the πίστις of Galatians must itself be a juridical quantity.[72]

This reasoning, however, is fallacious. Taylor is correct in saying that πίστις belongs to some kind of conceptual system in common with νόμος; this does not prove, however, that πίστις must be a "juridical quantity." From 3:11-12, it is clear that πίστις and νόμος are opposed not as rival juridical concepts but as alternative sources of *life*. Indeed, the whole point of the argument is precisely that πίστις is nonjuristic, that it is a source of life apart from the realm of law. Thus, Taylor's argument rests upon a misleading use of word statistics and linguistic evidence.

Taylor appears to be on firmer ground when he introduces a second point.

> The argument of chs. 2 and 3 of Galatians explicitly involves the conceptual analogy of a διαθήκη: a juristic transaction by which benefits are transmitted by one person to others. The διαθήκη of Galatians is a complex one, and one in which πίστις plays an integral and complex part.[73]

It is obviously true that Paul employs "the conceptual analogy of a διαθήκη." But is it true, as Taylor's formulation indicates, that this analogy is already operative in Galatians 2, and is it true that πίστις plays a part in the διαθήκη?

The first reference to the διαθήκη appears not in Galatians 2 but in Gal 3:15, when it is, to all appearances, introduced as a new idea in the discussion, drawn from Paul's exegesis of Genesis 17. The burden of proof surely rests heavily on anyone who asserts that this idea has informed the discussion prior to 3:15. But more damaging to Taylor's position is the fact that *precisely at the point where Paul develops the analogy of the διαθήκη* (3:15-18), *πίστις drops out of the discussion.* This is most striking at 3:18, where the earlier juxtaposition between νόμος and πίστις is supplanted by a juxtaposition between νόμος and ἐπαγγελία. (This cannot be explained as mere stylistic variation, since Taylor's interpretation takes πίστις as a fixed technical term for *fidei commissum*.) Again, when the theme of inheritance reappears in 4:1-7, πίστις is once again conspicuously absent. Conversely, in contexts where Paul ascribes soteriological efficacy to πίστις (2:16, 20; 3:8, 11, 22, 26), we hear noth-

---

72. Ibid.

73. Ibid., 61-62. Although Taylor says (63 n. 8) that "the διαθήκη of Galatians cannot be any of the various kinds of ברית known to the OT," he fails to discuss the proposal of E. Bammel ("Gottes ΔΙΑΘΗΚΗ [Gal III.15-17] und das jüdische Rechtsdenken," *NTS* 6 [1959-60] 313-19) that the Jewish מתנת בריא does indeed correspond to the features of the διαθήκη described by Paul in Galatians 3.

ing of the διαθήκη. This is especially apparent in Romans 3, in which Paul develops the justifying effects of πίστις Ἰησοῦ (Χριστοῦ) with no reference at all to the analogy of the διαθήκη. Thus the evidence decisively contradicts Taylor's claim that πίστις plays a part in the διαθήκη. Instead, the διαθήκη appears to be a temporary illustration introduced by Paul in 3:15-18 and echoed in 4:1-7. In no case does Paul bring the concepts of πίστις and διαθήκη into explicit relation with one another. Thus Taylor's assertion that πίστις is a "juristic" concept in Galatians remains unsupported.

(2) An equally grave difficulty with Taylor's hypothesis is created by his imprecise use of parallels from other ancient sources. He appeals to papyrus wills as evidence for the currency of the device of *fidei commissum* in the Greco-Roman world beyond Rome and to support his claim that "πίστις is the Greek word both generally and technically used to translate *fidei commissum*."[74] Taylor actually cites only one will as an example, though, as he indicates, examples of this type could be multiplied. He handles the evidence in the following manner.

> For example, by his papyrus will C. Longinus Castor leaves property τῇ πίστει of a certain person to be disposed of in a certain way. . . . Names and Latin technical words with no Greek equivalent are simply transliterated. . . . But what is obviously the technical *fidei commissum* appears in its Greek equivalent as πίστις.[75]

But let us consider the actual text to which Taylor refers: ὃς ἐάν μου κλη-[ρον]όμος γέ[νητ]αι, ὑπεύθυνος ἔστω δῶναι ποιῆσαι παρασχέθαι ταῦ[τα] πάντα [ἃ ἐ]ν ταύτῃ τῇ δικθήκῃ μου γεγραμμένα εἴη, τῇ τε πίστι [α]ὐτῆς παρακατατίθομαι.[76] This sentence in the will no doubt establishes the type of legal arrangement that Taylor has in mind, but does the word πίστι (= πίστει) actually translate the technical term *fidei commissum*? Hardly so. The sense of the last clause is correctly rendered by F. Preisigke: "Die Durchführung meines letzten Willens lege ich in ihre zuverlässige Hand."[77] The word πίστις simply and accurately translates the Latin *fides*, which, as Taylor himself points out elsewhere in his essay, refers to "the good faith — the reliability —

74. Taylor, "Function of ΠΙΣΤΙΣ ΧΡΙΣΤΟΥ," 70.
75. Ibid.
76. Text cited in accordance with L. Mitteis and U. Wilcken, *Grundzüge und Chrestomathie der Papyruskunde* (Leipzig: Teubner, 1912) 365. This text differs in some respects from the editio princeps (BGU 1.326), which Taylor cites, but it is identical in the crucial last clause of the quotation.
77. F. Preisigke, *Wörterbuch der griechischen Papyrusurkunden* (3 vols.; Berlin: Selbstverlag der Erben, 1925-31) 2.308-09.

of the testamentary heir."[78] In other words, even though the word πίστις occurs in a legal document, it bears its typical ordinary-language meaning, and it is not used as a technical term for a particular juristic device.[79]

Even more pertinent, however, is the fact that neither this text nor any other in the papyri or in the legal literature cited by Taylor provides a true parallel to Paul's expression ἐκ πίστεως 'Ιησοῦ Χριστοῦ. The legal documents entrust property to the good faith (τῇ πίστει) of various persons, but nowhere is the testamentary heir said to distribute benefits ἐκ πίστεως αὐτοῦ (or αὐτῆς). The absence of any such parallels weakens Taylor's case still further. He has shown that the term πίστις does appear in wills and legal documents, but he has failed to produce a single instance in which its usage resembles the Pauline idiom.

Taylor has rightly discerned that the argumentative coherence of Galatians is tenuous if one attempts to interpret the text in terms of the usual understanding of justification through believing in Christ. He has attempted to facilitate a unified reading of the argument through construing it as an extended exposition of a juridical transaction, on the analogy of the Roman *fidei commissum*. The analogy works out so neatly as an explanatory device that one might wish Paul *had* thought of using it, because it would clear up the logic of his argument so well; unfortunately, for the reasons indicated here, Taylor's solution cannot be accepted. His work, however, does point the way forward in several respects. His critique of the traditional understanding of justification is apt, and his quest for a coherent reading of the argument is exemplary. Furthermore, he rightly insists that "Christ's work alone" is the means of salvation in Paul. Although Taylor's interpretation of πίστις 'Ιησοῦ Χριστοῦ in terms of juridical terminology is to be rejected, his intuition that this enigmatic expression contains the key to understanding the logic of Paul's argumentation in Galatians is surely correct.

(b) Nils Dahl: Rabbinic Logic

Dahl looks to Jewish hermeneutical methods as the necessary background for understanding Paul's logic of argumentation. In the essay "Contradictions in

---

78. Taylor, "Function of ΠΙΣΤΙΣ ΧΡΙΣΤΟΥ," 72.

79. Taylor's one other example of πίστις as a legal technical term is legitimate. He cites a text which refers to αἱ κατὰ πίστιν γενόμεναι κληρονομίαι, which Preisigke (*Wörterbuch*, 2.310) translates as "hereditates fideicommissariae." Here πίστις means "trust" in the juridical sense, but this still does not offer a real analogy to the distinctive Pauline usage.

Scripture,"[80] Dahl adopts and refines an earlier suggestion by H.-J. Schoeps that Paul's discussion of scriptural texts in Gal 3:10-12 reflects "the treatment of contradictory scriptural passages in contemporary Jewish hermeneutics."[81] Schoeps proposes that Paul is using Rabbi Ishmael's thirteenth *middah* (exegetical principle), which he interprets as follows: "If two verses are contradictory, one should find a third verse in order to overcome the contradiction."[82] Paul finds Hab 2:4 ("The righteous one shall live by faith") to be in contradiction to Lev 18:5 ("The one who does them shall live by them"). Consequently, according to Schoeps, Paul adjudicates the contradiction by appealing to a third scriptural verse, Gen 15:6 ("Abraham believed God, and it was reckoned to him as righteousness"). There is a certain difficulty with this explanation, because the quotation of Gen 15:6 stands at the beginning of this section of the argument (Gal 3:6), and it is not explicitly presented as the solution to the apparent contradiction between Hab 2:4 and Lev 18:5. Schoeps thinks, however, that Gen 15:6 is "recapitulated in the word εὐλογία"[83] in verse 14.

Dahl agrees that Paul sets up the texts from Habakkuk and Leviticus as contradictory and that he deals with them in accordance with R. Ishmael's hermeneutical rule. But he understands the rule itself in a way different from Schoeps' explanation of it, and this understanding provides him with a way of analyzing the structure of Paul's argument in Gal 3:10-25. Dahl insists that the rule means, in accordance with a formulation of it ascribed to R. Akiba, "Two scriptural passages which correspond to one another yet conflict with one another, should be upheld in their place until a third passage comes and decides between them."[84] Dahl interprets this to mean that "the two scriptural passages should be upheld, each in its place; i.e., they should be so interpreted that they do not negate one another, but rather both remain valid, each with a specific meaning within its own context." The "third passage" as a means of resolving conflicts is mentioned, as Dahl points out, "only in a subordinate clause which adds a condition."[85] Normally *both* passages should be upheld; only in rare cases where some third passage renders this procedure impossible is this approach abandoned. Thus Dahl concludes that

> the task which confronted an exegete when he encountered an apparent contradiction in Scripture was not to find a third passage which could re-

80. Dahl, *Studies in Paul*, 159-77.
81. Ibid., 161.
82. Schoeps, *Paul*, 177-78.
83. Ibid., 178.
84. Dahl, *Studies in Paul*, 162.
85. Ibid.

solve this conflict. It was necessary first to establish which text contained the valid halakah, the correct statement, or the fundamental teaching. Then it was requisite to find a satisfactory explanation of the conflicting text to maintain its validity. This is clear from the typical rabbinic formulation of the problem: "One scriptural passage says . . . , but another passage says . . . . How are both of these passages to be upheld?"[86]

With this model for interpreting contradictory texts in mind, Dahl is able to outline persuasively the movement of Paul's argument in Gal 3:10-25. His conclusions[87] may be summarized as follows:

3:10-12 The contradictory texts juxtaposed
3:13-18 Demonstration of the fundamental validity of Hab 2:4
3:19-25 How is the contradictory passage (Lev 18:5) to be explained?

Dahl's model for grasping Paul's argumentative logic accounts much more satisfactorily than does Schoeps' view for Paul's insistence (3:21) that the Law is *not* really contrary to the promises of God; instead, the Law was, in Dahl's view, "a provisional, interim arrangement, valid only for pre-messianic times."[88] Thus the apparent contradiction is removed, and the validity of Lev 18:5 "in its place" is affirmed. In light of this analysis, Dahl draws the conclusion that "in no other place does Paul deviate more from the views of the rabbis. But in no other place is his style of argumentation more similar to that of the rabbis than in Galatians 3."[89]

As attractive as Dahl's hypothesis appears, there are several significant objections to be raised against it. First of all, Paul does not introduce the two passages as conflicting texts which pose an interpretive dilemma. Rather, they are introduced into the midst of a discussion in progress and, as Betz correctly observes, they "prove separate points in a consecutive argument."[90]

Second, verses 13-18 and 19-25 make no explicit reference to the passages whose respective validity they are supposed to explain, according to Dahl's analysis. This difficulty is perhaps not insuperable, but it is surely worth weighing. Third, even though Dahl is correct that Paul sees the Law as a provisional dispensation of God, it does not necessarily follow that the valid-

86. Ibid., 164.
87. See especially pp. 171, 174-75.
88. Ibid., 172-73.
89. Ibid., 175.
90. Betz, *Galatians*, 138 n. 8. Betz contends that the concepts of faith and law are juxtaposed here, not merely two scriptural texts.

ity of Lev 18:5 is thereby upheld. Lev 18:5 (as Paul interprets it in 3:12) claims that the Law has the power to give life to those who obey it, but Paul clearly denies that the Law ever possessed any such power (3:21b; cf. Rom 8:3). Thus, from Paul's perspective, Lev 18:5 must still be judged unconditionally false. Finally, Dahl's proposal does not explain how the exegetical discussion of 3:10-25 is related to its wider context, particularly the Abraham material in verses 6-9.

Nevertheless, though the particulars of Dahl's position are not adopted here, several of his observations remain valid and must be incorporated in our interpretation. First of all, Dahl rightly emphasizes that Paul is engaged in the interpretation of Scripture,[91] and that he handles the Scripture like a rabbi, alluding to whole passages through brief catch-phrases. Second, though the text does not support Dahl's view that Paul seeks to uphold the validity of Lev 18:5, the broader point stands: Paul, even while setting aside a part of scripture, still seeks to maintain continuity with the Jewish tradition and to ascribe meaning and positive value even to the Law that he now rejects. As we shall see, he tries to maintain this continuity (whether successfully or not the reader must judge) through a narrative "hermeneutic" which assigns to the Law a supporting role within an unfolding story.

(c) Hans Dieter Betz: Rhetorical Logic

Betz's commentary on Galatians carries through a thorough attempt to read Galatians as an "apologetic letter," an example of a clearly defined literary genre governed by the conventions of Greco-Roman rhetoric. According to Betz's hypothesis, the letter's argument is most readily understood when it is analyzed in terms of its rhetorical structure.[92] Betz's analysis yields the following broad outline of the letter.

---

91. The failure to give due weight to this fact is one of the difficulties with Taylor's essay.

92. Betz, *Galatians*, 14-25. For slightly more extensive discussion of the "apologetic letter" genre, see Betz's article "The Literary Composition and Function of Paul's Letter to the Galatians" (*NTS* 21 [1975] 353-79). It should be remarked in passing that Betz speaks with surprising confidence of the "apologetic letter" as an established literary genre in Greco-Roman antiquity. The authority whom he cites in support of this opinion, A. Momigliano, expresses himself with considerable reserve: "We have neither the letters (if letters they were) of Empedocles to Pausanias nor those of Alcmaeon of Croton (Diogenes Laertius 8.60 and 83), and we know too little about the epistolography of the Hellenistic period. . . . We cannot, therefore, see the exact place of Plato's letter in the history of ancient autobiographical pro-

I. Epistolary Prescript (1:1-5)
II. Exordium (1:6-11)
III. Narratio (1:12–2:14)
IV. Propositio (2:15-21)
V. Probatio (3:1–4:31)
VI. Exhortatio (5:1–6:10)
VII. Epistolary Postscript (Conclusio) (6:11-18)

Thus, the section of Galatians with which we are concerned is classified by Betz as the "probatio," the central argumentative section in which the "proofs" for the defense's case are presented. Betz discerns within the *probatio* a series of six arguments (plus one "digression") divided and characterized as follows.[93]

A. The first argument: an argument of undisputable evidence (3:1-5)
B. The second argument: an argument from Scripture (3:6-14)
C. The third argument: an argument from common human practice (3:15-18)
D. A digression on the (Jewish) Torah (3:19-25)
E. The fourth argument: an argument from Christian tradition (3:26–4:11)
F. The fifth argument: an argument from friendship (4:12-20)
G. The sixth argument: an allegorical argument from Scripture (4:21-31).

In Betz's view, the unity of the argument is to be found not so much in the material content of the various arguments as in the overarching apologetic purpose of the letter.[94] The arguments are presented seriatim; they support a common thesis, but the relationships among them are not entirely clear. In fact, Betz remarks that this section is characterized by "apparent confusion" and that "an analysis of these chapters in terms of rhetoric is extremely diffi-

---

duction. But one vaguely feels the Platonic precedent in Epicurus, Seneca, and perhaps St. Paul" (*The Development of Greek Biography* [Cambridge: Harvard, 1971] 62). Betz acknowledges that "the subsequent history of the genre is difficult to trace, since most of the pertinent literature did not survive" (*Galatians,* 15). It is noteworthy that Betz is forced to derive his parallels throughout the commentary not from actual "apologetic letters," but from handbooks on rhetoric.

93. Betz, *Galatians,* 19-22.

94. In this regard, Betz's position resembles that of Haeuser, who argued that the unity of the letter is best understood in terms of Paul's intention to defend himself against the charge that he did not consistently hold to a law-free gospel.

cult." This difficulty arises, according to Betz, because "Paul has been very successful — as a skilled rhetorician would be expected to be — in disguising his argumentative strategy."[95]

Thus, while Betz's analysis of the letter's rhetorical structure does in fact prove helpful in identifying various rhetorical devices and in determining the function of the large section (Gal 3:1–4:31) within this letter, it is of little help in grasping the construction of the argument *within* this section. Betz rightly maintains that in Galatians "in spite of the apparent confusion there is to be expected a clear flow of thought,"[96] but his formal analysis of the text, by treating Galatians 3 and 4 as a series of discrete arguments,[97] does not sufficiently address the problem of the material unity of the argument.

This criticism does not require a rejection of Betz's general theory about the composition of the letter. In looking for a substructure that provides material unity to Paul's theological formulations, I am raising a different question from the question pursued by Betz in his efforts to sketch out the *formal* structures that Paul employs to articulate his argument. However, I stand in firm agreement with Betz that it is appropriate to look for argumentative coherence in the central section of Galatians. The remainder of this chapter will seek to demonstrate this coherence not through the formal analysis of rhetorical structures, but through describing a *material* unity grounded in the "logic" of Paul's foundational gospel story.

2. What Is "Narrative Logic"?

I have suggested that Paul's thought is grounded in a narrative logic, i.e., in patterns of order that are proper to story rather than to discursive reasoning. The meaning of this claim must now be more carefully articulated. What is "narrative logic," and how does it differ from propositional or philosophical logic?

A story is made up of actions ordered in a chronological sequence that constitute, in Aristotle's term, the *mythos* of the story. These actions are not randomly ordered; they must bear a certain relation to one another so that the entire story can be perceived as a unity. Each new event must be an intelli-

---

95. Betz, *Galatians*, 129.

96. Ibid.

97. It seems odd, for example, to say, as Betz does, that a new "argument" begins in 3:26. In justice to Betz, however, it should be emphasized that many of his exegetical observations within the commentary point toward a unity of thought that reaches across the structural divisions proposed by his formal analysis.

gible — though not necessarily predictable — development of the events which precede it. As Aristotle recognized, a well-ordered story is one in which "the incidents are unexpected and yet one is a consequence of the other."[98] Ricoeur elaborates on this point.

> . . . A narrative conclusion can be neither deduced nor predicted. . . . This is why we have to follow it *to the conclusion*. Instead of being predictable, a conclusion must be acceptable. Looking backward from the conclusion over the episodes which led up to it, we must be able to say that this end required those events and this chain of actions.[99]

In short, the coherence of events in a narrative is characterized by *fitness* rather than by logical necessity. In this respect, narrative logic differs from a propositional logic, in which consequences follow necessarily from premises. If we ask why the events of a particular story are ordered as they are and not in some other way, the answer can only be "because that is the way it happened" or "because that is how the story is told." No explanation on grounds of strict logical necessity is possible.[100]

Thus far our observations have concerned the "logic" of narrative *sequence,* that aspect of narrative which Ricoeur calls the "episodic dimension." Equally important, however, is the logic of narrative *shape,* Ricoeur's "configurational dimension."[101] A story posits *patterns* of order and value. Certain networks of relationship among characters are established, and effects follow from some specified causes rather than from others. A "world" of possible and appropriate action is thus established by the story. In the case of stories that become foundational stories for a community, these patterns may take on a prescriptive-ethical significance: the "fittingness" of an action may be measured as a function of its correspondence to a particular narrative pattern. Here again, the "shape" of a story, which is closely related to the *dianoia*

---

98. Aristotle, *Poetics* 1452a.

99. Ricoeur, "Narrative Function," 182. See also his "Narrative and Hermeneutics," *Religion and the Humanities* (Research Triangle Park, NC: National Humanities Center, 1981) 42-46. Cf. C. L. Lloyd, *The Role of Narrative Form in Historical and Theological Explanation* (Ph.D. diss., Yale, 1968; Ann Arbor: University Microfilms, 1969) 178-80.

100. Of course, we have seen in Chap. III above that structuralism has succeeded in identifying certain constant patterns within narratives. These also constitute a sort of narrative logic. These patterns are of a very general nature, however, and might in fact be regarded, even if taken as normative rather than merely descriptive, as guides for measuring the fitness of various narrative possibilities rather than as rules that determine the necessary development of any given story.

101. See Chap. I.B.1.b above.

of which Frye speaks, is determined not so much by logical necessity as by the actual unfolding of the story. The constraints of narrative logic are thus determined by contingent and particular events rather than by "the necessary truths of reason."

In the remaining pages of this chapter, we must consider how these twin narrative properties of the Christ-story, its *sequence* and *shape*, become decisive for Paul as he constructs his argument in Galatians.

3. Patterns of Narrative Logic in Gal 3:15–4:11

(a) Participation in the Inheritance

In Gal 3:15, Paul introduces the metaphor of inheritance, which he then plays upon in various ways throughout the following discussion. The key to Paul's use of this metaphor is found in his assertion (vv. 16, 19) that Christ is the one heir of the promises made to Abraham.[102] This interpretation can have soteriological implications, however, only in light of the presupposition that finally becomes explicit in verses 26-29: all who are baptized into Christ become one in him and thus participate in the inheritance.

Even though this presupposition is not articulated until 3:26-29, its effects are evident throughout the argument. We have already noted the formulation of 3:14a, which declares that the Gentiles receive the blessing "in Christ Jesus," i.e., through participation in him. Likewise, although Paul speaks in verses 15-19 of Christ as the one seed to whom the inheritance is promised, he moves without comment or explanation in verse 22 to the affirmation that the promise is given to those who believe; thus, he gives evidence that a participatory soteriology informs his thought throughout. The "Christ" of verse 16 is an individual, as Paul insists, but he is an individual in whom the destiny of others is embodied, a "universal heir."[103] (A very similar idea appears in

---

102. The image of Christ as κληρονόμος appears to have been widespread in early Christianity. Paul employs it not only here but also in Rom 8:17, where Christians are described as συγκληρονόμοι Χριστοῦ. Again, in Heb 1:2, Christ is extolled as "heir of all things." An interesting further use of this metaphor appears in Mark 12:7 par., in the parable of the wicked tenants, which is the most explicitly christological of all the synoptic parables: when the tenants see the "Beloved Son," they exclaim οὗτός ἐστιν ὁ κληρονόμος. In all of these instances, the image of Christ as heir is connected with the metaphor of sonship (cf. also Gal 4:6-7). Galatians is unique, however, in portraying Christ as heir of the promises to *Abraham*.

103. See Schlier, *Galater*, 145. G. Klein (*Rekonstruktion*, 208), though obviously feeling little enthusiasm for this idea, concurs; Paul's interpretation of σπέρμα Ἀβραάμ "erklärt sich

Rom 8:17, which describes Christians as "fellow-heirs with Christ" [συγκλη-ρονόμοι Χριστοῦ], who participate in his suffering and glorification.) Thus, our participation in the inheritance depends upon the configuration of the story of Christ, a configuration in which we are included.

Paul also uses the inheritance metaphor to make two distinct points concerning the *sequential* logic of the gospel story. The first point is spelled out in verses 15-18: the promises to Abraham have the same irrevocable character as a human will.[104] The promises antedated the Law; consequently, the Law cannot impose ex post facto conditions or limitations on the fulfillment of the promises. The second point, which is closely related to the first, is stated explicitly in verse 19 and developed further in verses 22-25: the benefits of the inheritance are unavailable until the rightful heir (Christ) "comes" to receive them. Both of these points draw attention to the chronological element inherent in the metaphor of inheritance. The making of the διαθήκη, the interval before it takes effect, and its consummation are placed in a chronological sequence which Paul then uses as a basis for interpreting the place of the Law, as Cullmann and other advocates of *Heilsgeschichte* have emphasized.[105]

All of this helps to resolve a vexing question about the way in which Paul handles — or, in Beker's term, "bends" — the Abraham story. If, as we have affirmed, Abraham was already understood within Judaism as a figure whose faith had vicarious redemptive consequences for the people of God, why was there any need for Christ? The problem is particularly acute if, as I have argued, πίστις 'Ιησοῦ Χριστοῦ refers to a "faith in Jesus Christ" that corresponds to the pattern already established by Abraham in the Genesis story. What, in this case, does Christ contribute? Why not simply affirm the faith of Abraham as sufficient and interpret the figure of Jesus as a faithful follower of Abraham? There is, in one sense, no reason not to take this interpretive option; there is nothing intrinsically illogical about it. But for Paul — and here lies the crux of the matter — this option is rejected because that is not the way the story is told. The Abraham story is for Paul taken up into the Christ-story, and the Christ-story is understood, with the hindsight of narrative logic, as the fit sequel to the Abraham story. Looking back upon the Abraham story from the world established by the Christ-story, Paul perceives the

religionsgeschichtlich wohl so, dass Χριστός hier wie dort [i.e., 3:29] und in 1 Kor 12,12 in Aneignung gnostischer Begrifflichkeit als ekklesiologischer Begriff gebraucht ist."

104. This argument depends, of course, on a play on words which cannot be reproduced in English translation; διαθήκη in the Genesis texts means "covenant," but it is also the ordinary word for "will" (= last testament).

105. See especially Hester, "'Heir' und Heilsgeschichte."

proleptic character of Abraham as the recipient of a promise that was inherently unfulfillable in Abraham's own lifetime, a promise destined for fulfillment only in his seed. Thus, Beker's apt observations about Paul's surprising use of the Abraham story (see part A of this chapter) are best understood as pointers to the fact that the logic of Paul's argument is of a narrative character. Paul's interpretation of Abraham is "discontinuous" in the sense that it is not derivable from the Genesis story through critical exegesis or propositional logic, but it does affirm a positive continuity between Abraham and Christ (as prefiguration and fulfillment) within the gospel story.

(b) The Place of Law in the Narrative Structure

Paul's discussion of the promise to Abraham thus places it in narrative continuity with the christological story whose outlines we have already discerned in Chapter III above. The promise creates an expectation that remains unfulfilled "until the Seed to whom it was promised comes" (3:19). It is precisely this unfulfilled expectation which constitutes the "situation of lack" that Christ comes to remedy in the central action (topical sequence) of the gospel story; therefore, Paul's discussion in Gal 3:15-25 fills in some of the content of the story's initial sequence, of which we were able to form only a shadowy impression on the basis of Gal 4:3-6. The promise to Abraham may be understood as the "initial contract" that remained unfulfilled before the intervention of Christ, whose coming into the world signals the beginning of the topical sequence of the gospel story.[106]

This way of telling the story poses, however, a serious problem for Paul. If the time before the coming of Christ was "doch durchweg dunkel,"[107] if it was a time "frozen"[108] between promise and fulfillment, what was the purpose of the Law, which Israel had always regarded as God's ordinance for life and salvation? This is the question that Paul raises for consideration in verses 19-25. His an-

---

106. On the face of the matter, then, the narrative framework of Paul's thought in Galatians seems to differ somewhat from that which is manifested in Romans 5 and 1 Corinthians 15, where the initial sequence concerns Adam. Is this a different story, or yet another sequence in the same epic? Barrett (*First Adam*, 46) adopts the latter view and holds that Galatians 3 "combined with references made elsewhere to Adam, seems to make a clear, connected, and complete story." It is beyond the scope of this study to investigate this larger structure, but this would surely be a necessary part of any effort to write a comprehensive account of Pauline theology as reflection upon a narrative substructure.

107. Eckert, *Die urchristliche Verkündigung*, 103.

108. Boers, *Ghetto*, 82.

swer, unfortunately, is not a very lucid one, and it poses more exegetical difficulties than can be addressed within the scope of this study.[109] Without going into the problems in detail, however, it is possible to indicate in general terms how the Law is related to the narrative structure that we have identified.

Contrary to the opinion of some interpreters from Marcion onward,[110] Paul does not deny that the Law was given by God.[111] (It is given δι᾿ ἀγγέλων, not ὑπ᾿ ἀγγέλων.)[112] In what is perhaps the most surprising affirmation in the letter, he insists stoutly that the Law is not contrary to the promises (3:21),[113] an affirmation that seems to contradict his own radical juxtaposition of Law and promise in 3:18. When he attempts to explain, however, how the Law may be understood as *not* being κατὰ τῶν ἐπαγγελιῶν, he can do so only by saying that the Law does have, after all, a role to play in the drama of redemption: the role of jailer. During the initial sequence of the story, before the coming of Christ, "we were imprisoned under Law" (3:23). To all appearances, the law is the "Opponent" or enemy, the villain of the piece from whom Christ comes to liberate us (3:13, 4:5); in what sense, then, can Paul seriously maintain that the Law is not contrary to the promises? He can make this claim only in the sense that the Law, in spite of its negative role, remains under the sovereignty of the same God who made the promises, and that it plays the part this God has designed for it in the redemptive story; this is the meaning of verses 23-24.[114]

109. On the whole subject, see A. van Dülmen, *Die Theologie des Gesetzes bei Paulus* (SBM 5; Stuttgart: Katholisches Bibelwerk, 1968); H. Hübner, *Das Gesetz bei Paulus* (FRLANT 119; Göttingen: Vandenhoeck & Ruprecht, 1978); Luz, *Geschischtsverständnis*, 186-93; T. D. Callan, *The Law and the Mediator* (Ph.D. diss., Yale, 1977; Ann Arbor: University Microfilms, 1977); idem, "Pauline Midrash: The Exegetical Background of Gal 3:19b," *JBL* 99 (1980) 549-67; F. Hahn, "Das Gesetzesverständnis im Römer- und Galaterbrief," *ZNW* 67 (1976) 29-63; P. von der Osten Sacken, "Das paulinische Verständnis des Gesetzes im Spannungsfeld von Eschatologie und Geschichte," *EvT* 37 (1977) 549-87; for further bibliography, see Betz, *Galatians*, 163 n. 15.

110. See, for example, among recent representatives of the view that the Law is given by hostile angel powers, Klein (*Rekonstruktion*, 209-10) and Hübner (*Das Gesetz*, 28-31).

111. Defenders of the view that the Law, according to Paul, does come from God include Dahl (*Studies in Paul*, 173; idem, *Das Volk Gottes* [Oslo: Skrifter utgitt av Det Norske Videnskaps-Akademi i Oslo, 1941; repr. Darmstadt: Wissenschaftliche Buchgesellschaft, 1963], 216), van Dülmen (*Theologie des Gesetzes*, 44-45), Callan (*Law and Mediator*, 175), and C. H. Giblin ("Three Monotheistic Texts in Paul," *CBQ* 37 [1975] 537-43).

112. This observation is also made by Berger ("Abraham," 56).

113. Cf. Rom 3:31.

114. As these observations indicate, Paul thinks of God not only as Sender *in* the story but also as author *of* the story.

In contrast to other possible interpretive approaches, Paul determines the importance of the Law for the life of the Christian community by reflecting upon its location within the Christ-story. He neither rejects the Law unqualifiedly like Marcion nor embraces it unqualifiedly like the "Judaizers" nor allegorizes it like Philo; instead, he reasons about the Law within a system of coordinates determined by the gospel narrative structure. Consider these examples: (a) Christ died in order to redeem us and give us life; thus the Law must have been incapable of offering redemption and life (2:21). (b) He died, furthermore, by hanging on a tree, thus incurring the Law's curse; thus the Law is incompatible with the message of the crucified Messiah, and the Law must therefore have no continuing validity (3:13).[115] (c) The promise to Abraham came first in the story, and it is fulfilled only at the coming of the Messiah; thus the Law can neither supersede the promise nor fulfill it (3:15-18). In all these cases, Paul's theological reflection about the Law is grounded upon the shape and sequence of the gospel story.

(c) πίστις in the Narrative Pattern

In verses 23-25, Paul uses πίστις in a way that seems to differ significantly from his usage of it elsewhere in the letter. In these verses, "the Faith" seems to be a quasi-personified (or objectified) entity which is said to appear on stage at a specific point in the unfolding of the salvation-historical drama. We must inquire further into this peculiar usage in order to see how it relates to the christological narrative structure that we have discerned. Bultmann, despite his lively concern for the dimensions of individual faith, recognizes that πίστις here must have a different meaning.

> Though Gal 3:23-26 sketches the preparation and the "coming" of "faith," what is sketched is not the individual's development but the history of salvation.[116]

Likewise, Betz comments that πίστις in these verses "describes the occurrence of a historical phenomenon, not the act of believing of an individual."[117] What, then, is this "historical phenomenon"?

In order to answer this question, it is helpful to see that Gal 3:23-29 is

---

115. This point has been especially emphasized, of course, by Dahl; see, for example, *Studies in Paul*, 135.
116. Bultmann, *Theology*, 1.319.
117. Betz, *Galatians*, 176.

constructed on a pattern closely parallel to that of 4:3-7, which we have already examined in Chapter III.[118] This parallelism consists neither in surface syntax nor in verbal repetition but in the *narrative* pattern that the passages manifest, as the following outline demonstrates.[119]

3:23-29		4:3-7	
a) 23	Πρὸ τοῦ δὲ ἐλθεῖν τὴν πίστιν	a) 3	ὅτε ἦμεν νήπιοι
b)	ὑπὸ νόμον ἐφρουρούμεθα	b)	ὑπὸ τὰ στοιχεῖα τοῦ κόσμου
c)	συγκλειόμενοι εἰς τὴν μέλλουσαν πίστιν ἀποκαλυφθῆναι	c)	ἤμεθα δεδουλωμένοι.
d) 25	ἐλθούσης δὲ τῆς πίστεως	d) 4	ὅτε δὲ ἦλθεν τὸ πλήρωμα τοῦ χρόνου, ἐξαπέστειλεν ὁ θεὸς τὸν υἱὸν αὐτοῦ.
e)	οὐκέτι ὑπὸ παιδαγωγόν ἐσμεν	e) 5	ἵνα τοὺς ὑπὸ νόμον ἐξαγοράσῃ
f) 26	Πάντες γὰρ υἱοὶ θεοῦ ἐστε διὰ τῆς πίστεως	f)	ἵνα τὴν υἱοθεσίαν ἀπολάβωμεν.
g)	[Baptism — 3:27-28]	g)	[Spirit — 4:6]
h) 29	ἄρα τοῦ Ἀβραὰμ σπέρμα ἐστέ	h) 7	ὥστε οὐκέτι εἶ δοῦλος ἀλλὰ υἱός
i)	κατ' ἐπαγγελίαν κληρονόμοι.	i)	εἰ δὲ υἱός, καὶ κληρονόμος διὰ θεοῦ.

Paul uses two slightly different metaphors to describe the initial sequence. In 3:23, the initial dilemma is described as imprisonment, whereas in 4:3 it is called slavery. Either way, however, the pattern is the same. God's people are delivered from an initial state of deprivation by the coming of God's son (or of πίστις: see the comments below) and thus granted a new status as "sons" and "heirs." The correspondence between these two texts also reinforces the unavoidable identification between the Law and the στοιχεῖα τοῦ κόσμου which is such a peculiar feature of Paul's thought in Galatians. In

118. See Schlier's introductory remarks to Gal 4:1-11 (*Galater*, 188): "In diesem Abschnitt erläutert Paulus noch einmal das in 3:23-29 Gesagte. . . . Es ist also berechtigt, 4:1-7 nachträglich zur Aufhellung von 3:23ff. zu benützen, und besonders umgekehrt unsern Abschnitt im Zusammenhang mit 3:23-29 zu verstehen."

119. Gal 3:24 is not included in this outline because, from the point of view of the narrative pattern, it is a parenthetical remark that gives further information about νόμος, without advancing the action of the story. In structuralist terminology, 3:24 is a "qualification" rather than a "function." It should be noted, however, that the ἵνα clause in 3:24 does imply further content to the meaning of 3:25b and that its presence here may obviate the explicit manifestation of a topical sequence.

both cases, the metaphor is mixed with the idea that the victims of the slavery/imprisonment are minors who are temporarily prevented from receiving freedom and the inheritance. This mixing of metaphors is explicitly justified by Paul in the second case: "as long as the heir is a minor, he is no different from a slave" (4:1).

In spite of the similarities between the two passages, there is one important difference: in 4:4 there is an explicit "telling" of the topical sequence (cf. 3:13), whereas the narrative pattern in 3:23-26 skips directly from the initial dilemma (vv. 23-24) to a reflection upon its resolution (vv. 25-26). Paul moves from "once" to "now" without explicit mention of the Christ-event that accomplished the transition. That this event is presupposed as a necessary part of the story in verses 23-29 is shown not only by the corresponding patterns in 4:3-6 and 3:13-14 but also by the parenthetical remark of 3:24, which explains that the Law was a guardian εἰς Χριστόν.

How, then, is πίστις in 3:23, 25 to be understood? The commentators have suggested that it refers to a "mythico-historical period,"[120] or to a body of doctrine,[121] or to a new possible mode of disposing one's self toward God.[122] Each of these suggestions may reflect a facet of Paul's meaning, but none of them quite does justice to the fact that Paul speaks here of πίστις as a particular *event* that "came" at a specific point in the past, the very recent past, from Paul's perspective. This fact is most readily understood in terms of the narrative structure already sketched in this study. Note that in verse 25 Paul employs an aorist, rather than a perfect participle. His sentence should therefore be translated not as, "now that the faith has come . . . ," but rather as, "because the faith came. . . ." This event, as verses 19 and 24 prove, is bound closely together with the coming of Christ. Just as verse 19 explains that the Law was added "until the seed should come," so verse 25 declares that "since the faith came, we are no longer under a guardian." In both instances, the Law exercises a temporally limited function which is said to terminate with the coming of Christ (v. 19) or of πίστις (v. 25). Furthermore, this πίστις is said to be "revealed" (ἀποκαλυφθῆναι, 3:23); the only other occurrence of the verb ἀποκαλύπτω in Galatians is in 1:16, where its direct object is (God's) son: εὐδόκησεν ὁ θεὸς . . . ἀποκαλύψαι τὸν υἱὸν αὐτοῦ ἐν ἐμοί (cf. also 4:4).

120. Cf. Betz, Galatians, 175.
121. Cf. Lietzmann (An die Galater, 23): "Objektiv πίστις = 'Christentum,' Lehre von der Heilsbedeutung der subjektiven πίστις."
122. Cf. Bonnard (Galates, 75): "La venue de Jésus-Christ a inauguré le temps et donné la possibilité de la foi. Cette foi n'est pas la doctrine évangélique dans son ensemble . . . mais l'acte de l'homme répondant à la promesse de Dieu accomplie en Jésus-Christ; cet acte de soumission confiante caractérise les temps nouveaux. . . ."

All of these considerations urge upon us the conclusion that for Paul the coming of πίστις (vv. 23, 25) is virtually identified with the coming of Christ himself. Yet Paul does not speak explicitly here, as he does in verse 22, of Jesus Christ's own faith(fulness), nor can we suppose that Paul intends ἡ πίστις as a formal christological title. Why does Paul express himself in this odd way? What is the relationship, to pose Ebeling's question to this text, between Jesus and faith? Schlier proposes an answer that does justice to the foregoing exegetical observations.

> Der Glaube ist das Mittel (als solche auch das Prinzip) des Heils, Christus aber sein Grund. Mit dem Offenbarwerden des Heilsgrundes ist aber auch das Heilsmittel da. Christus Jesus setzt mit seinem Kommen objektiv den Glauben als den neuen Zugang zu Gott.[123]

Schlier does not elaborate on his suggestions here, but we may press for further clarity. In what way is Christ the "ground" of faith (as opposed to its object), and how does his "coming" establish faith as a new means of access to God?

On the basis of the exegetical investigations presented in this and the previous chapter, the answer, within the context of Galatians, is clear. Christ is the ground of faith because he is the one who, in fulfillment of the prophecy, lives ἐκ πίστεως. He thus proves to be the one true seed of the faithful Abraham and the heir of all the promises. His destiny, however, is not a merely individual one, because he acts as a universal representative figure, enacting (ἐκ πίστεως) a pattern of redemption which then determines the existence of others, to whom Paul refers as οἱ ἐκ πίστεως. These others participate in him and in his destiny not only vicariously but also actually: they are baptized into Christ (3:27) and they receive the Spirit, which in turn enables them to live ἐκ πίστεως, in conformity to the pattern grounded in Jesus Christ. This is the meaning of Gal 5:5: ἡμεῖς γὰρ πνεύματι ἐκ πίστεως ἐλπίδα δικαιοσύνης ἀπεκδεχόμεθα. Because the Christian's life is a reenactment of the pattern of faithfulness revealed in Jesus, it is futile to ask, in a formulation such as ἵνα ἐκ πίστεως δικαιωθῶμεν (3:24), *whose* faith is meant. It is of course "the faith of Jesus Christ," but it is also the faith of the Christian in whom, as Amos Wilder saw in his comments on Gal 2:20, "the world plot plays itself over."[124] Thus,

---

123. Schlier, *Galater,* 167. Cf. Ebeling, *Word and Faith,* 201-2: "Jesus is rightly understood only when he is not an object of faith but its source and ground." For further elaboration of this widely quoted opinion with reference to Pauline theology, see now Ebeling's *Dogmatik des christlichen Glaubens* (3 vols.; Tübingen: J. C. B. Mohr [Paul Siebeck], 1979) 2.520-22.

124. Wilder, *Early Christian Rhetoric,* 58.

the coming of πίστις is indeed the coming of a new possible mode of disposing one's self toward God, but this mode is possible precisely because it was first of all actualized in and by Jesus Christ.

(d) New Creation

These remarks bring us full circle to Gal 3:26-29, in which the theme of participation in Christ is most explicitly articulated. Betz calls this text "the goal toward which Paul has been driving all along."[125] This may be so, but it is also, as we have seen, the presupposition for Paul's argumentation all along. This "goal" appears as the unveiling of a premise that has sustained the argument from the beginning, not as a deduction from the foregoing argument. Gal 3:26-29 reveals Paul's starting place not only because it appeals to a baptismal tradition but also because it expresses the fundamental idea without which the reasoning throughout Gal 3:6-25 would be unintelligible: Christians are one in Christ and share his destiny. We have thus arrived at a conclusion diametrically opposed to Bousset's view that the "mystical thoughts" of these verses are an abrupt and incongruous interruption of a sober intellectual argument.

Christ is portrayed here not only as a representative figure but as the prototype of God's new creation. Dahl has pointed out that the phrase ἄρσεν καὶ θῆλυ in verse 28 is an allusion to Gen 1:27, a fact which shows that "Christ, as the image of God, is the prototype of redeemed mankind."[126] In Christ, "there is neither Jew nor Greek, neither slave nor free, no 'male and female.'" In Christ, the divisions of the fallen human order and even of the original creation are overcome and healed; that is why "neither circumcision nor uncircumcision means anything, but new creation" (Gal 6:15). The missing piece of the puzzle in Dahl's interpretation is that Christ, as the "prototype" (Hebrews, in which a representative christology is more explicitly developed, suggests the term ἀρχηγός) of the new humanity constitutes the new humanity precisely ἐκ πίστεως. By his faithfulness he triumphs over Law, sin, and death, and transmits "the promise of the Spirit" to his people. Thus he establishes πίστις as the distinctive mark of those who are "in" him.

125. Betz, *Galatians*, 181.
126. Dahl, *Studies in Paul*, 133.

(e) A Practical Application

Finally, a glance at Gal 4:8-11 will provide one more confirmation of the thesis that Paul reasons within a system of assumptions shaped by a narrative pattern. Paul notes with alarm that the Galatians "observe days and months and times and seasons" (4:10-11), and he expresses his disapproval by appealing once more to the sequential ordering of the gospel story. He interprets the Galatians' actions, whatever they may have been, as a reversion to the slavery of the initial sequence. To Paul this is as incomprehensible as it would be for the king's daughter, after being rescued by the knight, to choose to go back to the dragon. The logic of the story moves forward toward a final sequence in which Christians, empowered by the Spirit in the role of Helper, become free Subjects. How then, he asks the Galatians, can you return to slavery? The Galatians' actions must be an inappropriate response to the gospel story because the movement of that story is toward freedom.

Gal 4:8-11 points forward to the parenetic section that begins in 5:1: "For freedom Christ has set us free; stand fast therefore and do not submit again to a yoke of slavery." Thus, this passage illustrates in an illuminating way how the narrative structure of Paul's gospel provides the basis for his ethics.[127]

D. Conclusions

The purpose of this chapter has been to demonstrate that Paul's argument in Gal 3:1–4:11 is a unified attempt to think through the implications of a gospel story in which salvation hinges upon the faithfulness of Jesus Christ. The qualifications expressed in Chapter I should be kept in mind: any text is a complex entity shaped by numerous factors, and no claim is made here that this gospel story provides an exhaustive or sufficient explanation of how Galatians came to take its present form. The situation at Galatia, the Scriptures, rhetorical conventions, and Paul's own experiences, to name only a few of many possible factors, all operate as constraints and influences on the production of the letter. In the midst of this complex of variables, however, I have sought to show that Paul returns repeatedly to a narrative structure that operates as a constant factor in his efforts to wrestle through the practical and theological issues raised by the Galatian crisis.

---

127. For further discussion of the relation between narrative "world" and ethics, see Chap. VI.D below.

My thesis requires one crucial postulate about the character of the text: that it is strongly allusive. Its foundation and framework are for the most part hidden from view, implicit rather than explicit. Specifically, Paul's statement that before the Galatians' very eyes "Jesus Christ was publicly proclaimed as crucified" must be taken seriously, for it confirms that Paul had recounted for them at least the essentials of the Gospel story. He can assume that his readers know the story's *mythos*. The discussion therefore concerns its *dianoia*, "the point of telling the story."

The obvious and nearly inevitable criticism that might be raised against this interpretive procedure is that I am interpreting the text by positing a priori a narrative structure "behind" the text and then forcing the interpretation of the text to fit this structure. While this is an understandable objection, I reject it categorically. In the first place, the narrative structure is not "behind" the text; it is *in* the text, and its shape and sequence were determined through the analysis of specific passages in Galatians 3 and 4. This analysis can stand entirely apart from any theses about the text's "background," such as speculations about the identity and arguments of Paul's opponents or about antecedents in other ancient religious or literary texts. In the second place, the analysis in this chapter has been governed by an attempt to read the central section of Galatians as a unified whole. The theological models for my interpretation of passages in Gal 3:1-14 were derived not from external sources but from Gal 3:15-29, in which "participation in Christ" is the controlling soteriological motif. In short, I would contend that the interpretation proposed here offers the most satisfactory way of reading Paul's argument as a coherent piece of thinking.

The approach followed in this chapter does little to explain the text's *formal* structure. The narrative substructure does *not* dictate the outline of Paul's argument; instead, it serves as the ground in which the argument finds its material unity.

We have seen that Paul's appeals to this substructure as a warrant in his argument are of two different types: sometimes he appeals to the *sequence* of the narrative structure, and sometimes to its *shape*. The *sequence* argument is employed to show that the Law came later than the promise, that it has now been rendered obsolete by the coming of Christ, and that it is absurd for the Galatians to revert to practices proper to an earlier sequence in the story. The *shape* argument is closely linked to the text's participatory soteriology: the action of Jesus Christ in the gospel story defines the pattern of justification and life (ἐκ πίστεως). This pattern is employed to show that Gentiles are included in the promised blessing (= adopted as God's children) apart from adherence to Law, that divisions among God's people are dissolved in Christ, that righteousness and life are gifts of grace in which Christians participate because of Christ's πίστις, and that πίστις is consequently the distinguishing mark of the life given to those who live "in" him. The argument of Gal 3:1–4:11 finds its point of coherence in the story of the Messiah who lives by faith.

Chapter VI

Conclusion: Implications
for Pauline Interpretation

Because Paul's letters, as manifestly nonnarrative texts, stand within the NT canon in obvious contrast to the narrative forms of the Gospels, Acts, and Revelation, the narrative elements in Paul have understandably received relatively little attention. Indeed, Paul has often been perceived as the prototypical instance of a thinker for whom narrative expressions of Christian faith are in principle insignificant. The present study has sought to offer a corrective to this perception of Paul by concentrating on the presence — to put it more strongly, the centrality — of narrative elements in Paul's thought.

The preceding chapters have carried through an analysis of a single block of Paul's theological prose: Gal 3:1–4:11. This investigation has sustained the thesis that narrative elements are integral to Paul's argument in this text. Indeed, I have advanced the claim that Paul's reasoning is most fully comprehensible when this section of Galatians is understood as Paul's attempt to articulate in discursive language the meaning *(dianoia)* of a story whose protagonist is Jesus Christ. Of course, the text is not simply a theoretical exposition of the story's meaning; the letter is evoked by the particular crisis in Galatia, and the implications that Paul draws from the story are addressed to that situation. Nonetheless, we have seen that Paul responds to the situation by alluding and appealing to a Christ-story as the basis for his exhortations. In the shape and sequence of this story, Paul finds warrants that authorize his theological statements and constraints that pose limits to the logic of his argument.

If Paul's theological exposition in this central section of Galatians can be shown to rest upon a narrative substructure, we may reasonably ask whether this observation might be generalized to include other major passages in Paul's letters. Along the way, we have noted that texts such as 1 Corin-

thians 15, Phil 2:6-11, Rom 3:21-26, and Rom 5:12-21 presuppose and manifest, however fragmentarily, a narrative christology. Is it possible, then, that
the nature and method of Paul's theological language are best understood if
we see this language as grounded in a foundational "sacred story"? If so, what
might be the implications for our understanding of Paul and of his place
within early Christianity?

In this concluding chapter, we must draw together the results of the inquiry and attempt to suggest their potential significance for Pauline interpretation. Some fairly definite conclusions about the shape of Paul's theology
may be drawn on the basis of this investigation. My thesis also suggests, however, a broader range of implications about the historical and literary frame
of reference within which Paul should be read; while it is not possible to explore these complex implications in this study, this final chapter will seek to
indicate some of the directions in which further inquiry might proceed.

A. The Contours of Paul's Theology

If Galatians is interpreted as I have proposed in this investigation, several important consequences follow concerning the overall content and emphases of
Paul's theology. First and foremost, the results of this study suggest that for
Paul the obedience and faithfulness of Jesus Christ are of central soteriological significance; the accent of the gospel story lies upon his faithfulness in
accomplishing the promised redemption. The cross is not an isolated religious symbol; instead, it is the climactic event in the story of Jesus Christ,[1]
who was sent forth by God, who enacted the obedience of faith by giving
himself up in order to free humanity from the power of sin and death, "to deliver us from the present evil age according to the will of our God and Father"
(Gal 1:4). This act of obedience, which according to Romans 5 stands in typological antithesis to Adam's disobedience, is a representative action, in which
the fate of humanity is carried, or, to use a key term of Irenaeus, "recapitulated." Thus, Jesus' faith is not merely exemplary, as in nineteenth-century liberal theology, but vicariously efficacious.

In terms of the argument of Galatians, this story of Jesus Christ is cru-

---

1. Herein lies one of the ways in which my interpretation differs in emphasis from
Bultmann's. Bultmann also stressed the event-character of God's action in Christ, but he
tended to treat the event as punctiliar. My reading of Paul emphasizes that the salvation event
has temporal extension and shape; the event of the cross has meaning not as an isolated event
but as an event within a story.

cial because it demonstrates that the Galatians' well-intentioned desire to achieve righteousness through circumcision and/or "works of law" is absurd and self-defeating; anyone who has heard the gospel story, as Paul understands it, should realize that we are justified not by anything that we do but by Jesus Christ — indeed, if our interpretation is correct, through the πίστις of Jesus Christ, who loved us and gave himself for us (Gal 2:16, 20). That is the whole meaning (the *dianoia*) of the gospel story.

Second, because justification hinges upon this action of Jesus Christ, upon an event *extra nos*, it is a terrible and ironic blunder to read Paul as though his gospel made redemption contingent upon our act of deciding to dispose ourselves toward God in a particular way. The "grammar" of Paul's gospel — more precisely, of the gospel's topical sequence — places humanity in the role of "Receiver."[2] (This fact emerges with striking clarity in Gal 4:9: "But now knowing God — or rather, having been known by God, how can you turn again . . . ?" Paul starts to cast the Galatians in the role of active knowing subject, but he catches himself up short, perhaps for deliberate rhetorical effect, and re-words his sentence so that God is cast as the knower.) The logic of the gospel story requires that the deliverance of "those who believe" depend not upon their knowing or believing but upon the action of Jesus Christ, who faithfully discharges the commission of God. As Paul puts the matter in 2 Cor 5:18a, "Everything is from God, who reconciled us to himself through Christ."

Does this mean that the human faith-response to God's action in Christ is insignificant for Paul? By no means! It does mean, however, that "faith" is not the precondition for receiving God's blessing; instead, it is the appropriate mode of response to a blessing already given in Christ. As such, it is also the mode of participation in the pattern definitively enacted in Jesus Christ: as we respond in faith, we participate in an ongoing reenactment of Christ's faithfulness. This point must be spelled out carefully, because it is an elusive one. The gospel story is not just the story of a super-hero who once upon a time defeated the cosmic villains of Law, Sin, and Death and thus discharged us from all responsibility; it is also the enactment of a life-pattern into which we are drawn.[3] This is why Paul can say, "I have been crucified with Christ"

2. For further discussion of the problem of human responsibility, however, see part D, below.

3. Here attention may be drawn to another significant point of disagreement between Bultmann's interpretation and mine: the theological evaluation of narrative language. Whereas Bultmann regarded the language of story as "objectivizing," consigning narrated events to a fixed and dead past, I would want to insist that it is precisely the telling and re-telling of the story — the narrative *anamnesis* — which continues to make the salvation event present.

(Gal 2:19; cf. 6:15). The death and resurrection of Christ are the pivotal events in human history, cosmic events in which we are included vicariously: "One died for all; therefore, all have died. And he died for all, in order that those who live might no longer live for themselves but for the one who died and was raised for them" (2 Cor 5:14b-15). Because Jesus Christ is the proto-type of the new humanity,[4] those whom God calls are conformed to the pattern defined by him,[5] and the characteristic mark of this pattern is precisely πίστις. Thus, when Paul says ἐν πίστει ζῶ τῇ τοῦ υἱοῦ τοῦ θεοῦ τοῦ ἀγαπήσαντός με καὶ παραδόντος ἑαυτὸν ὑπὲρ ἐμοῦ (Gal 2:20), he means not only "I have life in consequence of the Son of God's faithful self-giving," but also "I participate in the pattern of faith enacted by the Son of God, who loved me and gave himself for me." Paul is saying neither that we are saved by believing in Christ nor that we are saved by believing as he did; rather, he is saying that because we participate in Jesus Christ, who lived ἐκ πίστεως[6] we also live ἐν πίστει.

So far, these observations about the contours of Paul's theology stand firmly on the exegetical foundation constructed in Chapters III-V, above. The following remarks about the nature of participation in Christ are more spec-ulative and should be taken as proposals for further investigation rather than as results of this study.

Our analysis of the narrative pattern of Paul's gospel story opens up one possible new approach to the much-debated problem of the relation between "participation in Christ" and "justification" in Paul's thought. These motifs are sometimes treated as unrelated ideas and sometimes even played off against one another. If, however, the gospel story portrays Jesus as the Mes-siah who is vindicated (= justified) ἐκ πίστεως and whose vindication is vi-cariously efficacious for others, the tension between the motifs vanishes. Christians are justified precisely because they participate in the crucified and justified Messiah, whose destiny embodies theirs. This compatibility of the two motifs appears most clearly in Gal 2:17, where Paul uses the expression δικαιωθῆναι ἐν Χριστῷ. Here justification and participation in Christ are merged, and it is clear that Paul intends this phrase to be synonymous with his words in the previous verse: ἵνα δικαιωθῶμεν ἐκ πίστεως Χριστοῦ. To be justified ἐκ πίστεως Χριστοῦ is the same thing as being justified ἐν Χριστῷ.

4. See the discussion of Gal 3:26-29 in Chap. V.C.3.d above.

5. Paul says this nowhere more clearly than in Rom 8:29: "For those whom he foreknew he also predestined to be conformed to the image of his Son, in order that he might be the firstborn among many brethren."

6. The formulation of this sentence reflects my interpretation of Gal 3:11 (see Chap. IV.B, above).

Thus, "justification" and "participation in Christ" do not belong to divergent theological spheres; for Paul, they belong together because he understands salvation to mean our participation in *Christ's* justification.[7]

Many interpreters have emphasized "participation in Christ" as the key theme in Pauline soteriology,[8] but there has been wide diversity of opinion concerning the nature of this "participation." Did Paul believe, in analogy to the mystery religions, that the sacrament of baptism magically transformed Christians into a new sphere of existence "in Christ"? Did he think, as Schweitzer contended, that this transformation was actually a physical one? Or, on the other hand, is all of the participatory language a mythological way of giving expression to the truth that through the Christ-event we are confronted with the possibility of a new self-understanding? Bultmann articulates the latter view succinctly.

> The union of believers into one *soma* with Christ now has its basis not in their sharing the same supernatural substance, but in the fact that in the word of proclamation Christ's death-and-resurrection becomes a possibility of existence in regard to which a decision must be made, and in the fact that faith seizes this possibility and appropriates it as the power that determines the existence of the man of faith.[9]

E. P. Sanders recognizes that neither of these alternatives adequately renders an account of Paul's thinking because both are reductionistic. Participation in Christ is not a magical fait accompli which deprives human choices of all significance; nor is it, however, reducible to a revised mode of self-understanding. Sanders' assessment of this matter may be quoted at length here, because it clearly poses the interpretive problem.

> In general, we may agree with what Bultmann and his successors wished to argue *against:* against magic, against viewing the soteriological event as taking place apart from man's will or as depriving him of it, against the possibility that Paul was interested in cosmological speculation for its own sake and the like. It must be wondered, however, whether the alternative as Bultmann proposed it — *either* cosmological speculation, magical transfer-

---

7. On the motif of the vindication or justification of the Messiah, see Hanson, *Paul's Technique*, 13-51; cf. Rom 6:7; 1 Tim 3:16.

8. See, for example, D. Somerville, *St. Paul's Conception of Christ* (Edinburgh: T. & T. Clark, 1897) 31-107; Wrede, *Paul*, 97-102; Schweitzer, *Mysticism;* Barrett, *First Adam*, 68-91; Whiteley, *Theology of St. Paul*, 130-37; J.A.T. Robinson, *The Body* (SBT 5; London: SCM, 1952) 45-48; Tannehill, *Dying and Rising;* E. P. Sanders, *Paul and Palestinian Judaism*, 463-68.

9. Bultmann, *Theology,* 1.302.

ence and the like, *or the ever-present demand to make a decision when faced with a demand which challenges one's self-understanding — does justice to Paul. . . . Being one body and one Spirit with Christ is not simply living out of a revised self-understanding, although that also may result. It seems to me best to understand Paul as saying what he meant and meaning what he said: Christians really are one body and Spirit with Christ. . . . But what does this mean? How are we to understand it? We seem to lack a category of "reality" — real participation in Christ, real possession of the Spirit — which lies between naive cosmological speculation and belief in magical transference on the one hand and a revised self-understanding on the other. I must confess that I do not have a new category of perception to propose here. This does not mean, however, that Paul did not have one.*[10]

The reading of Paul proposed in this study might in fact offer an approach toward what Sanders confesses himself unable to provide: a "new category of perception" within which Paul's statements might be understood. One widely recognized property of story is its power to lead hearers into an experience of identification with the story's protagonist. Precisely for this reason, stories can function as vehicles for the creation of community, as many individuals find a common identity within a single story. In the case of a story that becomes foundational for the self-understanding of a community, the identification of community members with the protagonist may be so comprehensive that it can be spoken of as "participation" in the protagonist's destiny. If Paul's gospel is the story of Jesus Christ, then we might participate in Christ in somewhat the same way that we participate in (or identify with) the protagonist of any story. We find that the story lays a claim upon us and draws us into its world; we recognize ourselves in the protagonist and feel that our own destinies are somehow figured in his story.[11] This recognition is not so much a "work" of the imagination as a spontaneous response elicited by the story. We find ourselves, in Via's phrase, "projected into the paradigm of the death and resurrection of Jesus."[12] Yet the transformation which the story works upon us is neither automatic nor magical; to the extent that it may change us, it does so by engaging our assent and imagination and will. In Via's language, we "decide for a model outside of [our-

10. E. P. Sanders, *Paul and Palestinian Judaism,* 522-23.

11. This approach may help to clarify the meaning of the term "vicarious," which I have used repeatedly in the foregoing pages. The idea remains in any case a difficult one, but it is not meaningless: our experience of intuitive identification with fictional figures provides at least a starting place for reflection upon the meaning of participation in Christ.

12. Via, *Kerygma and Comedy,* 66.

selves]";[13] we choose this paradigm rather than some other. Thus, our participation in Jesus Christ of the gospel story is "real" (particularly because Paul was firmly convinced that the events of the story "really happened" — see 1 Cor 15:12-17) without being magical. Our participation in Christ, which does also yield a new self-understanding, is both posited within and engendered by the story itself. Thus, Paul's participatory soteriology may best be understood as a function of his narrative christology.

I must reiterate that these remarks should be understood as suggestions for further reflection rather than as conclusive results of this investigation. The phenomenon of "participation" in narrative is a complex one in its own right; this language is usually employed with regard to a kind of momentary exercise of the imagination that projects the reader/hearer into a *fictional* world. In the case of Paul, the "participation" language clearly envisions a more permanent and "real" transformation of the hearers' existence on the basis of a story which is solemnly held to be nonfiction. Any thoroughgoing attempt to re-think Paul's soteriology with the aid of the category of story-participation would have to address this issue. That task lies, unfortunately, beyond the scope of this inquiry.

In any case, however, story-participation cannot serve as an exhaustive explanation of the phenomenon of "participation in Christ" for Paul. We must also allow due weight to other elements in Paul, such as "sacramental realism," immediate spiritual experience, and the fact of participation (κοινωνία) in a community that Paul regards as "the body of Christ." My suggestion, however, is that all these elements may find their common grounding in a story of Jesus Christ which is re-presented in the sacraments, which is the catalyst for the spiritual experience, and which serves as the foundational "sacred story" around which the community is gathered. Precisely because all these elements are dimensions or consequences of participation in the gospel story, they should not be played off against one another as they have sometimes been.

B. Paul's Place within Early Christianity

The interpretation of Paul proposed in this study also might encourage a re-evaluation of Paul's place within the development of early Christian thought. Although there have been some countertendencies recently, NT scholarship has long tended to view Paul as a solitary theological genius whose ideas were

13. Ibid.

misunderstood or ignored by his contemporaries and successors, because he so radically transcended his own spiritual milieu. Especially among German critics there has been significant resistance to any attempt to interpret Paul's thought within the framework of emergent confessional traditions in first-century Christianity. Even where there are signs that Paul is employing traditional christological formulations, many scholars have supposed that he must be subjecting them to radical critique and reinterpretation.[14] Typical is the view of Dieter Lührmann, who argues that Paul incorporated traditional materials in his letters in order to reinterpret them but that succeeding generations (as evidenced by the deutero-Pauline epistles), reinterpreted Paul's teaching in light of the older traditions embedded in his letters, rather than vice versa.

> Paulus und die Deuteropaulinen greifen zwar auf Traditionen zurück, die von der Versöhnung als einem kosmischen Geschehen reden, in das die Glaubenden hineingenommen sind. Paulus ordnet aber diese Traditionen seinem Verständnis unter, dass das Heil als Rechtfertigung dessen beschreibt, der nur aus Glauben lebt. . . . Für Paulus ist dies, wie z.B. der Galaterbrief zeigt, die einzig legitime Auslegung des Kerygmas. Demgegenüber nehmen Kol und Eph gerade diese Versöhnungs-traditionen zur Bestimmung dessen auf, was sie mit Heil meinen, und der Eph ordnet ihnen das unter, was Paulus als Heil bestimmt hatte.[15]

The considerations advanced in this study pose the question of whether Paul's exegesis of the traditions is as distinctive and individualistic as Lührmann and others suppose. Our examination of Galatians has shown, contrary to Lührmann's claim, that Paul does not "subordinate" the story of "atonement as a cosmic event" to his teaching about justification by faith; rather, his teaching about justification by faith presupposes and rests upon the story of the cosmic event whereby God reconciled the world to himself.[16] When Paul introduces traditional christological formulae (Gal 3:13-14; 4:4-6) — if indeed these are traditional formulae — into his argument, he presents them not as traditions which must be reinterpreted but as distillations

14. Of the many examples that could be cited here, Victor Hasler's essay "Glaube und Existenz: Hermeneutische Erwägungen zu Gal 2,15-21" (*TZ* 25 [1969] 241-51) may serve as a clear illustration of this approach. A notable exception is Conzelmann ("Bekenntnisformel").

15. D. Lührmann, "Rechtfertigung und Versöhnung: Zur Geschichte der paulinischen Tradition," *ZTK* 67 (1970) 448.

16. Cf. U. Wilckens, "Christologie und Anthropologie in Zusammenhang der paulinischen Rechtfertigungslehre," *ZNW* 67 (1976) 64-82, esp. 67, 72.

of the story upon which his argument depends. Thus, the narrative pattern that portrays redemption as a "cosmic event" is no less foundational for Galatians than for Ephesians. This does not mean that Galatians and Ephesians are theologically identical; the polyvalence of narrative allows the same story to be interpreted differently by different interpreters. By drawing attention to the importance of the Christ-story for Paul, however, the present study offers an impetus toward reflection upon often-overlooked elements of commonality between Paul and other early Christian writers.

Our investigation has identified as the basis of Paul's argumentation a Christ-story which bears significant affinities to certain christological statements in Hebrews: Jesus Christ is the archetypical (or prototypical) hero (ἀρχηγός) who, through his faithfulness unto death on the cross, wins deliverance and access to God for his people. No attempt has been made here to draw direct lines of historical connection between Paul and Hebrews, or between Paul and similar theological currents in the early church. This sort of historical inquiry would demand a full-length investigation in its own right.[17] It is clear, however, that the reading of Galatians advocated here places Paul within a theological "trajectory" that extends from the Philippians hymn through Hebrews and on into those patristic interpretations, particularly in Irenaeus and the Eastern Fathers, which portray the atonement as a great drama in which Jesus Christ triumphs over the powers of Sin and Death in order to give life to humanity.[18] Thus, this study suggests the possibility that, theologically speaking, Paul may have been less sharply distinctive within his contemporary environment than is often supposed. Although, to be sure, few

---

17. A number of recent studies have reopened important issues concerning Paul's relation to early Christianity. See E. Dassmann, *Der Stachel im Fleisch: Paulus in der frühchristlichen Literatur bis Irenäus* (Münster: Aschendorff, 1979); A. Lindemann, *Paulus im ältesten Christentum* (BHT 58; Tübingen: J. C. B. Mohr [Paul Siebeck], 1979); D. K. Rensberger, *As the Apostle Teaches: The Development of the Use of Paul's Letters in Second-Century Christianity* (Ph.D. diss., Yale, 1981; Ann Arbor: University Microfilms, 1981). These studies converge on the conclusion that, contrary to often repeated scholarly opinion, there was no widespread "orthodox" reaction against Pauline theology in the second century. This does not mean, of course, that Paul was either widely understood or influential during this period. Rensberger (*As the Apostle Teaches,* 57-58) judiciously notes that no one in the second century, with the possible exception of Marcion, was interested in "pure Paulinism"; Paul was one among many factors in the stream of traditions with which early Christian writers worked. Thus, the question is not whether the early church preserved Paul's christology; the question that I am posing here is whether Paul's christology/soteriology may legitimately be understood as standing in agreement with a narrative pattern manifested in a variety of other early Christian sources.

18. For a brief summary which argues broadly for the fundamental congruence of patristic christology with Paul's, see G. Aulén, *Christus Victor* (London: SPCK, 1931) 16-73.

of his contemporaries could rival the vigor and penetration with which Paul explored the implications of the gospel story, the basic narrative pattern of Paul's christology and soteriology was one that he held in common with "early catholicism."[19] Only when this fundamental commonality is duly recognized can Paul's distinctiveness be properly evaluated.

C. Paul's Gospel and the Gospel Genre

If a story about Jesus Christ is foundational for Paul's theological formulations, then we might reasonably ask about the relationship between Paul's gospel and the subsequently developed narrative genre of the "gospel." The origins of the gospel as a literary form are obscure, and NT scholars have remained divided over the question of whether this form constitutes a new genre invented by the evangelists or whether the Christian gospels should be considered to belong to an established Hellenistic literary genre, such as popular biography.[20] Clearly such a question cannot be answered by the present investigation, but my conclusions do relate to the problem in a potentially interesting manner.

If narrative elements are foundational even in such nonnarrative texts as the Pauline letters, this might lead us to hypothesize that the *kerygma* has an irreducible narrative dimension and therefore, as Dodd suggested, contains within itself the basic framework for the gospel genre.[21] While this idea is hardly a new one,[22] the prevailing tendency of NT scholarship has been to

---

19. Käsemann opens his essay on "Paul and Early Catholicism" (*NT Questions,* 236-51) by proposing the thesis that "Paul himself was a forerunner of early catholicism" (p. 238). It soon becomes clear, however, that in spite of the historical connection that Käsemann discerns, he regards the early church's handling of Paul as a fundamental distortion: very early, Paul's radical message became "ecclesiastically domesticated" (p. 24). Most of Käsemann's attention is directed to issues of sacraments and church order; I am suggesting here that a rather different picture might emerge in relation to christology.

20. For a summary of the debate over this issue, see C. H. Talbert, *What Is a Gospel?* For other views, see H. Koester, "One Jesus and Four Primitive Gospels," *Trajectories through Early Christianity* (Philadelphia: Fortress, 1971) 158-204; H. C. Kee, *Community of the New Age* (Philadelphia: Westminster, 1977) 17-30.

21. C. H. Dodd, "The Framework of the Gospel Narrative," *ExpTim* 43 (1931-32) 396-400. See also idem, *Apostolic Preaching,* 36-56. This suggestion does not imply, of course, an endorsement of Dodd's proposal that the kerygmatic framework preserves something like a traditional account of the historical course of Jesus' ministry.

22. See Koester, *Trajectories,* 161-62, and the references cited by Talbert, *What Is a Gospel?,* 18 n. 5.

distinguish sharply between the passion narrative (regarded as integrally re-lated to the *kerygma*) and mythological components of the gospel narrative (regarded as accretions to the *kerygma*).[23] Thus the *kerygma* is said to provide the "germ-cell" of the gospel form,[24] but not its structure or outline. In the present study, however, we have seen that in Galatians the *kerygma* of the cross (3:1, 13) is united in an organic fashion with the motifs of preexistence and incarnation (4:4-5); these elements are joined within the structure of a single continuous story. Thus, already present in Paul is a basic narrative pat-tern similar to that which informs the canonical Gospels, particularly Luke and John. The distinction between kerygmatic and mythological components of this pattern is based on modern criteria that do not arise from the text it-self. Both in Paul and in the Gospels, these elements are presented continu-ously within a single narrative plane.

In view of these considerations, we may venture the somewhat surpris-ing suggestion that Paul's letters mark a point within a historical develop-ment *toward* the formulation of "gospels," i.e., explicit literary articulations of the Jesus-story. As we have seen, Paul repeatedly alludes and appeals to as-pects of such a story. Contrary to the opinion of Eusebius, who thought that when Paul spoke of "my gospel" he was referring to the Gospel of Luke, Paul almost surely was not alluding to a written text but to a story-pattern that formed the basis for oral proclamation.[25] In view of the many possible ways of telling the Jesus-story, however, it is not hard to imagine the circumstances that would produce the impulse within early Christianity to set down a for-mal account of the story as it "ought" to be told; Luke's prologue bears wit-ness to precisely this impulse. Paul, however, stands at a slightly earlier stage in the process. He assumes that the Galatians know the story; after all, he himself told it to them. The argument concerns the implications of the story, not its content. The significant point, however, is that Paul's theological vi-sion is informed by a narrative structure, that he does appeal to the story-structure as a warrant. We know that there were streams of tradition within early Christianity which deemphasized or deliberately eschewed any narra-tive grounding for their spirituality, stressing instead sayings traditions (cf. the Gospel of Thomas) or immediate pneumatic experience. In contrast to these tendencies, Paul's theological sensibilities, by emphasizing the centrality

23. This tendency to associate the kerygma primarily with the passion narrative is traceable to the widely influential work of Martin Dibelius (*From Tradition to Gospel* [Cam-bridge/London: James Clarke, 1971] esp. 22-23).

24. Bultmann, *Theology,* 1.86.

25. Cf. the remark of Crites ("Narrative Quality of Experience," 308 n. 14): "Early Christian preaching was largely a story-telling mission."

of narrative elements of the tradition, move toward the ultimate production of written gospel narratives.[26] In fact, Paul's characteristic use of the term "gospel" to designate a narrative pattern might foreshadow the development of this term into a genre designation.[27]

These proposals raise a swarm of other problems that cannot be dealt with here. The most fundamental of these is the question of precisely how the narrative pattern that we have discerned in Galatians — a text written many years before the earliest synoptic Gospel — is related to the narrative structure and logic of the gospel texts. Is it really possible to discern within these texts a single underlying narrative substructure of which the various gospel texts (and fragmentary formulations in Paul) are "performances"? To ask this question is to ask the fundamental question of NT theology. While I do not presume to answer such a question here, I would like to call attention in this regard to Hans Frei's treatment of the four Gospels together as the telling of a story which manifests the identity of Jesus Christ; particularly noteworthy is his contention that the narrative logic of this gospel story unfolds a "pattern of exchange" in which Jesus "enacts the good of men on their behalf . . . in perfect obedience to God."[28] The tantalizing similarity between this gospel narrative pattern, as analyzed by Frei, and the narrative substructure of Galatians, as analyzed in this investigation, suggests that future inquiry might fruitfully explore the possibility of a fundamental congruity of narrative structure between Paul's gospel and the canonical Gospels.

D. Pauline Ethics: How Does the Christ-Story Shape Paul's Sense of Self and World?

Another important implication of the analysis offered in this work is that it provides some fresh possibilities for understanding the relation between theology and ethics in Paul. Let us examine this suggestion.

As we noted in the first chapter, one important function of stories is

26. Of course, the Gospels, unlike Paul, also incorporate the sayings traditions within a narrative framework, thus providing an interpretive context for them. This incorporation of sayings, along with traditional accounts of particular events from the life of Jesus, into a broader narrative structure is the distinctive literary/theological achievement of the canonical Gospels, and it distinguishes them significantly from the bare kerygmatic story-outline that we have traced in Galatians.

27. This possibility is suggested by J. A. Fitzmyer, "The Gospel in the Theology of Paul," *Int* 33 (1979) 339-50.

28. Frei, *Identity*, 74-84, 102-15.

that they can constitute a "world," a framework of order and value and expectation, within which people can live. Not all stories do this in the same way, however. Kermode's distaste for myth is based upon his conviction that myths depict a closed, static, reality and thus falsely sanction the status quo as absolute and unchangeable. Other kinds of stories, however, can present a more open and flexible vision of reality; Kermode prefers to call such stories "fictions."[29] In either case, the story portrays a worldscape in relation to which human beings may or must dispose themselves. The scope of possible and appropriate action is determined by the world that the story portrays.[30]

For this reason, some contemporary ethicists have emphasized the importance of stories as the medium through which character is formed and values are sustained.[31] Because we come to know our identity within certain stories, ethical reflection may, according to this view, most appropriately take the form of thinking about these stories which provide our sense of orientation. All of this suggests, in light of the findings of this investigation, that we might gain some significant insight into Paul's ethic by asking how his paradigmatic gospel story shapes his perception of self and world. In what way does the story of Jesus Christ inform Paul's understanding of the human task or — more precisely asked — his choices and directives in relation to concrete situations? The question thus posed deserves a book-length answer, but we may indicate briefly how it might be approached.

In *The Dark Interval,* John Dominic Crossan proposes a fivefold typology of narrative, which classifies narrative texts according to the stance they adopt toward "world." The typology ranges texts along a spectrum whose opposite poles are "myth" and "parable."

---

29. Kermode, *Sense of an Ending,* 39. In Kermode's view, the virtue of fictions as a mode of grasping reality is a function of their fictiveness. When we cease to hold them consciously to be fictive, they "degenerate into myth." Kermode has in mind here the Nazi myth of anti-Semitism, and he regards the "consciously false" quality of fictions as instrumental in shattering such degenerate and rigid thought-structures. In the case of Paul's gospel, however, we encounter a story consciously held as true which also has the power to challenge rigid thought-structures.

30. For a helpful discussion of this function of stories, with further bibliographical references, see Via, "Narrative World and Ethical Response," 123-49.

31. This perspective is expressed with particular clarity in the work of Stanley Hauerwas (see the works listed in the bibliography). See also R. W. Hepburn, "Vision and Choice in Morality," *Christian Ethics and Contemporary Philosophy* (ed. I. T. Ramsey; London: SCM, 1966) 181-95; Iris Murdoch, "Vision and Choice in Morality," *Christian Ethics and Contemporary Philosophy,* 195-218. For further bibliography, see J. Navone, *The Jesus Story: Our Life as Story in Christ* (Collegeville, MN: Liturgical Press, 1979) 172-209.

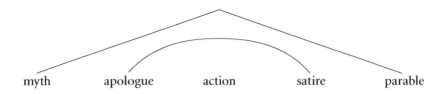

myth   apologue   action   satire   parable

Crossan describes the function of these different types of story as follows: "Myth establishes world. Apologue defends world. Action investigates world. Satire attacks world. Parable subverts world."[32] Now the Pauline *letter*, though it is not a narrative form, might plausibly be classed under the heading of apologue. But what about the Pauline *gospel?* How is this gospel related to "world," and how does it orient the individual in relation to "world"? Clearly, the gospel story is not susceptible to simple classification within Crossan's typological schema; seemingly it subverts and establishes world at the same time. As Beardslee has recognized, the Christ-story challenges Paul's self-understanding by confronting him continually with the event of the cross which, as Paul saw, is radically subversive of human expectations and judgments.[33] At the same time, it is clear that Paul sees in this story not only an overthrowing of the old order but also the establishing of a new one, a "new creation" (Gal 6:15); that is why he can make impassioned appeals to the story in order to argue that the Galatians ought to behave in certain ways and not in others. Unlike the "parable" (as defined by Crossan), Paul's gospel story does not simply bring us in touch with transcendence by shattering world and language and thus exposing their limits; it also posits a new "world" in which the Christian community might find its bearings.[34] Perhaps it would be more accurate to say, as John Cobb has suggested in a critique of Crossan, that the gospel *transforms* world.[35] Precisely because the story transforms world, it carries ethical significance.

But what sort of ethical guidance may be derived from the gospel story?

32. Crossan, *Dark Interval*, 59. Crossan has formed this typology by adding "myth" and "parable" to a typology worked out by S. Sacks (*Fiction and the Shape of Belief* [Berkeley: University of California, 1964]) for analyzing eighteenth-century novels.

33. See the discussion in Chap. I.A.2.d, above. In a general way, my views concerning Paul's ethics are indebted to Beardslee's perspective, as articulated in *Human Achievement and Divine Vocation in the Message of Paul* (SBT 31; London: SCM, 1961).

34. In my opinion, Crossan's analysis of the function of the parables of Jesus is one-sided; they too not only shatter world but also establish a new world. This question, however, cannot be taken up here.

35. J. B. Cobb, Jr., "A Theology of Story: Crossan and Beardslee," *Orientation by Disorientation*, 151-64; see esp. 159.

One possible inference can be set aside, though cautiously so: Paul does not present Jesus as the ethical ideal to be emulated by Christians. The *imitatio Christi* theme, which surfaces at various points in the NT, and perhaps in Paul's own thought in Philippians, does not appear explicitly in Galatians.[36] Participation in Christ for Paul must be distinguished from imitation or repetition of actions attributed to Christ.

At this point the model of narrative analysis developed in Chapter III proves helpful. Christ's redemptive action, now completed, constitutes the *topical* sequence of the story; this sequence was successfully carried through in his incarnation, life, death, and resurrection, and it would be pointless either to imitate it or to act as if it had never happened. Jesus Christ has fulfilled his mandate of bringing deliverance and the Spirit to his people. Paul sees himself and the Galatians (and all Christians) as the Receivers of the topical sequence. This means, however, that he and they are now thrust into the actantial role of Subject in the final sequence, with a new mandate from God: with the Spirit as Helper, they are charged to stand fast in their new freedom (5:1), to be servants of one another (5:13), to love the neighbor (5:14), and to bear one another's burdens (6:2). The mandate is addressed to a community which is thereby called to live in a disciplined and loving manner or, as Paul liked to put it, to walk by the Spirit (5:16, 25).

Thus the narrative model helps to account for the logic of Paul's movement from indicative (proclamation) to imperative (exhortation). The simultaneous presence of these emphases in Paul's thought is not to be explained solely as eschatological paradox; instead, it is the consequence of the fact that Paul's orientation to "world" is given by a narrative pattern. Christ's victory in the topical sequence has won freedom for humanity, but this freedom is neither an end in itself nor the end of the story: it is the necessary precondition that enables those who are redeemed to complete the story by carrying out their own mandate, by becoming active subjects who fulfill God's original purpose by loving one another. Thus, the final sequence of the story is played out in the experience of the Christian community, which finds itself as Subject, placed on the "axis of power" between the juxtaposed powers of Spirit and Flesh, which fill the actantial roles of Helper and opponent, respectively.

36. For studies of this theme, see the following: E. J. Tinsley, *The Imitation of God in Christ* (Philadelphia: Westminster, 1960); E. Schweizer, *Lordship and Discipleship* (SBT 28; London: SCM, 1960); A. Schulz, *Nachfolgen und Nachahmen* (SANT 6; Munich: Kösel, 1962); H. D. Betz, *Nachfolge und Nachahmung Jesu Christi im Neuen Testament* (BHT 37; Tübingen: J. C. B. Mohr [Paul Siebeck], 1967); J. H. Yoder, *The Politics of Jesus* (Grand Rapids: Eerdmans, 1972) 115-34; E. Larsson, *Christus als Vorbild* (ASNU 23; Lund: Gleerup, 1962; Copenhagen: Ejnar Munksgaard, 1962).

Interestingly, in Gal 5:13-26 the power of Flesh is manifest primarily in conflict and disunity, while the triumph of the Spirit (and thus the successful completion of the final sequence's task) is portrayed in images of harmony and unity within the community. Thus the goal toward which the gospel story drives is not so much authentic selfhood as authentic community. The community-oriented exhortations of Galatians 5 and 6 emerge naturally in Paul's thinking as the appropriate conclusion to the narrative movement to which the earlier chapters allude.

This discussion inescapably raises the perennial problem of the place of "works" in Paul. If salvation is by God's grace, what is the significance of human responsibility? On the other hand, if, as I have argued, the final sequence of the gospel story casts believers into the Subject role, have we lapsed back into making redemption dependent on our own works? As Paul would say, μὴ γένοιτο. Only a brief response to this range of issues is possible here. Three points must be stressed.

1. Redemption occurs in the topical sequence. The human action of faith-obedience in the final sequence does not complete an unfinished redemption; it is both the response to a completed redemption and the purpose for which the redemptive action was initiated by God.
2. The particular character of the gospel story works a subtle transformation in the Subject role. Christ's faithfulness is enacted in his giving himself up (Gal 2:20), his becoming a curse (Gal 3:13), his taking the form of a servant (Phil 2:7). The story of the cross, which portrays power as manifest in weakness, thus works an ironic reversal which cannot help but transmute our understanding of our own mandate as Subjects.
3. The Spirit given as our Helper effects a mysterious personal union with Christ. Thus the story does not simply shift from Christ as Subject in one sequence to humanity as Subject in the next. Instead, there is a complex overlay of two Subjects, so that Paul can attribute his own life and activity to "Christ in me" (Gal 2:20).

The formal model of narrative structure in Chapter III above explains the first of these three points very nicely, but it cannot really deal adequately with the second and third points, which, rather than being related to general properties of narrative structure, are bound up in the particularity of the story of Jesus Christ.

In any case, it is clear that the world established by the gospel story is not the frozen and unchangeable order which is usually associated with the world of "myth." The fixed order was precisely the state of slavery under the στοιχεῖα, whose power has now been broken, according to Paul's gospel story, by Christ's intervention; the new order thus created is one in which Christians live by the power of the Spirit, in freedom from the restraints of the Law. This new order is not a status quo to be protected but a vision to be realized — we might even say a task to be achieved — by "faith working through love" (5:6).

A word of qualification must be added here concerning the role of Christ as "ethical model." While Paul does not hold up the figure of Jesus Christ as an example to be imitated directly, there is in fact a pattern of correspondence between him and those who are "in" him. The Jesus Christ of the gospel story took the initiative to love and to give himself up (2:20), to bear vicariously the curse of the Law (3:13); thus, when Paul exhorts the Galatians to "bear one another's burdens and so fulfill the law of Christ" (6:2), we may see here a reflected image of the pattern enacted by Christ. When Paul says ἐν πίστει ζῶ τῇ τοῦ υἱοῦ τοῦ θεοῦ (2:20), he does not mean that he strives to emulate Jesus' faith but that his own new life in faith is "the shadow cast on the plane of experience"[37] by the transformation wrought through Jesus Christ's faith. This important distinction cannot be explored further here, but it is perhaps most readily understood in terms of the narrative framework described in this study. Our mandate is not a mandate to imitate Jesus' action of the topical sequence; however, his action empowers us to fulfill our mandate, as he did his, in obedience and faithfulness. There is an analogy between our role and Christ's role as Subject, but we are situated in a different sequence of the story, so that the specific content of the required obedience may differ. Wilder means something like this, I take it, when he says, "That which makes the peculiar mystery of life of the Christian is that the world plot plays itself over in him, yet in such a way that it is always unprecedented."[38] It may appear odd that my analysis of the story finds its final sequence to be played out in the life-experience of the Christian community. What has become here of the eschatological element, of the apocalyptic "final sequence" of resurrection and judgment? The answer to this question is that the story under consideration here is the story that is manifested in Galatians, which lacks the apocalyptic themes that appear so prominently elsewhere in Paul, particularly in texts such as Romans 8 and 1 Corinthians 15. On the basis of Galatians alone, it is not possible to know how (or whether) the present life of the community is related to the apocalyptic consummation of the drama of salvation. As I

37. P. Ricoeur, *The Symbolism of Evil* (Boston: Beacon, 1967) 274.
38. Wilder, *Early Christian Rhetoric*, 58.

have already remarked in Chapter V, a comprehensive account of the relation of Paul's theology to a narrative substructure would have to reckon with those passages that place the Christ-event within the framework of a story stretching from Adam to the eschaton. In Galatians, however, Paul traces the story backward no farther than Abraham and forward no farther than the immediately controverted future of the Galatian churches. This limitation of scope is imposed in part, no doubt, by the particular problem that Paul is addressing here: the role of the Jewish Law in a Gentile Christian community.[39] That Paul perceived the story stretching from Abraham to the present as a segment within a still larger story is demonstrated clearly by Romans, but it is beyond the scope of this study to trace out the structure of that larger story.[40]

The significant point with regard to Pauline ethics is this: the narrative substructure provides the "logic" that links the parenetic section of Galatians to the theological exposition of the central section. Interpreters of Paul have always found it difficult to explain how his ethic is grounded in his theology; this study poses the possibility that both are grounded in his gospel story.

E. The Character of Paul's Language

This investigation was begun with the intent of clarifying "the nature and method of Paul's theological language." Most of our attention has been focused on questions of *method* and upon the interpretation of a particular text; however, the conclusions drawn in the course of this study also bear significant implications for assessing the *nature* of Paul's langauge. Therefore, we may conclude the investigation with some general reflections upon the character of Paul's theological language as it appears in Galatians.

---

39. Koester (*Trajectories,* 145-46) thinks that Paul is working under restraints dictated by the polemical situation. He hypothesizes that Paul's opponents were Gnostic Judaizers who "emphasized the spiritual implications and the cosmic dimensions of the observance of the ritual law of the Old Testament." Consequently, "Paul consciously avoids any appeal to the first chapters of Genesis which played such a vital role in the mythological reinterpretations of the Old Testament tradition in apocalypticism and in wisdom speculations." This rather elaborate hypothesis, whatever its merits on other grounds, is hardly necessary to explain Paul's failure to discuss the creation story in Galatians. Indeed, if such matters were at issue, we would expect Paul to address them directly, as he does with Abraham and circumcision, rather than avoiding them.

40. The relation of the narrative substructure of Galatians, as analyzed in this study, to the more extensive narrative framework of apocalyptic thought is a problem which calls for further investigation.

Galatians must *not* be interpreted as if it were "foundational language." Paul writes in the mode of "primary reflectivity,"[41] and we understand the text properly only when we understand it as the explication of something else. A helpful analogy may be found in the relation between text and sermon. A sermon does not retell the story told in the text upon which it is based, but the story is pervasively presupposed by the sermon. To understand a sermon, therefore, we need to know not only something about the rhetorical conventions of the sermon genre and about the congregational situation to which the sermon is addressed but also about the text that the sermon seeks to explicate.[42] Galatians is not exactly a sermon (although it may well have been intended to be read aloud to the Galatian congregations), but it does stand close to the sermon on Funk's spectrum of language modes, clearly within the category of primary reflectivity. It is neither self-sufficient nor purely self-referential; instead, it constantly presupposes and elucidates the gospel story of Jesus Christ, as we have demonstrated. This means that the text is necessarily allusive in character, constantly pointing and appealing to something which finds only partial manifestation in the text. My project has been to follow Paul's pointers and allusions and thus to attempt to reconstruct as much as possible of the story that is presupposed by Paul in Galatians. This project in no way obviates or supplants other critical efforts to "understand" the text either in terms of rhetorical conventions or in terms of the historical situation in Galatia. My work should be seen as complementary to such efforts, all of which are necessary to a fully rounded interpretation.[43]

If, however, we recognize that the character of Paul's language in Galatians is highly allusive and that it depends heavily upon the foundational language of story, we must also reckon with another possible implication: perhaps Paul's language is less univocal and more "poetic" than the Western theological tradition has usually supposed. In the quest for clarity and accuracy, NT exegetes have tended to strive for *the* single right interpretation of Paul's theological expressions. This tendency is illustrated dramatically by Albrecht Oepke's denial that there could be any ambiguity in Paul's use of the phrase δικαιοσύνη θεοῦ: "An und für sich ist es wenig wahrscheinlich, dass

41. Funk, *Language, Hermeneutic, and Word of God,* 233. See the discussion of his typology of language modes in Chap. I.B.1.c., above.

42. By using this analogy, I do not intend to imply that the Christ-story which Paul is elucidating existed as a written text; at this stage it was a story passed along orally by many tellers, including Paul himself.

43. It is also true that our understanding of Paul might be enriched by further investigation of the "deeper" tensions which are figured forth by stories, though this study has not pursued questions of this type.

der scharfe und klare Denker Paulus sich einer so zweideutigen Redeweise bedient. . . ."[44] What if Oepke's assumption (in which he stands by no means alone) about the character of Paul's language is fundamentally wrong? Oepke seems to equate clarity of thought with univocal use of language. But this equation is surely mistaken, for there is also a poetic clarity of thought that seeks to expand rather than to delimit the referential horizons of language.

This study suggests indirectly that we must take more seriously the poetic functions of language for Paul. We must learn to read his exasperating syntax, alternatively impenetrably dense and tantalizingly elliptical, as a tapestry woven with the allusive and evocative language of faith. In Chapter IV above, this approach has been worked out in some detail with regard to Paul's phrase πίστις Ἰησοῦ Χριστοῦ, which, as we have contended, has more than one level of meaning.

A word of caution is necessary here: I am not proposing that NT exegesis should abandon the quest for *clarity* in interpreting Paul. I am advocating only that the presupposition of *univocity* be discarded. The texts and symbols which grasp and move us most profoundly are almost always polyvalent. I am proposing that Paul's language has something of that character, that it belongs less to the sphere of *wissenschaftliche Theologie* than to the sphere of confession, prayer, and praise.[45] If this is the case, accuracy of interpretation consists not in eliminating all possible ambiguities in the meaning of Paul's language but in tracing attentively its various overtones and ranges of implication. Such an approach, if applied consistently, would significantly alter the character of Pauline interpretation.

F. Conclusion

In summary, I have claimed that Paul's theological language is grounded in a narrative substructure, which is the story of Jesus Christ as outlined in Chapters III-V. Although this story is presupposed throughout Paul's argumentation, Paul never merely recites the foundational story, nor does he deliberate in a merely speculative manner upon its meaning, like a literary critic. Instead, Paul's language *enacts* the ongoing destiny of the foundational story because he sees himself and his churches as agents within the story's final sequence. His reflection and argumentation about the meaning of the gospel

---

44. Oepke, "Δικαιοσύνη θεοῦ bei Paulus," *TLZ* 78 (1953) 259.

45. Of course, in the case of Galatians, this language of confession, prayer, and praise is drafted into the service of polemical argumentation.

story derive their peculiar urgency from this fact. The recurrent impact and renewing power of Paul's letters within Christian history may be attributed in part to the organic relation between the story and Paul's interpretation of its meaning. Because it is rooted so firmly in a story which has the paradoxical capacity to subvert and establish world simultaneously (and thus to transform world), Paul's language becomes a living instance of a type of language that Ricoeur contemplates as a theoretical possibility: "a conceptual language which preserves the tensive character of symbolic language."[46] Our comprehension of Paul and of the logic of his argumentation may be advanced by grasping this tensive character of his theological language, a character which it derives from its integral relation to the story of Jesus Christ.

46. Ricoeur, "Biblical Hermeneutics," 36.

Selected Bibliography

A. Commentaries on Galatians

Betz, Hans Dieter. *Galatians*. Hermeneia. Philadelphia: Fortress, 1979.

Bligh, John. *Galatians in Greek*. Detroit: University of Detroit, 1966.

Bonnard, Pierre. *L'Épître de Saint Paul aux Galates*. CNT 9. Neuchâtel/Paris: Delachaux & Niestlé, 1953.

Bousset, Wilhelm. "Der Brief an die Galater." Pp. 28-72 in *Die Schriften des Neuen Testaments,* Vol. 2. 2nd ed. 2 vols. Ed. Johannes Weiss. Göttingen: Vandenhoeck & Ruprecht, 1908.

Bring, Ragnar. *Commentary on Galatians*. Trans. Eric Wahlstrom. Philadelphia: Muhlenberg, 1961.

Burton, Ernest De Witt. *A Critical and Exegetical Commentary on the Epistle to the Galatians*. ICC. Edinburgh: T. & T. Clark, 1920.

Calvin, John. *The Epistles of Paul the Apostle to the Galatians, Ephesians, Philippians, and Colossians*. Trans. T. H. L. Parker. Edinburgh: Oliver and Boyd, 1965.

Duncan, George S. *The Epistle of Paul to the Galatians*. MNTC. New York: Harper and Bros., 1934.

Guthrie, Donald. *Galatians*. The Century Bible, New Series. London: Nelson, 1969.

Lagrange, M.-J. *Saint Paul Épître aux Galates*. 2nd ed. Paris: Librairie Lecoffre, J. Gabalda, 1925.

Lietzmann, Hans. *An die Galater*. HNT 10. Tübingen: J. C. B. Mohr (Paul Siebeck), 1932.

Lightfoot, J. B. *The Epistle of St. Paul to the Galatians*. London: Macmillan, 1865; reprinted, Grand Rapids: Eerdmans, 1957.

Lührmann, Dieter. *Der Brief an die Galater*. Zürcher Bibelkommentare NT 7. Zürich: Theologischer Verlag, 1978.

Luther, Martin. "Lectures on Galatians." In *Luther's Works*, Vols. 26 and 27. Trans. Jaroslav Pelikan and Richard Jungkuntz. St. Louis: Concordia, 1963-64.

Lyonnet, S. *Les Épîtres de Saint Paul aux Galates, aux Romains*. Paris: Cerf, 1953.

Mussner, Franz. *Der Galaterbrief*. HTKNT 9. Freiburg: Herder, 1974.

Oepke, Albrecht. *Der Brief des Paulus an die Gatater.* 3rd ed. THKNT 9. Berlin: Evangelische Verlagsanstalt, 1973.

Ridderbos, Herman N. *The Epistle of Paul to the Churches of Galatia.* Trans. Henry Zylstra. NICNT. Grand Rapids: Eerdmans, 1953.

Schlier, Heinrich. *Der Brief an die Galater.* 14th ed. MeyerK 7. Göttingen: Vandenhoeck & Ruprecht, 1965.

Zahn, Theodor. *Der Brief des Paulus an die Galater.* HKNT 9. Leipzig: Deichert, 1905.

B. Studies Pertinent to the Interpretation of Gal 3:1–4:11

Allen, E. L. "Representative Christology in the NT." *HTR* 46 (1953) 161-69.

Aulén, Gustaf. *Christus Victor: An Historical Study of the Three Main Types of the Idea of the Atonement.* Trans. A. G. Hebert. London: SPCK, 1931; reprinted, New York: Macmillan, 1969.

Baird, William. "What Is the Kerygma? A Study of 1 Cor 15:3-8 and Gal 1:11-17." *JBL* 76 (1957) 181-91.

Bammel, Ernst. "Gottes ΔΙΑΘΗΚΗ (Gal III. 15-17) und das jüdische Rechtsdenken." *NTS* 6 (1959-60) 313-19.

Barr, James. *The Semantics of Biblical Language.* London: Oxford University, 1961.

Barrett, C. K. *From First Adam to Last: A Study in Pauline Theology.* New York: Scribner's Sons, 1962.

Barth, Karl. *Christus und Adam nach Rom 5: Ein Beitrag zur Frage nach dem Menschen und der Menschheit.* Theologische Studien 35. Zollikon-Zürich: Evangelischer Verlag, 1952.

—————. *Church Dogmatics* IV/1 and IV/2: "The Doctrine of Reconciliation." Trans. G. W. Bromiley. Edinburgh: T. & T. Clark, 1956.

Barth, Markus. "The Faith of the Messiah." *HeyJ* 10 (1969) 363-70.

—————. *Justification: Pauline Texts Interpreted in the Light of the Old and New Testament.* Trans. A. M. Woodruff, III. Grand Rapids: Eerdmans, 1971.

—————. "Jews and Gentiles: The Social Character of Justification in Paul." *JES* 5 (1968) 241-67.

—————. "The Kerygma of Galatians." *Int* 21 (1967) 131-46.

—————. "St. Paul — A Good Jew." *Horizons in Biblical Theology* 1 (1979) 7-45.

Bartsch, Hans Werner. "Der Begriff 'Glaube' in Römerbrief." Pp. 119-27 in *Kerygma und Mythos VI, 4: Hermeneutik, Mythos, und Glaube.* Ed. Franz Theunis. Hamburg/Bergstedt: Herbert Reich, 1960.

—————, ed. *Kerygma und Mythos.* TF 1. 4th ed. Hamburg/Bergstedt: Herbert Reich, 1960.

Beardslee, William A. *Human Achievement and Divine Vocation in the Message of Paul.* SBT 31. London: SCM, 1961.

Beker, J. Christiaan. "Contingency and Coherence in the Letters of Paul." *USQR* 33 (1978) 141-51.

—————. *Paul the Apostle: The Triumph of God in Life and Thought.* Philadelphia: Fortress, 1980.

Berger, Klaus. "Abraham in den paulinischen Hauptbriefen." *MTZ* 17 (1966) 47-89.

Betz, Hans Dieter. "Galatians, Letter to the." *IDBSup*, 352-53.

———. "Geist, Freiheit und Gesetz. Die Botschaft des Paulus an die Gemeinde in Galatien." *ZTK* 71 (1974) 78-93.

———. "In Defense of the Spirit: Paul's Letter to the Galatians as a Document of Early Christian Apologetics." Pp. 99-114 in *Aspects of Religious Propaganda in Judaism and Early Christianity*. Ed. Elizabeth Schüssler-Fiorenza. Notre Dame: University of Notre Dame, 1976.

———. "The Literary Composition and Function of Paul's Letter to the Galatians." *NTS* 21 (1974-75) 353-79.

———. *Nachfolge und Nachahmung Jesu Christi im Neuen Testament*. BHT 37. Tübingen: J. C. B. Mohr (Paul Siebeck), 1967.

Binder, Hermann. *Der Glaube bei Paulus*. Berlin: Evangelische Verlagsanstalt, 1968.

Blank, Joseph. *Paulus und Jesus: Eine theologische Grundlegung*. SANT 18. Munich: Kösel, 1968.

Bligh, J. "Did Jesus Live by Faith?" *HeyJ* 9 (1968) 414-19.

Boers, Hendrikus W. "Interpreting Paul: Demythologizing in Reverse." Pp. 153-72 in *The Philosophy of Order: Essays on History, Consciousness, and Politics (for Eric Voegelin on His Eightieth Birthday)*. Ed. P. J. Opitz and G. Sebba. Stuttgart: Klett-Cotta, 1981.

———. "Die Theologie Paulus im Lichte der Philosophie Platons." Pp. 57-77 in *Neues Testament und christliche Existenz: Festschrift für Herbert Braun*. Ed. H. D. Betz and L. Schottroff. Tübingen: J. C. B. Mohr (Paul Siebeck), 1973.

———. *Theology out of the Ghetto: A New Testament Exegetical Study concerning Religious Exclusiveness*. Leiden: Brill, 1971.

Bormann, Paul. *Die Heilswirksamkeit der Verkündigung nach dem Apostel Paulus: Ein Beitrag zur Theologie der Verkündigung*. Paderborn: Bonifacius, 1965.

Bornkamm, Gunter. *Paul*. Trans. D. M. G. Stalker. New York: Harper & Row, 1971.

Bousset, Wilhelm. *Kyrios Christos: A History of the Belief in Christ from the Beginnings of Christianity to Irenaeus*. Trans. John E. Steely. Nashville: Abingdon, 1970.

Bouttier, Michel. *Christianity according to Paul*. SBT 49. Trans. Frank Clarke. London: SCM, 1966.

———. "Complexio Oppositorum: sur les formules de 1 Cor 12:13, Gal 3:26-28, Col 3:10-11." *NTS* 23 (1976-77) 1-19.

———. *En Christ: étude d'exégèse et de théologie pauliniennes*. Études d'Histoire et de Philosophie Religieuses 54. Paris: Presses Universitaires de France, 1962.

Braun, Herbert. "Glaube im NT." *RGG*[3], 2.1590-97.

Bretscher, P. G. "Light from Galatians 3:1 on Pauline Theology." *CTM* 34 (1963) 77-97.

Bring, Ragnar. "Die Erfüllung des Gesetzes durch Christus." *KD* 5 (1959) 1-22.

———. "Die Mitten und das Gesetz. Eine Studie zu Gal 3:20." *KD* 12 (1966) 292-309.

Bruce, F. F. "Galatian Problems 3: The 'Other' Gospel." *BJRL* 53 (1971) 253-71.

———. "Galatian Problems 5: Galatians and Christian Origins." *BJRL* 55 (1973) 264-84.

Buber, Martin. *Two Types of Faith*. Trans. Norman P. Goldhawk. New York: Macmillan, 1951.

Bultmann, Rudolf. *Der Alte und der neue Mensch in der Theologie des Paulus.* Darmstadt: Wissenschaftliche Buchgesellschaft, 1964.

———. "Δικαιοσύνη θεοῦ." *JBL* 83 (1964) 12-16.

———. "πιστεύω, πίστις, κτλ." *TDNT*, 6.174-228.

———. *The Presence of Eternity: History and Eschatology.* The Gifford Lectures, 1955. New York: Harper & Bros., 1957.

———. *Theology of the New Testament.* 2 vols. Trans. Kendrick Grobel. New York: Scribner's Sons, 1951-55.

———. "Zur Auslegung von Galater 2,15-18." Pp. 394-99 in *Exegetica: Aufsätze zur Erforschung des Neuen Testaments.* Ed. Erich Dinkler. Tübingen: J. C. B. Mohr (Paul Siebeck), 1967.

Cabaniss, A. "The Gospel according to Paul." *EvQ* 48 (1976) 164-67.

Callan, Terrance D. *The Law and the Mediator: Gal 3:19b-20.* Ph.D. dissertation, Yale, 1976; Ann Arbor: University Microfilms, 1977.

———. "Pauline Midrash: The Exegetical Background of Gal 3:19b." *JBL* 99 (1980) 549-67.

Carré, Henry Beach. *Paul's Doctrine of Redemption.* New York: Macmillan, 1914.

Cavallin, Hans C. C. "The Righteous Shall Live by Faith: A Decisive Argument for the Traditional Interpretation." *ST* 32 (1978) 33-43.

Conzelmann, Hans. "Die Rechtfertigungslehre des Paulus: Theologie oder Anthropologie?" *EvT* 28 (1968) 389-404.

———. "Zur Analyse der Bekenntnisformel I Kor. 15,3-5." *EvT* 25 (1965) 1-11.

Cosgrove, Charles H. "The Mosaic Law Preaches Faith: A Study in Galatians 3." *WTJ* 41 (1978) 146-64.

Craddock, Fred. *The Pre-Existence of Christ in the New Testament.* Nashville: Abingdon, 1968.

Cullmann, Oscar. *Christ and Time: The Primitive Christian Conception of Time and History.* Rev. ed. Trans. Floyd V. Filson. Philadelphia: Westminster, 1964.

———. *The Christology of the NT.* Rev. ed. Trans. S. C. Guthrie and C. A. M. Hall. Philadelphia: Westminster, 1963.

———. *Salvation in History.* Trans. Sidney G. Sowers et al. New York: Harper & Row, 1967.

Dahl, Nils A. *The Crucified Messiah and Other Essays.* Minneapolis: Augsburg, 1974.

———. *Jesus in the Memory of the Early Church.* Minneapolis: Augsburg, 1976.

———. *Studies in Paul: Theology for the Early Christian Mission.* Minneapolis: Augsburg, 1977.

———. *Das Volk Gottes.* Oslo: Skrifter utgitt av Det Norske Videnskaps-Akademi i Oslo, 1941; reprinted, Darmstadt: Wissenschaftliche Buchgesellschaft, 1963.

Daly, R. J. "The Soteriological Significance of the Sacrifice of Isaac." *CBQ* 39 (1977) 45-75.

Daube, David. "The Interpretation of a Generic Singular in Galatians 3,16." *JQR* 35 (1944-45) 227-30.

Davies, W. D. "Paul and the People of Israel." *NTS* 24 (1977-78) 4-39.

———. *Paul and Rabbinic Judaism: Some Rabbinic Elements in Pauline Theology.* London: SPCK, 1948.

Deissmann, Adolf. *Paul: A Study in Social and Religious History.* 2nd ed. Trans. William E. Wilson. New York: George H. Doran, 1926.

Dietzfelbinger, Christian. *Heilsgeschichte bei Paulus?* Theologische Existenz Heute, N.F. 126. Munich: Kaiser, 1965.

―――. *Paulus und das Alte Testament: Die Hermeneutik des Paulus, untersucht an seiner Deutung der Gestalt Abrahams.* Theologische Existenz Heute, N.F. 95. Munich: Kaiser, 1961.

Dodd, C. H. *According to the Scriptures: The Sub-Structure of New Testament Theology.* London: Nisbet, 1952.

―――. *The Apostolic Preaching and Its Developments.* New York/London: Harper & Bros., 1936.

―――. "The Framework of the Gospel Narrative." *ExpTim* 43 (1931-32) 396-400.

Doughty, D. J. "The Priority of XAPIΣ: An Investigation of the Theological Language of Paul." *NTS* 19 (1972-73) 163-80.

Drane, J. W. "Theological Diversity in the Letters of St. Paul." *Tyndale Bulletin* 27 (1976) 3-26.

Dülmen, Andrea van. *Die Theologie des Gesetzes bei Paulus.* SBM 5. Stuttgart: Katholisches Bibelwerk, 1968.

Duling, D. C. "The Promises to David and Their Entrance into Christianity." *NTS* 20 (1973-74) 55-77.

Dunn, James D. G. *Christology in the Making.* Philadelphia: Westminster, 1980.

―――. "Paul's Understanding of the Death of Jesus." Pp. 125-41 in *Reconciliation and Hope: New Testament Essays on Atonement and Eschatology Presented to L. L. Morris on His 60th Birthday.* Ed. Robert Banks. Grand Rapids: Eerdmans, 1974.

Duprez, A. "Note sur le rôle de l'Esprit-Saint dans la filiation du chrétien. A propos de Gal 4,6." *RSR* 52 (1964) 421-31.

Ebeling, Gerhard. *Word and Faith.* Trans. James W. Leitch. Philadelphia: Fortress, 1963.

Eckert, Jost. "Paulus und Israel. Zu den Strukturen paulinischer Rede und Argumentation." *TTZ* 87 (1978) 1-13.

―――. *Die urchristliche Verkündigung im Streit zwischen Paulus und seinen Gegnern nach dem Galaterbrief.* Biblische untersuchungen 6. Regensburg: P. Pustet, 1971.

Edwards, Elizabeth G. *Christ, a Curse, and the Cross: An Interpretive Study of Gal 3:13.* Th.D. dissertation, Princeton Theological Seminary, 1972; Ann Arbor: University Microfilms, 1972.

E. Earle Ellis. *Paul and His Recent Interpreters.* Grand Rapids: Eerdmans, 1961.

―――. *Paul's Use of the Old Testament.* Grand Rapids: Eerdmans, 1957.

―――. *Prophecy and Hermeneutic in Early Christianity.* WUNT 18. Tübingen: J. C. B. Mohr (Paul Siebeck), 1978.

Eshbaugh, H. "Textual Variants and Theology: A Study of the Galatians Text of Papyrus 46." *JSNT* 3 (1979) 60-72.

Feuillet, A. "La citation d'Habaccuc II.4 et les huit premiers chapitres de l'épître aux Romains." *NTS* 6 (1959-60) 52-80.

Fischer, J. A. "Pauline Literary Forms and Thought Patterns." *CBQ* 39 (1977) 209-23.

Fitzmyer, Joseph A. "The Gospel in the Theology of Paul." *Int* 33 (1979) 339-50.

―――. *Pauline Theology: A Brief Sketch.* Englewood Cliffs, NJ: Prentice-Hall, 1967.

Flusser, David. "The Dead Sea Sect and Pre-Pauline Christianity." *Scripta Hierosolymitana* 4 (1958) 215-66.

Fridrichsen, Anton. *The Apostle and His Message.* Uppsala Universitets Årsskrift 1947/3. Uppsala: Almqvist and Wiksell, 1947.

Fuchs, Ernst. "Jesus und der Glaube." *ZTK* 55 (1958) 170-85.

Fuller, Daniel P. "Paul and the Works of the Law." *WTJ* 38 (1975-76) 28-42.

Funk, Robert W. *Language, Hermeneutic, and Word of God: The Problem of Language in the NT and Contemporary Theology.* New York: Harper & Row, 1966.

Furnish, V. P. *Theology and Ethics in Paul.* Nashville: Abingdon, 1968.

Gábriš, K. "Zur Kraft der Verheissungen (Zu Gal 3,15-22)." *Communio Viatorum* 11 (1968) 251-64.

Gaston, Lloyd. "Abraham and the Righteousness of God." *Horizons in Biblical Theology* 2 (1980) 39-68.

Giblin, Charles H. "Three Monotheistic Texts in Paul (1 Cor 8:1-13, Gal 3:15-29, Rom 3:27-31)." *CBQ* 37 (1975) 527-47.

Goffinet, A. "La prédication de l'Évangile et de la croix dans l'Épître aux Galates." *ETL* 41 (1965) 395-450.

Goodenough, E. R., and A. T. Kraabel. "Paul and the Hellenization of Christianity." Pp. 23-68 in *Religions in Antiquity: Essays in Memory of Erwin Ramsdell Goodenough.* Ed. Jacob Neusner. Leiden: Brill, 1968.

Goppelt, L. "Paulus und die Heilsgeschichte." *NTS* 13 (1966-67) 31-42.

Güttgemanns, Erhardt. *Der leidende Apostel und sein Herr: Studien zur paulinischen Christologie.* FRLANT 90. Göttingen: Vandenhoeck & Ruprecht, 1966.

———. *Studia Linguistica Neotestamentica.* BEvT 60. Munich: Kaiser, 1971.

Haeuser, Philipp. *Anlass und Zweck des Galaterbriefes: Seine logische Gedankenentwicklung.* NTAbh 11/3. Münster: Aschendorff, 1925.

Hahn, Ferdinand. "Genesis 15:6 im Neuen Testament." Pp. 90-107 in *Probleme Biblischer Theologie: Gerhard von Rad zum 70. Geburtstag.* Ed. Hans Walter Wolff. Munich: Kaiser, 1971.

———. "Das Gesetzesverständnis im Römer- und Galaterbrief." *ZNW* 67 (1976) 29-63.

Hanson, A. T. *Paul's Understanding of Jesus: Invention or Interpretation?* Hull: University of Hull Publications, 1963.

———. *Studies in Paul's Technique and Theology.* London: SPCK, 1974.

Hasler, Victor. "Glaube und Existenz. Hermeneutische Erwägungen zu Gal 2,15-21." *TZ* 25 (1969) 241-51.

Hatch, W. H. P. *The Pauline Idea of Faith in Its Relation to Jewish and Hellenistic Religion.* HTS 2. Cambridge: Harvard University, 1917.

Haussleiter, Johannes. "Der Glaube Jesu Christi." *NKZ* 2 (1891) 109-45, 205-30.

———. "Was versteht Paulus unter christlichem Glauben?" Pp. 159-82 in *Greifswalder Studien.* Gütersloh: Bertelsmann, 1895.

Hays, Richard B. "Psalm 143 and the Logic of Romans 3." *JBL* 99 (1980) 107-15.

Hebert, A. G. "Faithfulness and 'Faith.'" *Theology* 58 (1955) 373-79.

Heidland, Hans-Wolfgang. *Die Anrechnung des Glaubens zur Gerechtigkeit.* BWANT 4/18. Stuttgart: Kohlhammer, 1936.

Hengel, Martin. *The Son of God.* Trans. John Bowden. Philadelphia: Fortress, 1976.

Hester, James. "The 'Heir' and *Heilsgeschichte:* A Study of Galatians 4:1ff." Pp. 118-25 in *Oikonomia: Heilsgeschichte als Thema der Theologie.* Ed. Felix Christ. Hamburg/ Bergstedt: Herbert Reich, 1967.

Hooker, Morna D. *Jesus and the Servant.* London: SPCK, 1959.

———. *A Preface to Paul.* New York: Oxford, 1980.

Howard, George. "The Faith of Christ." *ExpTim* 85 (1974) 212-15.

———. "On the 'Faith of Christ.'" *HTR* 60 (1967) 459-65.

———. *Paul: Crisis in Galatia: A Study in Early Christian Theology.* SNTSMS 35. Cambridge: Cambridge University, 1979.

———. "Romans 3:21-31 and the Inclusion of the Gentiles." *HTR* 63 (1970) 223-33.

Hübner, Hans. "Existentiale Interpretation der paulinischen Gerechtigkeit Gottes: Zur Kontroverse Rudolf Bultmann-Ernst Käsemann." *NTS* 21 (1974-75) 462-88.

———. *Das Gesetz bei Paulus. Ein Beitrag zum Werden der paulinischen Theologie.* FRLANT 119. Göttingen: Vandenhoeck & Ruprecht, 1978.

———. "Gal 3,10 und die Herkunft des Paulus." *KD* 19 (1973) 21-31.

Hübner, Hans. "Identitätsverlust und paulinische Theologie. Anmerkungen zum Galaterbrief." *KD* 24 (1978) 181-93.

———. "Pauli Theologiae Proprium." *NTS* 26 (1979-80) 445-73.

Hultgren, Arland J. "The *Pistis Christou* Formulation in Paul." *NovT* 22 (1980) 248-63.

Hunter, A. M. *The Gospel according to St. Paul.* London: SCM, 1966.

Jacob, Edmond. "Abraham et sa signification pour la foi chrétienne." *RHPR* 42 (1962) 148-56.

Jeremias, Joachim. *Der Schlüssel zur Theologie des Apostels Paulus.* Stuttgart: Calwer, 1971.

———. "Zur Gedankenführung in den paulinischen Briefen." Pp. 146-54 in *Studia Paulina in Honorem Johannis De Zwaan Septuagenarii.* Ed. J. N. Sevenster and W. C. van Unnik. Haarlem: De Erven F. Bohn, 1953.

Jewett, Robert. "The Agitators and the Galatian Congregation." *NTS* 17 (1970-71) 198-212.

———. *Paul's Anthropological Terms: A Study of Their Use in Conflict Settings.* AGJU 10. Leiden: Brill, 1971.

Johnson, L. T. "Romans 3:21-26 and the Faith of Jesus." *CBQ* 44 (1982) 77-90.

Jones, P. R. "Exegesis of Galatians 3 and 4." *RevExp* 69 (1972) 471-82.

Käsemann, Ernst. "Konsequente Traditionsgeschichte?" *ZTK* 62 (1965) 137-52.

———. *New Testament Questions of Today.* Trans. W. J. Montague. Philadelphia: Fortress, 1969.

———. *Perspectives on Paul.* Trans. Margaret Kohl. Philadelphia: Fortress, 1971.

Keck, Leander E. *Paul and His Letters.* Philadelphia: Fortress, 1979.

Kertelge, Karl. *"Rechtfertigung" bei Paulus: Studien zur Struktur und zum Bedeutungsgehalt des paulinischen Rechtfertigungsbegriffs.* NTAbh, N.F. 3. Münster: Aschendorff, 1967.

———. "Zur Deutung des Rechtfertigungsbegriffs im Galaterbrief," *BZ* 12 (1968) 211-22.

Kittel, Gerhard. "πίστις Ἰησοῦ Χριστοῦ bei Paulus." *TSK* 79 (1906) 419-36.

Klein, Günther. *Rekonstruktion und Interpretation.* BEvT 50. Munich: Kaiser, 1969.

―――. "Righteousness in the NT." *IDBSup*, 750-52.

Knox, W. "The 'Divine Hero' Christology in the New Testament." *HTR* 41 (1948) 229-49.

Kramer, Werner. *Christ, Lord, Son of God*. SBT 50. Trans. Brian Hardy. London: SCM, 1966.

Lambrecht, Jan. "The Line of Thought in Gal 2:14b-2l." *NTS* 24 (1977-78) 484-95.

Larsson, Edvin. *Christus als Vorbild*. ASNU 23. Lund: Gleerup, 1962; Copenhagen: Ejnar Munksgaard, 1962.

Lindars, Barnabas. *New Testament Apologetic*. London: SCM, 1961.

Ljungman, Henrik. *Pistis: A Study of Its Presuppositions and Its Meaning in Pauline Use*. Lund: Gleerup, 1964.

Lohmeyer, Ernst. *Grundlagen paulinischer Theologie*. BHT 1. Tübingen: J. C. B. Mohr (Paul Siebeck), 1929.

Lohse, Eduard. *Märtyrer und Gottesknecht: Untersuchungen zur urchristlichen Verkündigung vom Sühntod Jesu Christi*. FRLANT, N.F. 46. Göttingen: Vandenhoeck & Ruprecht, 1955.

Longenecker, R. N. *Biblical Exegesis in the Apostolic Period*. Grand Rapids: Eerdmans, 1975.

―――. "The 'Faith of Abraham' Theme in Paul, James, and Hebrews: A Study in the Circumstantial Nature of NT Teaching." *Journal of the Evangelical Theological Society* 20 (1977) 203-12.

―――. "The Obedience of Christ in the Theology of the Early Church." Pp. 142-52 in *Reconciliation and Hope: New Testament Essays on Atonement and Eschatology Presented to L. L. Morris on His 60th Birthday*. Ed. Robert Banks. Grand Rapids: Eerdmans, 1974.

Lucchesi, E. "Nouveau Parallèle entre Saint Paul (Gal iii. 16) et Philon d'Alexandrie (*Quaestiones in Genesim*)?" *NovT* 21 (1979) 50-55.

Lührmann, Dieter. *Glaube im frühen Christentum*. Gütersloh: Gerd Mohn, 1976.

―――. "Rechtfertigung und Versöhnung: zur Geschichte der paulinischen Tradition." *ZTK* 67 (1970) 437-52.

Lull, David J. *The Spirit in Galatia: Paul's Interpretation of "Pneuma" as Divine Power*. SBLDS 49. Chico: Scholars, 1980.

Lütgert, Wilhelm. *Gesetz und Geist: Eine Untersuchung zur Vorgeschichte des Galaterbriefes*. BFCT I/22/6. Gütersloh: Bertelsmann, 1919.

Luz, Ulrich. *Das Geschichtsverständnis des Paulus*. BEvT 49. Munich: Kaiser, 1968.

Lyall, F. "Roman Law in the Writings of Paul — Adoption." *JBL* 88 (1969) 458-66.

McDonald, James I. H. *Kerygma and Didache: The Articulation and Structure of the Earliest Christian Message*. SNTSMS 37. Cambridge: Cambridge University, 1980.

Machen, J. Gresham. *The Origin of Paul's Religion*. New York: Macmillan, 1923.

Madvig, D. H. "The Missionary Preaching of Paul: A Problem in NT Theology." *Journal of the Evangelical Theological Society* 20 (1977) 147-55.

Malbon, Elizabeth Struthers. "'No Need to Have Anyone Write'?: A Structural Exegesis of 1 Thessalonians." Pp. 301-35 in *Society of Biblical Literature 1980 Seminar Papers*. Ed. Paul J. Achtemeier. Chico: Scholars, 1980.

Manson, T. W. "The Argument from Prophecy." *JTS* 46 (1945) 129-36.

————. "The Problem of the Epistle to the Galatians." *BJRL* 24 (1940) 59-80.

Mauser, Ulrich. "Galater iii.20: Die Universalität des Heils." *NTS* 13 (1966-67) 258-70.

Michel, O. *Paulus und seine Bibel.* BFCT 2/18. Gütersloh: Bertelsmann, 1929.

Minde, Hans-Jürgen van der. *Schrift und Tradition bei Paulus.* Paderborner Theologische Studien 3. Munich/Paderborn/Vienna: Schöningh, 1976.

Molland, Einar. *Das paulinische Euangelion: Das Wort und die Sache.* Oslo: I Kommisjon Hos Jacob Dybwad, 1934.

Müller, Christian. *Gottes Gerechtigkeit und Gottes Volk: Eine Untersuchung zu Römer 9–11.* FRLANT 86. Göttingen: Vandenhoeck & Ruprecht, 1964.

Munck, Johannes. *Paul and the Salvation of Mankind.* Trans. Frank Clarke. Richmond: John Knox, 1959.

Mundle, Wilhelm. *Der Glaubensbegriff des Paulus: Eine Untersuchung zur Dogmengeschichte des ältesten Christentums.* Leipzig: Heinsius, 1932; reprinted, Darmstadt: Wissenschaftliche Buchgesellschaft, 1977.

Mussner, Franz. *Theologie der Freiheit nach Paulus.* Quaestiones Disputatae 75. Freiburg: Herder, 1976.

Neugebauer, Fritz. *In Christus: Eine Untersuchung zum Paulinischen Glaubensverständnis.* Göttingen: Vandenhoeck & Ruprecht, 1961.

Oepke, Albrecht. "Δικαιοσύνη θεοῦ bei Paulus." *TLZ* 78 (1953) 257-64.

O'Neill, John C. *The Recovery of Paul's Letter to the Galatians.* London: SPCK, 1972.

O'Rourke, J. J. "*Pistis* in Romans." *CBQ* 35 (1973) 188-94.

Osten-Sacken, P. von der. "Das paulinische Verständnis des Gesetzes im Spannungsfeld von Eschatologie und Geschichte." *EvT* 37 (1977) 549-87.

Paulsen, Henning. "Einheit und Freiheit der Söhne Gottes — Gal 3:26-29." *ZNW* 71 (1980) 74-95.

Pollard, T. E. "Exit the Alexandrian Christ: Some Reflections on Contemporary Christology in the Light of New Testament Studies." *Colloquium* 13 (1980-81) 16-23.

Rad, Gerhard von. "Die Anrechnung des Glaubens zur Gerechtigkeit." *TLZ* 76 (1951) 129-32.

Richardson, Peter. "Pauline Inconsistency: 1 Cor 9:19-23 and Gal 2:11-14." *NTS* 26 (1979-80) 347-62.

Ridderbos, Herman. *Paul: An Outline of His Theology.* Trans. John R. DeWitt. Grand Rapids: Eerdmans, 1975.

————. *Paul and Jesus: Origin and General Character of Paul's Preaching of Christ.* Trans. David H. Freeman. Philadelphia: Presbyterian and Reformed, 1958.

Rigaux, Béda. *Saint Paul et ses lettres: état de la question.* Paris-Bruges: Desclée de Brouwer, 1962.

Robinson, D. W. B. "The Distinction between Jewish and Gentile Believers in Galatians." *AusBR* 13 (1965) 29-48.

————. " 'Faith of Jesus Christ' — A New Testament Debate." *Reformed Theological Review* 29 (1970) 71-81.

Robinson, J. A. T. *The Body: A Study in Pauline Theology.* SBT 5. London: SCM, 1952.

Robinson, James M. *Kerygma und historischer Jesus.* Zürich: Zwingli, 1960.

————, and Helmut Koester. *Trajectories through Early Christianity.* Philadelphia: Fortress, 1971.

Ropes, James Hardy. *The Singular Problem of the Epistle to the Galatians.* HTS 14. Cambridge: Harvard University, 1929.

Sanders, E. P. *Paul and Palestinian Judaism: A Comparison of Patterns of Religion.* Philadelphia: Fortress, 1977.

———. "Paul's Attitude toward the Jewish People." *USQR* 33 (1978) 175-87.

Sanders, Jack T. *The New Testament Christological Hymns: Their Historical Religious Background.* SNTSMS 15. Cambridge: Cambridge University, 1971.

Sanders, James A. "Habakkuk in Qumran, Paul, and the Old Testament." *JR* 39 (1959) 232-44.

———. "Torah and Christ." *Int* 29 (1975) 372-90.

Schein, Bruce E. *Our Father Abraham.* Ph.D. dissertation, Yale, 1972; Ann Arbor: University Microfilms, 1973.

Schenk, Wolfgang. "Die Gerechtigkeit Gottes und der Glaube Christi." *TLZ* 97 (1972) 161-74.

Schläger, G. "Bemerkungen zu πίστις Ἰησοῦ Χριστοῦ." *ZNW* 7 (1906) 356-58.

Schlatter, Adolf. *Der Glaube im Neuen Testament.* Stuttgart: Calwer, 1963.

Schlier, Heinrich. *Grundzüge einer paulinischen Theologie.* Freiburg: Herder, 1978.

Schmithals, Walter. *Paul and the Gnostics.* Trans. John E. Steely. Nashville: Abingdon, 1972.

Schmitz, Otto. *Die Christusgemeinschaft des Paulus im Lichte seines Genetivgebrauchs.* NTF 1/2. Gütersloh: Bertelsmann, 1924.

Schneidau, Norbert. *Die rhetorische Eigenart der paulinische Antithese.* Tübingen: J. C. B. Mohr (Paul Siebeck), 1970.

Schneidermeyer, W. "Galatians as Literature." *JRT* 28 (1971) 132-38.

Schoedel, W. R. "Pauline Thought: Some Basic Issues." Pp. 263-86 in *Transitions in Biblical Scholarship.* Essays in Divinity 6. Ed. J. C. Rylaarsdam. Chicago: University of Chicago, 1968.

Schoeps, Hans-Joachim. *Paul: The Theology of the Apostle in Light of Jewish Religious History.* Trans. Harold Knight. Philadelphia: Westminster, 1961.

———. "The Sacrifice of Isaac in Paul's Theology." *JBL* 65 (1946) 385-92.

Schrenk, Gottlob. *Studien zu Paulus.* ATANT 26. Zürich: Zwingli, 1954.

Schütz, John. *Paul and the Anatomy of Apostolic Authority.* SNTSMS 26. Cambridge: Cambridge University, 1975.

Schultz, Anselm. *Nachfolgen und Nachahmen: Studien über das Verhältnis der neutestamentlichen Jüngerschaft zur urchristlichen Vorbildethik.* SANT 6. Munich: Kösel, 1962.

Schweitzer, Albert. *The Mysticism of Paul the Apostle.* Trans. William Montgomery. London: A. & C. Black, 1931; reprinted, New York: Seabury, 1968.

———. *Paul and His Interpreters: A Critical History.* Trans. William Montgomery. London: A. & C. Black, 1912.

Schweizer, Eduard. *Lordship and Discipleship.* SBT 28. London: SCM, 1960.

———. "Zum religionsgeschichtlichen Hintergrund der 'Sendungsformel' Gal 4:4f., Rm 8:3f., Joh 3:16f., 1 Joh 4:9." *ZNW* 57 (1966) 199-210.

Smith, D. Moody. "Ο ΔΕ ΔΙΚΑΙΟΣ ΕΚ ΠΙΣΤΕΩΣ ΖΗΣΕΤΑΙ." Pp. 13-25 in *Studies in the History and Text of the New Testament in Honor of K. W. Clark.* Ed. B. L. Daniels and M. J. Suggs. Salt Lake City: University of Utah, 1967.

Somerville, David. *St. Paul's Conception of Christ: The Doctrine of the Second Adam.* Edinburgh: T. & T. Clark, 1897.

Stählin, Gustav. "Galaterbrief." *RGG*[3], 2.1187-90.

Stanton, G. N. *Jesus of Nazareth in New Testament Preaching.* SNTSMS 27. Cambridge: Cambridge University, 1974.

Stendahl, Krister. *Paul among Jews and Gentiles.* Philadelphia: Fortress, 1976.

Stenger, W. "Beobachtungen zur Argumentationsstruktur von 1 Kor 15." *LingBib* 45 (1979) 71-128.

Stowers, Stanley K. *The Diatribe and Paul's Letter to the Romans.* SBLDS 57. Chico: Scholars, 1981.

Stuhlmacher, Peter. *Gottes Gerechtigkeit bei Paulus.* FRLANT 87. Göttingen: Vandenhoeck & Ruprecht, 1965.

————. *Das Paulinische Evangelium I: Vorgeschichte.* FRLANT 95. Göttingen: Vandenhoeck & Ruprecht, 1968.

————. "Zur paulinischen Christologie." *ZTK* 74 (1977) 449-63.

Tannehill, Robert C. *Dying and Rising with Christ: A Study in Pauline Theology.* BZNW 32. Berlin: Töpelmann, 1967.

Taylor, G. M. "The Function of ΠΙΣΤΙΣ ΧΡΙΣΤΟΥ in Galatians." *JBL* 85 (1966) 58-76.

Thiselton, Anthony C. *The Two Horizons: New Testament Hermeneutics and Philosophical Description with Special Reference to Heidegger, Bultmann, Gadamer, and Wittgenstein.* Grand Rapids: Eerdmans, 1980.

Thüsing, Wilhelm. *Per Christum in Deum: Studien zum Verhältnis von Christozentrik und Theozentrik in den paulinischen Hauptbriefen.* NTAbh, N.F. 1. Münster: Aschendorff, 1965.

Tinsley, E. J. *The Imitation of God in Christ.* Philadelphia: Westminster, 1960.

Torrance, Thomas. "One Aspect of the Biblical Conception of Faith." *ExpTim* 68 (1957) 111-14.

Tyson, Joseph B. "Paul's Opponents in Galatia." *NovT* 4 (1968) 241-54.

————. " 'Works of Law' in Galatians." *JBL* 92 (1973) 423-31.

Vallotton, P. *Le Christ et la Foi.* Geneva: Labor et Fides, 1960.

Vanhoye, Albert. "Mediateur des Anges en Gal 3:19-20." *Bib* 59 (1978) 403-11.

Van Seters, John. *Abraham in History and Tradition.* New Haven: Yale University, 1975.

Via, Dan O. *Kerygma and Comedy in the New Testament: A Structuralist Approach to Hermeneutic.* Philadelphia: Fortress, 1975.

Vielhauer, Philipp. "Gesetzesdienst und Stoicheiadienst im Galaterbrief." Pp. 543-55 in *Rechtfertigung: Festschrift für Ernst Käsemann zum 70. Geburtstag.* Ed. J. Friedrich, W. Pöhlmann, and P. Stuhlmacher. Tübingen: J. C. B. Mohr (Paul Siebeck), 1976; Göttingen: Vandenhoeck & Ruprecht, 1976.

Wegenast, Klaus. *Das Verständnis der Tradition bei Paulus und in den Deuteropaulinen.* WMANT 8. Neukirchen: Neukirchener Verlag, 1962.

Wendland, Heinz Dietrich. *Geschichtsanschauung und Geschichtsbewusstsein im Neuen Testament.* Göttingen: Vandenhoeck & Ruprecht, 1938.

Wengst, Klaus. *Christologische Formeln und Lieder des Urchristentums.* SNT 7. 2nd ed. Gütersloh: Gerd Mohn, 1973.

Whiteley, D. E. H. *The Theology of St. Paul.* Philadelphia: Fortress, 1966.

Wikenhauser, Alfred. *Die Christusmystik des Apostels Paulus.* 2nd ed. Freiburg: Herder, 1956.

Wilckens, Ulrich. "Christologie und Anthropologie im Zusammenhang der paulinischen Rechtfertigungslehre." *ZNW* 67 (1976) 64-82.

——. *Rechtfertigung als Freiheit: Paulusstudien.* Neukirchen/Vluyn: Neukirchener Verlag, 1974.

Wilcox, Max. "The Promise of the 'Seed' in the New Testament and the Targumim." *JSNT* 5 (1979) 2-20.

——. "Upon the Tree: Deut 21:22-23 in the NT." *JBL* 96 (1977) 85-99.

Wilder, Amos N. *New Testament Faith for Today.* New York: Harper & Bros., 1955.

Williams, Sam K. *Jesus' Death as Saving Event: The Background and Origin of a Concept.* HDR 2. Missoula: Scholars, 1975.

——. "The 'Righteousness of God' in Romans." *JBL* 99 (1980) 241-90.

Wissmann, Erwin. *Das Verhältnis von ΠΙΣΤΙΣ und Christusfrömmigkeit bei Paulus.* FRLANT, N.F. 23. Göttingen: Vandenhoeck & Ruprecht, 1926.

Wrede, William. *Paul.* Trans. Edward Lummis. Boston: American Unitarian Association, 1908; reprinted, Lexington, KY: American Theological Library Association, 1962.

Wuellner, Wilhelm. "Toposforschung und Torahinterpretation bei Paulus und Jesus." *NTS* 24 (1977-78) 463-83.

C. Studies on Stories and Narrative Structure

Abrams, M. H. *The Mirror and the Lamp: Romantic Theory and the Critical Tradition.* New York: Oxford, 1953.

Adams, R. M., ed. *To Tell a Story: Narrative Theory and Practice.* Los Angeles: William Clark Andrews Memorial Library, UCLA, 1973.

Alonso Schökel, Luis. *The Inspired Word: Scripture in the Light of Language and Literature.* New York: Herder & Herder, 1965.

Alter, Robert. "A Literary Approach to the Bible." *Commentary* 60/6 (Dec. 1975) 70-77.

Aristotle. *The Poetics.* LCL. Trans. W. H. Fyfe. London: William Heinemann, 1927; New York: G. P. Putnam's Sons, 1927.

Armerding, Carl. "Structural Analysis." *Themelios* 4 (1979) 96-104.

Auerbach, Erich. *Mimesis: The Representation of Reality in Western Literature.* Princeton: Princeton University, 1953.

Barbour, Ian G. *Myths, Models, and Paradigms.* New York: Harper & Row, 1974.

Barr, James. *The Bible in the Modern World.* New York: Harper & Row, 1973.

——. "Story and History in Biblical Theology." *JR* 56 (1976) 1-17.

Barthes, R., et al. *Analyse Structurale et Exégèse Biblique: Essais d'interpretation.* Neuchâtel: Delachaux et Niestlé, 1971.

Barthes, Roland. "Introduction à l'analyse structurale des récits." *Communications* 8 (1966) 1-27.

————. *S/Z*. Paris: Seuil, 1976.

Beardslee, William A. *Literary Criticism of the New Testament*. Philadelphia: Fortress, 1970.

————. "Narrative Form in the New Testament and Process Theology." *Encounter* 36 (1975) 301-15.

————. "Openness to the New in Apocalyptic and in Process Theology." *Process Studies* 3 (1973) 169-78.

Black, Max. *Models and Metaphors: Studies in Language and Philosophy*. Ithaca: Cornell University, 1962.

Blanchard, Jean-Marc. "Searching for Narrative Structures." *Diacritics* 7 (1977) 2-17.

Borgman, Paul. "Story Shapes That Tell a World: King David and Cinema's Patton." *Christian Scholars Review* 9 (1980) 291-316.

Bremond, Claude. "La logique des possibles narratifs." *Communications* 8 (1966) 69-76.

————. "The Narrative Message." *Semeia* 10 (1978) 5-55.

Buechner, Frederick. *Telling the Truth: The Gospel as Tragedy, Comedy, and Fairy Tale*. New York: Harper & Row, 1977.

Calloud, Jean. *Structural Analysis of Narrative*. Semeia Supplements 4. Trans. Daniel Patte. Philadelphia: Fortress, 1976; Missoula: Scholars, 1976.

Cannon, Dale. "Ruminations on the Claim of Inenarrability." *JAAR* 43 (1975) 560-85.

Chabrol, Claude and Louis Marin. *Semiotique narrative: récits bibliques*. Paris: Didier/ Larousse, 1971.

Cobb, John B., Jr. "A Theology of Story: Crossan and Beardslee." Pp. 151-64 in *Orientation by Disorientation: Studies in Literary Criticism and Biblical Literary Criticism Presented in Honor of William A. Beardslee*. PTMS 35. Ed. Richard A. Spencer. Pittsburgh: Pickwick, 1980.

Collins, John J. "The Historical Character of the OT in Recent Biblical Theology." *CBQ* 41 (1979) 185-204.

Crites, Stephen. "The Narrative Quality of Experience." *JAAR* 39 (1971) 291-311.

————. "Angels We Have Heard." Pp. 22-63 in *Religion as Story*. Ed. James B. Wiggins. New York: Harper & Row, 1975.

Crossan, John Dominic. *The Dark Interval: Towards a Theology of Story*. Niles, IL: Argus, 1975.

————. "A Metamodel for Polyvalent Narration." *Semeia* 9 (1977) 105-47.

Culler, Jonathan. *Structuralist Poetics: Structuralism, Linguistics, and the Study of Literature*. Ithaca: Cornell University, 1975.

Culley, Robert C. "Structural Analysis: Is It Done with Mirrors?" *Int* 28 (1974) 165-81.

————. *Studies in the Structure of Hebrew Narrative*. Semeia Supplements 3. Philadelphia: Fortress, 1976; Missoula: Scholars, 1976.

Detweiler, Robert. "Generative Poetics as Science and Fiction." *Semeia* 10 (1978) 137-50.

————. *Story, Sign, and Self: Phenomenology and Structuralism as Literary Critical Methods*. Semeia Supplements 6. Philadelphia: Fortress, 1978; Missoula: Scholars, 1978.

Dundes, Alan, ed. *The Study of Folklore*. Englewood Cliffs, NJ: Prentice-Hall, 1965.

Dunne, John S. *A Search for God in Time and Memory*. London: Macmillan, 1967.

————. *Time and Myth*. Garden City, NY: Doubleday, 1973.

Eliade, Mircea. *Myth and Reality.* New York: Harper & Row, 1963.

———. *The Myth of the Eternal Return.* Bollingen Series 46. Princeton: Princeton University, 1954.

Entrevernes Group, The. *Signs and Parables: Semiotics and Gospel Texts.* PTMS 23. Trans. Gary Phillips. Pittsburgh: Pickwick, 1978.

Estess, Ted L. "The Inenarrable Contraption: Reflections on the Metaphor of Story." *JAAR* 42 (1974) 415-34.

Fackre, Gabriel. *The Christian Story.* Grand Rapids: Eerdmans, 1978.

Frei, Hans. *The Eclipse of Biblical Narrative: A Study in Eighteenth and Nineteenth Century Hermeneutics.* New Haven: Yale University, 1974.

———. *The Identity of Jesus Christ: The Hermeneutical Bases of Dogmatic Theology.* Philadelphia: Fortress, 1975.

Frye, Northrop. *Anatomy of Criticism.* Princeton: Princeton University, 1957.

———. *The Critical Path.* Bloomington: Indiana University, 1971.

———. *Fables of Identity: Studies in Poetic Mythology.* New York: Harcourt, Brace & World, 1963.

———. *The Stubborn Structure: Essays on Criticism and Society.* Ithaca: Cornell University, 1970.

Funk, Robert W. *Language, Hermeneutic, and Word of God: The Problem of Language in the New Testament and Contemporary Theology.* New York: Harper & Row, 1966.

Greimas, A. J. *Du Sens.* Paris: Seuil, 1970.

———. "Elements of a Narrative Grammar." *Diacritics* 7 (1977) 23-40.

———. "The Interpretation of Myth: Theory and Practice." Pp. 81-121 in *Structural Analysis of Oral Tradition.* Ed. P. Maranda and E. Köngäs Maranda. Philadelphia: University of Pennsylvania, 1971.

———. "Narrative Grammar: Units and Levels." *MLN* 86 (1971) 793-806.

———. *Sémantique Structurale.* Paris: Larousse, 1966.

Gros Louis, Kenneth R. R. et al., eds. *Literary Interpretations of Biblical Narratives.* Nashville: Abingdon, 1974.

Grosse, Ernst Ulrich. "Current Trends in French Narrative Research." *LingBib* 40 (1977) 21-54.

Gunn, Giles B. *Literature and Religion.* New York: Harper & Row, 1971.

Güttgemanns, Erhardt. "Introductory Remarks concerning the Structural Study of Narrative." *Semeia* 6 (1976) 23-125.

Hauerwas, Stanley. *Character and the Christian Life: A Study in Theological Ethics.* San Antonio: Trinity University, 1975.

———. "Jesus: The Story of the Kingdom." *Theology Digest* 26 (1978) 303-24.

———. "Story and Theology." *Religion in Life* 45 (1976) 339-50.

———. *Truthfulness and Tragedy: Further Investigations into Christian Ethics.* Notre Dame: University of Notre Dame, 1977.

———. *Vision and Virtue.* Notre Dame: Fides/Claretian, 1974.

Hendricks, William O. "Folklore and the Structural Analysis of Literary Texts." *Language and Style* 3 (1970) 83-121.

———. "Methodology of Narrative Structural Analysis." *Semiotica* 7 (1973) 163-84.

244

————. "The Structural Study of Narration: Sample Analyses." *Poetics* 3 (1972) 100-123.

Hepburn, R. W. "Vision and Choice in Morality." Pp. 181-95 in *Christian Ethics and Contemporary Philosophy*. Ed. Ian T. Ramsey. London: SCM, 1966.

Hirsch, E. D. *Validity in Interpretation*. New Haven: Yale University, 1967.

Holmer, Paul L. *The Grammar of Faith*. New York: Harper & Row, 1978.

Hopper, Stanley R., and David L. Miller, eds. *Interpretation: The Poetry of Meaning*. New York: Harcourt, Brace & World, 1967.

Ihwe, Jens. "On the Foundations of a General Theory of Narrative Structure." *Poetics* 3 (1972) 5-14.

Jakobson, Roman. "Linguistics and Poetics." Pp. 350-77 in *Style in Language*. Ed. T. A. Sebeok. Cambridge, MA: Technology, 1960; London: John Wiley & Sons, 1960.

Jobling, David. *The Sense of Biblical Narrative: Three Structural Analyses in the Old Testament*. JSOTSup 7. Sheffield: University of Sheffield, 1978.

————. "Structuralism, Hermeneutics, and Exegesis: Three Recent Contributions to the Debate." *USQR* 34 (1979) 135-47.

Johnson, Alfred M., ed. and trans. *Structuralism and Biblical Hermeneutics: A Collection of Essays*. PTMS 22. Pittsburgh: Pickwick, 1979.

Johnson, Luke T. *The Literary Function of Possessions in Luke–Acts*. SLBDS 39. Missoula: Scholars, 1977.

Jones, Hugh. "The Concept of Story and Theological Discourse." *SJT* 29 (1976) 415-33.

Kermode, Frank. *The Genesis of Secrecy: On the Interpretation of Narrative*. Cambridge: Harvard University, 1979.

————. *The Sense of an Ending: Studies in the Theory of Fiction*. New York: Oxford, 1967.

Kitagawa, J. M., and C. H. Long, eds. *Myths and Symbols: Studies in Honor of Mircea Eliade*. Chicago: University of Chicago, 1969.

Kort, Wesley A. *Narrative Elements and Religious Meaning*. Philadelphia: Fortress, 1975.

Krieg, Robert A. *The Theologian as Narrator: A Study of Karl Barth on the Divine Perfections*. Ph.D. dissertation, Notre Dame, 1978; Ann Arbor: University Microfilms, 1978.

Krieger, Murry. *A Window to Criticism*. Princeton: Princeton University, 1964.

Lévi-Strauss, Claude. *Structural Anthropology*. Trans. B. Jacobson and B. G. Schoepf. New York: Basic Books, 1963.

————. "Structure and Form: Reflections on a Work by Vladimir Propp." Pp. 115-45 in *Structural Anthropology*, Vol. II. Trans. Monique Layton. New York: Basic Books, 1976.

Lloyd, Charles L., Jr. *The Role of Narrative Form in Historical and Theological Explanation*. Ph.D. dissertation, Yale, 1968; Ann Arbor: University Microfilms, 1969.

Lynch, William F. *Christ and Apollo: The Dimensions of the Literary Imagination*. Notre Dame: University of Notre Dame, 1960.

McKnight, Edgar V. *Meaning in Texts: The Historical Shaping of a Narrative Hermeneutics*. Philadelphia: Fortress, 1978.

Maranda, Pierre, and Elli Köngäs Maranda, eds. *Structural Analysis of Oral Tradition*. Philadelphia: University of Pennsylvania, 1971.

Metz, Johann Baptist. "A Short Apology of Narrative." Pp. 84-96 in *The Crisis in Religious Language*. Concilium 85. Ed. J. B. Metz and J. P. Jossua. New York: Herder & Herder, 1973.

Miller, J. Hillis, ed. *Aspects of Narrative*. New York: Columbia University, 1971.

Mink, L. O. "History and Fiction as Modes of Comprehension." *New Literary History* 1 (1969-70) 541-58.

Murdoch, Iris. "Vision and Choice in Morality." Pp. 195-218 in *Christian Ethics and Contemporary Philosophy*. Ed. Ian T. Ramsey. London: SCM, 1966.

Navone, John. *The Jesus Story: Our Life as Story in Christ*. Collegeville, MN: Liturgical Press, 1979.

Nef, Frederic. "Introduction to the Reading of Greimas: Toward a Discursive Linguistics." *Diacritics* 7 (1977) 18-22.

Patte, Daniel, ed. *Semiology and Parables: An Exploration of the Possibilities Offered by Structuralism for Exegesis*. PTMS 9. Pittsburgh: Pickwick, 1976.

————. "Universal Narrative Structures and Semantic Frameworks." *Semeia* 10 (1978) 123-35.

————. *What Is Structural Exegesis?* Philadelphia: Fortress, 1976.

Patte, Daniel, and Aline Patte. *Structural Exegesis: From Theory to Practice*. Philadelphia: Fortress, 1978.

Petersen, Norman R. *Literary Criticism for New Testament Critics*. Philadelphia: Fortress, 1978.

Polzin, Robert. *Biblical Structuralism: Method and Subjectivity in the Study of Ancient Texts*. Semeia Supplements 5. Philadelphia: Fortress, 1977; Missoula: Scholars, 1977.

Power, William L. "Story and Theory in Christian Theology: Two Levels of Language and Logic." Paper presented at AAR/SBL meeting, New Orleans, 1978.

Price, Reynolds. *A Palpable God: Thirty Stories Translated from the Bible: With an Essay on the Origins and Life of Narrative*. New York: Atheneum, 1978.

Propp, Vladimir. *Morphology of the Folktale*. 2nd ed. Rev. and ed. L. A. Wagner; trans. L. Scott. Austin: University of Texas, 1968.

————. "Structure and History in the Study of the Fairy Tale." *Semeia* 10 (1978) 57-83.

Rastier, François. "Situation du récit dans une typologie du discours." *L'Homme* 11 (1971) 68-82.

Ricoeur, Paul. "Biblical Hermeneutics." *Semeia* 4 (1975) 29-148.

————. *The Conflict of Interpretations: Essays in Hermeneutics*. Ed. Don Ihde. Evanston: Northwestern University, 1974.

————. "Narrative and Hermeneutics." Pp. 37-56 in *Religion and the Humanities*. Working Paper #2. Research Triangle Park, NC: National Humanities Center, 1981.

————. "The Narrative Function." *Semeia* 13 (1978) 177-202.

————. *The Symbolism of Evil*. Trans. Emerson Buchanan. Boston: Beacon, 1969.

Robertson, David. "Hugh C. White on Roland Barthes, A Response." *Semeia* 3 (1975) 141-45.

————. *The Old Testament and the Literary Critic*. Philadelphia: Fortress, 1977.

Roth, Robert P. *Story and Reality*. Grand Rapids: Eerdmans, 1973.

Ruland, Vernon. *Horizons of Criticism: An Assessment of Religious-Literary Options*. Chicago: American Library Association, 1975.

————. "Understanding the Rhetoric of Theologians." *Semeia* 13 (1978) 203-24.

Sacks, Sheldon. *Fiction and the Shape of Belief*. Berkeley: University of California, 1964.

Schneidau, Herbert N. *Sacred Discontent: The Bible and Western Tradition*. Baton Rouge: Louisiana State University, 1976.

Scholes, Robert. *Structuralism in Literature: An Introduction*. New Haven: Yale University, 1974.

————, and Robert Kellogg. *The Nature of Narrative*. New York: Oxford, 1966.

Scott, Nathan A. *The Broken Center: Studies in the Theological Horizon of Modern Literature*. New Haven: Yale University, 1966.

Shea, John. *Stories of God: An Unauthorized Biography*. Chicago: Thomas More, 1978.

Spencer, Richard A., ed. *Orientation by Disorientation: Studies in Literary Criticism and Biblical Literary Criticism Presented in Honor of William A. Beardslee*. PTMS 35. Pittsburgh: Pickwick, 1980.

Stein, Gertrude. *Narration*. Chicago: University of Chicago, 1935.

Stroup, G. W. "A Bibliographic Critique." *Theology Today* 32 (1975) 133-43.

Szanto, George H. *Narrative Consciousness: Structure and Perception in the Fiction of Kafka, Beckett, and Robbe-Grillet*. Austin: University of Texas, 1972.

Tennyson, G. B., and E. E. Ericson, eds. *Religion and Modern Literature: Essays in Theory and Criticism*. Grand Rapids: Eerdmans, 1975.

TeSelle, Sallie McFague. *Speaking in Parables: A Study in Metaphor and Theology*. Philadelphia: Fortress, 1976.

Thompson, Leonard L. *Introducing Biblical Literature: A More Fantastic Country*. Englewood Cliffs, NJ: Prentice-Hall, 1978.

Todorov, Tzvetan. "Structural Analysis of Narrative." *Novel* 3 (1969-70) 70-76.

Toliver, Harold. *Animate Illusions: Explorations of Narrative Structure*. Lincoln: University of Nebraska, 1974.

Tolkien, J. R. R. "On Fairy-Stories." *The Tolkien Reader*. New York: Ballantine, 1966.

Uspensky, Boris. *A Poetics of Composition: The Structure of the Artistic Text and Typology of a Compositional Form*. Trans. V. Zavarin and S. Wittig. Berkeley: University of California, 1973.

Valdes, M. J., and D. J. Miller, eds. *Interpretation of Narrative*. Toronto: University of Toronto, 1978.

Via, Dan O., Jr. *Kerygma and Comedy in the New Testament: A Structuralist Approach to Hermeneutic*. Philadelphia: Fortress, 1975.

————. "Narrative World and Ethical Response: The Marvelous and Righteousness in Matthew 1–2." *Semeia* 12 (1978) 123-44.

Vickery, John B., ed. *Myth and Literature: Contemporary Theory and Practice*. Lincoln: University of Nebraska, 1966.

Weinrich, Harald. "Narrative Theology." Pp. 46-56 in *The Crisis of Religious Language*. Concilium 85. Ed. J. B. Metz and J. P. Jossua. New York: Herder & Herder, 1973.

Wellek, Rene, and Austin Warren. *Theory of Literature*. 3rd ed. New York: Harcourt, Brace & World, 1962.

Wheelwright, Philip. *The Burning Fountain: A Study in the Language of Symbolism.* Bloomington; Indiana University, 1968.

———. *Metaphor and Reality.* Bloomington: Indiana University, 1962.

White, Hayden. "The Structure of Historical Narrative." *Clio* 1/3 (June 1972) 5-20.

White, Hugh C. "French Structuralism and Old Testament Narrative Analysis: Roland Barthes." *Semeia* 3 (1975) 99-127.

———. "Structural Analysis of the Old Testament Narrative." Pp. 45-66 in *Encounter with the Text: Form and History in the Hebrew Bible.* Semeia Supplements 8. Ed. Martin J. Buss. Philadelphia: Fortress, 1979; Missoula: Scholars, 1979.

———. "A Theory of the Surface Structure of the Biblical Narrative." *USQR* 34 (1978-79) 159-73.

Wicker, Brian. *The Story-Shaped World: Fiction and Metaphysics: Some Variations on a Theme.* Notre Dame: University of Notre Dame, 1975.

Wiggins, James B., ed. *Religion as Story.* New York: Harper & Row, 1975.

Wilder, Amos N. *Early Christian Rhetoric: The Language of the Gospel.* 2nd ed. Cambridge: Harvard University, 1971.

———. *The New Voice: Religion, Literature, Hermeneutics.* New York: Herder & Herder, 1969.

———. *Theopoetic: Theology and the Religious Imagination.* Philadelphia: Fortress, 1976.

Wittig, Susan. "The Historical Development of Structuralism." *Soundings* 58 (1975) 145-66.

———. "Theories of Formulaic Narrative." *Semeia* 5 (1976) 65-91.

———. "A Theory of Multiple Meanings." *Semeia* 9 (1977) 75-103.

Zuck, John. "Tales of Wonder: Biblical Narrative, Myth, and Fairy Stories." *JAAR* 44 (1976) 299-308.

Appendix 1

Once More, ΠΙΣΤΙΣ ΧΡΙΣΤΟΥ

JAMES D. G. DUNN

1. Introduction

The revitalization of the old debate on the meaning of the Pauline phrase πίστις Χριστοῦ, and particularly as a transatlantic debate, has been one of the most stimulating features of the renewed interest in Pauline theology. The earlier phase was largely an in-house German debate, though W. H. P. Hatch was a prominent contributor.[1] The view that it meant "faith in Christ" (objective genitive) was the dominant opinion. But among advocates of the subjective genitive ("faith of Christ") was G. Kittel.[2] And notable variations included J. Haußleiter's *genitivus auctoris* (faith effected by Christ), A. Deissmann's *genitivus mysticus* (faith experienced in mystical communion with Christ), E. Wißmann's *genitivus confessionis* (confessing faith, acceptance of the Christian message), and O. Schmitz's "characterizing genitive" ("Christfaith").[3]

The opening blast of a new round of debate was sounded in Britain in the 1950s, initially by A. G. Hebert, on the basis of the Hebrew equivalent of πίστις = אֱמוּנָה "faithfulness" (hence the "faithfulness of Christ"),[4] followed

---

1. W. H. P. Hatch, *The Pauline Idea of Faith in Its Relation to Jewish and Hellenistic Religion* (HTS 2; Cambridge, MA: Harvard University Press, 1917).

2. Most recently H. W. Schmidt, *Der Brief des Paulus an die Römer* (THKNT 6; Berlin Evangelische, 1963) 66.

3. See the brief review of the debate in K. Kertelge, *'Rechtfertigung' bei Paulus* (NtA 3; Münster: Aschendorff, 1967, ²1971) 162-66; also R. B. Hays, *The Faith of Christ* (SBLDS 56; Chico: Scholars Press, 1983) 158-62.

4. A. G. Hebert, "'Faithfulness' and 'Faith,'" *Theology* 58 (1955) 373-79.

by T. F. Torrance,[5] responded to by C. F. D. Moule,[6] and squelched by J. Barr.[7] But the cudgels were taken up again on behalf of a subjective genitive reading in the 1960s, particularly on the North American side of the Atlantic, initially by R. N. Longenecker, G. M. Taylor, and G. Howard,[8] and with a substantial wave of support in the 1980s,[9] which has swept the interpretation back across the Atlantic.[10]

It would be natural at this point to note and review the main arguments in favor of the renewedly popular "faith(fulness) of Christ" interpretation. But that is another's brief. Mine is to restate the case for the objective genitive interpretation — "faith in Christ" — though in so doing I will naturally have to address at least the principal arguments brought in favor of a subjective genitive reading. To this task I therefore turn. But first a reminder of the basic data.

As is well known, the phrase itself appears seven times in three of the Pauline letters:

πίστις Ἰησοῦ Χριστοῦ — Rom 3:22; Gal 3:22;
πίστις Ἰησοῦ — Rom 3:26;

5. T. F. Torrance, "One Aspect of the Biblical Conception of Faith," *ExpT* 68 (1956-57) 111-14, 221-22.

6. C. F. D. Moule, "The Biblical Conception of 'Faith,'" *ExpT* 68 (1956-57) 157, 222.

7. J. Barr, *The Semantics of Biblical Language* (London: Oxford University Press, 1961) 187-205.

8. R. N. Longenecker, *Paul, Apostle of Liberty* (New York: Harper & Row, 1964) 149-52; G. M. Taylor, "The Function of πίστις Χριστοῦ in Galatians," *JBL* 85 (1966) 58-76; G. Howard, "On the 'Faith of Christ,'" *HTR* 60 (1967) 459-65; note also M. Barth, "The Faith of the Messiah," *HeyJ* 10 (1969) 363-70, with further bibliography 364-65 n.2; D. W. B. Robinson, "'Faith of Jesus Christ' — A New Testament Debate," *Reformed Theological Review* 29 (1970) 71-81.

9. S. K. Williams, "The 'Righteousness of God' in Romans," *JBL* 99 (1980) 272-78; also "Again *Pistis Christou*," *CBQ* 49 (1987) 431-47; L. T. Johnson, "Romans 3.21-26 and the Faith of Jesus," *CBQ* 44 (1982) 77-90; Hays, *Faith*, ch. 4; S. K. Stowers, "'Ἐκ πίστεως and διὰ τῆς πίστεως in Romans 3.30," *JBL* 108 (1989) 665-74; L. E. Keck, "'Jesus' in Romans," *JBL* 108 (1989) 443-60, here 452-57; R. N. Longenecker, *Galatians* (WBC 41; Dallas: Word, 1990) 87-88; otherwise D. M. Hay, "Pistis as 'Ground for Faith' in Hellenized Judaism and Paul," *JBL* 108 (1989) 461-76, here 473-75. The issue came to the fore in the Pauline Theology Group at the SBL meeting in 1988 but was postponed for full discussion to the 1991 meeting.

10. M. D. Hooker, "Πίστις Χριστοῦ," *NTS* 35 (1989) 321-42, the Presidential Address delivered in Cambridge at the 1989 SNTS meeting, reprinted in *From Adam to Christ: Essays on Paul* (Cambridge: University Press, 1990) 165-86; G. N. Davies, *Faith and Obedience in Romans: A Study of Romans 1–4* (JSNTS 39; Sheffield: JSOT, 1990) 106-10; and now I. G. Wallis, *The Faith of Jesus Christ in Early Christian Traditions* (SNTSMS 84; Cambridge: University Press, 1995).

πίστις Χριστοῦ Ἰησοῦ — Gal 2:16;
πίστις Χριστοῦ — Gal. 2:16; Phil 3:9;
πίστις τοῦ υἱοῦ τοῦ θεοῦ — Gal 2:20.

We should mention also Eph. 3:12 — ". . . Christ Jesus our Lord, in whom we have boldness and access in confidence διὰ τῆς πίστεως αὐτοῦ."

We will proceed by looking first at the form of the phrase itself. And since there is some danger of treating it in too isolated a fashion, we will then look at the way the phrase functions within the context and flow of the argument of each of the three undisputed Pauline letters in which the phrase (πίστις plus genitive referring to Christ) occurs. We will take the letters in their most likely chronological sequence — Galatians, Romans, Philippians. As a shorthand I will use πίστις Χριστοῦ throughout when referring as a whole to the five variations listed above.

2. The Form of the Phrase

There are three grammatical or formal points which should be clarified and put in their proper perspective at the beginning.

2.1. The force of the genitive construction

There is, of course, something seductively attractive about taking the phrase in its most literal English translation — "the faith of Christ." But here the seeming univocal meaning of the English genitive in no way reflects the inherent ambiguity of the Greek when the phrase is taken on its own. If lingering doubts remain, we need simply recall various related instances. (1) The parallel phrase, ἡ γνῶσις Χριστοῦ Ἰησοῦ, is used in close proximity to one of the seven occurrences of our phrase (Phil 3:8-9). No one would think to take "the knowledge of Christ Jesus" as any other than an objective genitive.[11] In this case the English form allows the objective force which seems to be excluded from "the faith of Christ." Similarly with ζῆλος θεοῦ in Rom 10:2, which clearly means "zeal *for* God."[12] (2) In Mark 11:22 we read ἔχετε πίστιν θεοῦ, which can hardly be taken in the sense, "Hold the faith of God," and

11. But see now Wallis, *Faith,* 122-23.
12. C. F. D. Moule, *An Idiom Book of New Testament Greek* (Cambridge: University Press, 1953) 40.

must mean "Have faith *in* God" (cf. the parallel in Matt 21:21 — ἐὰν ἔχετε πίστιν καὶ μὴ διακριθῆτε).[13] Here again, despite the attractiveness of a literal English rendering, no one would think to take the "faith of God" as anything other than an objective genitive;[14] compare also Acts 3:16, ἐπὶ τῇ πίστει τοῦ ὀνόματος αὐτοῦ, "by faith in his name," and 2 Thess 2:13, ἐν ἁγιασμῷ πνεύματος καὶ πίστει ἀληθείας, "by sanctification of the Spirit and faith in the truth."

We must therefore not be misled by the inflexibility of the literal English translation of our phrase, the "faith of Christ." And no one I assume would wish to argue on this basis.[15] There is, then, presumably, no dispute that the syntactical relation of the two words, πίστις and Χριστοῦ, tells us nothing to resolve our disagreement.

2.2. The absence of the definite article

What is the significance of the lack of the definite article in the phrase — πίστις Χριστοῦ, rather than ἡ πίστις Χριστοῦ.[16] I have in mind here the observation of E. D. Burton that when πίστις is accompanied by a subjective genitive "the article is . . . almost invariably present."[17] The point is weakened since the great bulk of the phrases cited by Burton speak of "your faith."[18] But

13. But Wallis, *Faith,* 71, nevertheless asserts that there are no unambiguous cases in the NT where πίστις plus genitive must be interpreted objectively.

14. Hays, *Faith,* 164, rightly notes that Mark 11:22 clearly establishes that πίστις plus objective genitive is NT, first-generation Christian usage. LSJ's failure to note any instance of πίστις plus objective genitive (Robinson 71-72) is of no consequence, since from the beginning Christianity developed its own distinctive "faith" vocabulary — πιστεύειν ἐπί/εἰς. The question, then, is whether and in what way πίστις plus genitive reflects that development. Hays is somewhat disingenuous when he argues that πίστις plus genitive meaning "faith in" cannot be demonstrated in the Pauline corpus (*Faith,* 164), since "faith in Christ" is the only form in which we might expect to find this distinctive Christian usage in Paul, and that is the very phrase which is at issue. More serious for Hays's case is the absence of a verbal equivalent to his understanding of πίστις Χριστοῦ, i.e., "Christ believed"; see further §3.3 below.

15. For further examples of the objective genitive see J. H. Moulton, *A Grammar of New Testament Greek,* Vol. III by N. Turner (Edinburgh: T. & T. Clark, 1963) 211-12.

16. The lack of a second definite article, τοῦ Χριστοῦ, can be adequately explained by the fact that Χριστός by this stage, in Greek-speaking Christianity, regularly functioned as a proper name.

17. E. D. Burton, *Galatians* (ICC; Edinburgh: T. & T. Clark, 1921) 482. The point is taken up by A. J. Hultgren, "*The Pistis Christou* Formulation in Paul," *NovT* 22 (1980) 248-63, here 253, though with a less cautious formulation ("invariably present").

18. This is the basis of the main critique of Hultgren by Williams, "Again," 432-33.

we should note three cases which may give Burton's point force for us.
(1) James 2:1 — ἔχετε τὴν πίστιν τοῦ κυρίου ἡμῶν. In this classic example of
Jewish-Christian paraenesis (James), it is very plausible to read the phrase as
a subjective genitive — "you hold the faith which our Lord Jesus Christ himself displayed."[19] (2) Rev 2:13 — "you do not deny my faith (οὐκ ἠρνήσω τὴν
πίστιν μου)," says the exalted Christ. (3) Rev 14:12 — "those who keep the
commandments and the faith of Jesus (τὴν πίστιν Ἰησοῦ)." In each case we
need to remind ourselves that the faithfulness of Christ (ὁ πιστός) is a particular theme of the seer (Rev 1:5; 3:14; 19:11), as, it would appear, of the more
characteristically Jewish-Christian documents in the NT (Heb 2:17; 3:2;
12:2).[20] So once again it is very likely that in each case the genitive is, if anything, subjective.

We should also simply mention Rom 3:3, τὴν πίστιν τοῦ θεοῦ, "the
faithfulness of God," a clear example of the definite article with the subjective
genitive. And perhaps we should include Col 2:12, διὰ τῆς πίστεως τῆς
ἐνεργείας τοῦ θεοῦ, which Hebert translates "through the faithfulness of the
working of God."[21]

It would appear, then, that Burton's observation has some force.
(a) The genitive phrase "the faith of Christ" *was* used within earliest Christian circles in reference to "the faith(fulness) of Christ" (subjective genitive).
But in the three arguably most clear examples which we have, the phrase
takes the form "*the* faith of Christ," where quite properly and naturally the
definite article denotes the particular faith(fulness) referred to — that of
Christ. Just as in the regular usage which Burton noted — "the faith, that is,
of you." (b) In contrast, it is probably more significant than at first appears
that *all* the phrases which come into dispute in Paul *lack* the definite article.
The fact that it is *all* the disputed cases does suggest that we are confronted
by a regular pattern of speech, where the lack of the definite article is in itself
almost sufficient to indicate that what is in view is *faith* (i.e., faith as exercised by believers in general), rather than *the faith* (i.e., the particular faith of
Jesus himself).[22]

---

19. It may be argued that ἔχετε is more naturally translated, "you hold on to your
[own] faith in our Lord" (cf. 2:18), and that the definite article refers back to the previously
mentioned "faith" (1:3, 6). On the other hand, our third example (Rev 14:12) speaks of
"those who keep . . . the faith of Jesus," where "keeping" is closely parallel to "holding."

20. This consideration has to be weighed against Hays, *Faith*, 187 n.113, who follows
Robinson in regarding the genitives of these texts as "broadly adjectival," denoting "the
[Christian] faith."

21. Hebert, "Faithfulness," 377.

22. Whether it is also significant that the clearest references to Christ's faithfulness

There are, however, two exceptions to the above patterns. One is Eph 3:12, cited above. Here it may be significant, even decisive, that the definite article *is* used — διὰ τῆς πίστεως αὐτοῦ. Should we therefore translate, "through the faith of him," that is, through Christ's faithfulness?[23] If so, it would simply confirm that Burton's observation is sound and that the definite article was the accepted way of indicating that the genitive was subjective in force. But in that case it may be all the more significant that the undisputed, or earlier (if you prefer) Pauline usage is so consistently anarthrous — a recognized way of signalling that the accompanying genitive is objective.

The other exception is potentially more disruptive of the pattern which seems thus far to have emerged. In Rom 4:16 Paul speaks clearly of "the faith of Abraham," where the Greek is again anarthrous — "the one who is ἐκ πίστεως Ἀβραάμ." Here is a key example which indicates that Burton was right to qualify his conclusion that the definite article "almost invariably" denotes the subjective genitive.[24] Whether it merely weakens the force of Burton's point ("almost invariably"), however, or disrupts it entirely, remains unclear. A factor of substantive importance in this case (Rom 4:16) is bound to be the fact that the phrase ἐκ πίστεως is a major leitmotiv in Romans.[25] It must be judged quite likely that Paul unconsciously slipped into (or maintained) the anarthrous use, because in his train of thought in this letter that was his principal prepositional phrase for "justifying faith."[26] It may well be, therefore, that Rom 4:16 should be regarded as a genuine exception (for understandable reasons) to what otherwise was an almost invariable rule within earliest Christian speech.

---

come in the more characteristically Jewish writings of the NT (James, Hebrews, and the Apocalypse of John), and that, in contrast, the anarthrous Pauline phrase comes in passages where Paul is in contentious dialogue with Jewish-Christian views, are points to which we will have to return.

23. So particularly M. Barth, *Ephesians* (AB 34; New York: Doubleday, 1974) 347; Wallis, *Faith,* 128-32. But note the following reference to "the faith" in 3:17, where the definite article points back to the already mentioned faith of 3:12, and where the reference can hardly be other than to the believers' faith through which Christ dwells in their hearts.

24. The issue does not hang on the genitive construction (see §2.1), as Keck, "'Jesus,'" 456 unwisely argues, but on the significance of the absence of the definite article.

25. Rom 1:17 (twice); 3:26, 30; 4:16 (twice); 5:1; 9:30, 32; 10:6; 14:23 (twice).

26. I use "justifying faith" as the shorthand for the faith summed up in Rom 5:1 — "Therefore, having been justified ἐκ πίστεως. . . ." The alternative, διὰ πίστεως, appears only four times, and all in the one section of the argument — Rom 3:22, 25, 30, 31.

2.3. Equivalent phrases

Finally, we need to clarify the possible significance of potentially synony-mous phrases. The deutero-Paulines seem to have developed the formula, "faith *in* Christ Jesus (πίστις [anarthrous] ἡ ἐν Χριστῷ Ἰησοῦ)" (1 Tim 3:13; 2 Tim 1:13; 3:15). An earlier version of it is Eph 1:15 — "your faith in the Lord Jesus (τὴν καθ᾽ ὑμᾶς πίστιν ἐν τῷ κυρίῳ Ἰησοῦ)" — the definite article in this case required, of course, to indicate the particular faith (καθ᾽ ὑμᾶς) in view. This could be significant, since it might indicate that a different phrase was current to denote "faith in Christ," and thus suggest that by "faith of Christ" Paul must have meant something else (Christ's faith). The difficulty of course is precisely that all the instances of the "in" phrase belong to the deutero-Pauline corpus and thus provide no evidence of Paul's own usage or of usage current at the time of Paul.[27] The deutero-Pauline usage therefore gives us no assistance in resolving the force of the genitive constructions in Paul.[28]

Much the same is true of the further variation Col 2:5 — "the firmness of your faith in Christ (τῆς εἰς Χριστὸν πίστεως ὑμῶν)." The problem is that ἡ εἰς Χριστὸν πίστις is a hapax legomenon in Paul, and though the verbal equiv-alent is used in the undisputed Paulines (Rom 10:14?; Gal 2:16; Phil 1:29), the issue of the Pauline authorship of Colossians muddies the discussion and makes it difficult to place much weight on the Col 2:5 usage either way.[29]

The only other variation is Phlm 5 — τὴν πίστιν, ἣν ἔχεις πρὸς τὸν κύριον Ἰησοῦν. But it is difficult to know how much weight to put on this iso-lated example.

---

27. The apparently close parallel of Gal 3:26 is almost certainly to be taken as sequen-tial rather than as integrated prepositional phrases — "for you all are sons of God, through faith, in Christ Jesus," rather than in the deutero-Pauline sense, "through faith in Christ Je-sus" (πάντες γὰρ υἱοὶ θεοῦ ἐστε διὰ τῆς πίστεως ἐν Χριστῷ Ἰησοῦ); so most, e.g., H. Schlier, *Der Brief an die Galater* (KEK; Göttingen: Vandenhoeck & Ruprecht, ⁴1965) 171; and Hays, *Faith*, 169-70. Similarly with the phrasing in Rom 3:25 — ἱλαστήριον διὰ (τῆς) πίστεως ἐν τῷ αὐτοῦ αἵματι — "an atonement, through faith, in his blood"; διὰ (τῆς) πίστεως is usually taken now as a Pauline insertion into a pre-Pauline formula (see, e.g., the bibliography and discussion reviewed in my *Romans* [WBC 38; Dallas: Word, 1988] 161-64). It may indeed be the case that a casual reading of these texts was what gave rise to the deutero-Pauline use. See further below, nn. 43 and 64.

28. The double variation from standard Pauline usage, in Eph 1:15 and 3:12, is typical of the slight distance from Pauline thought which convinces most scholars that Ephesians stems from the circle of Paul's (immediate) associates, after his death, rather than from Paul himself.

29. Elsewhere in the NT it occurs only in Acts 20:21, 24:24, and 26:18 (cf. 1 Pet 1:21).

All we can say, then, is that the deutero-Paulines developed a way of speaking of "faith in Christ" which Paul had not used. The absence of such usage from the undisputed Paulines, with the exception of Phlm 5, may, however, suggest that Paul did not need to use such forms because he had his own form — πίστις Χριστοῦ.[30] If faith was such an important motif for Paul, the absence of such phrases leaves the proponents of the subjective genitive with a somewhat surprising conclusion: *either* πίστις Χριστοῦ is Paul's way of speaking of "faith in Christ," *or* Paul, for some yet-to-be-explained reason, seems to have *avoided* speaking of "faith in Christ."

2.4

In short, not too much significance can be read out of the form of the phrase; though the lack of the definite article does seem to give some support to the inference that whoever's is the faith in view in the Pauline phrase πίστις Χριστοῦ, it would *not* be understood in earliest Christian circles as "the faith of Christ"; and the relative absence from the undisputed Paulines of other phrases denoting "faith in Christ" may indicate that πίστις Χριστοῦ filled that function for Paul.

3. Galatians

3.1

If I understand the arguments in favor of the subjective genitive reading of πίστις Χριστοῦ aright, there are two principal grounds for taking it as a reference to "the faith of Christ" in Galatians. Here and in the following section I refer particularly to the treatments of Hays and Hooker, the two most recent and thoroughgoing expositions of the view.[31] (1) In three of the four occurrences in Galatians there is reference also to the act of believing, using the verb πιστεύειν (Gal 2:16; 3:22); "another reference to the faith of believers would be redundant in a sentence which already refers to those who be-

30. Hultgren, "The *Pistis Christou* Formulation," 254. Williams, "Again," 433-55, surprisingly argues that Paul does not see Christ as the object of faith. But see the two preceding paragraphs, and Williams's attempt to turn πιστεύειν εἰς Χρίστον to his own account (442-43). See also below, n. 60.

31. Hays, *Faith*, 164-70; Hooker, "πίστις Χριστοῦ," 170-75. See also particularly Barth, "Faith of Messiah," 367-68; Williams, "Again"; and Wallis, *Faith*.

lieve."³² (2) The parallel with Abraham which dominates Gal 3:6-9 strongly suggests that πίστις Χριστοῦ is intended as a parallel to the reference to Abraham's faith. Hays develops the point in terms of a representative christology — ". . . Jesus Christ, like Abraham, is justified ἐκ πίστεως and . . . we, as a consequence, are justified *in* him."³³ For Hooker (followed by Wallis) the logic of Paul's argument is clear. The talk is of a sonship of Abraham understood in terms of sharing Abraham's faith. The logic indicates that *the* son of Abraham, Christ (Gal 3:16), also had faith, and that for others to share in that sonship they must share in the faith of the one true seed. This, she maintains, is the force of Gal 3:22: that the promise made to Abraham on the basis of faith is now fulfilled on the basis of Jesus Christ's faith.

3.2

Hays's argument is in danger of overkill. On the surface it seems that he merely wishes to deny that the other references in Galatians 3 point to Christ as the object of faith. In 3:2 and 5, πίστις denotes the Christian faith.³⁴ In 3:6-9 οἱ ἐκ πίστεως probably has the connotation, "those who are given life on the basis of [Christ's] faith."³⁵ In 3:11, ὁ δίκαιος ἐκ πίστεως ζήσεται (Hab 2:4), the reference is once again to Christ's faith,³⁶ the implication being (though Hays does not spell it out clearly) that this conclusion carries with it the ἐκ πίστεως of 3:12 and the διὰ τῆς πίστεως of 3:14.³⁷ In 3:23, 25 the "coming of the faith" is virtually identified with the coming of Christ himself,³⁸ with the consequence that the ἐκ πίστεως of 3:24 (as also 5:5) is best understood as referring, once again to "the faith [that is, of Jesus Christ]."³⁹

Thus, almost without realizing it, we find that every reference to πίστις in the body of Galatians has been swept up into the defence of the subjective

32. Hooker "πίστις Χριστοῦ," 173. So also, e.g., Williams, "Righteousness," 273-74; Keck, "'Jesus,'" 454, though I am puzzled at Keck's claim that "faith in *Christ*" (my emphasis) "separates Christ from justification, which now depends solely on human believing"; Wallis, *Faith,* 71 (three references in as many lines would be "strained").

33. Hays, *Faith,* 165-66; he argues back from Eph 3:12, without raising the issue of the significance of the definite article (see §2.2 above).

34. Hays, *Faith,* 143-49. Cf. 1:23.

35. Hays, *Faith,* 200-202.

36. Hays, *Faith,* 150-57; similarly Wallis, *Faith,* 111-12.

37. Hays, *Faith,* 206-12.

38. Cf. 3:26 (Hays, *Faith,* 169-70).

39. Hays, *Faith,* 228-32.

genitive. On Hays's logic even 3:2, 5 and 5:6 would most obviously be taken as a reference to Christ's faith: "the message of faith," that is, of Christ's faith (3:2, 5; also 1:23); "faith working through love," that is, Christ's faithfulness coming to effect through his (or God's) love (5:6).[40] More to the point, on Hays's thesis we have no clear reference to the "faith" of believers. There are two such references using the equivalent verb (2:16 and 3:22). But Hays leaves us with no noun counterpart, no noun to denote the Galatians' act of believing. Hays's thesis vacuums up every relevant reference to "faith" in Galatians in order to defend the subjective genitive reading of 2:16, 20 and 3:22.[41] This is nothing short of astonishing. It now appears that a text (Galatians) which has provided such a powerful charter of "justifying faith" for Christian self-understanding *nowhere* clearly speaks of that "faith."[42]

Two questions cannot be avoided. (1) If "faith" as a reference to *Christ's* faith filled such an overwhelmingly prominent role in Galatians, why does it appear at best fleetingly elsewhere?[43] On Hays's thesis Paul could speak of it as something well known, which would require no explanation when first mentioned in what is at least potentially ambiguous phrasing (2:16), an un-

---

40. "Through love" is occasionally taken as referring to God's love (G. S. Duncan, *The Epistle to the Galatians* [Moffatt; London: Hodder, 1934] 157-58), despite the obvious elaboration in 5:13-14 of the thought in 5:6.

41. Only 5:22, where πίστις is normally taken as denoting "trustworthiness" rather than "faith," would be exempt.

42. To argue that the phrase includes reference both to Christ's faith and to faith in Christ (so particularly Williams, "Righteousness," 276-78; "Again," 437, 443-46) is surely to overload it; to be meaningful to his readers such a phrase would have to be unpacked by Paul not only in terms of Christians believing (which he does) but also in terms of Christ believing (which he does not).

43. "Nowhere does the apostle speak plainly of Jesus as believing, trusting, or displaying *pistis* as 'faithfulness'" (Hay, "Pistis," 474). So far as Romans is concerned, Hays limits his case to Rom 3:21-26 (*Faith*, 170-74). If Rom 3:25 includes a pre-Pauline formulation, of which διὰ τῆς πίστεως was an integral part (so particularly S. K. Williams, *Jesus' Death as Saving Event* [Missoula: Scholars, 1975] 41-51; though see above, n. 27), it could be argued that πίστις there (in the pre-Pauline formula) referred to the well-known concept of Christ's faith (but see below, n. 66); though once again the thesis assumes an established and widespread usage which surpisingly (if so established and widespread) is otherwise hardly attested. And at the level of *Paul's* use of the formula, the echo of διὰ τῆς πίστεως in 3:30 and 31 hardly encourages the suggestion that Paul referred the πίστις in any case to *Jesus'* faith (despite Stowers; see below, n. 63), since the "faith" in question is clearly the medium by which justification comes to the believer, as in the case of Abraham (Rom 4). We should perhaps note that Hays does *not* take the "faith" references in 3:30-31 as referring to Christ's faith in his "'Have we found Abraham to be our forefather according to the flesh?' A Reconsideration of Rom 4:1," *NovT* 27 (1985) 76-98.

derstanding of the Christian message which could be summed up simply in the word "faith," that is, the faith of Christ (1:23; 3:2, 5, 23, 25). But where is the other evidence from outside the Pauline corpus that this was a recognized and central theme of early Christian preaching and self-understanding?[44] Where in the Gospel tradition, by means of which the first Christians maintained the memory of Christ's ministry, is there any emphasis on "the faith of Christ?" The fact that Hays's thesis makes Galatians stand out as so exceptional within the wide sweep of earliest Christianity must surely sound a warning note; the thesis is in danger of self-condemnation by *reductio ad absurdum*.

(2) Too little asked is the further question, What does "the faith of Christ" mean? To what does it refer? The answer is hardly clear.[45] The ministry of Jesus as a whole? The death of Christ in particular? The continuing ministry of the exalted Christ in heaven? Neither the first nor the last of these is a prominent theme in Paul. And while a reference to the death of Christ would fit well within Paul's theology, it is not clear how that would explain the διά forms of the phrase in 2:16 and 3:14, 26. What would Paul mean by saying "through Christ's faithfulness" in his life and/or on the cross? A more likely expression of the point would be διά plus accusative ("on account of"), equivalent to ἐκ plus the genitive ("on the basis of"), rather than διά plus genitive ("through" the medium of). It is true that Paul has a concept of the death of Christ as in some sense an ongoing event, if that is the right way to put it (cf. 2:19; 6:14), but he never expresses it in a διά formula. And if the reference

44. The verses reviewed in §2.2 (James 2:1 apart) do not provide strong evidence for first-generation Christian usage. Hooker, "πίστις Χριστοῦ," 178-79 suggests that the πίστις of 2 Cor 4:13 refers to Christ's faith. But a reference back to Christ's death and resurrection under that motif would be surprising here. (1) The "belief" is more naturally linked to the immediately associated Psalm quotation, "I believed"; elsewhere it is Paul's custom to quote scripture *after* an assertion, to back up that assertion. (2) The fuller phrase is "the same Spirit of faith" and is more naturally referred to the Spirit inspiring (or the spirit inspired to write) the words of the psalm. (3) The belief in the first clause is presumably the believing of the last clause; "the same spirit/Spirit" is the inspiring Spirit (inspired spirit) which brings belief to speech and witness. See further, e.g., V. P. Furnish, *2 Corinthians* (AB 32A; New York: Doubleday, 1984) 257-58.

45. Williams, "Again," illustrates the vagueness of the phrase as used in the current debate. At 444 he takes it to refer to "Christ's own openness to God," "the mode of personal existence which Christ pioneered" (thus unconsciously slipping into the language and motifs of Hebrews rather than of Paul). But in commenting on Gal 2:19-20 he takes "the faith of the Son of God" as defined by the relative clauses, "who loved me and gave himself for me" (445). And later on he defines it as "that relationship to God which Christ exemplified, that life stance which he actualized" (446) — but is this Paul?

is to the exalted Christ, then we would expect Paul to speak of Christ directly, rather than of his faith: thus in 6:14, δι' οὗ referring to Christ ("through whom"), as also in Rom 1:5 and 5:11.

I therefore find myself quite unconvinced by Hays's thesis.

3.3

Hooker does not try to be so ambitious, limiting the thrust of her exposition to the key reference 3:22 in context. For her the pressure to read 3:22 as a reference to Christ's faith grows out of the argument of 3:15ff. that Christ is the one true seed of Abraham. For her the logic is that Christ must therefore have shared Abraham's faith, have believed as Abraham believed. But is this Paul's logic? I think not.

Had it been so, Paul must surely have brought it out more clearly, that is, by saying directly that Christ believed as Abraham believed. Had that indeed been Paul's point, that Christ as Abraham's seed believed as Abraham believed, he could have said so quite straightforwardly. In 3:26 in particular rather than the potentially confusing "You are all sons of God through faith in Christ Jesus," Paul could have said so much more clearly, "You are all sons of God in Christ Jesus who believed." The lack of a verbal equivalent to the noun phrase, "the faith of Christ," is as weakening to Hooker's case as is the loss of a noun equivalent to the act of "justifying faith" (πιστεύειν) in Hays's case.[46]

More to the point, Paul's logic is manifestly different from that which Hooker follows. Paul's problem was to demonstrate that *non*-Jews could be counted Abraham's children. His answer was in terms of Gentiles believing as Abraham believed; they were his children because they shared his faith — "sons of" = sharing the same characteristic attitude and status before God (3:7).[47] But Jesus as a Jew did not require this special concession. And as Messiah he could be regarded as the "seed" of Abraham in a preeminent sense. Paul signals this difference in status between Christ and Christians by defining Christ's relation to Abraham solely in terms of the word "seed"; as "son" Christ is only to be understood as "God's son" (1:16; 2:20; 4:4, 6).

The logic of Paul's argument is that Christians are Abraham's children

---

46. See also above, n. 14.

47. "Son of" as denoting a share in a particular characteristic or quality would be familiar particularly to those familiar with semitic thought (BDB, בֵּן 8), but it was also a Greek idiom (BAGD, υἱός 1cδ).

by a *twofold* action — by sharing in Abraham's faith (3:7), and by being "in Christ" (3:28-29). The climax of the argument in 3:26ff. is quite clear: "you are all sons/children of God, (1) through faith, (2) in Christ Jesus."[48] The first phrase (1) sums up the line of argument in the first half of the chapter, the first half of the twofold action (3:1-14). The second phrase (2) sums up the force of the argument in the second half of the chapter (3:15ff). "Sons of Abraham" *through faith* are also "seed of Abraham" *in Christ* (3:28-29).

Hooker has thus merged the two strands of Paul's argument, and her thesis arises from the resulting confusion.[49] It does not follow that because Christ was Abraham's seed he shared Abraham's faith. By allowing that the οἱ ἐκ πίστεως of 3:6-9 refers to believers who share Abraham's faith,[50] Hooker has weakened her case regarding 3:22. For ἐκ πίστεως referring to Gentiles' faith, like that of Abraham in 3:6-9, probably has the same reference in 3:22: now that the promise has been fulfilled, the faith which "justified" in 3:6-9 can be defined more accurately as "faith in Jesus Christ" (the promised seed). In fact, as Hays seems to have appreciated, for the subjective genitive thesis to carry weight in regard to 3:22 it really does need to draw in all the other πίστις references with it. But that pushes us back into the *reductio ad absurdum* argument already exposed.

3.4

In pointed contrast to both Hays and Hooker, I would have to say that on the more natural reading, the text does speak precisely and consistently of "justifying faith," including the disputed πίστις Χριστοῦ passages.

a) In Gal 2:16 the antithesis between "works of the law" and πίστις Χριστοῦ is central, and is most naturally understood as Paul's way of posing the alternatives on the human side on the basis of which, ἐκ (according to the opposing Christian views), one might hope to be justified.[51] To speak of the redundancy of expression (one verb phrase, two noun phrases) is to miss the point. This is Paul's first clear statement on this theme so central to his own

48. See above, n. 27.
49. Williams, "Again," 437-47, and Wallis, *Faith,* 105-15, are open to the same criticism.
50. Hooker, "πίστις Χριστοῦ," 170-71.
51. Cf. B. L. Martin, *Christ and the Law in Paul* (NovTSupp 62; Leiden: Brill, 1989) 116. The choice of the hitherto unusual phrase πίστις Χριστοῦ may be simply explained by the rhetorical desire to have a simple two-word antithesis to ἔργα νόμου. The unusual parallel between πνεῦμα δουλείας and πνεῦμα υἱοθεσίας in Rom 8:15 is probably to be explained in the same way.

understanding. We should not be surprised, then, if he repeats himself in two synonymous formulations for the sake of emphasis and clarity. After all, he has no hesitation in emphasizing the correlated (οὐκ) ἐξ ἔργων νόμου no less than three times. So we can fairly translate ". . . knowing that a person is *not* justified by works of the law *but only* through faith in Jesus Christ,[52] we too *have* believed in Christ Jesus, *precisely* in order that we might be justified by faith in Christ, and *not* by works of the law. . . ."

b) In Gal 2:20 the πίστις τοῦ υἱοῦ τοῦ θεοῦ form is defined by the relative clauses, "who loved me and gave himself for me." But these are versions of the standard *pistis*-formula (confessional formula);[53] that is, they are most naturally understood as describing confessional faith rather than the act of Christ's faithfulness.

c) In 3:2 and 5 ἐξ ἀκοῆς πίστεως is best understood as "hearing with faith" or "the hearing which is faith,"[54] on the parallel not least with ὑπακοὴ πίστεως (Rom 1:5).[55]

d) The implication of 2:16 (synonymous formulations repeated for emphasis) is borne out in 3:6-9 where again it is most obvious to see the verbal and noun phrases used interchangeably.

3:6 — Abraham believed (ἐπίστευσεν) God, and it was reckoned to him for righteousness (εἰς δικαιοσύνην).

3:8 — God justifies (δικαιοῖ) the Gentiles by faith (ἐκ πίστεως).

The parallel is straightforward: God justifies on the basis of faith, whether the faith of Abraham or that of Gentiles. Abraham provides the pattern of faith. Those who express the same faith (3:6, 9) thus share in the same blessing (justification), are blessed with Abraham, the man of πίστις (3:9), and thus are truly his sons (3:7).[56] In contrast, to argue that the references here could only be understood in the light of the subsequent portrayal of Christ as alone the "seed" of Abraham (3:16) would mean that the crucial argument of 3:6-9 was likely to be lost on the Galatian audiences.

52. The argument here is not dependent on my understanding of the flow of thought between 2:15 and 16; see my "The New Perspective on Paul," *Jesus, Paul and the Law* (London: SPCK/Louisville: Westminster, 1990) 204 n. 25, 208-9, 212.

53. W. Kramer, Christ, *Lord, Son of God* (London: SCM, 1966) 118 (§26b).

54. See now S. Williams, "The Hearing of Faith ΑΚΟΗ ΠΙΣΤΕΩΣ in Galatians 3," *NTS* 35 (1989) 82-93.

55. Martin, *Christ*, 118. Contrast Wallis's labored formulation "the Spirit is received within or under the auspices of the dispensation of faith fulfilled in Christ" (*Faith*, 107-8).

56. See above, n. 47.

262

e) Likewise in 3:14 — ". . . in order that we might receive the promise of the Spirit through faith." Here too it is most natural to take the phrase διὰ τῆς πίστεως as a reference to the medium on the human side through, or to, which (cf. 3:2) the Spirit was given.[57] Had Paul wished to specify the divine medium through which the Spirit was given we would have expected something like "through whom,"[58] that is, through Christ himself A reference to Christ's faith is much less natural.

f) In 3:22 once again it is at least as plausible to take the double reference to faith/believing as Paul's way of reinforcing the importance of his argument — "in order that the promise which is by faith in Jesus Christ might be given [precisely] to those who believe." Apart from anything else, the reading is quite natural grammatically (§2.2) and avoids the problems posed by the sudden injection of thought of Jesus' faith already noted (§3.3).

g) Proponents of "the faith of Christ" interpretation seem to forget that Paul has a way of speaking of the divine source, medium, resource by means of which his saving power comes to effect. It is the word which in traditional Christian theology has always stood as the counterpart on the divine side to the human exercise of faith — "grace." 1:6 — God "who called you in the grace of Christ"; 1:15 — God "who called me through his grace"; 2:21 — "I do not annul the grace of God"; 5:4 — "you have fallen away from grace." The most natural reading throughout Galatians is summarized in the classic formulation — justified by grace through faith.

3.5

The irony of the subjective genitive reading of πίστις Χριστοῦ, therefore, is that in order to sustain it, other unqualified references to "faith" have to be taken as echoing or pointing forward to that meaning, "[Christ's] faith." Which leaves Paul's teaching on how Gentile and Jew receive the blessing of divine acceptance with a very large and unexplained hole in it. Conversely, if even a few of these intermediate references are taken as referring to human faith, the act of believing, the noun version of the verb phrase, it becomes increasingly difficult to maintain that the particular πίστις Χριστοῦ references point to something different.

---

57. The usual view, including now Williams, "ΑΚΟΗ ΠΙΣΤΕΩΣ," 88, arguing against Hays.

58. See above, §3.2(2).

4. Romans

4.1

Here the arguments are if anything more straightforward and focus on the double use of the phrase in 3:22 and 26.[59] (1) Again there is the problem of redundancy in 3:22 — διὰ πίστεως Ἰησοῦ Χριστοῦ εἰς πάντας τοὺς πιστεύοντας. (2) There seems to be a close parallel between πίστις Ἰησοῦ and πίστις Ἀβραάμ (3:26; 4:16). (3) Hays notes also the parallel with πίστις θεοῦ (3:3). (4) And Hooker presses the parallel between Christ and Adam; "if men and women are faithless, we may expect Christ to be faithful."[60]

4.2

(1) On the problem of redundancy the matter is resolved simply. "Why would Paul need to add εἰς πάντας τοὺς πιστεύοντας?" asks Hays. Precisely in order to emphasize the πάντας, is the obvious answer: "the righteousness of God through faith in Jesus Christ to *all* who believe." Students of Romans will not need to be reminded that this "all" is a thematic word in the letter, being used again and again, often with varying degrees of redundancy, and precisely as a means of emphasis (see particularly 1:5, 16; 2:10; 4:11, 16; 10:4, 11-13). The usage in 3:22 is simply part of a sustained motif.[61]

4.3

(2) The failure to be clear on whether Paul meant the "faith of Christ" or the "faithfulness of Christ" is a good deal more critical than has been appreciated by the proponents of the subjective genitive thesis. For in fact just such a distinction seems to have been crucial to Paul's exposition of Abraham's faith in

---

59. On 3:25 see above, n. 43 and below, §4.4.

60. Hays, *Faith*, 170-72; Hooker, "πίστις Χριστοῦ," 168-70. Hays also rightly notes that Romans is thoroughly theocentric, but draws the dubious conclusion that Christ is never unambiguously presented as an object of faith (as Williams, "Again," above, n. 30); this is surely to treat 9:33 and 10:11, 14 in too cavalier a fashion. Similarly the difficulty of making sense of the idea of God's righteousness being revealed through faith (in Jesus Christ) is greatly exaggerated in view of 1:17.

61. Keck, "'Jesus,'" 456, conveniently misses out the πάντας τούς in his quotation of 3:22.

chap. 4. The point which has been wholly ignored in the debate thus far is that Paul was in effect attacking the traditional Jewish understanding of Abraham which saw him as the archetype of *faithfulness*. As passages like Sir 44:19-21 and 1 Macc 2:52 (not to mention James 2:21-23) clearly show, Abraham was held up in Jewish piety as one of the supreme examples of "faithfulness" under trial, in his willingness to offer up Isaac. More to the point for Paul, as the same passages also show, Gen 15:6 was typically interpreted in Jewish circles by reference to Abraham's faithfulness thus displayed.[62]

Paul's response was twofold. First to insist that Gen 15:6 had to be understood prior to and independent of the later accounts both of Abraham's circumcision (4:9-15), and, by implication, of Abraham's offering of Isaac. And second, in consequence, to argue that Abraham's πίστις meant his faith, his naked trust in God's promise (4:16-22), and therefore *not* his "faithfulness." We must see, then, that for Paul's πίστις Χριστοῦ to be understood of Christ's faithfulness would be to play into the hands of his Jewish-Christian opponents: Abraham's faith (= faithfulness) was a prototype of Jesus' faithfulness and so could continue to serve as a model of Jewish-Christian covenant faithfulness. In sharp contrast Paul insists that Abraham was a model of *faith* = trust. But where then does that leave the parallel between 3:26 and 4:16? Did Paul intend to present Christ as an example of that same sheer naked trust? To what would he be referring, since a reference to Christ's faithfulness to death (the more natural parallel if parallel was sought) seems to be excluded? And why again does Paul fail to bring out the parallel more clearly? In point of fact he ends his exposition of Abraham's faith in the way that makes most sense of the objective genitive reading "faith was reckoned for righteousness to Abraham on our account also, to those who believe [as did Abraham — 4:17] in him who raised Jesus our Lord from the dead" (4:22-24). What is in view throughout is faith in the life-giving power of God (manifested in the conception of Isaac, and in the resurrection of Christ), not faithfulness (either of Abraham or of Christ).[63]

We may pursue the point a little further. For if Paul's intention had been to parallel Abraham's faith and Christ's, we would have expected a rather fuller and rather different treatment of Abraham, focusing precisely on Abraham's faith(fulness) in offering Isaac and paralleling it to Christ's faith-

62. See further my *Romans*, 200-201.

63. This also undermines Stowers's attempt to take the ἐκ πίστεως and διὰ πίστεως of Rom 3:30, 31 as references to Christ's faithfulness: "the heroic merit of Jesus was the means by which God provided an expiation" (670); "because of Abraham's faithfulness God established a covenant of righteousness for all his descendants" (673). But this interpretation cuts right against the grain of Romans 4.

(fulness) in offering himself on the cross. Now there is a generally recognized allusion to the offering of Isaac in 8:32 — "he who did not spare his own son. . . ."[64] The difference is that the parallel is between *God* and Abraham, not between Jesus and Abraham. This underlines the conclusion just drawn, that the point of chap. 4's exposition is to demonstrate what "justifying faith" is, to draw a parallel between Abraham's faith and the faith of all who believe in God's life-giving power, not to draw a parallel between Christ and Abraham.

4.4

(3) The reference to God is a reminder that Paul has a concept in Romans of what we might call simply "divine faith." Indeed, it is one of the major themes of the letter, often underestimated in significance because talk of "God's faith" is explicit as such only at 3:3. What is too easily missed is the fact that for a Jew like Paul talk of "the truth of God" carried the same connotation, since אֱמוּנָה and אֱמֶת could be translated equally by ἀλήθεια or πίστις. Hence the theme is actually very prominent in 3:3-7, a passage which is a railway junction for most of Paul's main lines of thought in the letter, and in the climax of 15:8.[65] In my judgment it is also present in the ἐκ πίστεως of 1:17, possibly in the διὰ (τῆς) πίστεως of 3:25,[66] and implicit in the quotation of 15:11,[67] as well as underlying the whole thrust of chaps. 9–11. What is noticeable throughout this theme is the variety of ways in which Paul refers to it and draws it in.

Of course it is arguable that πίστις Χριστοῦ is an equivalent reference to the faithfulness of Christ. But in contrast to the anarthrous πίστις Χριστοῦ, it is noticeable that the reference in 3:3 has the definite article (τὴν πίστιν τοῦ θεοῦ), in line with the "almost invariable" practice noted above (§2.2). And if, *ex hypothesi*, the faithfulness of Christ is so important for Paul, why then is it

---

64. See, e.g., my *Romans*, 501, and those cited there.

65. Δικαιοσύνη θεοῦ (3:5) overlaps with but is not synonymous with ἡ πίστις τοῦ θεοῦ, and ἡ ἀλήθεια τοῦ θεοῦ (3:3, 7), the first phrase, is the more general, embracing God's relationship as Creator to the world as a whole (3:5-6), hence its characteristic anarthrous form; whereas the last two phrases refer specifically to God's covenant faithfulness, hence the definite article.

66. This is more likely than a reference to the faithfulness of Christ, since what is being described is the action of God; but see above, nn. 27 and 43, and B. W. Longenecker, "ΠΙΣΤΙΣ in Romans 3.25: Neglected Evidence for the 'Faithfulness of Christ,'" *NTS* 39 (1993) 478-80.

67. See my *Romans* on each passage.

referred to only in the two grammatically ambiguous phrases in 3:22 and 26, in contrast to the far richer theme of God's faithfulness? Why no reference to Christ as πιστός, as he has to God elsewhere too (1 Cor 1:9; 10:13; 2 Cor 1:18; 1 Thess 5:24)?[68] We could push the argument still further. To understand πίστις Χριστοῦ as referring to *Christ's* faithfulness would not only weaken the emphasis on human faith (like that of Abraham) but also confuse and even divert attention from the emphasis on *God's* faithfulness. What Paul is calling for throughout Romans is for faith in God's faithfulness, faith like that of Abraham, faith in the one who now embodies in eschatological fulness that faithfulness, *God's* faithfulness, not Christ's.[69]

4.5

(4) Finally, as to the parallel between Christ and Adam (Hooker).[70] Perhaps all we need to note here is what Paul does *not* say. According to Hooker's statement of the subjective genitive thesis, the logic is simply crying out for Paul to make the precise antithesis which Hooker herself makes — between Adam's faithlessness and Christ's faithfulness. But Paul does not make it.[71] The sequence of antitheses in 5:15ff. was the ideal point at which to make clear beyond doubt that he was thinking of Christ as the prototype of faith. What would have been more natural, on Hooker's thesis, than that Paul should add to the antitheses between παράπτωμα and χάρισμα, between Adam's παρακοή and Christ's ὑπακοή, the further antithesis between Adam's ἀπιστία and Christ's πίστις? But he fails to do so. Does this not suggest that Hooker's logic has once again diverged from Paul's? The parallel/contrast between Adam and Christ is rich and resonant, but it evidently did *not* include the thought of Christ undoing Adam's faithlessness by means of his own faith in God.[72]

68. 2 Thess 3:3 and 2 Tim 2:13 are the only exceptions in the Pauline corpus.

69. The same is true of 2 Cor 1:17-22 — a reference to *God's* faithfulness, not Christ's (*pace* Hooker, "πίστις Χριστοῦ," 177-78), though we might speak of God's faithfulness incarnated in Christ (as does Torrance, "One Aspect," 114, elaborating Hebert, "Faithfulness," 375-76).

70. So also particularly Barth, "Faith," 366-67.

71. Despite Johnson, "Romans 3:21-26," 88-89.

72. Perhaps indicative of the state of the question is Hooker's expostulation, "If Paul does not use this idea, then he ought to!" ("Πίστις Χριστοῦ," 168). Since in Rom. 5:14-21 Paul resisted that inviting "ought," the implication is rather that he did *not* wish to speak of Christ's faith, even in one of the two most explicit Adam/Christ parallels.

4.6

For all these reasons I find myself being pushed strongly to the conclusion that the subjective genitive reading of πίστις Χριστοῦ in Romans is simply an example of mistaken exegesis.

5. Philippians

The one remaining example, in Phil 3:9, can be treated briefly. Hooker's arguments are simply the application of considerations we have already encountered. (1) The redundancy of two mentions of faith — "not having my own righteousness which is ἐκ νόμου, but that which is διὰ πίστεως Χριστοῦ, the righteousness ἐκ θεοῦ ἐπὶ τῇ πίστει."[73] (2) The parallel with Adam. In 3:7-8 Paul speaks of the reversal of values which marked his conversion. Hooker finds in the threefold use of ἡγέομαι ("I considered loss/rubbish") an echo of Christ's *kenosis* in 2:6-7 (ἡγήσατο), and suggests that the pattern of interchange between Christ and the believer, which she finds elsewhere in Paul, reappears here in another version. Christ's *kenosis* provides a model for Paul's own experience. This suggests that the διὰ πίστεως Χριστοῦ "ought to refer to the obedient self-surrender of Christ, that is, to his faithfulness."[74]

The parallel with Adam at this point, however, is rather remote, and the argument ignores the distinctiveness of the section in which the phrase occurs — 3:2-16. For the more immediate context is dominated by the same issues which have featured so strongly in the earlier passages. How is it that God reckons righteousness to humans? Is it because they are Jews, circumcised, of the race of Israel (3:4-5), who live fully "within the law" (3:6)? That was Paul's old view and status. It is that which he had reacted against. And once again the contrast he poses is in terms of faith — the righteousness which is through faith in Christ, the righteousness which is from God to that faith.

Three considerations strongly support this reading. (1) The repetition of both "righteousness" and "faith"; Paul was evidently concerned to emphasize a point here. Once again it is a matter of emphasis rather than of redundancy. (2) The lack of the definite article with the first reference to "faith" (διὰ πίστεως Χριστοῦ) once again probably tells against the reading "the faith of Christ" and indicates an objective genitive, "faith in Christ." (3) Conversely, it

---

73. So also Keck, "'Jesus,'" 455-56.
74. Hooker, "πίστις Χριστοῦ," 175-77; so also Wallis, *Faith,* 118-24.

is also to be noted that the second reference to faith is *not* anarthrous — ἐπὶ τῇ πίστει. This must mean that Paul was referring to the same faith both times — "the faith," that is, the faith just mentioned. His Greek would be scarcely intelligible if he meant the first πίστις to refer to Christ's faith and the second πίστις to "justifying faith." Once again, then, the subjective genitive reading overshoots the mark. In order to sustain the claim that the first reference is to Christ's faith, the second must be so interpreted as well; *both* of the crucial references must be referred to Christ's self-surrender on the cross. And at the crucial point in the brief polemic we find the same hole as before; the vital means by which the righteousness actually comes to the individual is left unexplained.

In short, here too a subjective genitive reading of the text begins to look more and more like a forced reading rather than the most natural reading of the text.

6. Conclusion

I should make it clear that the *theology* of the subjective genitive reading is powerful, important and attractive. For anyone who wishes to take the humanness of Jesus with full seriousness "the faith of Jesus" strikes a strong and resonant chord. Moreover, as a theological motif, it seems to me wholly compatible with Paul's theology; that is, not a component of Paul's theology but consistent with other emphases. As Hooker has noted, it follows naturally when we bring together the thought of God in Christ and the thought of God's faithfulness. It is an attractive variant on the Adam motif of Christ's obedience. None of this, however, is to the particular point at dispute. That focuses on the meaning Paul intended when he dictated the phrase πίστις Χριστοῦ. And on this point I remain wholly convinced that Paul intended his audiences to hear that phrase in the sense "faith in Christ."

This conclusion is based on the three major findings of the above discussion. (1) There are good grammatical grounds for affirming the objective genitive reading and denying the subjective genitive reading of πίστις Χριστοῦ. (2) The traditional "faith in Christ" makes consistently good sense of the line of thought in each case, with repetition serving to reinforce the claim being made. On the other hand, insistence on reading πίστις Χριστοῦ as a subjective genitive runs the risk of throwing other, clear lines of Paul's argument in some confusion. (3) Outside the phrase in dispute there is nothing that can be called a clear reference to Christ's faith (as such). At this point the agency of Christ in Paul is consistently described in other ways ("in/through/

to Christ"), but nowhere else in terms of Christ's own faith or faithfulness. A thesis built solely on a disputed phrase is usually likely to be wrong.

In consequence I find myself rather puzzled as to why the subjective genitive interpretation is being pushed with such fervor. In line with the above findings, the simplest and most coherent exegesis of the disputed phrase is surely to conclude that Paul did *not* intend to be understood as speaking of Christ's faith, but only of "faith in Christ."

Additional Note

In the debate at Kansas City my chief criticisms of Hays's paper were as follows.

Hays all the while seems to be working from what he perceives to be the narrative underlying Paul's theology as set out in his letters (his main thesis in *Faith*), *rather than from the actual argument of the letters themselves, and to do so in a way which ignores the terms and thrust of the argument actually used.* It is against the background of that underlying narrative that he reads *pistis Christou* as a reference to Christ's faith/faithfulness. The trouble is that neither Galatians nor Romans is a narrative but an argument. And it is the specific terms of these arguments themselves which determines the sense of *pistis Christou* as denoting faith in Christ.

a) Most striking is the way in which Hays treats Rom 3:21-26 in isolation from its immediate context — 3:19-20 and 3:27-31 (see below, pp. 282-84). (i) Thus he ignores the fact that the alternative against which Paul is polemicizing is *erga nomou* (3:19-20) — *pistis* as the opposite of *erga nomou*. The clear implication is that *pistis* is something on the human side of the salvation process. (ii) And when we look at the other end of the sequence (3:19-31), it is surely clear beyond dispute that *pistis* in 3:27-31 means human believing. How odd, then, if *pistis* in the central section should be so (exclusively for Hays) focused on Christ's faithfulness, whereas the follow through is exclusively focused on human faith. Something jars here. Hays has evidently taken his understanding of *pistis Christou* from the hypothesized underlying narrative rather than from the sequence and logic of the argument actually used by Paul.

b) The same is true with his treatment of Romans 4. When we understand the Jewish evaluation of Abraham and the context of the exposition of Gen 15:6 offered by Paul, it becomes clear how Abraham's *pistis* = trust offers a genuine and direct alternative to *erga nomou* (= works of the law, such as, not least, his circumcision and offering of Isaac). To argue that *pistis* = Abraham's faithfulness cuts quite against the grain of the argument. And for Abraham's *pistis* to be understood as a prefiguration of Christ's faithfulness would undermine Paul's argument, since it would be playing directly into the hands of those who opposed Paul (by maintaining the traditional view of Abraham as counted righteous because of his faithfulness when tested in the matter of Isaac).

c) The same problem arises for Hays from his reading of Galatians. A crucial factor is the consistency in the *pistis/pisteuein* references — a consistency demanded by the actual argument used. Hays seems to recognize this since, as I pointed out in my paper, the logic of his exposition virtually forces him to draw in *all* the *pistis* references to his thesis as denoting Christ's faith. But the most straightforward reading of the bulk of the *pistis/pisteuein* passages in Galatians is surely as references to the act/attitude of (human) believing. Thus the coherence of the flow of the argument actually used pushes strongly for the conclusion that all the *pistis* references (including *pistis Christou*) denote human faith. I do not recall Hays responding to one of my questions to him on this point: whether he would accept any of the *pistis* references in Galatians as denoting human believing in Christ. I'm still waiting for an answer.

The problem confronting Hays at this point is, once again, that he can sustain his interpretation of Galatians 3:22 in particular only by reading it against the underlying narrative which he reconstructs, rather than from the actual course of Paul's argument in Galatians 3. And in so doing he throws the actual argument of Galatians 3 into some confusion: what is the human response to the gospel to be if it is not *erga nomou?* According to Hays, and despite the most obvious reading of Galatians 3, Paul does not actually answer that question.

Appendix 2

Πίστις and Pauline Christology:
What Is at Stake?

RICHARD B. HAYS

Were there a Purgatory — though those of us who live and work in Paul's theological world have reason to suppose there is not — sinful scholars would surely be assigned the purifying ordeal of reading their own dissertations. Those who had especially many sins to atone for would be given the task of reworking their dissertations (perhaps, Sisyphus-like, ever anew) to conform to the wisdom conferred by experience. For my many sins, the Pauline Theology Group has given me a foretaste of purgatorial fire by asking me to revisit the question of how to interpret Paul's notoriously enigmatic expression Ἰησοῦ Χριστοῦ ("faith of/in Jesus Christ").

The discussion has moved forward significantly in the years since I completed my book *The Faith of Jesus Christ*,[1] and there have been several important new contributions to the debate.[2] Many interpreters of Paul have

---

1. R. B. Hays, *The Faith of Jesus Christ: An Investigation of the Narrative Substructure of Galatians 3:1–4:11* (SBLDS 56; Chico: Scholars, 1983).

2. Especially noteworthy are D. M. Hay, "*Pistis* as 'Ground for Faith' in Hellenized Judaism and Paul," *JBL* 108 (1989) 461-76; M. D. Hooker, "ΠΙΣΤΙΣ ΧΡΙΣΤΟΥ," *NTS* 35 (1989) 321-42 [her 1988 SNTS Presidential Address]; L. E. Keck, "'Jesus' in Romans," *JBL* 108 (1989) 443-60; D. Campbell, *The Rhetoric of Righteousness in Romans 3.21-26* (JSNTSup 65; Sheffield: JSOT Press, 1992); S. K. Stowers, *A Rereading of Romans: Justice, Jews, & Gentiles* (New Haven: Yale University Press, 1994); I. G. Wallis, *The Faith of Jesus Christ in Early Christian Traditions* (SNTSMS 84; Cambridge: Cambridge University Press, 1995); a series of important articles by S. K. Williams: "Again *Pistis Christou*," *CBQ* 49 (1987) 431-47; "Justification and the Spirit in Galatians," *JSNT* 29 (1987); "*Promise* in Galatians: A Reading of Paul's Reading of Scripture," *JBL* 107 (1988) 709-20; and "The Hearing of Faith: ΑΚΟΗ ΠΙΣΤΕΩΣ in Galatians 3," *NTS* 35 (1989) 82-93; and the detailed studies of D. Campbell: "The Meaning of

become convinced that the genitive in πίστις Ἰησοῦ Χριστοῦ should be understood to be subjective,[3] but others, such as J. D. G. Dunn, remain unconvinced, preferring instead the objective genitive interpretation: that πίστις Ἰησοῦ Χριστοῦ refers to "faith in Jesus Christ," the Christian's act of "faith directed toward Christ as the object."[4]

ΠΙΣΤΙΣ and ΝΟΜΟΣ in Paul: A Linguistic and Structural Perspective," *JBL* 111 (1992) 91-103; "Romans 1:17 — A *Crux Interpretum* for the ΠΙΣΤΙΣ ΧΡΙΣΤΟΥ Debate," *JBL* 113 (1994) 265-85.

3. Without presuming to offer a comprehensive bibliographical survey, I note the following supporters of this view who have taken a position on the question since 1981 (for earlier literature, see Hays, *Faith of Jesus Christ*, 139-91, and G. Howard, "On the 'Faith of Christ,'" *HTR* 60 [1967] 459-65; idem, "The Faith of Christ," *ExT* 85 [1974] 212-15); L. T. Johnson, "Romans 3:21-26 and the Faith of Jesus," *CBQ* 44 (1982) 77-90; B. Byrne, *Reckoning with Romans* (Wilmington, DE: Glazier, 1986) 79-80; T. L. Donaldson, "The 'Curse of the Law' and the Inclusion of the Gentiles: Galatians 3.13-14," *NTS* 32 (1986) 94-112; L. Gaston, *Paul and the Torah* (Vancouver: University of British Columbia Press, 1987), especially p. 12; M. L. Soards, "Assessing Paul's 'Faith' Talk in Galatians" (paper read in SBL Pauline Epistles Section, 1989); S. K. Stowers, Ἐκ πίστεως and διὰ τῆς πίστεως in Romans 3:30," *JBL* 108 (1989) 665-74; idem, *A Rereading of Romans: Justice, Jews and Gentiles* (New Haven: Yale University Press, 1994), 194-226; B. Witherington III, "The Influence of Galatians on Hebrews," *NTS* 37 (1991) 146-52; idem, *Paul's Narrative Thought World* (Louisville: Westminster/John Knox, 1994) 267-72; G. Howard, *Paul: Crisis in Galatia*, 2nd ed. (SNTSMS 35; Cambridge: Cambridge University Press, 1990); idem, "Faith of Christ," *ABD* 2.758-60; C. B. Cousar, *A Theology of the Cross: The Death of Jesus in the Pauline Letters* (Minneapolis: Fortress, 1990) 39-40; G. N. Davies, *Faith and Obedience in Romans* (JSNTS 39; Sheffield: JSOT, 1990) 107-12; R. N. Longenecker, *Galatians* (Word Biblical Commentary; Dallas: Word, 1990) 87-88, 93-94, 145; B. R. Gaventa, "The Singularity of the Gospel: A Reading of Galatians," in J. Bassler (ed.), *Pauline Theology, Volume I* (Minneapolis: Fortress, 1991), 147-59; J. L. Martyn, "Events in Galatia: Modified Covenantal Nomism versus God's Invasion of the Cosmos in the Singular Gospel: Response to Dunn and Gaventa," in J. Bassler (ed.), *Pauline Theology, Volume I*, 160-79; P. T. O'Brien, *The Epistle to the Philippians* (NIGTC; Grand Rapids: Eerdmans, 1991); F. J. Matera, *Galatians* (Sacra Pagina 9; Collegeville, MN: Liturgical Press, 1992); B. W. Longenecker, "ΠΙΣΤΙΣ in Romans 3.25: Neglected Evidence for the 'Faithfulness of Christ'?" *NTS* 39 (1993) 478-80; C. A. Davis, *The Structure of Paul's Theology* (Lewiston, NY: Mellen, 1995), 62-72; N. T. Wright, "Romans and the Theology of Paul," in D. M. Hay and E. E. Johnson (eds.), *Pauline Theology, Volume III* (Minneapolis: Fortress, 1995), 37-38; also the articles of Hooker, Keck, Williams, and Campbell (see n. 2 above). The NRSV has now given "the faith of Jesus Christ" a place in the footnotes as an alternative translation.

4. Dunn, *Romans 1–8* (Word Biblical Commentary; Dallas: Word, 1988) 178. Others continuing to assert the "traditional" (since Luther) objective genitive interpretation include J. Barclay, *Obeying the Truth: A Study of Paul's Ethics in Galatians* (Edinburgh: T. & T. Clark, 1988); F. F. Bruce, *Commentary on Galatians* (NIGTC; Grand Rapids: Eerdmans, 1982); G. F. Hawthorne, *Philippians* (WBC 43; Waco, TX: Word, 1983); M. Silva, *Philippians* (Wycliffe Exegetical Commentary; Chicago: Moody, 1988); R. Y. K. Fung, *The Epistle to the Galatians*

Indeed, at the 1988 meeting of the Pauline Theology Group, Prof. Dunn, observing the pronounced shift in North American scholarship towards the "faith of Jesus Christ" position, compared this movement to the headlong rush of the Gerasene swine into the sea. In response, I likened him to the Gerasene swineherds who begged Jesus to go away and leave them alone. Clearly, rhetorical tensions were rising, and the *kairos* for judgment was at hand. The steering committee of the Pauline Theology Group decided to ask Professor Dunn and me to elucidate our disagreement in a manner somewhat more exegetical and somewhat less dependent on typological interpretation of Mark 5. Hence, the present essay.

1. Framing the Question

Upon rereading *The Faith of Jesus Christ* ten years later, I remain unrepentant concerning the central thesis of my earlier work:[5] Paul's theology must be understood as the explication and defense of a *story*. The narrative structure of the gospel story depicts Jesus as the divinely commissioned protagonist who gives himself up to death on a cross in order to liberate humanity from bondage (Gal 1:4; 2:20; 3:13-14; 4:4-7). His death, in obedience to the will of God,

---

(NICNT; Grand Rapids: Eerdmans, 1988); G. W. Hansen, *Abraham in Galatians* (JSNTSup 29; Sheffield: JSOT Press, 1989); A. Hultgren, "The *Pistis Christou* Formulations in Paul," *NovT* 22 (1980) 248-63; W. Johnson, "The Paradigm of Abraham in Galatians 3:6-9," *TrinJ* 8 NS (1987) 179-99; S. Westerholm, *Israel's Law and the Church's Faith* (Grand Rapids: Eerdmans, 1988); V. Koperski, "The Meaning of *Pistis Christou* in Philippians 3:9," *LS* 18 (1993) 198-216; R. A. Harrisville, "ΠΙΣΤΙΣ ΧΡΙΣΤΟΥ: Witness of the Fathers," *NovT* 36 (1994) 233-41. Of course, all the older standard commentaries on Romans and Galatians represent the objective genitive interpretation, and this continues to be the majority view among European scholars.

A mediating position is taken by B. Dodd ("Romans 1:17 — A *Crux Interpretum* for the ΠΙΣΤΙΣ ΧΡΙΣΤΟΥ Debate?" *JBL* 114 [1994] 470-73), who is sympathetic to subjective genitive ("christological") readings of some of the key texts but who argues that each instance must be considered individually. C. H. Cosgrove (*The Cross and the Spirit: A Study in the Argument and Theology of Galatians* [Macon, GA: Mercer University Press, 1988] 57-58) takes a different tack, arguing that πίστις Χριστοῦ should be understood as metonymy for Paul's gospel of God's apocalyptic work in Christ: "Christ-Faith means God's eschatological action in Christ toward those who believe." This position is close to that of W. Schenk ("Die Gerechtigkeit Gottes und der Glaube Christi," *TLZ* 97 [1972] 161-74), who saw more clearly than most subsequent interpreters that Ernst Käsemann's apocalyptic interpretation of "the righteousness of God" also required a reinterpretation of Paul's understanding of πίστις.

5. I am, however, somewhat repentant about the methodological overkill of the piece. Some of the methodological preliminaries I would now gladly consign to the flames.

is simultaneously a loving act of faithfulness (πίστις) to God and the decisive manifestation of God's faithfulness to his covenant promise to Abraham. Paul's uses of πίστις 'Ιησοῦ Χριστοῦ and similar phrases should be understood as summary allusions to this story,[6] referring to Jesus' fidelity in carrying out this mission. Consequently, the emphasis in Paul's theology lies less on the question of how we should dispose ourselves toward God than on the question of how God has acted in Christ to effect our deliverance. Indeed, this last sentence is a tolerable summary of the message of Paul's letter to the Galatians.

I must, in all candor, confess some puzzlement that these theses can be regarded as controversial. Nevertheless, many learned readers of Paul disagree vigorously with some or all of these claims. How is the disagreement to be resolved? Should my earlier arguments be revised, supplemented, or improved? What is at stake in the debate?

The ongoing discussion of Pauline theology — within this group and elsewhere — has brought several matters into clearer focus since the writing of *The Faith of Jesus Christ,* and I have learned a number of things from specific critiques of my work. It has become increasingly evident that the interpretation of πίστις 'Ιησοῦ Χριστοῦ must be placed within the wider sphere of Paul's theology as a whole and — at the same time — within the sphere of the contingent argumentation of the letters in which this phrase appears.

With the wisdom of hindsight, I see six areas in which my earlier presentation of the evidence requires refinement and elaboration. They are as follows:

(1) The cultural/semantic background of Paul's πίστις language: how would Paul's uses of this terminology have been understood by his readers within the ancient Mediterranean world?

(2) The contingent circumstances of the letters to the Galatians and to the Romans: how does the πίστις Χριστοῦ language function within Paul's response to the politically sensitive Jew/Gentile issues that elicited these letters?

(3) Pauline christology: what is Paul's conception of the significance of Jesus' death, and how do other christological passages in his letters shed light upon the interpretation of Paul's πίστις Χριστοῦ expressions?

6. In the terminology of the dissertation (following Northrop Frye), the summarizing phrase πίστις 'Ιησοῦ Χριστοῦ encapsulates the *dianoia* of the story: its overall sense, in contrast to its *mythos* (plot line).

(4) The apocalyptic character of Paul's thought: how does the πίστις Χριστοῦ motif relate to Paul's conviction that God has acted through Christ to inaugurate the turn of the ages?

(5) Intertextual echoing of the OT as a generative factor in Paul's theology: does Paul's use of OT texts shed light on the passages in which the πίστις Χριστοῦ motif appears?

(6) Paul's insistence that the gospel constitutes the fulfillment of God's covenant promises to Israel:[7] what does πίστις Χριστοῦ have to do with the theme of God's faithfulness, which is particularly dominant in Romans?

When our question is located within the framework of these broader considerations, it becomes possible to give a more complete and satisfying account of the meaning of πίστις ᾽Ιησοῦ Χριστοῦ in Pauline theology. In the present essay, I do not attempt a systematic discussion of the above six topics (to do so would produce another book at least as long as the dissertation); instead, I offer a programmatic sketch of the way in which I now believe the question should be approached, considering the handful of πίστις Χριστοῦ passages in a way that is attentive to these factors. I shall concentrate primarily on Romans, for two reasons: (1) Because I dealt with Romans only glancingly in *Faith of Jesus Christ*, a fuller treatment of the problem there may be illuminating; (2) Romans — with its extended theological argument addressed to readers unfamiliar with Paul's teaching — gives us the best chance of placing the contested phrase in its proper theological context.

Little is to be gained by rehearsing the familiar arguments about syntax. I stand by my earlier judgment that the balance of grammatical evidence strongly favors the subjective genitive interpretation and that the arguments for an objective genitive are relatively weak.[8] Such syntactical arguments are, however, finally inconclusive. The objective genitive is a possible construal, and there are at least two passages where Paul does use the verb πιστεύειν with Χριστὸν ᾽Ιησοῦν (or the equivalent) as its object (Gal 2:16; Phil 1:29; cf. also Rom 10:12 and Col 2:5).[9] (It is an interesting fact — not always fully appreci-

---

7. See the important essays by N. T. Wright, *The Climax of the Covenant* (Edinburgh: T. & T. Clark, 1991).

8. See *Faith of Jesus Christ*, 164. For detailed evidence, see Howard's early essays on the topic (n. 3, above). The recent exchange between Hultgren ("*Pistis Christou* Formulations") and Williams ("Again *Pistis Christou*") demonstrates again how strongly the lexical and syntactical arguments weigh in favor of the subjective genitive.

9. This has always been the strongest evidence in favor of the objective genitive interpretation. See now, however, Williams' very provocative discussion of Gal 2:16 ("Again *Pistis Christou*," 442-44).

ated by defenders of the objective genitive interpretation — that such passages are relatively rare in Paul; more characteristically, he speaks of God [Rom 4:3, 5, 17, 24; Gal 3:6; cf. 2 Tim 1:12; Tit 3:8] or of the content of the proclaimed *gospel* [Rom 6:8; 10:9, 16; 1 Cor 15:11; 1 Thess 4:14] as the object of faith, or he uses the verb absolutely, with no expressed object.) Our interpretative decision about the meaning of Paul's phrase, therefore, must be governed by larger judgments about the shape and logic of Paul's thought concerning faith, Christ, and salvation. Indeed, rather than defining the debate as a dispute between subjective genitive and objective genitive readings, we would do better to speak — as some recent essays have suggested — of a distinction between the *christological* and *anthropological* interpretations of πίστις Χριστοῦ. The christological reading highlights the salvific efficacy of Jesus Christ's faith(fulness) for God's people; the anthropological reading stresses the salvific efficacy of the human act of faith directed toward Christ.

What is required is an attempt to understand how πίστις 'Ιησοῦ Χριστοῦ functions within the construction of Paul's arguments. The following survey, then, is offered not as a definitive exegesis of the pertinent passages but as a "reading," seeking to show how the subjective genitive makes sense out of the texts.

2. Πίστις Χριστοῦ in Romans

For methodological reasons, the investigation should begin with Paul's Letter to the Romans.[10] Because Paul had not founded the Roman church(es?) and had not previously taught there, his letter must set forth a relatively self-explanatory exposition of the gospel. Though he presupposes that the Romans do know a number of things about Jesus and the gospel[11] — he is, after all, writing to Roman Christians to whom he can say ἡ πίστις ὑμῶν καταγγέλλεται ἐν ὅλῳ τῷ κόσμῳ (Rom 1:8) — he cannot rely upon the signifying power of the compressed, allusive formulations that he employs in Galatians to remind his readers of his own earlier preaching. Thus, we have a better chance of grasping Paul's πίστις language if we "take our seat in the Roman congregation," as J. Louis Martyn might recommend, and listen to the way in which the discussion unfolds.

10. In *Faith of Jesus Christ,* I deliberately undertook to discuss Galatians because it seemed the more difficult case. Here I pursue a different tack.

11. See the discussion in Keck, "'Jesus' in Romans," for a reconstruction of what Paul assumes they do know.

Faith-Obedience (1:5)

In Rom 1:5, we encounter the thematic phrase ὑπακοὴ πίστεως ("obedience of faith"), which is to be understood as an epexegetical construction virtually equating the two nouns. Paul has received his apostleship from Jesus Christ "to bring about faith-obedience among all the Gentiles," who are called — as Paul explains later — to present their bodies as a living sacrifice (12:2) in obedience to God. Thus, from the letter's first sentence we find obedience and faith closely correlated. We also find that ὑπακοὴ πίστεως evidently describes a particular response to the proclaimed gospel. This supposition is confirmed by Paul's thanksgiving in 1:8 that "your faith" (i.e., the faith of the Roman Christians) is widely known. (It is worth noting that in the expression ἡ πίστις ὑμῶν the genitive is clearly subjective: Paul's sentence does *not* mean, "Faith in you Romans is proclaimed in the whole world.") Similarly, in 1:12, where Paul hopes that "we may be mutually encouraged by each other's faith," Paul thinks of πίστις, whatever its precise nuance, as an attribute or disposition characterizing the members of the church. Similar usages are to be found in 11:20, 14:1, and throughout chapter 4 (re: Abraham).

By Faith for Faith (1:17)

The next reference to πίστις, a crucial one for our purposes, appears in Paul's programmatic formulation of the gospel (1:16-17), where it is anchored by his citation of Hab 2:4. The fundamental assertion comes first: the gospel is "the power of God for salvation to everyone who believes (παντὶ τῷ πιστεύοντι), to the Jew first and also to the Greek." Paul here articulates four key motifs: (a) the gospel as God's saving power, (b) the importance of human response in faith, (c) the priority of Israel in God's saving design, and (d) the inclusion of the Gentiles. Following in v. 17 is the warrant for the claims of the previous verse: the righteousness of God is being revealed ἐκ πίστεως εἰς πίστιν, καθὼς γέγραπται· ὁ δὲ δίκαιος ἐκ πίστεως ζήσεται ("by faith for faith, just as it is written, 'the Righteous One will live by faith'").

For the purposes of our present discussion, I do not need to argue the case that the ἐκ πίστεως 1:17a refers to God's faithfulness eschatologicially revealed in the gospel, so that the phrase ἐκ πίστεως εἰς πίστιν means "from [God's] faithfulness for [our] faith." Dunn has already marshalled compelling arguments for this interpretation.[12] God's πίστις is his covenant faithfulness

---

12. *Romans 1–8*, 44. Campbell ("Romans 1:17 — A *Crux Interpretum*," 269), declaring

(cf. 3:3), which endures and overcomes all human unfaithfulness. When Paul affirms that the righteousness of God is revealed ἐκ πίστεως, he is pointing to the source of the revelation. The phrase "from faith for faith" then becomes a rhetorically effective slogan to summarize the gospel message of a salvation that originates in God's power and is received trustingly by the beneficiaries of that power. As J. Haussleiter remarked over a century ago, the Greek πίστις does not require the writer or reader to make the distinction between *"Treue"* and *"Glaube"*: both ideas are contained in the single term.[13] The difficulty of appreciating this semantic nuance contributes to the confusion surrounding the whole discussion of the meaning πίστις in Paul. (A similar reciprocal interplay of divine and human πίστις is found also, e.g., in Philo, *De Abr.* 273: ὃς τῆς πρὸς αὐτὸν πίστεως ἀγάμενος τὸν ἄνδρα πίστιν ἀντιδίδωσιν αὐτῷ, τὴν δι' ὅρκου βεβαίωσιν ὧν ὑπέσχετο δωρεῶν ["(God), marvelling at Abraham's faith towards him, repaid him with faith by confirming with an oath the gifts which he had promised"]. Here, however, Abraham's faith seems to elicit the divine πίστις rather than, as in Paul, vice versa.)

The Function of the Habakkuk Citation

Rom 1:17 provides decisive evidence that Paul's use of the peculiar locution ἐκ πίστεως is derived from Hab 2:4. When Paul first introduces the phrase, he explicitly cites the text to show the Romans where it comes from. As Douglas Campbell has pointed out, ἐκ πίστεως occurs in Paul's letters *only* in Romans and Galatians, that is, only in the two letters where he quotes Hab 2:4.[14] This observation supports my earlier suggestion that ἐκ πίστεως is an exegetical catchphrase that alludes to the Habbakuk text.[15] Once the phrase is established within the theological vocabulary of a particular letter, it can be used in contexts that have nothing to do with the exegesis of Habakkuk

---

that Rom 1:17 is "'the Thermopylae' of the πίστις Χριστοῦ debate in Romans," contends that it must be held "with blood and tears" by defenders of the christological interpretation and suggests (269 n. 16) that my concurrence with Dunn here constitutes premature surrender of a crucial point. This overstates the issue. Romans certainly is — as Dunn and I agree — about the eschatological faithfulness of God. To allow this interpretation of 1:17a does not necessarily determine all subsequent uses of πίστις in the letter, nor does it preclude a christological interpretation of 1:17b.

13. J. Haussleiter, "Der Glaube Jesu Christi und der christliche Glaube," *NKZ* 2 (1891) 136.

14. Campbell, "Πίστις and Νόμος," 100-101.

15. *Faith of Jesus Christ*, 150-57.

(e.g., Rom 14:23),[16] but it surely originates in Paul's reading of the prophetic passage.

Equally crucial, and certainly more controversial, is the suggestion that Paul understands Hab 2:4 as a messianic prophecy now brought to fulfillment through the death and resurrection of Jesus.[17] This is one interpretative proposal in *Faith of Jesus Christ* that has encountered much skepticism, even from critics who otherwise found the book's argument persuasive. It seems to me, however, that in Romans 1 a number of factors encourage us to give this messianic hypothesis a serious hearing.

Paul's quotation of Hab 2:4 in Rom 1:17 supports his assertion that the righteousness of God is revealed in the gospel (taking the antecedent of αὐτῷ ["it"] to be τὸ εὐαγγέλιον ["the gospel"] in 1:16). How, we should ask ourselves, is the righteousness of God revealed in the gospel? In the opening of the letter, Paul declares that the εὐαγγέλιον θεοῦ was "prepromised (προεπηγγείλατο) through his prophets in holy writings concerning his Son, . . . Jesus Christ our Lord" (1:1-4).[18] Thus, when we find a prophetic holy writing (Hab 2:4) quoted as the epigraph to Paul's exposition of the gospel, it is not unreasonable to suppose that Paul regards this text as a prefiguration of God's Son. If so, then Jesus Christ would be the means of the revelation of God's righteousness ἐκ πίστεως ("by faith"). (See below on Rom 3:21-26.)

This interpretation would be particularly attractive if it could be shown (1) that Hab 2:4 was already understood in first-century Judaism as a messianic prophecy and/or (2) that ὁ δίκαιος ("the Righteous One") was an established epithet for the eschatological deliverer.

(1) The first of these proposals was defended in *Faith of Jesus Christ* (1983, pp. 151-56); to my arguments there should be added the observations

16. In the discussion of this issue in the Pauline Theology Group in Kansas City, Robert Jewett raised the interesting possibility that passages such as Rom 14:22-23 might reflect a formula or slogan of one group in Rome, presumably the "strong" in faith. It is difficult to know how this intriguing hypothesis might be tested. In the absence of other evidence, it is simpler to treat the expression ἐκ πίστεως as Paul's own formulation, derived from his reading of Habakkuk.

17. This position is now also defended by Campbell, "Romans 1:17 — A *Crux Interpretum*," 281-85.

18. Most commentators prefer to connect the phrase περὶ τοῦ υἱοῦ αὐτοῦ (v. 3) directly back to εὐαγγέλιον θεοῦ (v. 1). This is a highly artificial interpretation, apparently influenced by the fact that Paul, unlike Matthew and John, does not usually argue that Jesus is the fulfillment of OT prophecy. But this objection fails to reckon with the fact that Paul is probably employing traditional language here. In any case, no hearer of the text of Rom 1:1-4, read aloud, would fail to connect περὶ τοῦ υἱοῦ αὐτοῦ with the immediately preceding phrase ἐν γραφαῖς ἁγίαις.

of August Strobel, *Untersuchungen zum eschatologischen Verzögerungsproblem auf Grund der spätjudisch-urchristlichen Geschichte von Habakuk 2,2ff*,[19] and now also D.-A. Koch, "Der Text von Hab 2.4b in der Septuaginta und im Neuen Testament,"[20] both of whom accept the position, already taken by T. W. Manson, C. H. Dodd, and A. T. Hanson, that the LXX has rendered the text of Hab 2:2-4 in a way that shows unmistakable signs of a messianic interpretation.

(2) The second proposal, that ὁ δίκαιος is a common messianic title, seems to me to be beyond dispute. In addition to the clear NT evidence (Acts 3:14, 7:52, 22:14, 1 Pet 3:18 [echoing Isa 53:11], and 1 John 2:1 — I leave aside the disputed Pauline passages), we have evidence in the Similitudes of Enoch (see 1 Enoch 38:2; 53:6; cf. also 39:6; 46:3; 48:2; 62:5ff.) of a figure called the Righteous One who appears at the scene of eschatological judgment as a revealer and executor of divine justice. Since I have gathered these texts and discussed their exegesis in an essay elsewhere,[21] I will not repeat my arguments here. The point is simply that first-century Jews and Christians were well acquainted with the use of "the Righteous One" as a title for the agent of God's eschatological justice.[22]

These arguments suggest that a messianic interpretation of Hab 2:4 is both historically possible and contextually meaningful in Rom 1:17. It remains to be seen whether the development of Paul's argument will sustain the hypothesis that God's righteousness is somehow revealed through the πίστις of the Righteous One, Jesus Messiah.

---

19. (NovTSup 2; Leiden: Brill, 1961), especially pp. 47-56.

20. *ZNW* 76 (1985) 73 n. 25.

21. "'The Righteous One' as Eschatological Deliverer: A Case Study in Paul's Apocalyptic Hermeneutics," in J. Marcus and M. L. Soards (eds.), *Apocalyptic and the New Testament: Essays in Honor of J. Louis Martyn* (JSNTSup 24; Sheffield: JSOT Press, 1988) 191-215.

22. For a different, nonmessianic interpretation of Hab 2:4 in later rabbinic Judaism, see Ecclesiastes Rabbah on Eccl 3:9 ("What gain has the worker from his toil?"): "Solomon said: Since there are times for all things, what advantage has the labourer in his work and the upright man in his uprightness? . . . R. Isaac b. R. Marion said: *But the righteous shall live by his faith* (Hab. II,4) means that even the Righteous One who lives for ever lives from His faith" (*Midrash Rabbah* VIII, trans. A. Cohen [London: Soncino, 1939] 83). Here "the Righteous One" is interpreted as a reference to God, not the Messiah. This is in keeping with the well-known tendency of rabbinic literature to deemphasize messianic themes. Nonetheless, if the rabbis could speak of God himself as living by faith (even though this is admittedly an unusual text), the early Christians might have found no awkwardness in speaking of the faith of Jesus the Christ.

The Faith of Jesus Christ Manifests God's Righteousness (3:21-26)

In Rom 1:18–3:20 Paul depicts, in stark contrast to the righteousness of God, the ungodliness and unrighteousness of God's human creatures. Gentile and Jew alike, they have failed to glorify God. With or without the Law, they have turned away into rebellion and delusion. The whole world stands under the wrath of God, subject to God's righteous judgment. In the midst of this devastating indictment of human unrighteousness, Paul pauses to reflect plaintively on the situation of God's chosen people (3:1-20), those who were supposed to be "a priestly kingdom and a holy nation" (Exod 19:6). Tragically, despite the privileges with which they were entrusted (3:2: ἐπιστεύθησαν — note the continuing wordplay), they too have fallen under the power of sin (3:9), as Israel's own Scriptures forcefully attest (3:10-20).

All of this ineluctably forces the critical question that surfaces in 3:3: "Will their faithlessness (ἀπιστία) nullify the faithfulness of God (τὴν πίστιν τοῦ θεοῦ)?" Will God's election of a people turn out to be fruitless? Of course, Paul's question (introduced by μή) demands a negative answer. The faithfulness of God — his resolute adherence to his covenant — demands that he be true even if everyone be false. In 3:3-8, Paul emphatically rejects the notion that God's faithfulness can be thwarted, and he asserts three apparently synonymous attributes of God: ἡ πίστις τοῦ θεοῦ, θεοῦ δικαιοσύνη, and ἡ ἀλήθεια τοῦ θεοῦ ("the faithfulness of God, God's righteousness, and the truthfulness of God," 3:3, 5, 7).[23] He does not yet, however, explain *how* God is to prevail over human unrighteousness. Is it merely through the act of pronouncing condemnation, as 3:9-20 might suggest?

The answer at last comes in Rom 3:21-26. How does God's πίστις/δικαιοσύνη prevail? The righteousness of God has been made manifest (note the perfect tense πεφανέρωται) διὰ πίστεως ᾽Ιησοῦ Χριστοῦ ("through the faithfulness of Jesus Christ"), whom God put forward to demonstrate his own righteousness. This notoriously dense passage contains dozens of exegetical difficulties, but I propose the following interpretation. God has solved the problem of human unrighteousness and Israel's unfaithfulness by putting forward as a sacrifice the one perfectly faithful human being, Jesus. Though others rebelled and refused to give glory to God, he remained faithful. His death is an act of πίστις: human πίστις — the counterweight to Israel's ἀπιστία ("unfaithfulness") — because it is an act of perfect obedience through which many will be made righteous vicariously (5:19), and divine

23. See the analysis of this passage in R. B. Hays, "Psalm 143 and the Logic of Romans 3," *JBL* 99 (1980) 107-15.

πίστις because it affirms God's unbreakable love: "God proves his love for us in that while we still were sinners Christ died for us" (5:8). (Here we might want to give serious consideration to David Hay's suggestion that πίστις can mean "pledge" or "objective basis for faith": "Jesus is a pledge or assurance from God that makes human faith possible."[24]) Christ's death is — mysteriously — an act of divine love and faithkeeping (cf. 15:8).

The pivotal point in this discussion is the meaning of δικαιοσύνη θεοῦ. As long as interpreters maintained the notion that this phrase signified a status of righteousness imputed by God to believers, it was possible to make sense of Ἰησοῦ Χριστοῦ in 3:22 as an objective genitive: the status of righteousness is conferred through the believer's faith in Jesus Christ. (This reading leaves the phrase εἰς πάντας τοὺς πιστεύοντας ["for all who believe"] as a peculiar redundancy and renders the choice of the verb πεφανέρωται ["has been made manifest"] puzzling, but I let these issues pass for now.) However, it should be beyond dispute that the "righteousness" in question in 3:21-22 is God's own righteousness (subjective genitive), just as in 3:3-7 and 3:25-26.[25] Paul is framing an argument concerning theodicy, insisting that God's way of dealing with humanity through the gospel is a manifestation of his justice, not an arbitrary dissolution of his promises to Israel. Romans 3 is a defense of God's justice.[26] Once that point becomes clear, the objective genitive interpretation of πίστις Ἰησοῦ Χριστοῦ becomes virtually unintelligible. What would it mean to say that God's justice has been made manifest through our act of believing in Jesus Christ? This, if it means anything at all, verges on blasphemous absorption in our own religious subjectivity. God's eschatological justice can only have been shown forth by an act of God: Paul's claim is that the death of Jesus is just such an apocalyptic event.

24. Hay, "*Pistis* as 'Ground for Faith,'" 472. I differ from Hay's proposal because it seems to me to accord insufficient attention to the way in which Rom 3:1-8 functions to define πίστις θεοῦ as God's covenant faithfulness. Still, it makes far better sense of Rom 3:22 than does the objective genitive interpretation. One problem with Hay's article is that he fails to give sufficient weight to his own observation that "In the LXX, which uses *pistis* fifty-seven times, the 'evidence' sense is generally absent" (462). Given the importance of the LXX in constituting Paul's theological vocabulary, this fact deserves more attention, especially since in Romans and Galatians Paul seems to be grounding his discussion of faith in Genesis and Habakkuk.

25. Cf. Hays, "Psalm 143." I would now contend — on the basis of OT sources of the language — that δικαιοσύνη θεοῦ means God's covenant faithfulness. See my article on "Justification," *ABD* 3.1129-33.

26. For a fuller exposition of this interpretation, see R. B. Hays, *Echoes of Scripture in the Letters of Paul* (New Haven: Yale University Press, 1989) 36-54.

In light of these observations, it is still not easy to decide whether the difficult διὰ (τῆς) πίστεως ("through faith") in 3:25 refers to God's faithfulness (probably not directly), Christ's faithfulness in accepting death on the cross (the likeliest option),[27] or the faith whereby hearers of the gospel receive the atoning benefits of Christ's death (since δικαιοσύνη θεοῦ ["God's righteousness"] is, after all, manifested εἰς πάντας τοὺς πιστεύοντας ["for all who believe," 3:23]). If Paul means the last of these three possibilities, he certainly has not made himself very clear. The emphasis of the whole passage is on God's action in putting forward Jesus Messiah, who enacts the faith-obedience that Israel failed to render, who thereby glorifies God as faithless human creatures had failed to do and constitutes, through his resurrection, the beginning of a new humanity (cf. chaps. 5 and 6),[28] whom God has "predestined to be conformed to the image of his Son" (8:29). Because this manifestation of God's saving righteousness has taken place χωρὶς νόμου ("apart from law"), through Christ's action, the new humanity includes Jews and Gentiles without distinction. Nonetheless, the faithfulness of Jesus is at the same time the manifestation of God's covenant faithfulness (here again, the wordplay on πίστις is important) to Israel, as Paul will argue in Romans 9–11 and 15:8-9.

The paragraph concludes in 3:26 with the affirmation that God's act of putting forth Jesus Christ was undertaken "so that [God] himself might be just precisely by justifying[29] the one who shares the faith of Jesus." I continue to resist the temptation of reading, with D L Ψ 33 614 et al., δικαιοῦντα τὸν ἐκ πίστεως Ἰησοῦν (= "by justifying Jesus ἐκ πίστεως"). This manuscript tradition shows that a significant number of interpreters in the church later found no difficulty with the idea that Jesus was justified by faith, but the meaning of Paul's expression (reading τὸν ἐκ πίστεως Ἰησοῦ ["the one who shares the faith of Jesus"]) is better illuminated by the parallel expression in Rom 4:16: τῷ ἐκ πίστεως Ἀβραάμ ("to the one who shares the faith of Abraham"). The parallelism between 3:26 and 4:16 is a fatal embarassment for all interpreters who seek to treat Ἰησοῦ as an objective genitive.

27. I am persuaded on this point by S. K. Williams, *Jesus' Death as Saving Event* (HDR 2; Missoula: Scholars Press, 1975) 41-51.

28. The discussions of Keck, Hooker, and Wright, though differing in emphasis from one another, are particularly alert to these themes.

29. I take the καί to be epexegetical.

The Faith of Abraham (4:1-25)

One argument frequently urged against understanding πίστις Ἰησοῦ Χριστοῦ as "faith of Jesus Christ" is that when Paul wants to offer a "model" of faith, he points not to Jesus (as does the Letter to the Hebrews — see especially Heb 12:2), but to Abraham. This argument, however, neglects the contextual argumentative purpose of Paul's appeals to the figure of Abraham.

In the case of Galatians, Paul does not pick Abraham out of the air as an example. We should probably accept the suggestions of C. K. Barrett[30] and J. Louis Martyn[31] that Abraham was introduced into the Galatian discussion by Paul's opponents, the Jewish-Christian "Teachers" who were urging the Galatians to receive circumcision as Abraham did. Paul, seizing the opportunity afforded by Gen 15:6, offers a subversive counterreading of the Abraham story that seeks to enlist Abraham against the Teachers (see especially Gal 4:21).

In the case of Romans 4, Paul brings Abraham into the argument neither because he is looking for models of faith, nor because he is seeking in some general way to explain how justification takes place. Rather, he appeals to Abraham in defense of the claim that his gospel does not nullify the Law (Rom 3:31). The structure of the argument positively requires him to produce evidence *from Scripture* that will demonstrate the continuity between Torah and gospel. To cite kerygmatic traditions about Jesus here would not serve his purpose at all. His argument requires a *scriptural* warrant for the claim that God will justify Jews and Gentiles alike ἐκ πίστεως/διὰ τῆς πίστεως ("by faith/through faith," 3:30).[32]

Consequently, the fact that he points to Abraham rather than Jesus as a paradigm for faith proves nothing one way or the other about the meaning of πίστις Ἰησοῦ Χριστοῦ. Abraham appears in Paul's exposition because his story provides an analogically provocative set of *biblical* images that Paul can use to reinforce his gospel story.

Indeed, much critical discussion of Paul's use of the Abraham story —

30. "The Allegory of Abraham, Sarah, and Hagar in the Argument of Galatians," in J. Friedrich et al. (eds.) *Rechtfertigung: Festschrift für Ernst Käsemann* (Tübingen: J. C. B. Mohr [Paul Siebeck], 1976 and Göttingen: Vandenhoeck & Ruprecht, 1976) 1-16.

31. "A Law-Observant Mission to Gentiles: The Background of Galatians," *SJT* 38 (1985) 307-24.

32. Against Stowers ("Ἐκ πίστεως and διὰ τῆς πίστεως"), I continue to regard these expressions as synonymous. To posit a distinction here would be to undo the whole point of Paul's argument, which is to insist that "there is no distinction," that Jews and Gentiles are now related to God on precisely the same terms through the grace of Jesus Christ.

and here I include my own analysis of Galatians 3 in *Faith of Jesus Christ* —
goes subtly astray by failing to appreciate that Paul is working backward from
his gospel into a typological/literary interpretation of the OT text. Abraham
is of interest to Paul not as a "historical" figure but as a metaphorical figure in
Paul's symbolic world. He is theologically valuable to Paul because his story
prefigures certain aspects of the gospel that Paul preaches.[33] So, for example,
Paul claims that Abraham received circumcision after faith was reckoned to
him as righteousness (Gen 15:6), not before, in order that he might be the
symbolic father figure both of Gentile believers and of circumcised believers
(Rom 4:9-12). Likewise, Paul writes that Gen 15:6 was "written not for [Abra-
ham's] sake alone, but for ours also, to whom it is going to be reckoned, to
those who place their trust in the one who raised Jesus our Lord from the
dead" (Rom 4:23-24). Abraham typologically prefigures Christian believers,
whose faith — note carefully — is said to be directed not toward Jesus but toward the God who raised Jesus.

Adam and Christ (5:12-21)

The final crucial passage in Romans for assessing the meaning of Paul's references to the "faith of Jesus Christ" is the typological contrast between Adam
and Christ in Rom 5:12-21. Adam is "a type of the coming one" (i.e., Jesus)[34]
in that he is the progenitor, the typological embodiment, the ἀρχηγός ("cap-
tain," to borrow a term from Hebrews) of a people. His sin carries vicarious
consequences (condemnation) for all who are "in" him. Jesus Christ, on the
other hand, by his act of righteousness (δικαίωμα, 5:18), his obedience
(ὑπακοή, 5:19), effects justification for all who are "in" him. Of course, the act
of obedience in view here is Christ's death (5:6-11). The passage does not use
the word πίστις, but in light of the virtual synonymity established in 1:5 between πίστις and ὑπακοή, it is difficult to suppose that this terminological difference is particularly significant.[35] Luke Johnson's cogent argument that
Rom 5:15-21 is the plain explication of "the faith of Jesus" in Rom 3:21-26

---

33. A similar point could be made about Adam in Romans 5 and Moses in 2 Corinthians 3.

34. Note the way in which Paul here applies the messianic epithet ὁ μέλλων ("the coming one") to Jesus Christ without explanation or comment; the usage is analogous to his
equally casual use of ὁ δίκαιος ("the righteous one"). In both cases, he expects the reader to
recognize the epithet as a term of reference to the Messiah.

35. *Contra* Cosgrove, *Cross and Spirit*, 55-56; idem, "Justification in Paul: A Linguistic
and Theological Reflection," *JBL* 106 (1987) 665 n. 32.

has never been seriously countered.[36] In any case, Romans 5 shows unmistakably that Paul regards Jesus' death as an act of obedience that carries the destiny of many; furthermore, Romans 6 goes on to contend that his death is not merely vicarious but that through baptism we have entered a union with Christ in such a way that his death and resurrection define a pattern for our obedience as well. If — as I have been contending — πίστις Ἰησοῦ Χριστοῦ is a summary description of Christ's faithful death, then those who are "conformed to the image of God's Son" (8:29), crying as he did "Abba, Father" (8:14) will also share in his πίστις, being conformed to it. That is surely the sense of the expression τὸν ἐκ πίστεως Ἰησοῦ ("the one who shares the faith of Jesus," 3:26).

One of the liabilities of the traditional interpretation of justification through believing in Jesus, as Schweitzer perceptively noted, is its inability to explain how Romans 5–8 are related to Romans 1–4. E. P. Sanders reemphasized this point, of course, in *Paul and Palestinian Judaism*. Whereas Schweitzer and Sanders both attributed the disjunction to a lack of internal systematic coherence in Romans, I would suggest that the difficulty lies in the "objective genitive" (i.e., *anthropological)* misinterpretation of πίστις Χριστοῦ — hence, more in Luther than in Paul. A great strength of the subjective genitive (i.e., *christological*) construal is that it allows us to read Romans 1–8 as a theologically coherent discussion in which Paul's christology and soteriology are correlated in such a way that "justification by faith" and "participation in Christ" are virtually synonymous. As Morna Hooker formulates it, "Justification is a matter of participation; so, too, is believing: . . . even the believer's initial response — his faith — is a sharing in the obedient, faithful response of Christ himself."[37] Of course, this suggestion would have to be worked out much more fully than is possible here.[38] In any case, the foregoing sketch at least begins to demonstrate how the "faith of Jesus Christ" construal helps us to make sense out of the letter to the Romans as a whole. After surveying the evidence, Leander Keck concludes that ". . . in every case, construing πίστις Ἰησοῦ as the fidelity of Jesus not only removes

36. Johnson, "Romans 3:21-26," 87-89. See also R. Longenecker, "The Obedience of Christ in the Theology of the Early Church," in R. Banks (ed.), *Reconciliation and Hope* (Grand Rapids: Eerdmans, 1974) 142-52; Keck, "'Jesus' in Romans," 457.

37. Hooker, "ΠΙΣΤΙΣ ΧΡΙΣΤΟΥ," 341. Concerning the relation between justification and participation, see my comments in *Faith of Jesus Christ,* 250-54 (pp. 212-15 in the present edition).

38. Another important part of the interpretative task would be to show how my interpretation of πίστις Ἰησοῦ fits — or fails to fit — the discussion of Christ, faith, and Israel in Rom 9:30–10:21. But that is a project for another day.

unwarranted awkwardness from Paul's statements but clarifies the key point — the role of Jesus in salvation."[39]

3. Other Texts: Some Observations

Besides the passages in Romans, some form of the πίστις Χριστοῦ formulation occurs in Gal 2:16, 2:20, and 3:22, in Phil 3:9, and — for what it may be worth — in Eph 3:12. Space limitation precludes a full discussion of these passages here. I have already written rather extensively on Galatians, and we already have in print other excellent discussions of the material. On Phil 3:9, see Hooker, "ΠΙΣΤΙΣ ΧΡΙΣΤΟΥ," 331-33. On the Galatians passages, see Sam Williams, "Again *Pistis Christou*."[40] For the record, let it be said that I agree with Williams that there is a remarkable convergence of our conclusions, despite our different approaches and some differences in detail. (I do still hope, for example, to convince him that Paul understands Hab 2:4 as a messianic prophecy.) His treatments of Gal 2:16 and 3:23-25 are particularly helpful. For the purposes of discussion I would like to highlight a couple of points where Williams' analysis seems particularly illuminating, before adding a few thetic remarks of my own (along with one significant retraction of my earlier position) concerning these texts.

Williams's Exposition of πίστις Χριστοῦ in Galatians

Rather than conceding that ἡμεῖς εἰς Χριστὸν Ἰησοῦν ἐπιστεύσαμεν ("we believed in Christ Jesus," Gal 2:16) designates Christ as the "object" of faith — as exegetes on both sides of this question have almost always done — Williams notes the parallel expression εἰς Χριστὸν ἐβαπτίσθητε ("you were baptized into Christ," Gal 3:27) and proposes that εἰς Χριστὸν Ἰησοῦν ἐπιστεύσαμεν should be understood, in the same way, as "transfer terminology."

> Just as Paul can say that one comes to be "in Christ" by being baptized into Christ, so he can say that one *believes* into Christ. In this second expression, too, *eis* implies movement, change, the transfer from one order of existence into another. Thus, to "believe into Christ" is the *means* by which one comes to be "in Christ." That means is adopting the life-stance, *pistis*, which marked

39. L. Keck, "'Jesus' in Romans," 454.
40. *CBQ* 49 (1987) 431-47.

Christ's own relationship to God, the life-stance of which he is the eschatological exemplar. To adopt this stance is to trust and obey Him who raised Jesus from the dead, to believe *like* Christ, and thereby to stand *with* Christ in
that domain, that power field, created through his death and resurrection.[41]

The value of this interpretation is evident in the good sense it enables Williams to make out of Gal 3:23-25, where πίστις is said to be something that
"has come" and can be "revealed." Williams explains as follows: "Faith comes
in that Christ, the single *sperma* of Abraham, actualizes and exemplifies faith.
In his trusting obedience, his complete reliance on God as trustworthy and
true, Christ *reveals* faith." Consequently, "Christian faith is Christ-faith, that
relationship to God which Christ exemplified, that life-stance which he actualized and which, because he lived and died, now characterizes the personal
existence of everyone who lives in him. Christ is not the 'object' of such faith,
however, but rather its supreme exemplar — indeed, its creator."[42]

Williams would concede, I think, that his explanations of the passages
are broadly paraphrastic, intended to "unpack" the connotative freight of
Paul's metaphorical language.[43] One might translate ἡμεῖς εἰς Χριστὸν
Ἰησοῦν ἐπιστεύσαμεν in a less theologically loaded way, such as "we have
placed our trust in Christ Jesus." It seems to me, nonetheless, that Williams's
proposals have considerable heuristic power. Among other things, this approach helps to account for the way in which Paul's frequent appeals to the
pattern of Christ's death and resurrection function in Pauline ethics.[44]

I would want, however, to engage Williams in discussion at several
points. First of all, his way of describing πίστις Ἰησοῦ Χριστοῦ leans heavily toward what he calls a "minimal reading" of Paul's metaphorical language of
participation in Christ, with the result that he downplays the vicarious elements of Paul's story of salvation. I would prefer to speak less of Jesus as "exemplar" and somewhat more of Jesus as the σπέρμα ("seed") whose apocalyptic destiny of death and resurrection reshapes the destiny of those who are now
"in" him. Note, for instance, the remarkable claim of Gal 2:19b-20a: "I have
been crucified with Christ; it is no longer I who live, but it is Christ who lives in
me." Or again, Gal 6:14-15: ". . . the world has been crucified to me and I to the
world. For neither circumcision nor uncircumcision is anything — but new

---

41. Ibid., 443.

42. Ibid., 438, 446.

43. See Williams' useful comments on the metaphorical character of Paul's language
(ibid., 439).

44. On this theme in Paul's ethics, see R. B. Hays, *The Moral Vision of the New Testament: Community, Cross, New Creation* (San Francisco: HarperSanFrancisco, 1996) 27-32.

creation!" One hardly does justice to this sort of language by speaking of Christ merely as an exemplar of faith. Second, I would emphasize more firmly than Williams does that Paul's πίστις language is thematically intertwined with his exegesis of OT texts (especially Hab 2:4 and Gen 15:6) and with the affirmation of God's faithfulness to his covenant promises. But these are points for ongoing discussion between interpreters who are in substantial agreement.

A Retraction

In *Faith of Jesus Christ,* I argued that Galatians 3 "depicts Abraham not as an exemplary paradigm for faith but as a representative figure in and through whom others are blessed."[45] This now seems to me to be an overly precise and rationalistic distinction; it may have a certain heuristic usefulness, but it posits a dichotomy where I suspect Paul saw none. I still hold that Gal 3:8-9 presents Abraham as a representative figure "in" whom the word of Scripture blesses those who are his children. But those who are his children stand in this relationship to him precisely insofar as they share his orientation toward God in faith (3:6-7). If we accept (for the sake of argument) Williams' reading of πίστις Ἰησοῦ Χριστοῦ, it becomes clear at once that there is a sense in which Abraham is the prefiguration both of Christ and of those who are in Christ. Christ is Abraham's σπέρμα ("seed," 3:16), and those who are Christ's are τοῦ Ἀβραὰμ σπέρμα ("seed of Abraham," 3:29). Abraham is the biblical type to whom the promise was given, Christ the eschatological antitype through whom the promise becomes effectual for those who are "children of promise" (4:28), Abraham's sons (3:7).

This way of putting the matter resolves my concern about the fact that Abraham's theocentric faith is not properly analogous to christocentric Christian faith. In fact, on this understanding, *both* Abraham and Jesus are paradigms for Christian faith and Christian faith itself is — properly understood — theocentric. If the analogies still do not work out in a neatly systematic fashion, that is because Paul's use of the Abraham story remains metaphorical in character. Abraham is a metaphor for the truth now disclosed in the faith of Jesus Christ.[46]

45. *Faith of Jesus Christ,* 205-6 (p. 177 in the present edition).

46. I hasten to head off protests by insisting that metaphor is constitutive of all thought and that to describe an assertion as "metaphorical" is not to denigrate its seriousness or truth. See, e.g., G. Lakoff and M. Johnson, *Metaphors We Live By* (Chicago: University of Chicago Press, 1980). For a particularly helpful treatment of metaphors in Pauline theology, see S. Kraftchick, "A Necessary Detour: Paul's Metaphorical Understanding of the Philippian Hymn," *HBT* 15/1 (1993) 1-37.

Observations on Gal 2:20 and 3:22

I would reiterate for the Group's attention a few exegetical points that must be addressed in any decision about the interpretation of πίστις Ἰησοῦ Χριστοῦ. For the sake of brevity I will formulate these as thesis statements.

Gal 2:20 —

(1) The syntax of the sentence poses a difficulty for the objective genitive interpretation. The definite article τῇ sets the whole phrase to the end of the sentence (τοῦ υἱοῦ τοῦ θεοῦ ... ὑπὲρ ἐμοῦ ["the Son of God ... for me"]) in apposition to πίστις ("faith"). The sentence should therefore be translated as follows: "I no longer live, but Christ lives in me; and the life I now live in the flesh I live by faith — that is, by the faith of the Son of God who loved me and gave himself for me." If Paul intended to designate "the Son of God" as the *object* of the verbal idea in the noun πίστει, he certainly chose a very odd way to do it.

(2) The aorist participles modifying τοῦ υἱοῦ τοῦ θεοῦ ("the Son of God") serve to specify what Paul means when he refers to "the faith of the Son of God." Keck comments, "if Paul is writing about the *Son's* πίστις, then the christological clause exegetes this πίστις as Christ's self-giving."[47] The purpose of the sentence as a whole is to emphasize Christ's agency in shaping Paul's life.

(3) The syntactical parallelism between this sentence and Rom 5:15 should be carefully observed.

Rom 5:15 ἐν χάριτι τῇ (τοῦ ἑνὸς ἀνθρώπου Ἰησοῦ Χριστοῦ)
Gal 2:20 ἐν πίστει τῇ (τοῦ υἱοῦ τοῦ θεοῦ)[48]

In Rom 5:15, the grace of God is manifested in the grace of Jesus Christ; in Gal 2:20, the life of God is manifested in the faithfulness of Jesus Christ. The subjective/christological interpretation of the genitive in Gal 2:20 brings this theological parallelism into sharper focus: in both texts, Jesus' death is interpreted as the means through which God's lifegiving power is made effective in those for whom Jesus died.

47. Keck, "'Jesus' in Romans," 455.
48. Rom 5:15: *by grace, that is of the one man Jesus Christ*
    Gal 2:20: *by faith, that is of the Son of God*
For discussion of this parallelism, see Hays, *Faith of Jesus Christ,* 168 (pp. 154-55 in the present edition).

Gal 3:22 —

(1) The RSV made hash of this sentence by translating ἐκ as "to": ". . . that what was promised *to* faith in Jesus Christ might be given to those who believe." The NRSV offers only minimal improvement by changing "to" to "through." The sense of the passage is significantly clarified, however, if we read the phrase ἐκ πίστεως Ἰησοῦ Χριστοῦ ("by the faith of Jesus Christ") as a modifer of δοθῇ ("given") and translate, ". . . so that what was promised might be given through the faithfulness of Jesus Christ [i.e., his death on the cross for us, as in 2:20] to those who believe."

(2) This kerygmatic pattern, beginning from Christ's πίστις as source of salvation and moving to the human response of πίστις in return, corresponds precisely to the interpretation given above of Rom 1:17 (ἐκ πίστεως εἰς πίστιν ["by faith for faith"]) and Rom 3:22 (διὰ πίστεως Ἰησοῦ Χριστοῦ εἰς πάντας τοὺς πιστεύοντας ["through the faithfulness of Jesus Christ for all who believe"]). It also corresponds to the sequence of exposition in Gal 2:16, where the affirmation that a person is justified only διὰ πίστεως Ἰησοῦ Χριστοῦ ("through the faith of Jesus Christ") precedes the account of the answering response, καὶ ἡμεῖς εἰς Χριστὸν Ἰησοῦν ἐπιστεύσαμεν ("we also placed our faith in Christ Jesus").

In sum, though the evidence of Galatians, taken by itself, is less compelling than the evidence of Romans, it appears that Paul's allusive formulations in Galatians are intended to recall his preaching to them about a Jesus who was "publicly exhibited as crucified" (Gal 3:1) in obedience to the will of the Father (1:4, 4:4) in order to set free those who had been slaves (4:3-7, 5:1) and to bring them, in unity with him, into the blessing that had been promised to the children of Abraham (3:13-14, 29). Jesus' act of giving himself up to death is precisely the act of burden-bearing to which Paul refers when he speaks of "the πίστις of the Son of God who loved me and gave himself for me" (2:20).

4. What Is at Stake?

What difference does it make whose faith is meant in Paul's compressed πίστις formulations? Clearly, we keep having the argument not only because the evidence is sufficiently ambiguous to sustain vigorous disagreement but also because there are serious theological issues at stake here. It may be useful to articulate precisely what we take these issues to be, so that we can see what we are really arguing about. In conclusion, I offer a sketch of the theological questions that I see as critical consequences of the present debate.

(1) **The relation between Christology and soteriology in Pauline theology.** One of the driving motivations of my work on the πίστις Χριστοῦ question has been the desire to understand how the death of Jesus can be understood to be the source of salvation. In the standard Lutheran-Reformation accounts of justification by faith, there was always a puzzling arbitrariness, a lack of "inner connexion between Christology and the doctrine of justification."[49] I still cannot, I am sorry to say, offer a satisfactory elucidation of this mystery. George Lindbeck reminds me that it is not without reason that the church has never formally dogmatized any particular theory of the atonement. It does seem to me, however, that the christological interpretation of πίστις 'Ιησοῦ offers a more promising approach to the problem than does the now-traditional anthropological (objective genitive) exegesis. Williams puts the point aptly: "Christians are justified by that faith which derives its very character from [Jesus'] self-giving obedience, that faith which was first his and has now become theirs."[50] That is what it means to say that the righteousness of God is revealed by faith for faith. By no means should this be understood to mean that Christians are saved by their own Herculean faithfulness; indeed, the central emphasis of the christological interpretation of πίστις 'Ιησοῦ Χριστοῦ is precisely that we are saved by Jesus' faithfulness, not by our own cognitive disposition or confessional orthodoxy.

(2) **The humanity of Jesus.** Some opposition to the christological interpretation may be rooted in an implicitly docetic Christology. If Jesus was a real human being, it is hardly scandalous or inappropriate to speak of his faith/fidelity toward God. Did Paul think of the Jesus who died on the cross as a human being? Formulas such as Gal 4:4-5, Rom 1:3-4, and Phil 2:6-8 suggest that he did.

(3) **Experiential-expressive vs. "narrative" theology.** The besetting danger of the anthropological ("objective genitive") interpretation, with its emphasis on the salvific efficacy of individual faith, is its tendency to reduce the gospel to an account of individual religious experience, or even to turn faith into a bizarre sort of work, in which Christians jump through the entranceway of salvation by cultivating the right sort of spiritual disposition. (Luther no doubt stirs and curses in his tomb whenever his seed commit this theological blunder.) The narrative account of salvation as won ὑπὲρ ἡμῶν ("for us")

---

49. G. Ebeling, *Word and Faith* (Philadelphia: Fortress, 1963) 203. A larger section of this passage is quoted as an epigraph to Chapter IV in *Faith of Jesus Christ.*

50. Williams, "Again *Pistis Christou*," 444.

through the faithfulness of Jesus attempts to preclude this theological misstep, emphasizing not only the *extra nos* of salvation but also its public, corporate character. Bultmannians past and present fret, of course, that this emphasis on the narrative character of the gospel will objectify the word and render it inert.

(4) **The cruciform character of Christian obedience.** The particular interpretation of "the faith of Jesus Christ" that I have promulgated has the effect of stressing the pattern of correspondence between Jesus and the believing community: those who are in Christ are called to live the same sort of faith-obedience that he revealed. From a theological point of view, this has the distinct advantage of explaining how Pauline ethics is christologically grounded (Philippians, not discussed in this essay, is a lovely illustration of the point — see especially Phil 1:27–2:13); from a practical point of view, this has the distinct disadvantage of summoning us to live lives of costly self-sacrificial burden-bearing.[51]

(5) **The righteousness of God as covenant-faithfulness.** A theological judgment on this issue is not strictly tied to one's exegetical decision about πίστις Χριστοῦ, but I would suggest that there is some positive correlation between the christological ("subjective genitive") construal and an affirmation of the centrality of Israel/covenant themes in Paul's theology.[52] The key is to recognize that Paul's defense of God's faithfulness to Israel in Romans 3:3-5 (ἡ πίστις τοῦ θεοῦ = θεοῦ δικαιοσύνη) is linked to his affirmation that the righteousness of God (δικαιοσύνη θεοῦ) has been manifested through the faithfulness of Jesus Christ (διὰ πίστεως Ἰησοῦ Χριστοῦ, 3:21-22). The issues here are complicated, and their systematic interrelation still must be sorted out more clearly: Dunn, with whom I am in agreement about the covenant-faithfulness motif, rejects the "faith of Christ" interpretation. Martyn, on the other hand, who emphatically disagrees with Dunn's account of Paul as a covenant theologian,[53] agrees with me about πίστις Ἰησοῦ Χριστοῦ. Future analysis of the πίστις Χριστοῦ problem should seek to show how the various interpretive options are related to these other major themes in Paul's proclamation.

So, as the debate continues, advocates of each position must pursue not only critical exegesis but also constructive theological work. The fire will test what sort of work each has done.

51. For a more extensive discussion, see R. B. Hays, "Christology and Ethics in Galatians: The Law of Christ," *CBQ* 49 (1987) 268-90; idem, *Moral Vision of the New Testament*, 27-32, 197.

52. For a preliminary attempt to articulate this correlation, see Wright, "Romans and the Theology of Paul" (in Hay and Johnson [eds.], *Pauline Theology, Volume III*), 37-38.

53. "Events in Galatia," in Bassler (ed.), *Pauline Theology, Volume 1*, 160-79.

Postscript: Reflections on the Debate

The Pauline Theology Group's discussion of the πίστις Χριστοῦ issue was — seen in retrospect — not a trip through the purgatorial flames but rather a foretaste of the eschatological feast: friends and colleagues gathered at table, reflecting on Scripture together. Rarely have I found an academic *Ausein-andersetzung* so enjoyable. J. D. G. Dunn's paper (in this volume) represents the best attempt I have seen to *argue* the case for the objective genitive interpretation (usually it is simply asserted apodictically). I remain unconvinced by his arguments, but the whole discussion has been advanced by this serious and edifying exchange of views. Thanks are due also to Paul Achtemeier for focusing the issues in a helpful way that facilitated the discussion. Looking back on the discussion, I would like to add several concluding comments to clarify issues that arose during the debate.

Responses to J. D. G. Dunn

(1) If Paul takes the expression ἐκ πίστεως from Hab 2:4 — as we can infer from his citation of this text in Rom 1:17 and Gal 3:11 — then Dunn's entire discussion of the presence or absence of the definite article in this expression is irrelevant. I note for the record that in the Group's discussion Dunn conceded this point.

(2) Dunn contends that Paul wants "to argue that Abraham's πίστις meant his faith . . . and therefore *not* his 'faithfulness.'"[54] If that is the case, why does he refer to Abraham in Gal 3:9 as ὁ πιστὸς Ἀβραάμ ("the faithful Abraham")?

(3) Indeed, Dunn's whole argument depends on making a clear distinction between "faith" and "faithfulness." I challenge him, however, to show that it was semantically possible in Hellenistic Greek to make such a conceptual distinction. The single word πίστις carries both connotations. Therefore, Dunn's distinction is anachronistic, a semantic fallacy.[55]

---

54. See above, p. 265.

55. A similar reservation may be lodged against Paul Meyer's careful attempt (in Group discussion) to distinguish between "trust" and "faithfulness." Meyer wants to resist the notion of Jesus as "Promethean believer" by interpreting Paul's language to refer to Jesus as sufferer: his πίστις is his steadfast trust in God in the face of death on a cross. This formulation no doubt captures an important part of the meaning of πίστις Χριστοῦ for Paul, but I do not understand either how such an interpretation can be construed as dissonant with the christology of Hebrews (as Meyer suggested it was) or how one can limit the semantic range of πίστις to *exclude* the connotations of fidelity/faithfulness.

(4) Dunn asks "where is the other evidence from outside the Pauline corpus" that the faithfulness of Jesus was "a recognized and central theme of early Christian preaching?"[56] This is a very odd question. Dunn's own paper sketches out the evidence of this theme in James, Revelation, and Hebrews. I would add Eph 3:12 and the Pastorals, and Ian G. Wallis has now provided extensive documentation for the prevalence of this motif in early Christianity, including patristic sources.[57] In light of this evidence, it appears that Paul would be exceptional if the theme were absent from his theology. (I would have expected the opposite critique: that the christological interpretation of πίστις Χριστοῦ reads the christology of these other texts, such as Hebrews, back into Paul!) Indeed, it seems to me that the force of Dunn's question can be turned back upon him: where is the NT evidence *outside* the Pauline corpus for an objective genitive usage of the expression πίστις Χριστοῦ = "faith in Christ"?

(5) Dunn asks whether I would accept any of the πίστις references in Galatians as denoting human believing in Christ. Since I have already noted that the verb ἐπιστεύσαμεν in Gal 2:16 is used to refer to "human believing in Christ," Dunn's question pertains to constructions using the noun. This is an interesting question, and not as easily answered as Dunn supposes. Let us for the moment set aside the contested constructions with Ἰησοῦ Χριστοῦ or equivalent (2:16, 20; 3:22) and consider the other appearances of the noun πίστις in Galatians. In several cases, πίστις functions by metonymy for "the gospel," referring to the content of what is preached and believed (1:23; 3:2, 5; 3:23, 25; 6:10). In one case, the noun appears in a list of "the fruit of the Spirit" (5:22). All of the other occurrences appear in the prepositional phrases ἐκ πίστεως (3:7-9, 11-12, 24; 5:5) and διὰ τῆς πίστεως (3:14, 26). To be sure, several of these passages do refer to what Dunn calls "human believing"; this is clearest in 3:7-9, 3:14, 26, 5:5, and 5:26. In none of these cases, however, is an "object" of faith designated, although the linkage between 3:6 and 3:7 suggests that οἱ ἐκ πίστεως ("those of faith") must, like Abraham, be those who have faith in *God*. Nothing is said in 3:7-9 — or in any of these other passages — about "faith in Christ." Thus, to respond directly to Dunn's question, I would say that there are no cases in Galatians where the noun πίστις unambiguously denotes "human believing *in Christ*." The fact that Paul repeatedly uses the noun without a specified object suggests — as I have argued above — that he is thinking primarily of the trust toward God that was prefigured by Abraham and definitively enacted by Jesus Christ in such a way that it now shapes the life of all who are "in Christ." As Paul writes in Gal 3:22, the fulfillment of the promise is given "*by* the faith(fulness)

56. See above, p. 259.
57. Wallis, *Faith of Jesus Christ in Early Christian Traditions* (see n. 2, above).

of Jesus Christ (ἐκ πίστεως Ἰησοῦ Χριστοῦ) *to* those who believe (τοῖς πιστεύουσιν) The faith(fulness) of Jesus Christ is the means of the transmission of the blessing to others who now participate in his life and therefore reflect the same trusting relationship to God that broke into human experience through his death and resurrection (3:23, 25).[58]

(6) The most crucial difference between Dunn and me lies in the extent to which we are willing to read Paul's language as *multivalent* and *metaphorical*. Whereas Dunn wants to press at every point for a univocal sense, I see Paul using language with connotative complexity. Some of Paul's πίστις expressions are multivalent; for example, if we ask whether in Gal 3:14 Paul means that we receive the promise through Christ's faithfulness or through our faith, the best answer is probably, "Yes, both." The expression διὰ τῆς πίστεως enfolds both semantic possibilities.

Furthermore, the noun πίστις does not have precisely the same sense in every case. Πίστις θεοῦ, πίστις Χριστοῦ, πίστις Ἀβραάμ, and πίστις ἡμῶν ("the faithfulness of God, the faith[fulness] of Christ, the faith of Abraham, and our faith") are not identical; rather, they are *analogically* related to one another. The "mapping" of one concept onto the other is not strictly isomorphic, because the correspondences are metaphorical.[59] As πίστις is predicated of us rather than of Christ, its meaning shifts slightly because the relation between Christ and believers is one of analogy rather than simple identity. Similarly, when Paul uses the language of crucifixion with Christ (Gal 5:24; 6:14), carrying the dying of Jesus (2 Cor 4:10-12), having the mind-set of Christ Jesus (Phil 2:5-11), and imitation of Christ (1 Cor 11:1; 1 Thess 1:6), he does not mean that our actions mimic the example of Jesus in a woodenly literal way; rather, he means that there is a significant metaphorical correspondence between the life-pattern defined by Christ's death and the suffering experienced by those who are in Christ. The precise nature of this correspondence must be discerned in the contingent circumstances of each believing community. The relation between our faith and the faith of Christ is similarly metaphorical: our faith answers and reflects his — indeed, *participates in* his — because according to Paul it is God's design for us "to be conformed to the image of his Son" (Rom 8:29).

58. It should be said clearly that for Paul, πίστις Χριστοῦ refers to Jesus' obedience to death on the cross: in other words, the meaning of the phrase is focused on the kerygma's narration of his self-giving death, not on the whole ministry of Jesus of Nazareth. This narrower punctiliar sense — focused on the cross — is the only meaning supported by Paul's usage.

59. For a helpful discussion of metaphorical "mapping," see Kraftchick, "Necessary Detour."

Index of Authors

Index of Scripture References

Made in the USA
Lexington, KY
24 June 2018